King of the Action Thriller

ALSO BY BRIAN HANNAN
AND FROM MCFARLAND

*The Magnificent '60s: The 100 Most Popular Films
of a Revolutionary Decade* (2022)

*In Theaters Everywhere: A History of the Hollywood
Wide Release, 1913–2017* (2019)

The Gunslingers of '69: Western Movies' Greatest Year (2019)

*Coming Back to a Theater Near You: A History
of Hollywood Reissues, 1914–2014* (2016)

The Making of The Magnificent Seven:
Behind the Scenes of the Pivotal Western (2015)

King of the Action Thriller
Films from the Mind of Alistair MacLean

BRIAN HANNAN

McFarland & Company, Inc., Publishers
Jefferson, North Carolina

LIBRARY OF CONGRESS CATALOGING-IN-PUBLICATION DATA

Names: Hannan, Brian, 1954– author
Title: King of the action thriller : films from the mind of Alistair MacLean / Brian Hannan.
Description: Jefferson, North Carolina : McFarland & Company, Inc., Publishers, 2026. | Includes bibliographical references and index.
Identifiers: LCCN 2026001333 | ISBN 9781476695334 paperback ∞
ISBN 9781476655833 ebook
Subjects: LCSH: MacLean, Alistair, 1922-1987—Criticism and interpretation | Film adaptations—History and criticism | Action and adventure films—History and criticism | BISAC: PERFORMING ARTS / Film / Screenwriting | PERFORMING ARTS / Film / Genres / Action & Adventure | LCGFT: Literary criticism | Film criticism
Classification: LCC PR6063.A248 Z66 2026 | DDC 823/.914—dc23/eng/20260120
LC record available at https://lccn.loc.gov/2026001333

ISBN (print) 978-1-4766-9533-4
ISBN (ebook) 978-1-4766-5583-3

© 2026 Brian Hannan. All rights reserved

No part of this book may be reproduced or transmitted in any form or by any means, electronic or mechanical, including photocopying or recording, or by any information storage and retrieval system, without permission in writing from the publisher.

Front cover image: Poster art of the 1961 film *The Guns of Navarone* featuring Gregory Peck, David Niven, and Anthony Quinn (Columbia Pictures/Photofest)

Printed in the United States of America

*McFarland & Company, Inc., Publishers
Box 611, Jefferson, North Carolina 28640
www.mcfarlandpub.com*

To Dillon Kastner,
for getting the ball rolling

Acknowledgments

I am indebted to Dillon Kastner, who put his father Elliott's vast archive at my disposal, responded promptly to my queries and offered continuous encouragement. Lord David Puttnam, Tom Reeve, Richard Morris-Adams and Daniel Unger took time out of their busy schedules to speak to me, answer my follow-up questions and clarify points. The staff at the Margaret Herrick Library of the Academy of Motion Picture Arts and Sciences in Los Angeles spent several days guiding me around their Alistair MacLean Collection and, in particular, allowed me a quiet note of personal satisfaction by pointing out my previous books sitting on their shelves. Mary Huelsbeck, assistant director of the Wisconsin Center for Film and Theater Research at the University of Wisconsin–Madison, was particularly helpful in relation to the United Artists records for *Breakheart Pass*. Jennifer Mylrea-Young, archivist at the HarperCollins archives in Bishopbriggs, outside Glasgow, opened up the publisher's Alistair MacLean Collection. The Glasgow University Library Archives & Special Collections made available to me a BBC radio dramatization of *The Guns of Navarone*. Dave Worrall and Lee Pfeiffer of *Cinema Retro* shared with me some of their files. Glasgow film critic Eddie Harrison kept up a steady stream of encouragement and offered suggestions. Last but not least, my wife Anne Marie provided loving and unwavering support as she has done for over a dozen books.

Table of Contents

Acknowledgments	vi
Preface	1
Introduction	3
ONE. Soon to Be a Major Motion Picture: The Bestseller Bounty	9
TWO. *The Secret Ways* (1961)	15
THREE. *The Guns of Navarone* (1961)	22
FOUR. *The Satan Bug* (1965): When Alistair MacLean Quit, Part I	33
FIVE. *Ice Station Zebra* (1968): When Alistair MacLean Quit, Part II	39
SIX. *Where Eagles Dare* (1968)	48
SEVEN. *When Eight Bells Toll* (1971)	66
EIGHT. *Puppet on a Chain* (1971)	80
NINE. *Fear Is the Key* (1972)	91
TEN. *Caravan to Vaccarès* (1974)	98
ELEVEN. *Breakheart Pass* (1976)	104
TWELVE. *Golden Rendezvous* (1977)	111
THIRTEEN. *Force 10 from Navarone* (1978)	117
FOURTEEN. *Bear Island* (1980)	128
FIFTEEN. The Last Movie Hurrah: *The Hostage Tower* (1980) and *River of Death* (1989)	138
SIXTEEN. Television Endgame: *Death Train* (1993), *The Way to Dusty Death* (1995), *Night Watch* (1995), *Air Force One Is Down* (2013)	148
SEVENTEEN. The Final Mystery: What Happened to *Caribbean*?	160
EIGHTEEN. Unmade, Sequels, Remakes	167
Conclusion	173
Appendix: Box Office	175
Chapter Notes	183
Bibliography	212
Index	215

Preface

Like many teenagers of my generation, I grew up on Alistair MacLean novels. Receiving one of his thrillers for Christmas or your birthday made you the envy of your school buddies. I was too young to see *The Guns of Navarone* in the cinema on initial release, catching up with it on reissue about the same time as I realized that the roadshow was not solely devoted to musicals like *The Sound of Music* (1965) and *Oliver!* (1968). You could view an all-guns-blazing war picture like *Where Eagles Dare* (1968) in 70mm or bask in Cinerama for the thriller *Ice Station Zebra* (1968) without having to race to catch them for the one week they were screened at your neighborhood theater, since in my home town of Glasgow, Scotland, they played for months. *Where Eagles Dare*, in particular, had a long lease of life in the United Kingdom, was reissued a couple of times, and then turned up on TV as regularly as *The Magnificent Seven* (1960), *The Great Escape* (1963) and the Bond films. Of course, when Hollywood's long tail encompassed VHS and DVD, there was every excuse to rent and buy these movies. Like many movie devotees, I soon had a physical VHS-DVD library and it gradually occurred to me that Alistair MacLean pretty much occupied an entire shelf on his own, just as his novels had on my bookcase. Not possessing an encyclopedic knowledge of Hollywood, it took me some time to realize how rare it was for an author to have so many movies made out of his books.

Where Eagles Dare remained a driving force in the continuing appreciation of Alistair MacLean, and once I started attending the annual Bradford Widescreen Festival, I was able to enjoy screenings of that movie and *Ice Station Zebra* in all their roadshow glory. I introduced the 4K screening of *The Guns of Navarone* at this festival after dipping my toes in MacLean waters with the publication of my book about the making of the film. I have to confess that other characters took precedence over MacLean. Producer Carl Foreman, a refugee from the Joseph McCarthy hearings, had a huge battle on his hands to develop the picture, from avoiding a revolution, to seeing first-choice stars slip away, and then watching the actors being sidelined by injury or illness.

My overwhelming interest is in the movies of the 1960s. Following my last book, *The Magnificent '60s* (2022), I was deluged by readers asking why I had limited my examination of that period to 100 movies. So I started watching a 1960s movie every night and writing about them in a blog called, unimaginatively, themagnificent60s. Having reviewed a number of Alistair MacLean pictures, I had the most amazing piece of good fortune. Unbeknownst to me, Dillon Kastner, a fan of my blog, was the son of Elliott Kastner, whose production outfit was behind *Where Eagles Dare*, *When Eight Bells Toll* (1970), *Fear Is the Key* (1972) and *Breakheart Pass* (1975). Out of the blue, he sent me his father's archive. That gold mine proved an irresistible temptation. I was hooked and started working on this book.

Introduction

He was the world's best-selling author. He was the highest-paid screenwriter in Hollywood. He didn't learn to speak English until he was six.

"I'm a businessman, not a writer," claimed the self-effacing Alistair MacLean.[1] While his narrative skills attracted readers by the millions, his understanding of the publishing and entertainment industries made him the most business-savvy author since Charles Dickens. MacLean had an instinctive understanding of synergy. In Hollywood, "property" was king. This was real estate of a different commercial kind, an item on which many fates depended, and which could be used to raise the millions of dollars required to make a movie. And, virtually alone among authors of his generation, and certainly unique among screenwriters, his name acquired marquee status, carrying above-the-credit status. He was often billed above actors, ensuring that movies could be marketed as Alistair MacLean pictures, promising to deliver a certain experience, akin to a Sherlock Holmes mystery. In the 1950s and 1960s, his books were translated onto the screen at a startling rate, a total of 18 making the transition.[2] *The Guns of Navarone* (1961), *Where Eagles Dare* (1968) and others were the biggest blockbusters of their day, while others like *Puppet on a Chain* (1970) and *Fear Is the Key* (1972) not only attracted a cult following but reinvented the chase picture. His books spanned World War II and the Cold War, espionage often a consideration; his gift for authenticity ensured that he was at home in the Wild West or at a racetrack. A number of elements made his novels stand out from the other bestsellers of the day. Unlike Harold Robbins (*The Carpetbaggers*), he didn't rely on sex, nor a retelling of history in the vein of James Michener (*Hawaii*), nor explore institutions in the manner of Arthur Hailey (*Hotel*).[3] He wasn't interested in contemporary issues. He didn't have a series character like James Bond,[4] which allowed his thrillers to be cherry-picked by a far wider range of producers and Hollywood studios. Although his main characters were loners, often with a disfigurement or major flaw, they were sufficiently different to be interpreted by a very diverse group of actors. You could argue that he re-purposed the thriller and invented the mission war novel. By the late 1950s, the former was polarized between the critically acclaimed novels of Graham Greene and Eric Ambler and the sexed-up pulp of Mickey Spillane. MacLean's books were defined by serious purpose, dedicated professionals rather than amateurs stumbling onto a conspiracy. The aftermath of the Second World War saw the advent of many mission pictures, most of them based on real events and documentary or gung-ho in style. *The Guns of Navarone* ushered in a new type of mission book–mission film, short on exposition and training and overloaded with tension.

Authors rarely become brand names. They may become bestsellers, well-known to readers and within the book trade; even when appreciated by critics, their fame rarely extends beyond the publication arena. The adjectives Dickensian, Chandleresque, Shakespearean and Tolkienesque are shorthand for describing a type of character or a fictional world; they are the biggest accolade that can be bestowed upon an author, that their work has transcended the specific arena of publishing and entered the vocabulary. You can be a multi-million–selling author and still the impact of your work will be limited; nobody has created adjectives around the door-stopping sagas of Leon Uris and James Michener or the thrillers of James Patterson. The contemporary ancillary opportunities available to the likes of Stephen King and J.K. Rowling have ensured they have become brands, their names above the titles of movies made from their novels, promising a certain kind of experience and, in broader terms, creating a marketing gold mine. For over two decades, Alistair MacLean was a brand name. The only author whose sales came close was Agatha Christie and yet her mysteries, set in an impossibly English landscape, lacked the full international penetration of the harder-edged thrillers of MacLean. In her lifetime, her two most famous characters, Hercule Poirot and Miss Marple, barely made a dent on the big screen. But the pull of MacLean was such that his name was not just above the titles of the movies but emblazoned across the posters, as if that was all the marquee lure an audience required. As *Where Eagles Dare* producer Elliott Kastner put it, "Alistair MacLean is the first bestselling author equally talented as novelist and screenwriter. This puts him astride the entertainment industry like a golden colossus."[5] Peter Snell, producer of *Bear Island* (1979), concurred: "He's simply an author everyone knows. The films have a guaranteed audience and that's hard to beat, knowing you have an audience before you begin."[6]

Bestsellers had underpinned Hollywood from the outset, studios believing they were a safer bet because the resulting films were pre-sold. Then directors became more demanding, their name superseding the names of the authors of the source material, to the extent that audiences often believe that a movie has emerged from the imagination of a director rather than originating elsewhere (*Poor Things*, 2023, a case in point). So it is Martin Ritt's *The Spy Who Came in from the Cold* (1965) and Francis Ford's Coppola's *The Godfather* (1972). But after the first few adaptations of MacLean thrillers, it was never Brian G. Hutton's *Where Eagles Dare* or Geoffrey Reeves' *Puppet on a Chain* or Don Sharp's *Bear Island*. These movies were identified with their author.

From the outset, MacLean's films attracted variable budgets—very big for *The Guns of Navarone*, *Where Eagles Dare* and *Ice Station Zebra* (1968), the last two designated 70mm roadshows,[7] and considerably smaller for *The Secret Ways* (1961) and *The Satan Bug* (1965). In later films, it was apparent that the author's name was as big a draw as any of the stars, and that you could make a film based on one of his books without going to the expense of recruiting a major marquee name. George Maharis, Sven-Bertil Taube, Anthony Hopkins and David Birney were virtual

Alistair MacLean drew on his World War II experiences for his debut novel *HMS Ulysses* (its first edition cover pictured) and his sophomore effort *The Guns of Navarone*. He served mostly aboard HMS *Royalist*, a light cruiser which saw action in the Arctic, the Mediterranean and the Far East. Beginning as an able seaman, he ended the war as a leading torpedo operator.

unknowns when cast in the leading roles in *The Satan Bug*, *Puppet on a Chain*, *When Eight Bells Toll* and *Caravan to Vaccarès* (1974), respectively. Audiences knew what they were going to get; if a director added more exciting action sequences (for example, the speedboat chase through Amsterdam canals in *Puppet on a Chain* or the car chase in *Fear Is the Key*), that was a bonus.

English was a foreign language for MacLean. Though born in Glasgow in 1922, the son of a Church of Scotland minister, he was brought up in a small town in the Scottish Highlands and spoke Gaelic until age five, when he began attending school. He was drafted into the Royal Navy at 19 on what proved a five-year stint, seeing action in the North Sea, the Atlantic, the Mediterranean and Aegean Seas and the Far East. These experiences provided authentic material for several books. Postwar, as a schoolteacher in Glasgow, he tried his hand at short stories to generate extra income. After winning a competition in a national newspaper,[8] he was encouraged to write *H.M.S. Ulysses*, the tale of a doomed wartime convoy. It was a massive bestseller (an unprecedented 250,000 copies in hardback[9]) and the film rights sold for £30,000[10]; this income allowed him to become a full-time writer. His prospects were cemented by the publication in 1957 of *The Guns of Navarone*: Four hundred fifty thousand copies sold in six months and the film rights were purchased by Carl Foreman, who planned a multi–million-dollar, star-laden picture for Columbia.

But the first movie to roll off what would become the MacLean assembly line was a lesser-known, smaller-budgeted affair, *The Secret Ways* (1961).[11] Thereafter, films based on his works appeared at regular intervals.

Never happy with his treatment either by publishers or Hollywood studios, MacLean made his resentment known in distinctive fashion. In response to feelings that his editors were being condescending, MacLean twice in the 1960s went on strike and, if investment in a hotel venture had gone according to plan, he might have given up writing for good. As it was, he decided to teach his publisher a lesson and write books (*The Dark Crusader* and *The Satan Bug*) under the pseudonym Ian Stuart, to give him the freedom to take his writing in a different direction and to prove he was not dependent on the brand-name of Alistair MacLean.

For an author, MacLean was unusually involved in the filmmaking process. Most writers, perhaps attracted by Hollywood mystique and the hefty sums paid out for film rights, generally entertain some interest, at least initially, in participating in the movie machine. But, equally usually, they become disaffected by the ruthlessness of a business where the screenwriter is on the lowest rung of the ladder. William Goldman is usually held up as the best example of someone who straddled both fields with equal success, but of his original works, only *Butch Cassidy and the Sundance Kid* (1969) was a big movie hit, and his fame largely rested on adaptations: *Harper* (1966), *All the President's Men* (1975) and *A Bridge Too Far* (1977). You could as easily argue that he learned from MacLean to write books that were cinematic and enjoy the financial triple whammy of book sales, selling the film rights and writing the screenplay.[12]

MacLean's annoyance was initiated by the liberties taken by screenwriter-producer Carl Foreman on *The Guns of Navarone* and subsequent treatments that he felt were not true to his novels, especially when, as it must seem to every author, a screenwriter attempts to improve on the original. His antipathy might well have remained as ill-concealed umbrage except for an intervention by American agent-turned-producer Elliott Kastner, who had set up a London office. Kastner invited the novelist to write an original screenplay in a deal that was extremely advantageous to MacLean, permitting the author to retain the publication rights.[13] It's fair to say that MacLean in creating *Where Eagles Dare* plundered his previous mission opus *The Guns of Navarone*, but jacked up the suspense and action. Kastner then signed up to make another three films based on MacLean novels.[14] That experience sparked the idea within MacLean that better movies could be made of his books if only he were more creatively involved. So he teamed up with Geoffrey Reeve, untested on the big screen and best known as a director of commercials, to make *Puppet on a Chain*. Reeve subsequently helmed *Caravan to Vaccarès* (1974). MacLean's second wife Mary also got the producing bug, and she proposed to make movies from a quartet of his books. After their divorce, she held on to these rights and tied up with producer Peter Snell, who later pulled together *Bear Island* (1979) and the televised versions of various books.

Not all the films made from the thrillers were box office smashes. With their big budgets and all-star casts, *The Guns of Navarone* and *Where Eagles Dare* were the most commercially successful, the latter now mentioned in the same hushed tones as two other seminal 1960s war movies, *The Great Escape* (1963) and *The Dirty Dozen* (1967). *Ice Station Zebra*, while in the same league from a budget perspective, didn't match their box office. *Fear Is the Key* and *Puppet on a Chain* are the standouts among the more modestly-budgeted movies, although there are plenty of advocates for *When Eight Bells Toll*, *Breakheart Pass* (1975), *Golden Rendezvous* (1977), *Force Ten from Navarone* (1978) and *Bear Island*. In recent years, after the global pandemic, *The Satan Bug* has picked up a new audience.

Never mind the marquee value of an author; the hold Alistair MacLean exerted over producers and studios remained nothing short of remarkable especially when, ostensibly, some of the films did relatively poorly at the U.S. box office. But the global reach of the bestselling author and the idea that the films could be marketed on his name alone meant that, even if the movies did not hit the commercial bullseye, they would still do well enough to be worth the risk once foreign markets and ancillary revenue were taken into consideration.

From the critical perspective it's a mistake to imagine that MacLean was underrated as a thriller writer. While he would never gain the lead review in the *New York Times Review of Books*,[15] his books were critiqued in colossal numbers; most of the critics rated him as among the best practitioners of the genre. It's true that later in his career, the critics became snippier but that was always the case, as novelists as eminent as Philip Roth, John Updike and Cormac McCarthy can attest. MacLean might have felt aggrieved that his literary merits were not "discovered" by critics in the way of Ross Macdonald (the Lew Archer series) and John D. MacDonald (the Travis McGee series) as the more routine aspects (repeat character and repeat locale, for example) of these works were ignored in favor of what might as easily be described as self-indulgent prose, rich on metaphor and description and lax on the narrative thrust that had become MacLean's trademark. MacLean was also highly irregular for a novelist, of the popular or literary variety, in that he changed styles and writing approach five times, when the vast majority of writers, once established, and whether popular or literary, rarely ventured from the tried and tested.

From the outset, one of MacLean's hallmarks was his use of time: events telescoped to just a few days, and chapter headings often consisting of a time identification. He was fond of unusual locales. The Arctic was a favorite; his various jaunts took in Florida, Amsterdam, San Francisco, the Sierra Nevada, Yugoslavia, the Far East, Nova Scotia, Provence, the Gulf of Mexico, the Caribbean, Alaska, the Amazon and the west coast of Scotland. The more remote the region, the more tension he could extract. His heroes were usually self-deprecating and often came with a physical or mental flaw. His debut novel *H.M.S. Ulysses* was not a thriller, more a human-interest documentary-style novel in the vein of *The Cruel Sea*.[16] While the Second World War provided the backdrop for the next few novels, the author was already moving away from the style that had brought him instant fame, these works more easily fitting into the adventure category. *The Last Frontier* and *The Secret Ways* marked another change, testing the new waters of espionage, setting the hero down in politically hostile territory and, critically, racking up the narrative speed. At this point, his stories were told in the third person but with *Fear Is the Key*, published in 1961, he switched to first person, limited point-of-view providing greater immediacy.

The final development was mastery of cinematic style. Once he began writing his books first as screenplays, beginning with *Where Eagles Dare*, the novels took on a different tone again. And with his greater involvement in the movie process, what was often seen in his later books as laziness was, to the more discerning eye, the result of eliminating unnecessary information and stripping the story to the bare bones. The author had a loyal fan base. Among unexpected supporters, actress Emma Thompson "confessed a fondness."[17]

Hollywood played a role in MacLean's success in one other significant way. He achieved recognition just as the U.S. studios were beginning to latch onto novels as a marketing tool. The growth of the movie tie-in paperback and novelizations of films played a vital role in expanding the publishing marketplace, one of the few genuine examples of creative synergy, a marketing crossover paying off for both parties. Book sales brought moviemakers greater exposure, while covers featuring Hollywood stars increased public recognition. The part played by this commercial symmetry is explained in Chapter One.

Primarily, this book sets out to explore the Alistair MacLean cinematic phenomenon. Starting with *The Secret Ways*, each film will be addressed chronologically in turn: examining its cinematic qualities; the circumstances under which it was made; how it reflected the author's creative situation at the time, and how these might impact on the film; and the changes made to turn book into film, taking a behind-the-scenes look at each production.

There is another aspect to the MacLean movie story. Because his cinematic impact was pervasive over three decades, he reflected dramatic changes in the way movies were financed, made and sold. While a number of his movies originated within the Hollywood system, from major companies like Columbia, MGM and United Artists, his name was as synonymous with independent production. Many producers made their first foray into the industry on the back of an Alistair MacLean book; this indicated the global sway he held. It was often believed that his name was a substitute for investment, that a budget could be trimmed, or shorn of a major star, because MacLean had so powerful a marquee standing, especially outside the U.S.

Each movie receives its own chapter, except for the last six, spanning 1980 to 2013; they are accounted for over two chapters. In addition, in Chapter Seventeen, I discuss an extraordinary find: an original screenplay (written in the 1960s) which was turned into neither book nor film.

At one time or another, all MacLean's novels were optioned and what happened to those which never reached the screen is the subject of Chapter Eighteen. For ease of reference, box office is dealt with in the appendix.

Chapter One

Soon to Be a Major Motion Picture
The Bestseller Bounty

Alistair MacLean turned up just in time to take advantage of two new publishing phenomena exploiting the synergy between movies and publishing. A 1960s novelist lucky enough to hit the bestselling jackpot could generally count upon another financial bounty when Hollywood came calling. Studios believed that bestsellers came with the double bonus of a ready-made story and a ready-made audience. The industry recognized the benefit of making pictures out of properties that had already gained a wide readership, hence the continual adaptation of Shakespeare and Dickens from the silent era onwards. A novel's combined hardback and paperback sales in the U.S. could amount to a couple of million copies, with double that number or more overseas, and of course some books hit the sales stratosphere—*Gone with the Wind*, *The Grapes of Wrath* and *Valley of the Dolls*, for example. In addition to selling a book to the movies, publishers learned that slapping the tagline "Soon to be a major motion picture" and adorning a cover with stills from a movie tie-in edition boosted sales. For studios, such promotion ensured advance buzz. In the 1960s, there were many more bookstores than now. The 125,000 U.S. outlets included not just bookstores but locations targeting passing trade. Newsstands, hotel lobbies, railroad stations, department stores, street kiosks, airports and drugstores all boasted racks of paperback books with glossy covers. Like fan magazines, book covers in shop windows brought free promotion. From the studio perspective, buying the rights to novels was often cheaper than original screenplays. Although studios paid substantial sums for some books, most were purchased for relatively small fees.[1] Books were usually optioned for relatively insignificant amounts rather than bought outright, substantial payment only forthcoming if a movie entered production. In the 1960s, except for 1965, the top bestseller in the *Publishers Weekly* annual ranking was turned into a movie. On average, about four Top Ten bestsellers a year were made into pictures. In 1962, the figure was seven: *Ship of Fools* (film released in 1965), *Youngblood Hawke* (1964), *Fail Safe* (1964), *Seven Days in May* (1964), *The Prize* (1963), *The Agony and the Ecstasy* (1965) and *The Reivers* (1969). Six were adapted in 1965 and five in 1963. Generally, books so chosen went into speedy production.[2] Nine of the number-one films every year of that decade at the U.S. box office originated from publishing or Broadway.

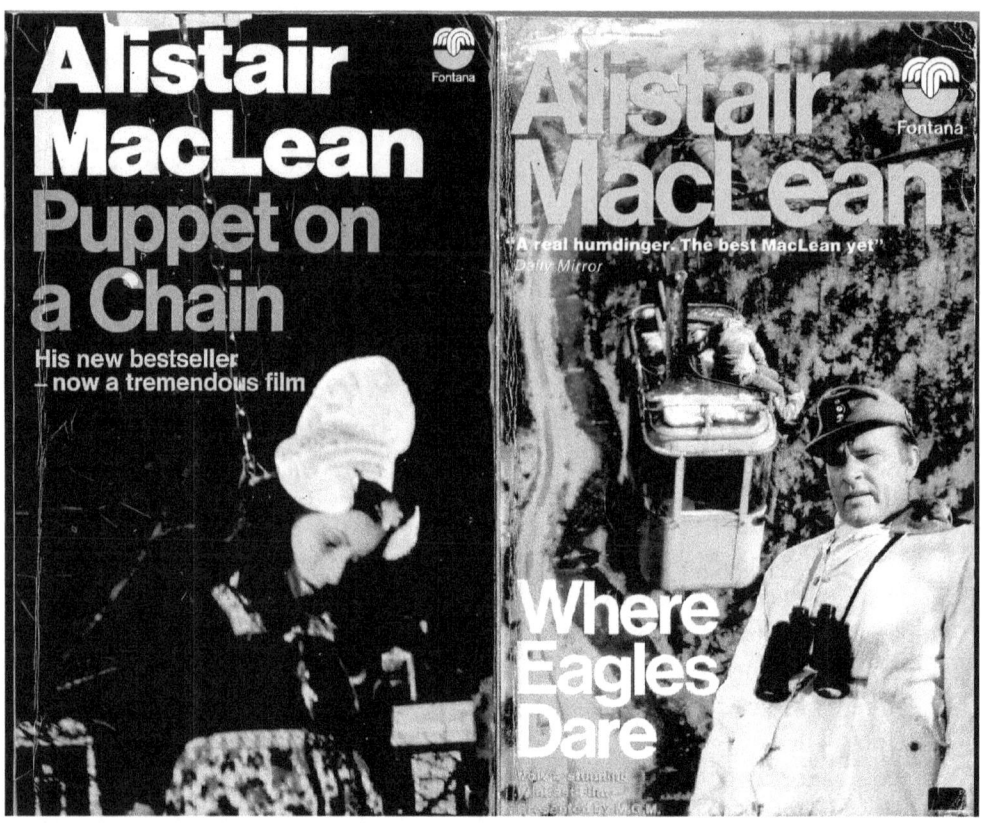

Alistair MacLean's *Where Eagles Dare* and *Puppet on a Chain* were among the hundreds of movies promoted by major studios through paperback movie tie-ins. In 1969 alone, MGM sent a dozen movies down this route; in addition to *Where Eagles Dare* and *Ice Station Zebra*, others included *The Appointment*; *Goodbye, Mr. Chips*; *The Shoes of the Fisherman*; and *2001: A Space Odyssey*.

More than any other author of the 1960s, Alistair MacLean had his novels plundered by Hollywood. His books were ideally suited to take advantage of the movie tie-in. Prior to the 1960s, moviemaking and publishing were generally viewed as completely separate entities, only crossing over when books were sold to Hollywood. Up to the mid–1950s, Hollywood had far better, more effective marketing tools at its disposal. By 1955, promotional plugs were worth about $350 million a year. In 1948, for example, *Mr. Blandings Builds His Dream House* amassed $5 million in merchandising, the booklet listing all the participants running to 72 pages.[3] Anything that could be sold on the back of a picture—furnishing, clothes, vehicles—provided a mountain of free advertising through manufacturers, suppliers and retailers investing in support marketing.

But by 1960, as television advertising more straightforwardly pitched such goods towards the public, that well of merchandising dried up. Film publicists casting about for new exploitation outlets latched onto paperbacks. The paperback industry was booming, shifting over 280 million copies a year. Dell came to realize the "remarkable sales impact of books which have tie-ins with a motion picture" and noted that "in most instances book sales prior to the picture will be equaled following the release of the picture."[4] Publishing executive William C. Engel, pointing to the movie tie-in for *Psycho*, reprinted three times in two months, reckoned that a "big spectacular picture will stimulate sales of a paperback."[5] Bantam was equally buoyant, issuing 32 books in the movie tie-in business on the basis that films increased sales by 50 percent.[6]

Sometimes the first glimpse of a movie's advertising came on a paperback book cover. While hardcover books were generally plain, little on offer but title and author, paperback specialists Dell, Avon, Pocket Books, New American Library, Bantam, Fawcett and Ballantine reveled in colorful designs positioned to take advantage of movie advertising campaigns. Some studios, like Columbia regarding *The Interns* (1962),[7] spent money promoting the books they had bought in order to keep the titles on the bestseller lists until it was time for the movie to appear—a device later used by Paramount to turn *Love Story* (1970) into a bestseller in the first place. "Virtually every production we release is linked to a publisher, it all depends on who offers the best promotion," explained Twentieth Century–Fox's Perry Lieber,[8] insisting on publication aligned to the movie release date. United Artists could count on paperbacks to support ten of its 1961 releases: *Judgment at Nuremberg*, *The Young Doctors*, *Paris Blues*, *Sergeants 3*, *Something Wild*, *Birdman of Alcatraz*, *The Miracle Worker*, *The Happy Thieves*, *What a Wonderful Life* and *Jessica*.[9]

It was an odd relationship in many respects. Studios paid publishers for book rights; then, when these properties were turned into films, they helped publishers sell more books by furnishing movie artwork and stills, free of charge, for the covers. Every copy printed was one more piece of advertising for the film, often in places where a studio would not normally advertise. Publishers targeted potential moviegoers in ways that were too difficult or too expensive for studios. Book designers did not need to come up with original covers if they could simply adapt movie artwork. Occasionally, tie-ins would include a photo spread or run movie credits. If movie tie-ins encouraged moviegoing, then the reverse was equally true, as movie advertising resulted in increased book sales.

By the mid–1960s, every studio was knee-deep in movie tie-ins. In 1965, Dell had 47 titles sold to studios either for imminent or future production. Among those, *The Collector*, *Genghis Khan* and *Lord Jim* were slated for Columbia; *Harlow* for Embassy; *The Sound of Music* (based on the von Trapp Family book) for Twentieth Century–Fox; *How to Murder Your Wife* and *The Knack* for United Artists; *The Amorous Adventures of Moll Flanders* for Paramount; *Assault on a Queen* and *The Bride Wore Black* set for Seven Arts; and *The Cincinnati Kid* and *The Loved One* lined up for MGM.[10] That same year, MGM placed *Operation Crossbow*, *The Yellow Rolls-Royce*, *The Sandpiper*, *She*, *Joy in the Morning*, *Once a Thief*, *Lady L* and *Doctor Zhivago* with publishers other than Dell.[11] In 1966, Paramount had nine deals with a variety of paperback houses to promote *Is Paris Burning?*; *Oh, Dad, Poor Dad*; *Seconds*, *Hurry Sundown*; *Funeral in Berlin*; *The Swinger*; *Alfie*; *El Dorado*; and *Warning Shot*.[12] Disney, which had long been the master of merchandising, set up a new deal with Scholastic Publishing to target schools and libraries.[13] Studios learned to instigate bookshop window displays promoting their forthcoming product. By the end of the decade, the movie tie-in bandwagon was in full swing. In 1968, Twentieth Century–Fox pacted with a dozen different publishers for 19 pictures including *Bandolero!*, *Star!*, *The Devil's Bride*, *Planet of the Apes*, *The Boston Strangler* and *The Sweet Ride*. *Doctor Dolittle* came out in 26 different editions through various publishers.[14] In 1969, the National Association of Theater Owners (NATO) tied in with National Library Week for a cross-promotion promoted under the tagline "Read These Important Books—See These Important Films." Libraries backed pictures sourced from novels included *True Grit*, *Belle de Jour*, *Goodbye, Columbus*, *John and Mary* and *Topaz*. In return, NATO distributed posters advertising library involvement via 5000 theaters.[15] The same year, Bantam Books ran a trailer in 100 cinemas for its own "film festival tie-in" of eight books: *Goodbye, Mr. Chips*; *John and Mary*; *Bob & Carol & Ted & Alice*; *Hail, Hero!*; *Marooned*; *Topaz*; *A Dream of Kings*; and *Women in Love*.[16]

There was another development, accentuating the marketing power of paperbacks: the novelization, the hidden secret of 1960s Hollywood. The novelization revolutionized the way films were marketed. By the end of the decade, virtually every film released was accompanied by a book tie-in, either a bestseller sold to Hollywood, or a film script turned into a paperback. Except in particular circumstances, studios virtually gave away screenplays to publishers to be turned into novels in return for the marketing they could provide. "Producers looked at tie-in in books primarily as an exploitation aid, not a source of income," explained Patricia Johnson of paperback specialist Gold Medal Books. "Motion picture companies with no more—and often much less—than a rough script are being besieged by droves of publishers vying for the right to novelize original scenarios."[17] Novelizations were usually short—about 60,000 words—and therefore attractively priced for the reading public. They could sell as many as half a million copies. "What a publisher does for a film concern," said Johnson, "is it creates a nationwide market, a popular anticipation of a film before it would ordinarily be more than a vague glimmer in the public consciousness."[18] One of the earliest novelizations was for the Rat Pack heist picture *Ocean's 11* (1960) and it showed the format to which publishers readily adhered. As you might expect, the cover featured a still from the movie incorporating the main stars. But there was also, by dictate of the Writers Guild of America (the screenwriters union), mention of the original scriptwriters in the same size of typeface as the authors who transformed the script into a novel. Very rarely did the original screenwriter undertake this task. For a start, most considered it beneath their dignity. But, secondly, they got paid anyway. The screenwriter automatically received one-third of the fee the publisher paid the studio and the same share of royalties. By the mid-1960s, the WGA was negotiating for a set fee of $6000 (about $50,000 equivalent now) so a nice amount for no work but less appetizing for a full-time screenwriter to do the whole job.[19]

There were exceptions. When Robert Bloch turned his original screenplay *The Couch* (1961) into a novel,[20] it was in response to his experience with *Psycho*. Prior to the Hitchcock film, his novel had sold 4000 copies in hardback. The success of the film shifted 500,000 copies in paperback.[21] But he was not as assiduously wooed

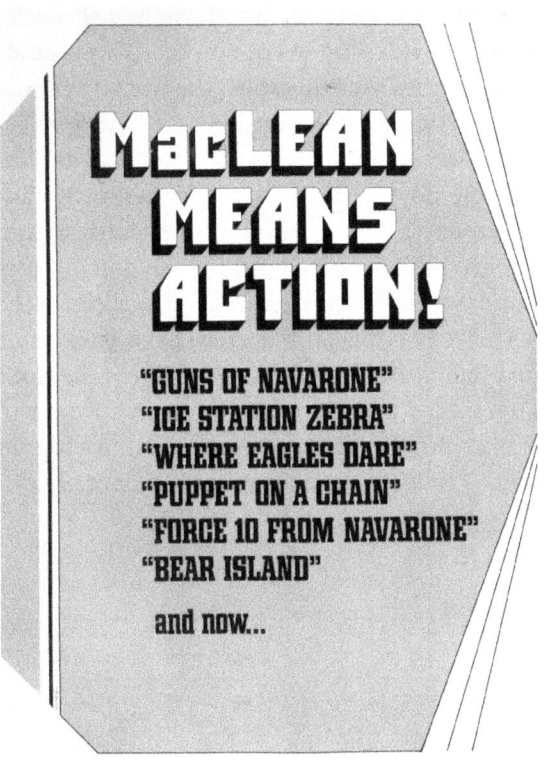

MacLean was the major pre-selling point for *The Hostage Tower*. When promoting a new film by a major star, ads sometimes listed previous hits. MacLean was one of the few writers to be so honored (advertisement from *Screen International*, October 20, 1979, page 40).

by publishers as Arthur C. Clarke and Stanley Kubrick, jointly credited for the novelization of *2001: A Space Odyssey*. Unusually, the novelization appeared first in hardback. Delacorte-Dell forked out a $150,000 advance and offered a 15 percent royalty rate. In addition, Clarke-Kubrick refused the hardback publisher a share of the paperback spoils.[22]

When Isaac Asimov agreed to novelize the script of *Fantastic Voyage* (1966), that was perceived as a publishing coup.[23] Famed Western writer Louis L'Amour novelized James R. Webb's script of *How the West Was Won* (1962).[24] Irving Shulman was a well-known novelist when called upon to turn *West Side Story* (1961) and *The Notorious Landlady* (1962) into novels.[25] Novelist-screenwriter Adela Rogers St. Johns (*The Girl Who Had Everything*, 1953) novelized *King of Kings* (1961),[26] and crime writer Jim Thompson tackled James Lee Barrett's script of *The Undefeated* (1969).[27] Marvin H. Albert—better known later for the Tony Rome private eye novels filmed with Frank Sinatra—was a relatively unknown journeyman when he penned the novelizations for a string of movie comedies including *Come September* (1961); *Lover Come Back* (1962); *Move Over, Darling* (1963); *The Pink Panther* (1963); *The Great Race* (1965); and *Strange Bedfellows* (1965). Similarly, David Westheimer, a year before his bestselling *Von Ryan's Express*, knocked out the book of *Days of Wine and Roses* (1962) from the J.P. Miller screenplay.[28] But, mostly, novelizations were produced by journeymen—Richard Wormer (*Operation Crossbow*, 1965),[29] Alan Caillou (*Khartoum*, 1965),[30] Ed Friend (*Alvarez Kelly*, 1966),[31] John Burke (*Privilege*, 1968), Richard Meade (*Rough Night in Jericho*, 1967),[32] Jackson Donahue (*Divorce American Style*, 1967),[33] Michael Avallone (*Krakatoa—East of Java*, 1968),[34] and Joseph Landon (*Stagecoach*, 1966).[35] No genre was safe. Even musicals were plundered. *West Side Story* was later joined by *My Fair Lady* (1964), *Funny Girl* (1968) and *Paint Your Wagon* (1969),[36] an unexpected bestseller thanks to Clint Eastwood and Lee Marvin on the cover. From the movie perspective, books were seen as "silent salesmen," alerting the public well in advance of other publicity about forthcoming attractions.[37]

The combination of the movie tie-in and the novelization expanded the market for books with Hollywood links. With the widening of the market to accommodate movie tie-ins, novelists were seen as prime movie real estate, their books viewed more enthusiastically by book retailers, particularly when the writers were serial producers of filmable material. Especially in the popular market, this was an ace. More than any other author, MacLean wrote novels that were marketed in the widest possible way, receiving three bites at the apple. Initial sales of the hardback from bookstores were augmented when the paperback hit the stands in the much larger book outlet arena, with a third opportunity when the movie tie-in[38] appeared. In the 1960s and 1970s, a novelist's backlist was prized because when a new paperback came out, it was generally accompanied, often in a dump-bin,[39] by copies of his previous works. Since MacLean was virtually guaranteed to produce a new book every year, and the bulk of his novels were turned into movies, he proved a marketing kingpin for his publishers. A new MacLean was not just an event, but an unprecedented marketing tsunami.

Chapter Two

The Secret Ways (1961)

It was something of a fluke that *The Secret Ways* was the first Alistair MacLean movie to reach the big screen. Three other adaptations appeared to have a much better chance of beating it into release. The leading contender was *H.M.S. Ulysses*. Such was the wave of public acclaim that greeted MacLean's debut novel on publication in 1955 that it seemed a foregone conclusion that the movie version would follow. Robert Clark, managing director of the top British studio Associated British, had bought the rights pre-publication for £30,000, initially looking upon it as a successor to the box office hit *The Dam Busters* (1955), and he looked almost triumphant when pictured with MacLean at the book launch.[1] Although the purchase price was a substantial sum at the time for a British novel, it soon proved an incredible bargain given the fact that the novel went on to sell an unprecedented 250,000 copies in hardback and more in paperback. Even before the movie version had been cast, Clark had dispatched in 1955 "advance camera and sound crews" to "the Home Fleet in Arctic waters" to shoot "essential background material."[2] Production hotted up two years later when Michael Anderson, director of *The Dam Busters* and Oscar-nominated for *Around the World in 80 Days* (1956), signed on to direct, with filming due to begin in 1958.[3]

Columbia snapped up the rights to the author's second book, *The Guns of Navarone*, which had appeared in 1957 and was an immediate bestseller. Third out of the traps was *South by Java Head*, published a year later. The rights went, again pre-publication, to British producer Daniel Angel (*Reach for the Sky*, 1956),[4] with Daniel Fuchs (*Love Me or Leave Me*, 1955) assigned the screenplay.[5] Angel had a deal with Twentieth Century–Fox to make this and *The Sheriff of Fractured Jaw* (1958), a comedy Western starring Kenneth More and Jayne Mansfield.[6] *The Last Frontier* (title changed in the U.S. to *The Secret Ways*[7]) and *Night Without End* were both published in 1959. As the former ended up with actor Richard Widmark, marking his second outing in the producer's chair, and the latter with the experienced production team of George Seaton and William Perlberg, responsible for the big-budget hits *The Bridges at Toko-Ri* (1954) and *The Proud and the Profane* (1956) (both with William Holden), it seemed a foregone conclusion that experience would win out. "I've exhausted my war service pretty thoroughly," MacLean said in the run-up to publication of *Night Without End*, a thriller about an airliner that crash-lands in Greenland.[8] Perlberg-Seaton planned to team Holden and Debbie Reynolds,[9] set the budget at $3.5 million[10] and hired British thriller writer Eric Ambler (*The Wreck of the Mary Deare*, 1959) for the screenplay.[11] But, in fact, the bigger the budget, the harder it

The first cross-marketing attempt to cash in on the author's fame. References to *The Guns of Navarone* would follow the author through many films. The British premiere in London was attended by Agatha Christie, considered for many years MacLean's rival for the tag of the world's best-selling author (Hannan collection).

seemed to reach the finishing line. When Associated British hit financial troubles, *H.M.S. Ulysses* was set to one side. When the stars pulled out of *Night Without End*, that went on the back burner. Disappointing box office for *The Sheriff of Fractured Jaw* put an end to *South by Java Head*. The derailment of these projects should have left *The Guns of Navarone* as the front-runner. But producer Carl Foreman, fighting a losing battle with Columbia over a roadshow release, incurred excessive delay, allowing *The Secret Ways* to steal its release thunder by one week.

The Widmark Way

"Acting's too ephemeral for a full-time job," lamented Richard Widmark,[12] echoing the views of many actors on realizing such skills were not so difficult to acquire. "The reason I made *The Secret Ways* "is that I like spy thrillers. I've been in this business quite a long time and to survive you have to do all kinds of pictures, you can't just specialize on just one kind."[13] Widmark wasn't just branching out into a different genre, he was developing a completely new set of skills: turning producer. Although making his Hollywood breakthrough around the same time as tough guys Burt Lancaster and Kirk Douglas, and receiving an Oscar nomination on debut for the film noir *Kiss of Death* (1947), Widmark missed out on the elevation to top billing in big-budget movies (when the occasion arose saddled with second male lead rather than out-and-out star), seemingly stuck with a snarling persona, and the changes he sought were as much to re-establish his acting career as swing into production. His Heath Productions outfit cut its teeth on *Time Limit* (1957), a Korean war drama in which he starred with a strong supporting cast (Richard Basehart, Dolores Michaels, Martin Balsam and Rip Torn) and a surprise director, Oscar-winning actor Karl Malden, helming his first picture. Widmark had bought the rights to *Time Limit* from Warner Brothers at a time when big studios were running shy of small pictures. Widmark purchased the rights to *The Secret Ways* in March 1959, one month after American publication by Doubleday,[14] with the intention of beginning production before the year was out.[15] He fronted the book deal with his own cash, not signing until months later a two-film deal with Universal, for whom he had starred in John Sturges' *Backlash* (1956).[16] Also on his production schedule were *The Seven File* for United Artists and the bullfighting drama *Wounds of Honor*, which he would direct but not star.[17] The *Secret Ways* budget was set at $1 million. "I enjoy production," Widmark claimed. "I like to act but over the years I find that I can do more, and I enjoy setting things up and seeing them through."[18] But he could hardly have been happy with his experience on *The Secret Ways*. Screenplay issues prevented Widmark meeting his initial start date of late 1959, filming set for England and an undefined European country.[19] Peter Viertel (*The Old Man and the Sea*, 1958) had first crack,[20] followed by Scotsman William Templeton[21] who, having written *1984* (1956), was expected to have a firm grasp of the Cold War elements. But it was left to Widmark's wife Jean Hazelwood to take the screenwriting credit, even though this would be her movie debut and she never made another film.

Finalizing actors proved equally last minute. German female lead Sonia Ziemann, virtually a veteran with nearly two decades experience, signed up only a few weeks before production began,[22] Austrian Senta Berger, making her Hollywood debut, a couple of weeks after,[23] and looking "set for discovery in America."[24] Director Phil Karlson was recruited a few months before shooting began.[25] Access being denied to Communist-controlled Hungary, where the story was set, Widmark elected to shoot in Austria. "You can't beat a genuine location," he noted, having not chosen one, but something similar: "[T]he backstreets of Vienna could easily double for Budapest."[26]

Obstacles arose once filming finally got underway on August 1, 1960.[27] Rather than importing crews from Britain or America, Widmark chose the budget-conscious idea of utilizing a German-only team. Problems abounded. "Shooting in Vienna was murder," he observed, complaining, with a very American sense of entitlement, that there was "very little English spoken" (the British tended to make the same complaint) and that it was "difficult to find interpreters" (as if such people should be in ready supply in case Hollywood comes calling).[28] Widmark recalled that it was "like fighting World War II all over again—you have the Austrians and the Germans fighting like mad with the English and the Americans." Language barriers, technical obstacles and cultural clashes exacerbated different working practices, one example being that foreign crews were not accustomed to going out into the street and shooting all night for five consecutive weeks.[29] Nor, presumably, were they keen to be filming so close to the borders. Much of the filming, according to assistant producer Euan Lloyd (later producer of *Shalako*, 1969) in a six-minute documentary, was "done directly under the guns of Communist guards only yards away."[30] Worse, star and director were soon at odds. Widmark had little regard for directors: "There are to me about eight to ten efficient directors in the world."[31] He didn't count Karlson among that figure. When the director took ill for a week with a virus, Widmark took over the directorial reins.[32] Three weeks later, the director quit over creative differences regarding the ending,[33] and again Widmark replaced him. Release was delayed due to Widmark's other commitments. After completing his part, he was away from mid–October shooting John Ford's *Two Rode Together* and not able to return to post-production until December.[34] The biggest problem was avoiding making an overt political statement. "I was trying to make an adventure story, a sheer adventure story. But some of it [politics] just creeps in." Exiled Hungarians in Detroit complained that the movie did not go far enough in depicting the reign of terror. "They had been in contact with the Hungarian Secret Police," said Widmark, "had gone through this torture, which seems corny with the dope, the needle and the steam room. But it's not incredible, it goes on every day of the week there."[35]

Once this production wrapped, Widmark forged ahead with plans to make *The Tiger's Roar* from the Jack Davies novel as a vehicle for Trevor Howard. But this and his other two features did not come to fruition and the star did not wear the producer's hat again until *The Bedford Incident* in 1965, his last stab at production. Working with Widmark inspired Ziemann to set up her own production arm, announcing *Next Stop Paradise*, based on husband Marek Hlasko's novel, in which she would star. (That did not get off the ground either.[36]) Senta Berger won the female leads in *Major Dundee* (1965) and *Cast a Giant Shadow* (1966).

The Film

This gritty, realistic thriller has much in common with *The Quiller Memorandum* (1965) with spies stalked through dark cobbled streets. To pay off his gambling debts, Michael Reynolds (Widmark), posing as a journalist, agrees to smuggle resistance leader Jansci (Walter Rilla) out of Hungary; Jansci is on the Soviet hit list after the failed 1956 uprising. Assisting him is Jansci's daughter Julia (Sophie Ziemann) and Elsa (Senta Berger) as a budding femme fatale. In a city of staircases and tunnels and echoing footsteps, authorities keep close tabs on visitors. The first time Reynolds escapes their notice, he is beaten up and it takes considerable skill, dodging through cinemas and creeping along ledges, to make any headway in his assignment. Various complications ensue, not least that Julia despises Reynolds and that Jansci does not want to flee his country. Reynolds, who starts out as anything but your standard good guy, ends up less mercenary. Mostly it is atmospheric cat-and-mouse with ruthless opposition partial to the odd spot of torture. Once it gets going, it is mostly chase and mostly unlikely for the escapees to succeed. That Reynolds is distrusted by those he is trying to help and that he doesn't want to be here at all, forced into adventure by adverse personal circumstances, stokes up the tension. Widmark doesn't quite abandon his snarling persona but manages some deft comedy when trying to play a journalist accommodating his hosts. Berger makes a striking debut, Ziemann less impressive, but veteran character actor Wolf Rilla has the brooding and charismatic presence of a leader. Vienna, generally not considered a soulless city, does a great job standing in for Budapest.

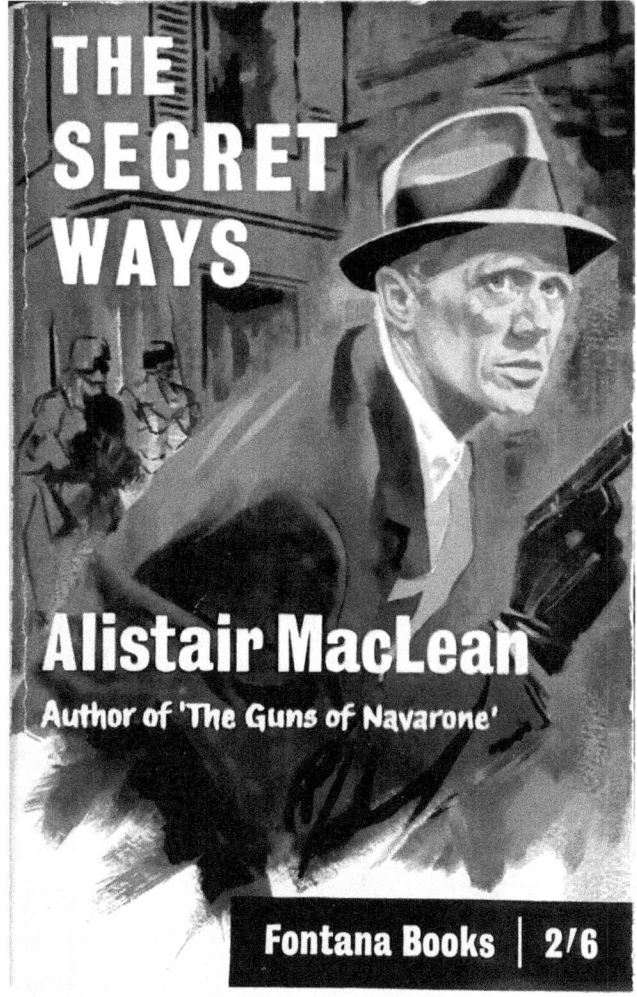

A Heath Production for Universal-International
Starring Richard Widmark and Sonja Ziemann

The Secret Ways, which is set in Hungary, takes place a couple of years after the Hungarian Uprising of 1956 and features dissidents. One of the film's stars, Wolf Rilla, was a real-life dissident whose family had fled Germany when Hitler came to power.

This was one of many Widmark bids to gain greater control of his career and provide himself with more interesting leading roles than the standard villains or tough guys that Hollywood marked him down for. While there's less out-and-out action for MacLean devotees brought up on *Where Eagles Dare* and *Fear Is the Key*, there are still considerable rewards from an intelligent screenplay and the crackle of pursuit. But it should be viewed more as a late entrant to the Hollywood cloak-and-dagger genre than a precursor of the 1960s Bond-style spy adventure. It's effective without being too memorable.

Book into Film

You might ask yourself why Richard Widmark bought the book if he was going to ignore so much of the author's brilliant story. In the original version, hero Reynolds (Widmark's character) does not simply fly into Vienna as in the film but has already crossed the Austrian border into Hungary in a blizzard after hitching a lift in a truck but now is stranded on foot in subzero temperatures, 30 miles from Budapest. This is not the only change authorized by Widmark, wearing his producer's hat. His Reynolds is a freelance gun for hire, clearing a gambling debt. He is hired by an American spy ring compared to MacLean's British secret service agent, intensely trained for 18 months for a mission to rescue British ballistic missile expert Professor Jennings with the help of Hungarian Resistance leader Jansci (Hungary at the time was part of the Soviet bloc). Widmark eliminated the character of Jennings, concentrating on getting Jansci out of Hungary. While Jansci remains a Resistance leader, Widmark turns him into a scholar and nothing to do with missiles. Combining characters was not unusual in the movie business and may have been necessary to streamline the plot. But if the idea was to simplify the storyline, that hardly explained of Elsa, who didn't exist in MacLean's novel. Her sole purpose is to provide Widmark with casual romance—testament in Hollywood terms to a hero's irresistible attraction. This was MacLean's first shift away from the trio of war novels which had rocketed him into the bestseller class and, in a major change of style, created the non-stop thriller template underpinning the subsequent *Fear Is the Key* (published in 1961), *When Eight Bells Toll* (1966) and *Puppet on a Chain* (1969), which saw loners or secret agents endure horrific physical abuse as they battled the odds.

MacLean's Reynolds enters Budapest a captive, rather than as in the Widmark version merely catching a train. He meets Julia in Vienna. But in the book, Reynolds meets Julia, along with her father, only after the secret agent is captured by the Resistance. In the book, Reynold's abduction occurs in the first 20 pages, in the film at the halfway mark. From the outset, MacLean thrusts his hero pell-mell into action with nary a let-up but in the film that tension is dissipated by punctuating the action with romance and various political meanderings.

Perhaps Widmark shied away from the MacLean plot due to budget constraints; the novel is certainly more intense and continuously action-packed. Starting with a blizzard and ending in a perilous river crossing, the novel has several scenes which would have looked stupendous on screen. The story Widmark ignored involved the scientist in danger of being removed from Hungary and returned by the authorities to the Soviet Union, forcing Reynolds to affect a rescue on board a train, in a devil-may-care episode worthy of James Bond, by separating one carriage from the rest. There follows a 400-kilometer chase to the Austrian border where, pursued by Hungarian secret police, they cross the Danube. In a final twist, while the professor and Julia are safe, Jansci refuses to leave his native country. It's common practice in translating novel into screenplay, for the adaptor to delete, alter or embellish plot, characters, time scale and even locale. Sometimes the screenwriter simply comes up with a more believable plot (as in *Blindfold,* 1966) or is required by the sheer length of the novel to make considerable changes. Here, it's quite obvious that MacLean had a far better narrative than the film Widmark opted to make; the novel's blizzard, train and river-crossing scenes are far more exciting than anything in the finished picture.

However, Widmark & Co. manage to make an enjoyable picture by not following the original story. The role of gambler-gone-bad was more appropriate to the Widmark screen persona than a secret service agent. (Outside of the humorous *Our Man in Havana*, 1959, there were not many of those around until a few years later.) The film introduced Senta Berger to a wider audience and the plot as it stands made a lot of sense.

Chapter Three

The Guns of Navarone (1961)

The Secret Ways was an easy ride compared to the travails endured by *The Guns of Navarone*. Welcome to big-budget Hollywood and another inexperienced producer. Oscar-nominated[1] screenwriter Carl Foreman (*High Noon*, 1952) had no films to his name when he was hired by Columbia as a producer in 1957,[2] after the company had purchased the MacLean novel in February 1957.[3] As part of a major investment in British production,[4] Columbia viewed it as its top release of 1959. The movie went through three screenwriters and three directors, was nearly closed down on account of a civil war and the actors strike of 1960, nearly killed David Niven, injured Gregory Peck, saw its budget rocket and its release delayed two years.[5] In addition, thanks to fleeing his native land as a result of McCarthys anti–Communist purge, Foreman was persona non grata in the United States, an issue that could severely hamper his career.[6] His political stance had cost Foreman a lucrative deal after *High Noon*,[7] and while he was able to work under a pseudonym in Britain,[8] none of his other projects came to fruition[9] and he was forced to appear before HUAC in 1956 to clear his name.[10] Columbia okayed a huge $5 million budget[11] for *Guns of Navarone*, with the aim of putting together an all-star cast.[12]

Foreman's first idea was to pair William Holden and Alec Guinness,[13] the stars of the blockbusting Oscar-winning *The Bridge on the River Kwai* (1957).[14] When that proved fruitless, he could have landed Cary Grant except for his excessive financial demands.[15] Foreman entered into negotiations with Burt Lancaster, Richard Burton, James Mason, Jack Palance, Brian Keith, Dan O'Herlihy,[16] Dean Martin and Louis Jourdan[17] and British stalwarts John Mills and Trevor Howard.[18] Kenneth More (*Reach for the Sky*, 1956) should have been a shoo-in but he had upset his boss at Rank, who refused to authorize a loan-out.[19]

Eventually, Foreman settled on a genuine star cast of five-time Oscar nominee Gregory Peck,[20] two-time Oscar winner Anthony Quinn and Oscar winner David Niven with Britisher Anthony Quayle, Welshman Stanley Baker and American James Darren in supporting roles.[21] Envisaging an old-fashioned talent hunt for the (in *Variety* parlance) "lone femme role,"[22] Foreman screen-tested 30 Swedish actresses.[23] Annette Stroyberg won the role[24] but dropped out and was replaced first by Ina Balin (until she preferred *From the Terrace*, 1960) and then by rising star Gia Scala (*The Angry Hills*, 1959). Perhaps the biggest name he failed to hook was opera superstar Maria Callas,[25] whose worldwide popularity put her in a class of her own. Callas nibbled at the bait but failed to bite. She was replaced by Greek star Irene Papas.

Chapter Three. The Guns of Navarone (1961)

With the exception of David Lean, Foreman had his pick of the cream of British directors. He considered Michael Anderson (*The Dam Busters*, 1955), Carol Reed (*The Key*, 1958), Guy Hamilton (*The Colditz Story,* 1955) and J. Lee Thompson (*Ice Cold in Alex*, 1958)[26] before plumping for Alexander Mackendrick, a stalwart of Ealing Studios. Although born in Boston, Mackendrick had grown up in Scotland. His debut *Whisky Galore!* (1949) was followed by *The Man in the White Suit* (1951) and *The Ladykillers* (1955), but it was his handling of the big American stars Burt Lancaster and Tony Curtis in the unflinching *Sweet Smell of Success* (1957) that contributed most to his getting the job. Shooting was initially scheduled to begin in the spring of 1959[27]; by the time it got underway, Foreman had opened his production account with *The Key* (1958) starring William Holden and Sophia Loren.[28] Locations sounded out for *The Guns of Navarone* included Italy[29]; Foreman considered shooting interiors in Belgrade[30] and even floated the notion of converting a Greek passenger ship into a studio.[31] Filming in Cinerama, which would have made it the first drama in that format, was briefly an option.[32] Eric Ambler, a thriller writer with a dozen screenplays to his credit,[33] was assigned the script.[34] At under two hours, it was deemed too short for what Foreman—a self-confessed "didactic writer"[35]—had in mind and so the producer took over screenwriting duties.[36] Thanks to major tax benefits and government cooperation,[37] Foreman was all set to shoot somewhere in Greece, finally selecting the island of Cyprus. But following a hunch,[38] he switched location to the neighboring island of Rhodes—and just in time, because civil war broke out in Cyprus.[39] Once that crisis was averted, the project was hit by the actors strike, a situation exacerbated by star

The Guns of Navarone is set during World War II. One of the film's British stars, David Niven, had been a professional soldier, graduating from the British military college Sandhurst, before switching to acting. He rejoined the Army on the outbreak of war in 1939 as a lieutenant, then joined the commandos and took part in D-Day.

Gregory Peck being very active in the Screen Actors Guild.[40] No sooner was that hurdle cleared than Mackendrick pulled out, citing a bad back.[41] Foreman briefly took over as director,[42] but Columbia, worried about him spreading himself too thin and balked at the idea of him tackling the role full-time. J. Lee Thompson re-entered the equation.[43]

Filming was now due to begin on January 2, 1960, with two units, one directed by Mackendrick and the other by Foreman, both filming background and mass scenes. The units would merge in March with the stars arriving in April. The original schedule called for six months of location work followed by a month of special effects in London. In the event, filming began on February 8 with the performers beginning their roles in late March.

The scale of the production was daunting. Greece supplied 1000 troops, fully equipped for combat, and specialist mountain corps, as well as a dozen destroyers, small planes, launches, rescue boats, helicopters, M24 Chaffee Light Tanks, American half-trucks, M8 Greyhound Scout Car, other combat vehicles, howitzers, mortars and machine-guns. Virtually the entire manpower, and senior commanding officers, of the Greek army and navy were at the film's disposal. The crew was granted unrestricted access to all historical sites. An abandoned German fortress dating back to the war, complete with barbed wire, was used as a German stronghold. A local 60-foot caique, utilized as the boat ferrying the team to the cliffs, lacked room for a full crew once massive lights and generators were mounted. A full-scale replica was built for the storm sequences, filmed in the studio in England.[44] Consultants included Brigadier D.J.T. Turnbull, General Fritz Bayerlein and Commander G.W. Stedman, who made available electronic specialists, harpoon-gunners and beach-landing specialists.[45] The Greeks supplied Brigadier General Veros, Admiral Eifas, Capt. George Stephanides (in charge of a dozen Greek destroyers) and explosives expert Commander John Theogolitis. Lt. Evangelos Tsakirakis and other army mountaineers scaled the cliffs beyond the village of Lindos, dropping ropes that the camera crew could attach to themselves in order to film the action.[46] The Greeks loaned half a dozen Royal Hellenic frigates while the Harbor Defence motor launch *Bezane*, on loan from the Royal Navy, was turned into the German E-Boat.[47]

As much as possible, the production used original locations but in other instances, such as the Marine Gate in the Old City of Rhodes doubling up as the fortress,[48] Shepperton Studios matte artists added a background that included the gun batteries and cliffs. However, for long shots of the fortress, a different location was used, 30 miles away: Lindos, with mattes providing the fortress elements. The Acropolis at Lindos was the backdrop, unadorned, for a scene where Peck's team prowls the ruins and for another in which German troops hunt them down. The total production unit comprised 120 people. There were two light and sound trucks, a mobile food commissary, five cars for props and cameras and two buses for the rank-and-file crew. Reaching the 23 major locations involved traveling a total of 12,600 miles and consuming 8500 gallons of gas. A boat bringing 21 tons of generators and lighting equipment was hit by a gale and could not land; coming to the rescue was the U.S.S. *Courier*, a Coast Guard ship whose main task was to broadcast *Voice of America* programs. There were 500 extras.

Since many locations were inaccessible by road, a convoy of donkeys was hired at the rate of $2.67 per day. Caterer Phil Hobbs flew in milk daily from Athens, imported marmalade from London and used Dutch canned butter. By mid–April, the crew had devoured 7240 loaves, 3210 turkeys, 1550 chickens, 1870 pounds of veal, 1850 pounds of beef, 855 pounds of pork, 520 pounds of ham, 365 pounds of lamb, 6000 heads of lettuce, 9900 eggs, 1200 pounds of cheese and 56,600 cups of tea.

The barrage of heavy fire by the guns was simulated by powerful underwater explosions. The Greek air force and infantry were involved in the attack on the fictional town of Mandrakos, location of the wedding. The sequence utilized various locations: the Isodia Theotokou church in Koskinou, four miles from Rhodes, while the restaurant was situated opposite what is now the international airport at Paradisi. For the climax, when the raiders infiltrate the fortress, the production used a mixture of original locations, the Gate of Saint Athanasios and Argyrokastro Square in the Old Town, with sets built at Shepperton.[49]

With Foreman very much a hands-on producer and embittered over Columbia's lack of faith in his untried directorial ability, Thompson had his work cut out for him. The producer tried to exert his authority by refusing to answer any script problems in private, instead doing so in front of the cast. The stars, too, were initially wary of each other, in part because Quinn and Niven outranked Peck, the bigger marquee name, in the Oscar stakes, but they bonded over games of chess. Gia Scala was "off-key" from the start because of Thompson's insistence that she cut her hair to disguise her as a man. Niven's biggest problem was "smoking with apparent enjoyment" since he was a lifelong non-smoker.[50] However, the actors responded to Thompson's work methods: He rehearsed entire scenes for two or three hours. He avoided storyboarding except for rudimentary diagrams that only he could understand. "It's an actor's picture," said Quinn.[51]

Thompson's biggest failure was sinking a Greek navy boat by overriding the expert and insisting on more explosives.[52] Despite their differences, Thompson appreciated Foreman the screenwriter: "He really brought up all these moral and ethical issues ... infused the story with much more meaning ... into something that was far more sophisticated."[53]

King Paul and Queen Frederica of Greece were guests on the final day of the location shoot, April 30.[54] Then the production shifted to Shepperton for interiors such as the mountain cave, the snow scene (though not the snow soldiers), the ruins (though not the exteriors) and the monastery (though not outside), as well as action scenes including mountain climbing, storm and blowing up the guns. The producer had initially wanted mountaineering scenes filmed on location with doubles, but instead they were shot in the studio with a horizontal camera and actors crawling along a floor, the final result an intricate jigsaw. The cliff foot was built in the studio; the cliff face was sometimes a painted matte, the actors watching from below shot on location, the rock face a studio floor plus blue screen, interspersed with stunt doubles on location and stuntman in the studio handling Anthony Quayle's fall.

The storm scene, shot over a long period in a water tank, was dangerous. A water tank is trapezoid, back wider than front, where the camera is placed, one end about twice the width of the other, sloping sides preventing waves bouncing back. On Shepperton's flooded Stage H, the biggest in Europe, jet engines and wind machines powered 250,000 gallons of water down four giant chutes. While a miniature was used for long shots, most filming involved a larger boat rocked on hydraulics with water blasted against the actors. Special effects created the climactic tidal wave. Filming lasted ten days, so arduous that only two shots a day were achievable.[55] Peck suffered a deep gash on the head after catching his coat on the hydraulics. He was washed overboard; had the hydraulics been working that day, he would have been crushed.[56] Quinn injured his back, Niven and Quinn reopened old war wounds, Darren almost drowned.[57] Filming the gun sequence, Niven nearly died.[58]

The titular guns did not conform to any particular vision. They were not specified in the book where the author simply had Mallory imagine that they were nine-inch guns, then 12-inch, then that they were the biggest guns he had ever seen, monsters. In essence, they had to be massive and menacing. It has generally been assumed they were based on coastal guns at Leros, but those were much smaller. In fact, the Navarone guns were so enormous they would have been physically impossible to erect in the cave they occupied. Vibrations from the guns, which in Foreman's version wrecked many buildings in the town, should have done similar damage to the rock on which they stood. The gun set was the largest ever built, three storeys high, and it included a working elevator. Construction took five months and cost £100,000. Production designer Geoffrey Drake and set designer Maurice Fowler based their guns on the Big Berthas, which were 280mm (11 inches), used by the Germans in both wars, with a range of 21 miles, further if, as here, radar-controlled. Three separate gun sizes—60-foot, 30-foot and 15-foot to create the necessary scale—were manufactured by a British munitions company and weighed 15 tons. Excessive rain caused the plaster roof of the exterior set to fall in; the cost of rebuilding was £20,000. Luckily, the 50 men working on the 100-foot-high steel scaffolding holding the set together had finished construction for the day when the accident occurred, otherwise such a catastrophic collapse would have seriously endangered production.

Looking out to sea from the gun cave, the audience was given two views. One perspective was filmed on location and the other was achieved not by blue screen but from strips of silver paper strung across fields on the backlot with the backing a painted matte.[59] Six cameras filmed the destruction of the guns. To set charges to the hoist, David Niven was required to stand chest-deep in water. The reasons for this were never clear. In the book, the lift had a floored well but, presumably to add to the excitement, Foreman had filled the bottom of the lift with water. Niven contracted septicemia, either because the water infected a cut lip or due to contamination in the water. He was rushed to intensive care. For some time, it was touch and go whether he would survive. But he did and returned to complete his scenes.

The movie was now running late. It had been scheduled to finish at the start of August; shooting limped on until September 21. As a consequence, the budget soared by about 20 percent to nearly $6 million. When filming wrapped with 445,000 feet of exposed footage and 85,000 feet shot for television use, Foreman was

Chapter Three. The Guns of Navarone (1961) 27

Carl Foreman (in dark glasses), in his capacity as writer, confers with Anthony Quinn prior to the first take of Scene 246 of *The Guns of Navarone* (courtesy of *Cinema Retro* magazine).

exhausted. "I came into this business as a writer and now look at me," he said, "businessman, father figure, a politician, I have to play nursemaid to stars and spend all day juggling egos."[60]

Understandably, Foreman needed a break.[61] His marriage had broken up and his father had died. Columbia, keen to recoup costs as soon as possible, was taken aback by Foreman's plans for the picture's release. He clamored for roadshow[62] and argued that time spent tub-thumping the picture across Europe[63] and the U.S. was marketing gold. As well as the paperback and, unusually, a reprint of the hardback featuring scenes from the film, promotional tie-ups included food (cheese from Crete, olives from Kalamae, figs from Smyrna, pistachio nuts from Aegine, plus recipes by the stars), ideas targeting the fashion industry such as "Navarone Blue" used in bedspreads, and clothes in classical Grecian style by top designers and highlighted in department stores and magazines. There were Navarone shirts, ties and slacks, plus watches, a haircut and even a toy.[64]

The movie world-premiered in London (with Queen Elizabeth II in attendance) on April 27, and opened in the U.S. in July. It was critically acclaimed and nominated for five Oscars, including Best Picture, Director and Adapted Screenplay.[65]

The Film

The truth is, nobody knew quite what to expect. Carl Foreman and Alistair MacLean appeared to be unlikely bedfellows. War films generally presented straightforward narratives, not laced with twists like savage beats on a drum. And mission films such as this were in their infancy, *The Magnificent Seven* (1960) the closest comparison. But the opening is almost prosaic, verging on the heavy-handed, as a narrator (James Robertson Justice) attempts to link, for six minutes, the legends of ancient Greece with a modern one about destroying the Guns of Navarone preventing the rescue of 2000 men trapped on a different Greek island. Attempts to bomb the gun have failed. Mountaineer Captain Mallory (Gregory Peck), his leave curtailed, joins a team composed of explosive experts Major Franklin (Anthony Quayle) and Corporal Miller (David Niven), mechanic and ruthless killer "Butcher" Brown (Stanley Baker), Resistance contact Pappadimos (James Darren) and Stavrou (Anthony Quinn). With no time to waste on character introduction *à la The Magnificent Seven*, they are identified economically, Brown playing with his knife, Pappadimos with a pistol, Miller lying idle. Stavrou expecting betrayal soon finds it, rooting out a spy. They set off on an old tub of a boat.

The first action displays character. Attacking a German patrol boat, Mallory takes the initiative but Miller crouches out of sight and a hesitant Brown is saved by Pappadimos. Relationships are revealed, Miller and Franklin sharing an unspoken bond. Stavrou hates Mallory for accidentally causing the death of his family, thus stoking up internal division. Franklin muses that the Germans knew they were coming. Two bravura scenes follow in quick succession, storm and virtuoso mountaineering, group activity and individual action, searing noise and virtual silence. When they reach the cliff top, there's no time to savor triumph. The injured Franklin needs rescue, food and medical supplies are lost. Taking charge, Mallory questions Brown over his apparent cowardice. In the first stab at the futility of war, Brown confesses he's sickened by killing. Mallory answers a buzzing telephone in German. For a moment, we think he has got away with it, but the German on the other end is not fooled. The next day, Franklin, knowing he is a liability, tries to crawl away. To prevent Franklin committing suicide,

Chapter Three. The Guns of Navarone (1961)

and Stavrou doing the job for him, Mallory tells the major that the mission has been abandoned. Almost instantly, another music cue, drumbeats, soldiers approaching, Stavrou picking the enemy off to let his comrades escape. Night, and they wait in the St. Alexis ruins. Franklin is delirious. Stavrou and Pappadimos on guard duty drag a body into the cave, dump it face-down on the ground. Turned over, it is, unexpectedly, a young woman. A female voice off-screen growls, "Don't move." Surprise #1: Their contact is a woman, Maria (Irene Papas). Surprise #2: she is Pappadimos' sister. Surprise #3: The unconscious woman is Anna (Gia Scala), rendered mute after being whipped by the Germans until the white of her bones showed. Surprise #4: When the pursuing Germans arrive, the cave is empty.

The fourth day: soldiers patrol, a plane is sighted overhead, Germans search a village, Franklin's leg has turned gangrenous. They are shelled by mortar, attacked by dive bombers. A decision about Franklin had been made, but we don't see the discussion, just Franklin carried into hospital. But it's a trap. Anna, Mallory and Stavrou escape and find a table in the village square to watch a wedding. Pappadimos blends in by joining a traditional song. Marching boots signal an end to jollity; the team surrenders. They are interrogated by the S.S. but Stavrou quickly turns the tables and they escape, leaving Franklin behind.

Almost as temporary relief, budding romance between Maria and Stavrou flowers in elliptical fashion. They hole up in a monastery. It's exposition time. Mallory expects the captured Franklin to mislead the Germans. Miller confronts Mallory over his cold-blooded use of Franklin, underscoring the theme of war's brutality. Mallory's conscience is troubled: Was his treatment of Franklin "the civilized thing?" He finds succor by kissing Anna. Franklin, tortured, refuses to talk, but the German have truth serum.

The last day: They enter Navarone. Franklin talks, sirens sound, troops move out. One hour and 48 minutes of screen time have elapsed, we're almost exactly two-thirds in. Act Three opens with a famous scene, Miller taking center stage: "The party's over, someone's stepped on the cake." Sabotage. "Which means there is a traitor in this room." Pointing the finger at Anna, he rips the dress from her back. No scars show. Anna whimpers, "I cannot stand pain." And she may well have been echoing the fears of every man in the room, the need to be brave in the face of everything. A woman admits to cowardice that in a man would have been repellent. Self-interest rather than self-sacrifice. "They said they would put me into their brothels. They said they'd torture me." We have seen Franklin tortured. The villain is a beautiful woman; it's churlish to even accuse her of being weak. Mallory is appalled; they had kissed, he has fraternized with the enemy. But who will kill her? "Who is more guilty?" taunts Miller. "The man who gives the order or the man who has to do it with his own hands?" The crying girl cowers. Mallory takes aim. There is a quiet pop. Anna turns from Mallory to her killer. Maria.

Emotional high point over, now it's back to the action—and tension. Stavrou and Pappadimos hold off the Germans. Mallory and Miller get inside the fortress. An alarm attracts more soldiers, pounding on the doors. Brown dies stealing a boat. Maria's brother is killed trading fire with the Germans. The Allied convoy can be seen at sea. The tale now has so many areas to cover, it's not hard to ratchet up the tension between the saboteurs, the advancing ships, the encroaching Germans, the countdown, the massive guns. Mission is accomplished in spectacular fashion.

Book into Film: The Carl Foreman Translation

Characters, genders and narrative were changed and elements, out of place in a straightforward action picture, added as Foreman the screenwriter took instructions from Foreman the producer. Altering the gender of partisans Louki and Papayanis from male to female was more than a commercial ploy—a war movie minus women potentially excluded half the audience—and heightened the drama, adding a layer of fascinating interaction. When the part of Maria went to Irene Papas, her love interest became Stavrou and as she was such a strong character that made Quinn more interesting but also brought out other aspects of World War II. While British and American women played a negligible part in the actual conflict, that was not true of conquered nations, Greek women presented here as fighters and victims, not passive love interests. Switching Papayanis to the female Anna both provides Mallory with romantic yearnings and underscores emotional betrayal.

The other key change was to add to the MacLean mix an extra Greek, Pappadimos, an exile returning to fight for his country, and younger brother of Maria. Foreman divided the characteristics of the novel's Lt. Andy Stevens, Royal Naval Volunteer Reserve, among three people: his boyishness to Pappadimos, reticence to fight bordering on cowardice to Brown, broken leg to Major Franklin. There was no Franklin in the book and thus no debate about leadership; Mallory's authority is never questioned. The inclusion of Franklin created high drama when he was sidelined and brought out tension with Mallory and between Mallory and Miller. The Mallory-Andrea antagonism is a Foreman invention; in the book, they are simply colleagues. Altering their backstory creates conflict. And given Franklin's absence in the book, then Miller's friendship with him is another filmic device. Having the subordinate Miller played by the upscale David Niven twisted public preconception. Mallory was more vicious in the book, kicking the partisan, but that action wouldn't sit well with a top Hollywood star.

Foreman both simplified and complicated the narrative. In the original, they took a convoluted route to Navarone, involving launch, plane and motor torpedo boat before setting off in the battered old caique. Foreman excised much of this and MacLean's second encounter with the Germans, instead directing the team straight into the storm. In the book, they are saved by Mallory's mountaineering skills but Foreman separates landing and climbing and also eliminates Andrea saving Mallory from falling. At the top of the cliff, MacLean had Mallory not answering the phone, while in the film he did. It made little difference to the outcome. Either way, the Germans came, but it was more dramatic the Foreman way, for it demonstrated Mallory's language skills and again heightened tension because, for a moment, the audience believed Mallory had fooled the Germans.

Chapter Three. The Guns of Navarone (1961)

The idea of betrayal was a constant in both film and book, but for Foreman this reflected deep-seated feelings about the HUAC episode, and in the film he dramatized the impact of the actions of betrayers on their victims. Foreman eliminated most of the book's drawn-out rescue of the soldier on the mountain to keep the action moving. In both versions, the man was badly hurt, with gangrene setting in quickly, and he became a liability. The route to Navarone differed enormously from book to film.Perhaps the greatest example of Foreman's dramatic skills was the encounter with the partisans. The heart of the action was the same as in the book except, of course, Foreman changed the partisans into women and made one of the women the older sister of one of the men. So now, in the film, the emotional hub, rather than the narrative purpose, of each member of the team (now including the partisans) had been revealed. Everyone had an emotional core, and as the film moved into its second half, other relationships developed in a way not possible in the book, Maria with both her brother and Andrea; Mallory with Anna; Miller, the makeshift medic, safeguarded Franklin. In the book, the Germans captured them in a hut, rather than a hospital. The good German and the evil German were MacLean's ideas but in the book, Andrea's trick failed and they were rescued another way. Foreman complicated their entrance to Navarone; the team was now expected rather than a surprise. MacLean held up the action by holing up the invaders in an abandoned house. But the discovery of sabotaged fuses is pure MacLean, as is the "Exhibit A, Exhibit B" speech; but Foreman brings everyone into the scene rather than just Mallory and Miller. In the subsequent questioning of the traitor, MacLean had Miller, rather than Maria, do the killing. Foreman made much more of the Germans attacking the doors with sledgehammers and oxyacetylene cutters. Planting the explosive in the hoist came from the book; MacLean's hoist wasn't flooded. And there was no fight to the death for Brown, as in the film.

What Foreman chose to retain, what he dropped and what he embroidered provided a fascinating journey into the mind of the screenwriter. Take three examples at the film's outset. In the book, we are given far more of the background of Commander Jensen, which Foreman ignored. Instead, he introduced two new elements: that Mallory has never met his boss, and that Jensen personally reflected on the futility of war rather than conveying it to Mallory. The Richard Harris "bloody" speech was pure Foreman. And the screenwriter dispensed with another MacLean character at HQ, Monsieur Eugene Vlachos, who directs them to the partisans and who imparted one piece of information that Foreman used to greater dramatic effect (the Germans punish anyone helping the Allies). It was Foreman's idea to foreground the movie with the historic and legendary status of the island, emphasizing the ruins, adding domesticity, employing the wedding scene to bring into focus the local people and their customs and songs. Foreman's sense of place was exceptional whereas MacLean's was sketchy. Foreman also created more confrontation and more twists, and his understanding of pace was undeniable. He enhanced relationships between characters and built up the themes of betrayal. The other major addition was the anti-war sentiment. The novel's Stevens expressed concerns about some actions proposed by Mallory and on a few, isolated occasions, MacLean's characters acknowledged the barbarity of war. But in a more forceful way, conscience was at the forefront of Foreman's mind in constructing his screenplay and it rarely relinquished center stage. And it's this that gave the movie its soul.

Chapter Four

The Satan Bug (1965)
When Alistair MacLean Quit: Part I

Scroll down the credits for *The Satan Bug* (1965) and there's no mention of Alistair MacLean. Instead, the source material is credited to Ian Stuart. Yes, it's a pseudonym. But you might be asking yourself: Why did a world-famous thriller writer employ a pseudonym? Pseudonyms were generally used, most often in genre fiction, for two reasons. Firstly, during this period, authors, except of the status of Agatha Christie or Georges Simenon, were expected to limit output to one book a year. Salvatore Lombino used the pseudonym Ed McBain for his *87th Precinct* series,[1] while British author John Creasey had 28 pseudonyms.[2] The second reason was when a famous author in one genre wished to experiment with another; recently J.K. Rowling turned to crime under the name Robert Galbraith.

MacLean fell into neither of these categories. An unexpected success, the Scottish schoolteacher hit the jackpot in 1955 with his debut *H.M.S. Ulysses*, a straightforward war novel, and followed up with *The Guns of Navarone* in 1957 and another four thrillers in four years under his own name, the last being *Fear Is the Key* (1961). By this point, he had become exceedingly annoyed at the treatment his manuscripts received at the hands of his publisher Collins which had strongly advised he set aside his third book *South by Java Head*, complaining there were too many incidents.[3] The author felt "very much like a pupil under severe pressure from a master."[4]

While no doubt every author gets picked up for momentary lapses or for elements of the story that need reconsideration,[5] MacLean was annoyed that his publishers were tinkering with his output rather than falling over themselves to worship their cash cow. MacLean also felt that his books only sold so well because his name was attached. Every book was "by the author of *H.M.S. Ulysses*" or, after the fantastic success of the movie, "by the author of *The Guns of Navarone*." He was beginning to feel more unwelcome commodity than cherished asset. Unusually, from a financial perspective, having sold millions of copies of books plus revenues from film sales, he was able to assert his authority in a way that could damage his tormentors. This would not prove to be the last time MacLean turned the publishing industry on its head. As much as he was innovative in his writing, giving birth to an entire new category of novel later taken up by Geoffrey Jenkins, Desmond Bagley, Brian Callison and Robert Ludlum and laying the groundwork for the later Lee Child, he viewed his business from a different perspective. Part of the problem lay in his self-deprecating approach to his work. "I'm not a novelist, I'm a storyteller," he said. "There's no art in what I do, no mystique…. The plotting, yes, I enjoy that. But the writing is a pain." MacLean gave the impression that he simply tossed off novels whereas any seasoned observer would recognize depths of skill and talent, not least because of the plotting and pace. He was one-off. Nobody could work out why he was so compulsively readable. But while MacLean failed to acknowledge in public his undoubted gift, he objected to his publishers allowing editors to take him to task with continuous severity, almost resenting his success.

Matters had come to a head with *Fear Is the Key* (1961), his least successful book so far, and one that involved a deliberate change of writing style. "What I'm trying to do is develop a technique of completely impersonal storytelling in the first person,"[6] he explained, the reader seeing action unfold as if through the eye of a camera. His publishers, who measured success only in terms of sales, took the opportunity to gloat, expecting him to listen to their superior wisdom and toe their line. But for MacLean, this was a clash too far and he took himself off to renowned agent Curtis Brown,[7] who welcomed him with open arms and none of the niggling that marked his dealings with the publishers. While Collins would remain his British publisher, Curtis Brown took on the task of invigorating foreign rights. After snaring what they expected to be a golden goose, you can guess at Curtis Brown's reaction on being told that the first book the agency would handle would be under the pseudonym Ian Stuart.

Set in Australia, *The Dark Crusader* (retitled *The Black Shrike* for U.S, readers) concerned a hunt for missing scientists. Collins hated this book, complaining about over-complicated plot, boring characters and improbable action. MacLean was incensed: "If

Although *The Satan Bug* top-lined the relatively unknown George Maharis, the producers at one time had hopes of recruiting a major star. The script was sent to Charlton Heston, Oscar-winning star of *Ben-Hur* (1959), but he turned it down (Hannan collection).

the book is as bad as you say and you obviously lack faith in it, can you genuinely imagine that I believe you will honestly and sincerely get behind it in promotion, publishing and selling?"[8] Desperate to retain the author and hoping that this experiment would be short-lived, Collins agreed to publish it. Naturally, the only way to ensure that it didn't vanish into the oblivion that faced most new authors, Collins gave the book "by a new author" a heavy publicity campaign. The poorer sales did not dampen MacLean's ardor for his pseudonym, and he went on to produce *The Satan Bug* by Ian Stuart, his faith in his decision justified when a Hollywood director of the caliber of John Sturges (*The Magnificent Seven*, 1960), seeing far greater potential in the novel than the publishers, snapped it up for production.

Myth has it that both *The Dark Crusader* and *The Satan Bug* played by the rules laid down by the author. But that did not turn out to be the case. The U.S. paperback edition of *The Satan Bug* (published by Popular Library in 1962) reveals the author's real identity on the back cover. In due course, the book was reissued under the MacLean moniker and is a far better example of the cinematic style the author was attempting to achieve than *The Dark Crusader*. It became the template for his later books.

Top-Name Director John Sturges

With *Gunfight at the O.K. Corral* (1957), *The Magnificent Seven* and *The Great Escape* (1963) in his portfolio, John Sturges was one of the best-known and most respected Hollywood directors, a far cry from the likes of Phil Karlson and head-and-shoulders above J. Lee Thompson.[9] *The Satan Bug* had not been immediately snapped up by Hollywood[10] when touted around studios by H.N. Swanson and Co. in 1962. A year later, it ending up on Sturges' slate as the first project in a four-picture deal with the equally highly regarded Mirisch Brothers, who released product through United Artists.[11] The director was keener on *The Hallelujah Trail* (1965), filmed as a 70mm Cinerama roadshow, and *Hour of the Gun* (1967), but *The Satan Bug* was greenlit first because of the production difficulties inherent in developing Westerns.[12] When Sturges was initially connected with *The Satan Bug* in 1963, it was left open whether the movie would be filmed abroad or the U.S.[13] In the event, a foreign location was avoided, and to minimize travel, Sturges decided to shoot in and around the desert area close to his home turf of Palm Springs and the Joshua Tree National Park.[14] Screenwriters James Clavell (*The Great Escape*) and Edward Anhalt (*Becket*, 1964) were called in to Americanize and update an English-set thriller.

"We aren't losing any of the suspense quality by moving it to America,"[15] averred Sturges. He was not a director known for "message pictures,"[16] but he recognized the implicit threat of biological warfare for "its terror potential" and envisioned a powerful climax in the evacuation of Los Angeles. He swapped the married, lame and disfigured hero for a hip loner in the Steve McQueen mold. It would have been quite a different picture if first choice star Charlton Heston had not turned it down.[17]

Co-producer Walter Mirisch admitted to being "disappointed that we had not been able to get a major star"[18] and settled instead on George Maharis (*Quick Before It Melts*, 1964), graduate of television's *Route 66* (1960–1963). Also plucked from television were Richard Basehart, the star of *Voyage to the Bottom of the Sea* (1964–68), and Frank Sutton from the comedy *Gomer Pyle, USMC* (1964–69). Initially cast as the general's daughter was Joan Hackett (*The Group*, 1966)—it would have been her movie debut—but she was replaced by Anne Francis.[19]

Sturges' biggest problem was creating imposing research facility Station 3. Sticking it underground saved a chunk of cash, since interiors were minimalist. "The set cost us nothing," said Sturges. "We had to build the thing big enough to make it look right. But this was a budget picture.... All you have to do (underground) is build a lot of ventilation stacks up in the air and a cement thing with a door."[20] To build tension, the set was lit with an ominous amber glow.

It proved impossible to achieve the one effect Sturges had set his heart on: the panic-crazed evacuation of Los Angeles. City officials put a block on the gridlock called for in the script. Recalled Sturges, "The sons-of-bitches wouldn't let me stop traffic ... we didn't get the panic on the streets, the motorists trapped on the freeways ... the nightmare of the evacuation." The director was forced to resort to "glass shots" and background noise to create the sense of pandemonium, the gridlock limited to the roadblock.[21] Also hampering production was a sense that the director's mind was not fully on the job. John Gay, screenwriter of the forthcoming *The Hallelujah Trail*, was often on set conferring between shots with Sturges. "Obviously, that's where his mind and heart were," complained Edward Asner. The laughter that Sturges and Gay enjoyed while dreaming up ideas for the comedy Western seemed at odds with the mood of the pandemic thriller. "The smaller things suffered because of that big thing to come," said producer Robert Relyea.[22]

The Satan Bug had its world premiere in West Germany, where Richard Basehart was a big name. Even with Sturges on board, the movie only cost $1.79 million, distinctly small potatoes for the period. The hiring of Maharis was the first in a series of casting moves that saw MacLean pictures saddled with virtual unknowns, on the assumption that the author's name was the chief marketing tool.

Another Message Picture

The subject matter—a manufactured pandemic—would certainly resonate these days, after Covid, but the emphasis then was on the dangers of a nuclear winter. From a documentary-style start, it segues into detective thriller, then chase. It has a couple jaw-dropping moments of tension, several clever twists, some sleight of hand, distinctive cinematography that utilizes twilight, an eerie score from Jerry Goldsmith (*Planet of the Apes*, 1968) and a scene of mass slaughter that presaged apocalyptic movies common a few decades later. Maverick investigator Barrett (George Maharis) is called in to investigate murder at top-secret biochemical establishment Station Three—and the theft of the Satan Bug, a chemical weapon that can destroy the world in weeks. Barrett determines it is an inside job, masterminded by a lunatic messiah. With General Williams (Dana Andrews) and his daughter, Barrett's old flame Ann (Anne Francis), Barrett tracks down mad Charles Reynolds Ainsley (Edward Asner). After a stolen chemical weapon paralyzes Florida, Barrett must stop Reynolds dropping the Satan Bug on Los Angeles. Director Sturges blows apart all the conventions of the genre and, boy, does he enjoy playing with the audience. The hero takes 15 minutes to arrive and the second main character General Williamson (Dana Andrews) another 30 minutes. We shift from docu-drama to pure detection to a manhunt that is way ahead of its time. General Williams marshals an air-sea-land operation that pulls a police web so tight, it seems the villains cannot escape—but that is just another device to throw the audience off track. Most spy thrillers take place in glorious color or in noir night, but here we are either in broad desert daylight, with vistas so wide and dirty-brown nothing can escape the camera, or in murky twilight where anyone could get away, so that when we reach Los Angeles, civilization is like a lush new world. In the arid desert, water is like an oasis of blue.

By now, quite a lot of the bad guys in this kind of thriller were narcissists, delighted to step into the spotlight and take on the good guys, but once again Sturges lets us nibble on this juicy bone before yanking it away. The bad guy may be well known but, like John Wick or the Equalizer these days, he has left no trace on the public records. There are a few standout scenes: Barrett entering the bug vault in full Hazchem outfit with every squeak of his accompanying hamster setting the viewer on edge; newsreel footage of roads littered with corpses; a roadblock played for laughs; and in the noir tradition, Ann turns up too often for coincidence. That kind of playing on expectation goes on, too, as Asner tones down his usual screen belligerence to a whisper. Barrett is always behind the eight ball, never getting the drop on the opposition, and, unlike James Bond, he has no time for sexual dalliance. There's overmuch exposition at the start and especially once the picture picks up pace but, that said, the tension remains taut. Maharis is excellent as the smart detective, but former Hollywood superstar Dana Andrews (*Laura*, 1944) steals the show as the tight-lipped general. Anne Francis (*Girl of the Night*, 1960) proves a spunky girlfriend while Richard Basehart has a plum as the chief scientist.

Book into Film

Not unexpectedly, director John Sturges shifted the action of MacLean's Doomsday-scenario thriller from Britain to the U.S., the locale of the secret chemical facility from lush English countryside to desert, and from above to below ground. Not unusually, either, wholesale changes were made to character names: MacLean's Pierre Cavell is altered to Lee Barrett, chief scientist Dr. Gregori becomes Dr. Hoffman, General Cliveden turns into General Williams, while his daughter Mary emerges as Ann. MacLean's Cavell was far from the handsome Hollywood hero, walking with a limp and face scarred. Mary is his wife and not, as in the Sturges version, an ex-flame.

Sturges inserted a 15-minute prologue. The initial scenes at the plant are screenwriter invention though Clavell and Anhalt draw on material presented as backstory in the original. MacLean went straight into the action with the attempt to recruit Cavell for nefarious purposes, inviting the reader to learn about his past.

There are other differences between book and film. Sturges widened out the action, so that the idea of mankind in complete peril is more obviously cinematically achieved. (In the book, a small village is wiped out after a nerve gas attack with London the main objective for the Satan Bug.) In addition, the general plays a greater on-screen role and, in some respects, controls the manhunt.

But the narrative thrust of film and book go their separate ways. Barrett, a Korean War vet, operates in standard espionage territory, while Cavell is more of an old-fashioned detective, interviewing suspects. While Barrett, with the help of the general, closes in on the suspect responsible for the panic, Cavell had to investigate myriad possibilities before fixing on the culprit.

Perhaps the most important change is that MacLean's hero solves the mystery primarily through his own skill while Barrett is less self-reliant. Cavell often informs his mystified superiors that he knows exactly what is going on. In the novel, Cavell spots the real reason for the theft of the Satan Bug, realizing it is merely a front for an audacious heist, the scheme a method of clearing out central London in order to carry out a series of thefts in a city deserted by police. However, the idea of a robbery to end all robberies had been adequately covered in *Goldfinger* the previous year and Sturges focused instead on an audience fearing wholesale slaughter rather than worrying whether a James Bond–type hero would survive. Sturges correctly calculated that audiences would respond more to the paranoia pervasive at the time than individual derring-do. In some respects, Sturges created a template for future movies that threatened swathes of the population such as *The Andromeda Strain* (1971), *The Cassandra Crossing* (1976), *Black Sunday* (1977) and *Outbreak* (1985). Silent destruction touched on implicit human fear of unknown powers at work. The screenwriters did lift complete sections from the book: the initial interrogation of Cavell-Barrett, how the dogs were silenced at the facility, the nerve gas attack on the imprisoned pursuers (a farm in the book, an abandoned gas station in the film) and Barrett's insistence that the bad guys take away Ann immediately prior to this attack. But most of the Sturges film veers so far from the MacLean blueprint that it relies heavily on screenwriter imagination.

It would be interesting to know why they deprived Barrett of more personal ties, for in the novel it is the wife who is endangered, not an old flame, and the investigator's best friend is among the casualties at the facility.

CHAPTER FIVE

Ice Station Zebra (1968)
When Alistair MacLean Quit: Part II

Alistair MacLean had another nasty surprise in store for his publishers. After a five-year tax exile in Switzerland, the author had returned to Britain in 1962, setting up home first in Farnham, Surrey, followed by a brief hiatus in Ireland before settling down in a Georgian mansion with a two-acre estate in Haslemere, Surrey. Having abandoned the pseudonym, two books were published that year under the Alistair MacLean brand name: the thriller *Golden Rendezvous* and his first non-fiction work *All About Lawrence of Arabia*. It might have appeared to his publishers that the crisis was over.

But in 1963, while delivering the manuscript of *Ice Station Zebra* to publisher Ian Chapman of Collins, MacLean dropped a bombshell. Financially independent, fed up with the high-and-mighty attitude of his editors, and depressed by sales of *Fear Is the Key*, disillusioned by the act of writing itself,[1] he announced that he had written his final book. The goose had laid its last golden egg. This time he was giving it up for good. He planned to become a hotelier and, after examining over 100 premises, had purchased the 400-year-old Jamaica Inn in Cornwall,[2] immortalized by the Daphne du Maurier book and Alfred Hitchcock film. The place was a solid going concern, takings from accommodation and food augmented by income from three bars and a souvenir shop. MacLean intended becoming a hands-on manager and felt immediately more at home dealing with the public in this atmosphere rather than in correspondence with fans. His younger brother Gillespie was an established hotelier, and eventually his older brother Ian, a high-flyer at Shell, became involved.

Despite MacLean calling time on publishing, Hollywood did not give up on him. The box office accrued by *The Guns of Navarone* and the surprising success of another British war film, *Sink the Bismarck* (1962), in the U.S.[3] revived interest in *H.M.S. Ulysses*. *Night Without End*, with new director Richard Wilson, was still on the cards at Paramount.[4] Actor Laurence Harvey, going down the Richard Widmark route of taking control of his career, had purchased *The Golden Rendezvous* as a vehicle for his directorial debut.[5] But the big news was that another independent outfit, Filmways, one of a new breed of high-profile independent production companies, had acquired *Ice Station Zebra* in 1964. Headed by Martin Ransohoff, Filmways had started out in commercials before progressing to documentaries and television sitcoms; *Mr. Ed* (1961–66) and *The Beverly Hillbillies* (1962–1971) were early

The first attempt to film *Ice Station Zebra* had a different cast and screenwriter from the eventual movie. Only director John Sturges was retained. Even the main advertising image, seen here, did not survive. Note that the name of Alistair MacLean was not as prominent as it would later become (Hannan collection).

successes. Segueing into the movies, Ransohoff quickly built up an impressive roster of big-budget, prestigious projects, attracting the likes of Julie Andrews (*The Americanization of Emily*, 1964), Richard Burton and Elizabeth Taylor (*The Sandpiper*, 1965) and Steve McQueen (*The Cincinnati Kid*, 1965). A tie-up with MGM ensured his output received wide release and top-level marketing.[6] Ransohoff initially hired MacLean to do an *Ice Station Zebra* treatment[7]; the first writer to tackle an actual screenplay was Ring Lardner, Jr., who had written *The Cincinnati Kid*. His first draft, measuring 157 pages (i.e., over two and a half hours of screen time), was delivered on September 30, 1964. Spring 1965 was set as a start date.[8]

Lardner's version introduces an element of romance while sticking roughly to the original tale. An American, Carpenter, is dispatched to the submarine *Resolute* with orders for Commander Swainson to beat a Russian ice breaker to Ice Station Zebra. His secret mission is to prevent Hungarian refugee and now top American scientist Dr. Lukas from falling into Russian hands. At Zebra, the survivors of a fire include Lukas, the Russians Petrov and Professor Federin, Captain Folsom, the Englishman Grant and a female, Dr. Nikov. Russian Lt. Cherenko is parachuted in from the ice breaker. Carpenter is suspicious of Lukas. Carpenter finds the cylinder from a secret camera but the film is missing. Once all are back on board the sub, everyone is stripped, including Nikov, who is unconscious at this moment. When she wakes, she becomes flirtatious towards Carpenter. Later, after a fire on the sub, Carpenter gives Nikov mouth-to-mouth resuscitation. The missing film is smuggled on board in a cast set by Nikov. She is made to strip again. The Russian ice breaker takes off all the Russians including Nikov. Lukas, not a traitor after all, has dumped the film in the ocean via the garbage chute but without a dye marker. Among the incidents keeping tension high are: the sub finding a hole in the ice which then closes, Carpenter and his chosen team endangered on the surface by moving ice, sabotage in the torpedo room, the fire, and a bomb planted on the sub.[9]

But this narrative didn't pass muster and Lardner was quickly replaced by Oscar-winning Paddy Chayefsky (*The Americanization of Emily*)[10] with shooting pushed back to late summer. Aware of MacLean's gripes about being excluded from

The Guns of Navarone once Carl Foreman had installed himself as screenwriter, the producer arranged a meeting between the author and Chayefsky.[11] Ransohoff's directorial "short list" included Fred Zinnemann (*High Noon*, 1952), Robert Mulligan (*To Kill a Mockingbird*, 1962), Sidney Lumet (*Fail Safe*, 1964) and Stanley Donen (*Charade*, 1963). The first three proved unavailable; Donen was attractive because of his "earlier enthusiasm for the book." The producer would not countenance John Frankenheimer and there was a "question mark" over Norman Jewison.[12] Other directors addressed themselves directly to the potential star. "I am deeply enthusiastic," declared David Miller,[13] who was, in any case, at $200,000, considered too expensive.[14]

When John Sturges was selected, he had reservations over the screenplay, which he felt suffered from "excessive length," a "needlessly confusing" plot and "an ineffectual ending."[15] Charlton Heston rejected the movie: "I liked the script but not the part."[16] That hardly mattered as Ransohoff subsequently brought together a stellar cast: *Guns of Navarone* alumni Gregory Peck and David Niven (as Dr. Jolly). For the role of the captain, Sturges expressed "reservations" about Jason Robards[17] and Ransohoff's choice, Robert Webber.[18] In came George Segal (*The Quiller Memorandum*, 1966).[19] Sturges promised Peck, "We have a good chance of curbing some of the wayward moves of Chayefsky and Ransohoff."[20] However, the three stars wanted to act against type. Peck, having played a submarine commander in *On the Beach* (1959), wished the role of an American secret agent, Niven his British equivalent, with Segal an unusual choice for an authority figure. Then Peck objected to the way his character was portrayed, bristling at being unmasked as a double agent working for the Russians.[21]

Electing in 1967 to shoot in Cinerama ensured roadshow release[22] and still with Peck and Segal on board, Ransohoff announced a February[23] start date; later the start date became June.[24] John Sturges, loaned out by Mirisch,[25] was paid a whopping $500,000[26] despite not flying quite as high as when he had helmed *The Satan Bug*. Sturges was associated with a "composite screenplay" running an "incomplete" 137 pages, with various sections dated between September 20, 1965, and October 5, 1965. After the rewrites, the submarine was now known as the *Dolphin*. Carpenter remains the protagonist but doesn't reveal his real mission, the missing film, until page 72. The sabotage on the submarine (the flooding of the torpedo room) was intended to delay the vessel and give the Russian agent at Zebra enough time to send the film up in a weather balloon, but the sky wasn't clear enough. Captain Halliwell and others were shot by the Russian agent who set fire to the camp to hide the evidence. Dr. Jolly is the villain.[27] Sturges later contributed a 24-page outline "to be used as a guideline in the preparation" of the picture.[28]

Sturges' big-budget 70mm Western *The Hallelujah Trail* (1965) and *Hour of the Gun* (1967) had flopped. Steve McQueen's motor racing epic *Day of the Champion* and *The Yards of Essendorf* were shelved. But his mastery of the action picture made him first choice for *Ice Station Zebra*. Objecting to the existing script, he brought in W.R. Burnett (*The Great Escape*, 1963) and Harry Julian Fink (*Major Dundee*, 1965). When the screenplay still proved stubbornly overly patriotic, Sturges threatened to quit, but with Ransohoff already in the hole to the tune of $1.7 million, that was a non-starter. As a last resort, Sturges called in Douglas Heyes (*Beau Geste*, 1966), who beefed up the MacLean story, completely changing the ending, introducing the U.S. vs. U.S.S.R. race to the Arctic, and a bunch of new characters including those played by Jim Brown and Ernest Borgnine, who had previously worked together on *The Dirty Dozen* (1967).[29] Not only did Heyes alter a great deal, but Sturges claimed improvisation was often the order of the day. "We made it up as we went along," he said, "adding a whole bunch of gimmicks—the homing device, the capsule in the ice, the blowtorch.... I don't think it had any political significance. It just dealt with an existing phenomenon in an interesting way."[30]

But by now Ransohoff had lost his stars. Peck pulled out in November 1966.[31] The replacements were of a lower pedigree. Rock Hudson, once a huge star after his comedy pairings with Doris Day and others, was now in a career trough after *Seconds* (1966) and *Tobruk* (1967); he campaigned for the role of the sub commander. Laurence Harvey was briefly in the frame for a top role.[32] British television star Patrick McGoohan, who had not made a movie since *Dr. Syn* (1963), was an unlikely candidate for the second lead. Sturges saw in him as the "same excitement" as Steve McQueen.[33] His inclusion was the result of a sharp increase in his popularity Stateside after fans bombarded the networks to bring back the *Danger Man* (1964–67) series (renamed *Secret Agent* for American consumption) after it had initially underwhelmed. The "old-fashioned hero with morals" was a feature of the series' advertising campaign[34]

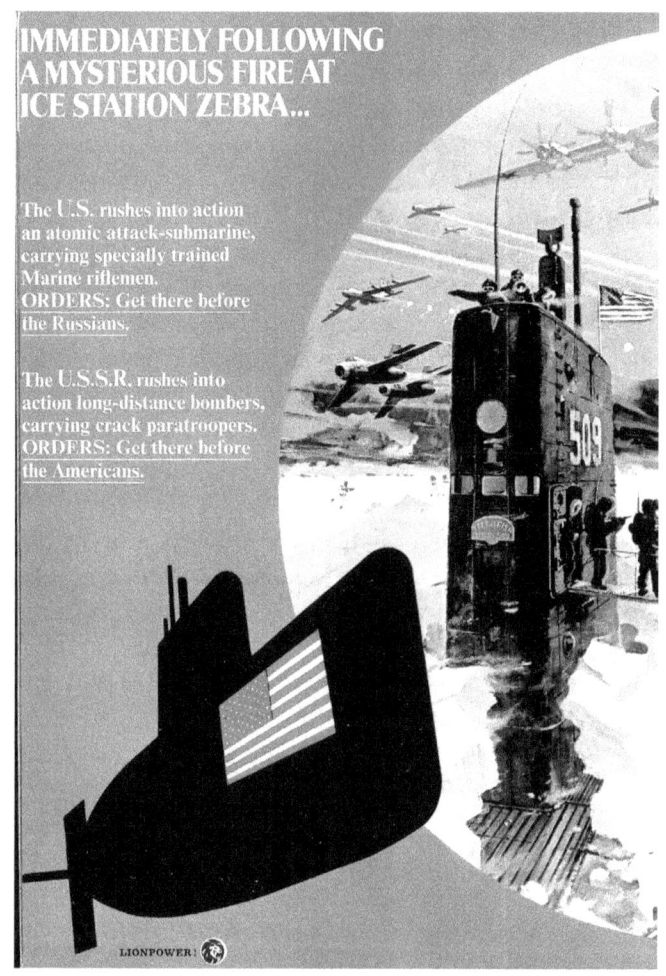

The reason for the film's title was never explained in the movie version of *Ice Station Zebra*. In fact, "Zebra" was then the word used in NATO's phonetic alphabet for navigation and aviation. According to Jack Webster's biography of MacLean, originally MacLean considered using the title *Drift Ice Station Zebra* because the location was drifting on the moving Arctic ice pack (from the Elliott Kastner Archive, courtesy of Dillon Kastner).

and McGoohan was written up in the *New York Times*.³⁵ The rest of the cast members were unknowns, newcomers with potential, or, like Ernest Borgnine, solid supporting actors.

Sturges was a gadget nut and particularly interested in the space race, tracking by ham radio the launch of the Russian Sputnik 1, concerned that the Americans had been beaten. While Moon landings remained some way off, the next battleground for global supremacy was nuclear submarines, of which Sturges was in awe.

Principal photography began in mid–June 1967 and finished 19 weeks later.³⁶ The initial $8 million budget topped out at $10 million. The non-nuclear *U.S.S. Tronquil* stood in for the *Tigerfish* while the *U.S.S. Blackfin* doubled for some sequences at sea. The vessel's interiors dominated MGM's soundstages with a 16-foot superstructure as the centerpiece and hydraulics creating the tilting and rocking effects. The art department scoured marine salvage yards for genuine parts—gyroscope, periscope, instrument panels, hatches etc. The interior was built in six sections, totaling 600 feet, plus a conning tower the height of a five-story building. Some scenes were shot on the MGM backlot. On Lot 3, the Process Tank was drained of three million gallons of water and turned into the Arctic landscape, including the weather station, with a cyclorama for the sky. A Matthew Yuricich matte painting enhanced the snowscape.³⁷ Aerial shots of Greenland ice floes and fjords doubled for Siberia; to capture the wild ocean, Sturges and cameraman John M. Stephens (responsible for *Grand Prix*'s [1966] racing sequences) took a helicopter ride 30 miles out from the coast of Oahu where a 45-knot wind created "monumental" seas. A ten-foot miniature in a tank permitted shots underwater and cameras attached to the *Tronquil*'s deck and conning tower achieved the unique sub's-eye view.³⁸ A second unit captured footage at the Gareloch, Arrochar and Loch Lomond in Scotland. The submarine seen in port in Scotland was actually filmed at the Submarine Support Facility in San Diego, as was the helicopter scene. Background for the Russian jets filmed near the North Pole.³⁹

Ice Station Zebra world-premiered on October 23 at Los Angeles' Cinerama Dome, its lobby decked out with a submarine 20 feet long and 12 feet high.⁴⁰ For the movie's nationwide release, MGM ordered 425 prints (exceeding the record set by 1967's *The Dirty Dozen*), including 75 in Cinerama.⁴¹ While 15 major cities were immediately targeted,⁴² there was an unexpected two-month delay in reaching New York because MGM was reluctant to yank *2001: A Space Odyssey* out of the city's Pacific East Cinerama while it remained so surprisingly potent.⁴³

The Sturges Version

The John Sturges Cold War thriller twists and turns as Americans in a nuclear submarine and the Soviet Union race to the Arctic to retrieve a fallen space capsule containing a deadly secret. The movie is thoroughly enjoyable hokum, filmed in Cinerama 70mm with an earworm of a booming theme from Michel Legrand and mostly outstanding special effects.

Like a James Bond movie, it begins in outer space with both Americans and Russians tracking a satellite as it enters the atmosphere. It lands four hours ahead of schedule, and off-course, in the Arctic, a later twist revealing that it technically belongs to the Soviets. As one man comes to retrieve it, another stands back, watching. Then we cut to nuclear submarine Commander Ferraday (Rock Hudson) being dispatched from Scotland on what he believes is a last-gasp mission to save the stricken weather station dubbed Ice Station Zebra. Despite his seniority, the real reason for his journey is withheld. He is forced to carry as passenger an arrogant British secret service agent, David Jones (Patrick McGoohan), who refuses to divulge the object of the voyage. Also on board is a squad of raw Marines.

Once at sea, Ferraday stops to take helicopter delivery of Russian defector Boris Vaslov (Ernest Borgnine), a buddy of Jones', and Capt. Anders (Jim Brown), tasked with knocking the Marines into shape. Thanks to sabotage, the vessel is flooded and almost sinks.

When the sub reaches its destination, the movie switches from adventure into more straightforward detective territory, more sabotage, arson, murder, suspects and the ominous approach of the Russians. Then a traitor is uncovered and all is revealed. We end on a shoot-out and the kind of climax that keeps the peace. While the plot shifts like a tectonic plate, it's the submarine section that proves most riveting. The underwater photography is superb in part thanks to an invention by second unit cameraman Stephens, which could film for the first time a continuous dive. Whether the sub is submerging, surfacing and puncturing the ice or in danger of sinking and being crushed, it's the vessel that takes center stage, a significant achievement in the days before CGI. Not all the effects are quite so top-notch, there's some dodgy back and front projection, and the Arctic landscape looks fake. But in general, especially with streamlined control panels, jargon spat out at pace, and sub interiors that appear realistic, the result of two years' research, it's a more than solid job, delivering the core of an action picture. The Super Panavision cameras create astonishing visuals, capturing in enormous detail the bow spray, the massive icebergs, the gleaming intricacy of the controls, and even the sea parting under the weight of the sub. And there's something inherently dramatic in the commander slapping down the periscope.

Rock Hudson is back to straightforward leading man duty after the departure into paranoia in *Seconds* although he is burdened with chunks of exposition and having to develop a stiff upper lip in response to the secret agent's reluctance to confide in him. He comes more into his own in the face-off with the Russians. The tight-lipped, brusque, provocative McGoohan has a ball as mischief-maker-in-chief, keeping everyone else on tenterhooks. Ernest Borgnine invests his character with wide-eyed charm at the same time as the audience doubts his credentials. Jim Brown has little more than an extended cameo as the Marine chief. In smaller roles, you can spot future Oscar-winning producer Tony Bill (*Castle Keep*, 1969, another Filmways project) and veteran Lloyd Nolan.

There are some anomalies. Having a squad of soldiers aboard indicates to the audience, if not to the commander, that trouble is expected. Keeping Ferraday ignorant of the real purpose of the mission renders him a bystander for much of the picture and reduces his screen authority. And allowing Jones to be duped by Vaslov undermines his credentials. Whatever criticism Sturges had of MacLean's prose, it was nothing compared to the turgid, lengthy exposition required to make sense of the new storyline (chasing down a British camera that the Russians stole from the Yanks). But in his second bout with MacLean, Sturges keeps a tighter grip on the proceedings, the bigger budget ensuring that the movie mixes thriller elements with high adventure and well-orchestrated slugs of action.

Book into Film

The film changed the entire thrust of the book, introducing the U.S. vs. Russia theme and climaxing with the firefight on the ice. As Gregory Peck had complained, audiences wouldn't take to an American double agent, so that was changed to Russian defector Vaslov, who was actually a triple agent.

Ice Station Zebra was not successful as a roadshow. However, when given a general release, it performed better than expected in its initial weeks. MGM was so delighted that it trumpeted the box office figures (advertisement, *Box Office* November 25, 1968).

The submarine commander took on a more central role in the film compared to the book, and other characters were introduced. Structural changes abound. The movie reaches Zebra at the halfway mark, while in the book it's barely a quarter of the way through. The film switches the sinking to earlier, renders transmissions "garbled," brings the traitor on board from the outset, forces the sub to break through the ice, and turns the book's mere possibility of being crushed by ice into reality. Many liberties were taken with MacLean's work but there is little to match the arrogance of director Sturges in deciding that the author's original ending just wasn't good enough. Setting aside the achievements of *The Magnificent Seven* (1960) and *The Great Escape* (1963), Sturges was known for lapses of cinematic judgment, namely in switching completely the tone of *The Satan Bug* (1965) and assuming that audiences shared his sense of humor with *The Hallelujah Trail* (1965). According to Glenn Lovell, Sturges' biographer, the director had "cringed" when presented with the Chayefsky screenplay, claiming the book had no "finish"; it was closer, in Lovell's words, to Agatha Christie than Ian Fleming. You have to ask if Sturges, or Lovell for that matter, had ever read MacLean's astonishing tour de force of an ending. The MacLean version climaxes in the claustrophobic submarine rather on the wide-open Arctic. And the novel takes to the ultimate the problems of confinement. You would have thought Sturges would have little problem with deadly incarceration given that had been a main element of *The Great Escape*, especially in the scenes with Charles Bronson. (In the film, the Russian defector uses claustrophobia as an excuse to snoop.) What Sturges passed up was what films like the box office smash *The Poseidon Adventure* (1970) and *Das Boot* (1981) later imagined so well: the sheer terror of being trapped underwater. MacLean's book envisages the survivors of the fire at Ice Station Zebra rescued and returned to the submarine with the knowledge in the mind of David Jones (Patrick McGoohan in the film) that among them is a murderer, a Russian spy who caused the fire. The vessel is then subjected to further sabotage. An engine room fire causes the submarine to stop. That in turn causes the temperature to plummet, leaving the men in an "ice cold tomb." Worse, they are running out of oxygen. Carbon monoxide is poisoning the atmosphere. In a short time, 100 will be dead. And to top it all, they have lost their bearings, the compasses don't work, they are traveling in a circle. Can you imagine the possibilities? Absolute chaos. Not just thick acrid smoke everywhere, men strewn unconscious, the fire still burning, panic, terror, but a vessel slowly becoming an underwater grave with a killer still on the loose. Sturges could not imagine the possibilities. Perhaps he had not read the book either and Chayefsky had skipped through that part of the novel to get to the "trial," the uncovering of the traitor that had been deemed too much like Agatha Christie. But *The Guns of Navarone*, one of the most successful movies of all time, had a similar scene in which a surprise traitor was unmasked.

The ending Sturges slapped on the picture had its genesis in a couple of lines from the book where the British secret agent explained that Russian airplanes had come to the Arctic on the pretext of participating in the rescue but were, in reality, looking for the film from the satellite. All the stuff about the new type of camera being stolen by the Russians and of film containing sensitive information about American missile sites needing to be recovered had come from the book. In the MacLean version, the traitor would dump the film out into the sea via the garbage chute but tagged with a floating device and a yellow marker so it could be picked up by a Russian vessel. Instead, Sturges went for some kind of direct confrontation with the Russians, a shoot-out on the ice. It seemed a mighty odd decision, given the opportunities in 70mm Cinerama for a full-scale panic on board an immobilized submarine drifting to its doom. To make his version work, Sturges drafted a squad of Marines eventually led by Capt. Anders (Jim Brown). The introduction of Russian defector Boris Vaslov (Borgnine) makes less sense, especially as, skulking around the submarine, he is obviously up to no good. In the novel, the British secret agent is the younger brother of the scientist at the weather station, giving him a secondary reason for his mission, and the potential for emotional reaction on finding his sibling dead.

Sometimes screenwriters just seem to earn their keep by changing names for no apparent reason. The book's Commander Swanson becomes Ferraday (Rock Hudson), British agent Dr. Carpenter is renamed David Jones minus medical degree, and even the submarine switches from *Dolphin* to *Tigerfish III*. All the initial sabotage comes from the fertile mind of the author. Long before Arthur Hailey (*Hotel*, *Airport*) set his tales against a background of operational minutiae and Tom Clancy, beginning with *The Hunt for Red October*, invented a brand-new publishing genre focusing on military hardware, MacLean reveals an extraordinary grasp of how a nuclear submarine works and the vicissitudes of weather and what exactly might go wrong, from a fire on board to a loss of speed. Neither would you recognize Rock Hudson in MacLean's description of the submarine commander as "short, plump [and] a pink cherubic face." MacLean's British agent is less arrogant and acerbic than the film's David Jones and, in MacLean's typical style, keeps much more information to himself, revealing it at appropriate moments spaced through the book. That Dr. Carpenter, the narrator, knows massive amounts about everything means that he does not need to showboat like David Jones to prove he is in charge. Sturges can't find a cinematic equivalent to the author's mesmeric accumulation of fact—tiny details like the 1000 bricks kept aboard to ensure that discarded waste sinks to the bottom—that testifies to authenticity. The book is a turbo-charged thrill ride. That the final piece of sabotage and its consequences lasts nearly 50 pages is proof of MacLean's skill at writing page-turners.

Much as I enjoyed the film as it stands, it's just a shame that Sturges did not follow the author into his astonishing climactic tour de force.

CHAPTER SIX

Where Eagles Dare (1968)

Alistair MacLean had yet another curveball to throw at his publishers. In so doing, he broke the cardinal rule relating to film rights, took novelization into a far more profitable sphere than anyone could have imagined, and re-invented himself. In the process, he made himself the most sought-after novelist of the era.

Selling film rights had always been the preserve of the publisher, who took a half-share of the proceeds. MacLean changed that. With *Where Eagles Dare*, he kept all the receipts from the rights to himself. And he hit another curveball in the direction of the movie producers. Usually, in acquiring a screenplay, the producer retained the publication rights, and might sell to a paperback house the opportunity to hire another writer to whip up a novelization. But MacLean retained those rights. The thriller he based on his screenplay he sold to his publishers, knowing it already came with the kind of movie tie-in potential that would augment future sales. And as a final coup, he became a one-man movie machine, someone who could play both ends. If MacLean had epitomized the fabled author who struck it rich at the first time of asking, he was entering new territory, the writer who had Hollywood at his beck and call.

That MacLean returned to writing at all, after abandoning the business in the wake of delivering *Ice Station Zebra* to his publisher and embarking on a new profession as a hotelier, was the result of a leap of faith by American producer Elliott Kastner, another independent[1] with a hefty dose of determination. He was formerly an agent with MCA; it took four years before his ambition translated into a movie. In 1962, he teamed with Oscar-winning screenwriter Abby Mann (*Judgment at Nuremberg*), and it appeared that his producing career would start with a bang after he secured

... *The Jerry Gershwin–Elliott Kastner Picture*

Where Eagles Dare

Royal Premiere this Wednesday. Richard Burton, Clint Eastwood star in Alistair MacLean's epic story of British adventure in World War II. Boxoffice, on the grand scale.

The Royal Premiere of *Where Eagles Dare* took place on January 22, 1968, in the presence of Princess Alexandra. It was attended by all the stars except Clint Eastwood, who was then shooting *Two Mules for Sister Sara* (from the Elliott Kastner Archive, courtesy of Dillon Kastner).

Chapter Six. Where Eagles Dare *(1968)*

the Italian trio of Sophia Loren (*El Cid*, 1961), financier Carlo Ponti (her husband) and director Vittorio De Sica (*The Condemned of Altona*, 1961) for the company's debut feature *The Children of Sanchez*.[2] They also splurged $150,000 for the rights to William Faulkner's novel *Light in August*.[3] When neither film materialized, the partners split. Kastner surfaced the following year as a gun for hire, producing *Honeybear, I Think I Love You* with Warren Beatty for the independent ECA.[4] That, too, fell by the wayside but, meanwhile, he had formed an alliance with Stan Shpetner to film *Tropic of Cancer* on a $2 million budget in France for Embassy, *Hanno's Doll* with Jane Fonda for Columbia, and had bought the rights to 1959 Broadway hit *The Fifth Season*.[5]

His movie debut was Universal's *Bus Riley's Back in Town* (1965) with Ann-Margret.[6] Switching his production base to London, he formed Winkast with producer Jerry Gershwin and persuaded Peter Sellers to star in *The Bobo* (1966). His biggest success came after parlaying $1000 for the rights to the Ross Macdonald novel *The Moving Target* and another $5000 for a screenplay by William Goldman[7] into a $3.3 million private eye picture, *Harper* (1966) with Paul Newman, along the way netting a cool half-million for himself.[8] He had secured Warren Beatty for just $100,000 to star in the romantic thriller *Kaleidoscope* (1966).[9] Though not quite in the Ransohoff-Filmways league of production prestige, Winkast capitalized on early success, with a planned $42 million outlay in 1966 on 14 pictures, including five for Warner Brothers.[10]

Aware that Alistair MacLean had no books to sell, his entire portfolio already snapped up, Kastner went down another route. He made contact with the author in October 1965[11] and suggested that MacLean write an original screenplay, offering $200,000 plus a half-share of the profits and the book rights.[12] After convincing the author that he had an ear for cinematic dialogue, and that his plots were ideal, Kastner handed MacLean some sample screenplays.[13] Kastner specified that he wanted a World War II adventure involving a "woman or two" but with the emphasis on tension. "I want the clock ticking," Kastner specified.[14] Although MacLean was interested, he told the producer he was too busy to commit. Kastner was later surprised to learn that, unbeknownst to his publishers, MacLean had already renounced his retirement (the hotels sidelined)[15] and was working on *When Eight Bells Toll*.

The official deal for *Where Eagles Dare* was struck on January 20, 1966.[16] Eight weeks later, MacLean delivered the screenplay.[17] Interestingly, MGM was not the producer's first port of call. Paramount rejected the opportunity, the studio's G.H. Ornstein complaining about "so many twists and turns ... that I don't know where I am half the time."[18]

Kastner had only one star in mind and was prepared to ante up the million dollars it would require. Despite being stonewalled by Richard Burton's agent, Kastner managed to cold call on him in a restaurant in Nice in 1966 and seeded the notion that the actor take a break from heavy-hitting dramas like *Who's Afraid of Virginia Woolf* (1966), *The Spy Who Came in from the Cold* (1965) and *Becket* (1964) and try his hand at something that might appeal more to his children. But the pursuit was less straightforward than legend, and the producer, suggested.[19] Burton already had a full slate. He was heading to Rome to film *The Taming of the Shrew* (1967), to be followed by *The Comedians* (1967) and the musical remake of *Goodbye, Mr. Chips*, while squeezing into his already overloaded schedule the cherished vanity project *Doctor Faustus* (1967). In August 1966, Kastner pursued Burton to Rome, but failed to see him. Although the actor was in possession of a script, Kastner was unsure whether he had read it, so he sent this telegram:

> Am hopeful you have read Alistair MacLean's *Where Eagles Dare*. Am convinced that once you have, *The Comedians* or any other project will take second position. With *Virginia Woof, Taming of the Shrew, Doctor Faustus* and *Chips* next year, timing most propitious you programming big action suspense film and best in world is *Where Eagles Dare*. I urge you to read it if you have not as yet.

Kastner ended on a wan note, hoping, presumably, to apply some pressure: "As must make decision alternative casting."[20] Possibly he played down the importance of his offer to Burton. He was putting the actor in the million-dollar league. That positioned him, at this point in the Hollywood hierarchy, ahead of Steve McQueen, John Wayne and Paul Newman. Previously, the only stars whose marquee value entitled them to a million bucks were Marlon Brando, Elizabeth Taylor and Audrey Hepburn. In fact, once you counted in Burton's later share of the profits,[21] this would be the single highest-paid role of the decade. So there was every inducement for Burton to agree. But it wasn't until May of the following year that his involvement was announced.[22]

It's highly likely that the delay in securing Burton had one beneficial side effect. Had Burton agreed in 1966, it's doubtful if Clint Eastwood's name would have entered the frame since *A Fistful of Dollars* was not released in the U.S. until 1967, three years after its initial Italian launch. *Fistful of Dollars* was quickly followed by a sequel. Burton had an "equally strong preference" regarding his co-star, favoring Rod Taylor or Richard Boone, or Eastwood, though it had been "difficult" to knock Robert Webber out of the equation. (In retrospect, Webber seems to be a surprising choice but he had made a big impression in a smaller role in *Harper*.) Kastner was keenest on Boone (*Hombre*, 1967): "[T]he more I think of Boone the more I like him."[23] MGM had its own ideas about who would be most suitable, suggesting Paul Newman, Lee Marvin, James Garner and George Peppard, combinations that could put the studio in the hole for way upwards of a million dollars[24]; pairing Burton with either Newman or Marvin,[25] for example, totaled $1.6 million or $1.75 million depending. However, these were not the only names that popped up. Kastner tossed about casting ideas while working on *The Bobo*. Steve McQueen was the only name scored off a list of stars (considered for the role of Schaffer) which included Anthony Quinn, Rod Steiger, George Segal, James Coburn, Robert Mitchum, Lee Marvin, George Maharis, David Janssen, Rock Hudson and James Garner. Michael Caine, another early possibility, was tied up until 1968.[26] Marlon Brando,[27] Tony Curtis and Richard Harris also came into the frame as well as lesser-known names like James Arness, Vittorio Gassman and Tony Franciosa.[28] Under later consideration were Dean Martin, George C. Scott, Sidney Poitier and Kirk Douglas.[29] Actresses under discussion included Anne Bancroft, Françoise Dorléac, Virna Lisi, Lee Remick, Elke Sommer, Claudia Cardinale and Jane Fonda,[30] the last two exciting particular interest[31] along with Anouk Aimée.[32] Diana Rigg was

Chapter Six. Where Eagles Dare (1968)

For *Where Eagles Dare*, MGM's marketing team stoked advance interest via a series of adverts that were only seen in the trade press (pre-selling advertisement, *Independent Film Journal*, November 26, 1968).

unavailable.³³ Burton was "very bullish" on Leslie Caron but "approving Mary Ure in second position."³⁴ Shirley Eaton was the front-runner for Heidi³⁵ although Director Brian G. Hutton had his eye on Elke Sommer.³⁶

The names submitted for the role of Admiral Rolland were Michael Redgrave, Harry Andrews, James Mason, *Guns of Navarone* alumni Anthony Quayle and James Robertson Justice and eventual choice Michael Hordern.³⁷ For Col. Turner,³⁸ initial discussion revolved around the likes of Nicol Williamson³⁹ and Denholm Elliott; Patrick Wymark, the actor finally cast, did not make that early list.⁴⁰ A clue as to how big a picture this was aiming to be: the inclusion of such top names as Trevor Howard, Kenneth More and Michael Redgrave for the relatively insignificant role of the pilot.⁴¹ Hardy Kruger was the obvious choice for the Gestapo officer, with Darren Nesbitt initially not under consideration. For Col. Kramer, Anton Diffring made it onto the list along with Herbert Lom and another obvious choice, Curd Jürgens.⁴² Other unlikely names suggested for supporting roles included Roger Moore and British singer-comedian Harry Secombe.⁴³ Charles Bronson were among those rejected.⁴⁴

The biggest obstacle to hiring Eastwood was his price: His agent was holding out for $400,000. Kastner proposed a deal of £250,000 upfront and the rest deferred.⁴⁵ In the end, Eastwood's agent won.⁴⁶ On top of his $1 million, Burton would receive ten percent of the rentals (what the studio is left with out of the overall gross once the cinemas have taken their cut), $6340 towards hiring a Rolls-Royce and other cars, $10,490 for his personal staff and up to $50,000 in other expenses. Part of Burton's contract called on the producers to acquire the services of the star's production adviser Richard McWhorter plus his business manager, chauffeur and personal makeup artist.⁴⁷ Eastwood would have to get by on less than $20,000 in living and other expenses.⁴⁸ The production fee was set at $250,000 though Kastner's expenses tallied $27,083.⁴⁹ By comparison, salaries for supporting stars were minute. Although Mary Ure received $75,000, Michael Hordern (for one week) and Patrick Wymark (for two) picked up $5000 apiece, Vincent Ball $4000 and Olga Lowe $3000 for two weeks compared to Ingrid Pitt—she got the role after the intervention of her lover, a producer⁵⁰—$2000 for eight weeks. Others in the main received between $1000 and $2000.⁵¹ Offsetting the costs, MacLean agreed to defer $100,000.⁵²

Burton brought his own problems. For tax purposes, he could not spend too long in Britain. Given that Burton's preferred location was France, Kastner investigated the prospect of a French-British co-production. As late as October 1967, this remained a possibility⁵³ even after being knocked back by the French Board of Trade.⁵⁴ To suit his own program, Burton wanted filming to start in November 1967,⁵⁵ not the planned January 1968. While Kastner instructed the actor to "lose a few pounds" and get his hair cut,⁵⁶ a bigger potential issue was Burton's fear of "working at certain heights."⁵⁷ You might wonder at how someone could struggle with looking out a castle window and even Burton would know he was not expected to climb atop a cable car in reality, but this referred to the first draft of the script (see below). However, Burton was also chasing a production credit, as was his production advisor Richard McWhorter,⁵⁸ producer of *Doctor Faustus*.⁵⁹

Chapter Six. Where Eagles Dare (1968)

Although Kastner had praised MacLean's screenplay ("the best I've ever read"), the general consensus was that, at 167 pages,[60] it was too long. Co-producer Gershwin had some serious reservations over the romance ("kicked under the rug") and the revelations of the double agents.[61] Director Brian G. Hutton undertook a rewrite. However, this was more of a fine tuning than a major overhaul. While in the main Hutton's task was subtracting (he eliminated for example a burgeoning romance between Schaffer and Heidi), he added significant sections which increased tension, namely the conflict between the castle commandant and the Gestapo officer, plus Mary getting caught out on her Dusseldorf recollections. He eliminated an early cliff scene but extended the final action sequence. Most of the killing was down to Hutton. In the MacLean version, Germans tended to be knocked out or tied up rather than shot. Burton was delighted with the Hutton rewrite and did not "want to change one word."[62] Second unit director Yakima Canutt suggested the escaping trio jump from the cable car into the river rather than onto dry land.[63] The final draft was 132 pages.[64]

In those days, scripts had to pass muster with the Production Code, the Motion Picture Association of America's self-regulated censorship system. They complained that use of the words "Jesus" and "goddam" were unacceptable and they insisted there be "no undue or indecent exposure of Mary as she changes her dress."[65] British censor John Trevelyan promised a "U" certificate as long as the violence was not accompanied by screams and cries of pain "which would intensify the action to a point unacceptable for children."[66]

"I knew who I wanted to direct this movie before Alistair MacLean had even written it," declared Kastner. That didn't account for Jules Dassin (*Topkapi*, 1964) turning the project down[67] nor for Kastner drawing up a list of other contenders in 1966. Hutton, who was included on the list, was up against such American luminaries as Oscar winners John Huston (*The Sandpiper*, 1965), Fred Zinnemann (*A Man for All Seasons*, 1966) and Norman Jewison (*In the Heat of the Night*, 1967) plus Sidney J. Furie (*The Ipcress File*, 1965) as well as a British contingent headed by double Oscar winner David Lean (*Lawrence of Arabia*, 1962),[68] Oscar winner Carol Reed (*Oliver!*, 1968), Basil Dearden (*Khartoum*, 1965) and Terence Young (*Dr. No*, 1962).[69] Later contenders were Ken Annakin (*Battle of the Bulge*, 1965), Guy Hamilton (*Goldfinger*, 1964), Michael Anderson (*Operation Crossbow*, 1965), Jack Clayton (*The Innocents*, 1961), Elliot Silverstein (*Cat Ballou*, 1965), Sydney Pollack (*This Property Is Condemned*, 1966) and Robert Mulligan (*To Kill a Mockingbird*, 1962). Of course, this could all be camouflage, to cover his back against outrage from MGM at handing such a sizable budget to an inexperienced director. But Kastner had an ace to play. Burton had director approval. Kastner told MGM, "No Brian Hutton, no movie,"[70] and got his way even though Hutton had only two features to his name, *The Wild Seed* (1963) and *The Pad* (1966). He had spent three years setting up *The Wild Seed*, costing $250,000 and shot over 22 days, *The Pad* took 19 days.[71]

Hutton and Kastner had met at age eight at primary school in New York, attended junior high and college together, and worked in the William Morris agency mail room. Kastner's professional relationship with Hutton predated his partnership with

Gershwin. He had bought Hutton's screenplays *The Violent Land*[72] and *Gabriel and the Angels* and another co-written by Hutton with Stephen Kandel, *Taylor Made*.[73] To give the director more experience before tackling the big-budget war picture, Kastner arranged for him to direct *Sol Madrid* aka *The Heroin Gang* (1968). By Hutton's admission, after being forced to replace John Cassavetes with Rip Torn during shooting, and with star David McCallum depressed after wife Jill Ireland left him for Charles Bronson, "it was a total disaster." Hutton also said: "How Elliott ever convinced MGM to continue with me to direct *Where Eagles Dare* is a miracle." He later contended that he took on the "multi-million-dollar bonanza" in the hope that "maybe I'd have the name and leverage to do what I wanted."[74] He signed up in April 1967 for a $75,000 fee. Hutton also had previous experience with Clint Eastwood, working with him on the unproduced *To Kill a King*.

The scale of the production didn't prove off-putting. "I was too stupid to be intimidated by anything," said Hutton. "I just put one foot in front of the other. I had a great producer in Elliott Kastner. He stood by me." Hutton could hardly contain his enthusiasm for the project: "It is hard for me to sit still and continue to work on *Sol Madrid* when I am in such great anticipation of getting over there and getting into things."[75] If he had any doubts, it was "how to handle" the star.[76] Apparently his honesty got him off on the right foot with Burton. The story goes that, on meeting the star,

Where Eagles Dare was far more successful overseas than in the United States. In Sweden, Alistair MacLean films were so popular that they were brought back time and again. At the Draken cinema in Stockholm, *Where Eagles Dare* was revived, for runs of about eight weeks, in 1972, 1974, 1975, 1978, 1980, 1982 and 1984 (from the Elliott Kastner Archive, courtesy of Dillon Kastner).

he introduced himself: "My name is Brian Hutton. My last two films were flops."[77] Turned out Burton was just as edgy, and on the first day of shooting apologized for his own nerves.[78]

You could argue that second unit director Yakima Canutt[79] was just as critical to the producer's plans. Audiences might not have been as keen on the over-wordy *Ben-Hur* (1959) had it not been for the action scenes—nautical battle and chariot race—filmed by Canutt, here paid $16,875[80] and involved in early location scouting in Austria and Switzerland.[81]

MacLean's imagining of the Schloss Adler had been very specific and it was down to the production team to find a location that suited. The producers were torn between Austria[82] and Switzerland as the main location.[83] Location manager Kent McPherron's discovery of Hohenwerfen[84] and its majestic castle, built in 1077,[85] was deemed a "sensational" find.[86] While cast and crew were housed in Salzburg, location work was split between the villages of Werfen, 20 miles away, and Lofer and Ebensee. Filming at the castle itself was limited: Only the courtyard, a couple of interiors, an exterior wall and part of the castle base were utilized. The rest was reimagined through matte paintings and model work at MGM's Borehamwood studio.[87] The picturesque Werfen, nestled below the castle, provided railway station, river and bridge, and was dressed up with military vehicles and soldiers in uniform, repurposed signage and the erection of roadblocks. Several of Lofen's main streets were adapted, and one of the hotels in the main square turned into the inn where Heidi works.[88]

The location shoot was complicated: While Werfen had a castle, it wasn't linked to the village by a cable car. So the production headed for Ebensee, whose cable car ran two miles into the peaks. It wasn't the actors who engaged in hand-to-hand combat there on the roofs of the cable cars. Stuntmen Alf Joint and Joe Powell doubled for the stars and often worked without "protective lifelines" and in 60-mile-an-hour winds. Canutt, responsible for this element of the shoot, said, "With the wind blowing and the cars bouncing and swinging, it was very thrilling." Commented Hutton, "They took unbelievable risks."[89]

That was an understatement. The fight between Smith and the two traitors took place several thousand feet above the ground at Ebensee. Cameras were draped over one cable car in every conceivable position. Jumping from rock to cable car was a dicey proposition.[90] Not all the cable car work went according to plan, and some re-shooting back in the studio (using front projection) was required. Once both pieces of footage were edited together, few had any complaints.[91] On Stages 4 and 5 at Borehamwood was built a set to accommodate arrival of the cable cars at the castle, the header station and its interiors.[92]

The budget of *Where Eagles Dare* began at $4.7 million and soon escalated to $5.3 million. It began shooting on January 2, 1968, and ended 17 weeks later, on April 26. The initial budget allowed for 34 days spread over six weeks on location (with Canutt remaining behind a further fortnight "to blow up a railway station, a bridge, cars and lorries, a castle and at least three aircraft"[93]) and 55 days over 11 weeks in the studio, followed by 16 weeks for editing and post-production. Kastner managed to save some money by "eliminating about 14 pages from the script."[94] An extra

$263,000 was spent after unforeseen weather conditions in Austria necessitated that the second unit remain an extra four weeks on location. Some scenes shifted from location to studio. Unexpected repairs to vehicles and increased costs relating to transportation, site rental and catering were only partly offset by cast savings of around $16,000.[95] Mary Ure complained that journeys to the location, expected to take one hour, could take three times as long.[96]

"Everything went wrong," recalled Hutton. "There were explosions that went wrong and just about everything went wrong once or twice. I was over budget and over schedule."[97] In a country where blizzards could hamper shooting, they had to occasionally fork out $250 a day for fake snow. The second unit spent two extra days in April shooting in Switzerland after airfields in Austria lacked the necessary snow.[98] The best way to save money was to trim the script and so various remedies were actioned, including cutting the pivotal Gold Drawing Room scene—where the traitors are exposed—by eight pages.[99] Even as shooting concluded, costs continued to rise. By October 1969, there was still "a discrepancy" accounting for another $220,000.[100]

Cast salaries totaled $1.96 million and for the production unit $373,000; the

The stars of *Where Eagles Dare* in the scene at the inn: left to right, Clint Eastwood, Ingrid Pitt, Mary Ure and Richard Burton (from the Elliott Kastner Archive, courtesy of Dillon Kastner).

complete directorial team earned $227,000. Set construction amounted to $578,000 with props another $131,000, cameras $316,000 and lighting $205,000 plus $70,000 for full-size effects. Transportation came to $234,000, set operation $339,000, location expenses $708,000, music $31,000 and studio overhead $749,000. Stunt double Tom L. Dittman was hired at $800 per week plus $25 per day expenses.[101] Hutton stayed at Eaton House in the heart of Mayfair; the three-month tab was £1,161.[102] There were "heavy additional costs incurred in the U.S. on conversion of the film from 35mm to 70mm and additional costs in final redubbing."[103]

With filming commitments placing restrictions on Richard Burton and Clint Eastwood, publicists alighted on Ingrid Pitt as eminently promotable. Bayley Sillick said, "If she's free and willing, she could do an European tour."[104] Attempts were made to sell her as a sex symbol, the stills photographer offering "additional material of Ingrid Pitt in the semi-nude" and there were suggestions of a session with "one of the glamor photographers" with a view to winning a spread in *Playboy* magazine.[105] Maximum publishing-film synergy was achieved: The hardback book "easily topped" the British bestseller charts for July and August 1967.[106] The movie tie-in paperback arrived in time to provide a marketing fillip in the run-up to release; some bookshop windows were devoted entirely to its promotion. Enterprising retailers used props such as Nazi insignia, guns, stuffed eagles, castles, parachutes and figures[107] to attract the attention of the prospective reader. Even Richard Burton helped out: "Publishers are anxiously awaiting a Richard Burton quote attendant to the release of the hardback in the U.K."[108] By this point, overall sales of MacLean's books in the U.S. topped 10,000,000 copies, a landmark figure.[109]

The final budget: $8.2 million excluding legal fees[110]; advertising was estimated at $1.8 million, with another $760,000 for foreign territories.[111] That meant, just to break even, using the standard MGM calculation of 2.2 times the budget,[112] the movie would have to rack up just over $18 million—or a gross of $36 million–plus. Despite the rising cost, MGM remained buoyant about the outcome, Maurice Silverstein commenting, "[T]he enthusiasm you feel has certainly been infecting us all here."[113] A decision on whether to open the movie in roadshow was taken after completion.[114] In the event, the movie made its global debut in December 1968 in Japan, where Eastwood was marketed as "America's Toshiro Mifune."[115] In an "unprecedented" move, MGM's other 70mm blockbuster *Gone with the Wind* was shifted out of the Empire in London's Leicester Square to make way for an eight-week roadshow run of *Where Eagles Dare*.[116] MGM took the general release route in the U.S., hoping to emulate the box office of *The Dirty Dozen* two years earlier. As noted previously, MGM also switched the release dates with *Ice Station Zebra* in the U.K. Whereas in the U.S. the submarine caper had opened first, in Britain it was the other way around, though both were more easily slotted into roadshow.

A few years later, there was talk of a *Where Eagles Dare* sequel (see Chapter Eighteen), but that was never a possibility until MGM had recouped all its costs from the expensive original.

Murder, Mystery, Action!—The Film

With the exception of the jaunty defiant whistle of *The Bridge on the River Kwai* (1957) and *633 Squadron* (1964), this genre was not known for iconic scores. Forty-odd seconds after *Where Eagles Dare* opens with a view of snow-topped mountains and an insistent ominous drumbeat, an airplane races out of the darkness towards the camera. It turns and plunges down icy ravines to a swelling earworm of a theme. Just past the three-minute mark, the music cuts out and, after a brief glimpse of an anonymous pilot, the camera pans for a few seconds along the faces of soldiers sitting in silence until we switch to Admiral Rolland (Michael Hordern) briefing an increasingly apprehensive group on an impossible rescue mission of a captured American general, vital to D-Day, hidden away in an impregnable Austrian castle. No time is wasted on the kind of individual character introduction that marked *The Magnificent Seven* (1960) or the bonding exercise that swallowed up the first half of *The Dirty Dozen* (1967). It also dispenses with the normal anti-authority stance of war movies and the jostling for position and standard personality clash between personnel.

What we don't know is that the admiral is spinning a yarn: What unfolds is a mystery as much as an action picture, a story divined by a mind more fiendish than Agatha Christie. Mary (Mary Ure), the mysterious woman tagging on to the end of the parachute drop, is a hint that something is amiss and that the audience will be duped and duped again. You get the impression that the poker player in the screenwriter had watched a mountain of war movies and determined to raise the stakes to an unprecedented degree. We soon learn that Major Smith (Richard Burton) knows a lot more than he's willing to admit, but doles out this information in miserly fashion, scarcely even confiding in his American sidekick Lt. Schaffer (Clint Eastwood). A mysterious death indicates the presence of a traitor. The major, pretending the radio isn't working, slips away to meet Mary, a secret agent with, unknown to her, a specific essential part to play in the scheme, and with whom he has a romantic inclination. But the most important element of the early section is to show how impenetrable the castle is, the area swarming with crack German troops and Gestapo.

When they finally reach the town, Smith has another rendezvous with Mary, revealing that the supposed captured American Brigadier General Carnaby is actually lowly actor Cartwright-Jones (Robert Beatty). Schaffer is later let in on the secret. After another team member is murdered, Smith meets with undercover agent Heidi (Ingrid Pitt), a barmaid who can get Mary into the castle, but their situation is immediately compromised by the appearance of a German patrol. Surprisingly, rather than attempting to flee, Smith surrenders, and he and Schaffer are bundled into a car, from which escape proves easier. We also get the first sign that the film is going to take violence ... *not* to the blood-spattered extremes of *The Wild Bunch* (1969), but to exceptional heights for a war picture.

Mary attracts an unwelcome admirer, local Gestapo chief Major von Hapen (Derren Nesbitt) who attempts to bully castle commandant Col. Kramer (Anton Diffring). The other three captured Brits—Captains Christiansen (Donald Houston),

Berkeley (Peter Barkworth) and Thomas (William Squire)—are herded into a cable car for interrogation up in the castle. The close-mouthed major springs his biggest surprise yet: He and Schaffer are taking the same cable car, but traveling on the roof, not inside. So now, *à la The Guns of Navarone*, the tone shifts to perilous adventure. At the other end, Mary is waiting at an open window, necessitating a further perilous climb, that allows castle access. In another twist, the captured trio are not treated as prisoners but friends, knocking back brandy while the Germans interrogate the fake general. Before Cartwright-Jones can be drugged with truth serum, Smith and Schaffer interrupt the proceedings. Rather than turning his weapon on the enemy, Smith aims it at Schaffer, disarming him, before explaining that he is a double agent, Johann Schmidt, working clandestinely for the Germans, proceeding to prove his credentials through contact with a high-ranking German officer. Smith holds the floor, accusing the prisoners of plotting to assassinate Hitler and in consequence forcing them to prove their innocence by writing down the names of German agents in Britain.

In general release, *Where Eagles Dare* garnered $1.89 million from 197 theaters (advertisement, *Variety*, July 16, 1969).

But this is a double bluff. Smith is not a double agent after all, and the mission was not to rescue a general but to unmask traitors. It's a stunning *coup de théâtre*, an even greater twist than *Guns of Navarone*'s "trial" scene. However, the tables are turned by the arrival of von Hapen, suspicious of Mary. And it twists again on Mary's unexpected appearance. Killing the Germans and having set off booby traps in parts of the castle, the commandos flee with two of the traitors—Thomas sacrificed—and the actor. On reaching the cable car, Christiansen and Berkeley overpower Schaffer and commandeer the cable car. Smith leaps on the roof, avoids bullets spraying from below and is then involved in a nerve-jangling physical fight. Once he survives that, Smith, Schaffer, the actor and the two women appropriate a snowplow. Pursued by a posse of Germans, and after blowing up a bridge, they eventually make it to the airfield where a British plane is waiting.

The final twist: Admiral Rolland's number two, Col. Turner (Patrick Wymark), pulls a machine-gun on them, revealing himself as the leader of the traitors. But he failed to reckon on Rolland and Smith being one step ahead. His weapon is missing a firing pin. Rather than face the hangman, he jumps out a door.

The bravura plotting, the turning of the mystery tale on its head, information withheld not to misguide the audience but because Smith doesn't know who to trust ... even without the action, this would have set *Where Eagles Dare* on another level in terms of the standard crime picture. In mashing-up genres—war, thriller, crime, spy and you can throw in car chase—MacLean pulls off the biggest coup of his career. It's exquisitely structured, the layering of impossibilities, the twists and turns, each one topping the last, the death-defying stunts (decades before CGI limited accidental death, this was genuinely perilous stuff), to the unraveling of the central conceit. And it breaks every rule in the book. There's no explicit tension between the personnel, none of the usual war tropes, no mention of husband-wife-child back home, romantic inclination remaining repressed and very British, though just enough to add a scintilla of emotion, no sentimental hogwash (even *The Dirty Dozen* indulged in that). Smith isn't superhuman in the way of James Bond, but he is calm under pressure and incredibly resourceful (the book reinforces this more). Even so, the obstacles faced are so realistic that it's a wonder he survives. And for once it's surely entitled to be dialogue-heavy—the exposition that Clint Eastwood abhorred—because so much ongoing explanation is vital to the story, teasing the audience in a way no other mystery movie would dare.

In some respects, as far as mystery is concerned, it stands out for what it doesn't do. It doesn't over-egg the pudding, there are no red herrings and no list of suspects. Audience members are left to make up their own minds who among the group could be the traitor, not realizing, perhaps in a nod to *Murder on the Orient Express*, that it's all of them. Nor, come the car chase, are our heroes driving a souped-up supercar, just a superannuated bus that happens, given it is winter, to wear a snowplow.

Nor are the women superfluous, neither eye candy nor powerless. The first time we meet Mary, she's wielding a machine-gun, and she blasts away from the back of the bus along with the best of them. Heidi has been risking her life all this while as a double agent under the eyes of the Gestapo. If there's any narrative flaw, you might complain that the bad guys are underwritten, no explanation given as to reasons for their betrayal. But that might have tipped the movie in the wrong direction, introducing unnecessary timber to a skeletal frame. The biggest surprise, again playing with the nascent Eastwood screen persona, is that he is not the tough guy's tough guy. He makes two grave errors that endanger the mission: He fails to kill a German before he can hit an alarm switch, and he allows the two remaining traitors to escape. Otherwise he is cold-blooded enough and, since Burton is driving the bus, does the lion's share of the killing at that point. Richard Burton, having just scored the fifth of his Oscar

Chapter Six. Where Eagles Dare (1968)

MGM boss Maurice Silverstein (left), *Where Eagles Dare* producer Elliott Kastner and rising star Ingrid Pitt. Pitt was being considered for a big role in *Shalako* (1969) with Sean Connery and Brigitte Bardot (from the Elliott Kastner Archive, courtesy of Dillon Kastner).

nominations for *Who's Afraid of Virginia Woolf?* (1966), reins in the angst, and seems to enjoy the freedom of avoiding emotional entanglement. Mary Ure had only made four pictures the whole decade, the last *Custer of the West* (1967) with husband Robert Shaw, and with demure features was an unlikely candidate, outside of villainesses in the *Deadlier Than the Male* (1967) vein, for the action female lead.

At the time the movie was being made, Burton was a star, Eastwood a fast-rising one,[117] Ure an Oscar nominee. Director Brian G. Hutton was a nobody, three flops in five years, owing the gig to a form of what today would come close to nepotism, Elliott Kastner being a childhood friend and supporter. But he was essential to pulling it all together. MacLean opened his book with the plane, but he didn't commission the music, he didn't translate his imagination onto the screen, didn't work out the details; the screenplay was a template, not the finished article. And you can see how much has to be put into turning a piece of writing for the screen into something more solid by comparing the author's novel to the screenplay. Hutton dictated tempo, emotion, high points and low points, mixing blunderbuss and fine tuning to mesh all-out action with clever dialogue, almost measuring out the dramatic beats, holding his nerve when he must have been tempted to give the audience a greater nod, and especially ensuring that emotion did not get in the way of the classic scenes. And of course, everyone came out humming the theme music.

Book into Film

This proved to be the best-ever MacLean adaptations and the most faithful version of a MacLean novel. Although written first as a screenplay, it was quickly turned into a novel that was published in summer 1967; the novel demonstrates the author's superb narrative skill, every bit as thrilling a ride as the film. For once, every excision is justified and not at the whim of the producer. There's no screenwriter, as in the four previous adaptations, completely altering the storyline or, as in *Ice Station Zebra*, a director eschewing the dialogue-heavy reveals (the author's hallmark) in favor of tipping the wink to the audience, nor a producer intent on infusing the story with his own perspective, as with Carl Foreman and his anti-war sentiments in *Guns of Navarone*. While MacLean is fleshing out his screenplay in the novel, the basic structure remains the same, the author treating it as a blueprint on which to expand situation and character rather than sticking to the bare bones of the narrative as was more common with a novelization. The filmic changes are done for the purpose of disentangling over-complication, speeding up action and occasionally adding spice to character.

But the bulk of the dialogue is taken verbatim from the original script. As was often the case in the translation of book to screen, names were changed. The most obvious, for simplicity, was to truncate Col. Wyatt-Turner to Turner. To avoid confusion with the leading character Major Smith, Berkeley is substituted for Torrance-Smythe. Rolland is promoted from vice-admiral to admiral and Carnaby from lieutenant-general to brigadier-general. The less easily pronounced Captain Von Brauchitsch is dumped in favor of von Hapen.

You wouldn't know it from the film but Schaffer, from Montana, hates horses, a recurrent refrain in MacLean's screenplay and the book. The whistling of Lorelei, another recurring device, is used more sparingly in the film. Throughout the MacLean screenplay and novel, Schaffer continually refers to Smith as "boss" but that is junked completely. And his increasing feelings for Heidi never appear; presumably the filmmakers decided that one romance was enough for an action picture. You may recall the book of *The Guns of Navarone* was totally devoid of romance; Carl Foreman, altering the gender of the Resistance fighters, introducing that element. And it's a shame this particular romantic component was eliminated because, as ever, MacLean is a dab hand at revelation: in his screenplay, he explains that Heidi was actually British and later, at a critical point, to relieve the tension, that her real name is Ethel.

MacLean went straight from writing the screenplay to turning out the book. So the book reflects his initial work, rather than phasing in Hutton's rewrites. But anyone coming to the book first might make the mistake of believing the filmmakers deleted certain scenes rather than, as was occasionally the case, MacLean adding sections to the book that were not in his version of the screenplay. His opening scene was wordy whereas the scene filmed removes all dialogue. The nonchalant Wing Commander piloting the plane, who loses all his jaunty dialogue in the final version, has his lines reinstated, and then some, in the book. Also, in the book, Harrod is presented as fearful. The flashback to Admiral Rolland outlining the mission, dealing with objections and raising the stakes, is primarily MacLean.

The first big change is the location of their drop. MacLean posited them on the edge of a plateau, ensuring a dangerous climb down (rather than up as in *Navarone*) and they sleep in tents whereas director Brian G. Hutton has found them safer shelter. However, when Smith goes off in search of the radio codebook, requiring a dangerous climb upwards, an attempt is made on his life.

One of the joys of reading MacLean is the depth of his research. Only this author would know the best way to sleep in the snow. Unroll, rather than pitch, your tent, place your sleeping bag on one half, snuggle in and cover yourself with the other half, let the snow fall and you'll be both invisible and warm. That's roughly the advice he gives Mary when he locates her and, in an instant, in one of those flashes of writing inspiration, he hints at their relationship when Smith completes that task for her. Given that in the film, they're neither on a cliff nor hiding in tents, this scene is eliminated, as is the scene of Smith checking on her in the morning.

As Schaffer and Smith watch the castle and town through binoculars, the American is privy to some new information, that Turner was a spy in Germany for most of the war, penetrating the German High Command. But that doesn't make it into the film either. And it's not obvious in the film that the infiltrators park their gear in a left luggage office. At the inn, Smith claims to be Himmler's son, but in the film he becomes Himmler's brother. When Smith and Mary meet again, she exclaims at how well the new dress fits her. Smith explains it was made to measure, a clever and casual route into the revelation that Carnaby is a plant. While the latter plot point remains in the movie, the earlier dialogue disappears. When the German officer appears at the inn hunting for deserters, in the film Smith surrenders, but in the screenplay and book it's Heidi who turns them in. When Mary and Heidi are alone, the German asks her

Alistair MacLean (left) with *Where Eagles Dare* producer Elliott Kastner. Alistair MacLean was a regular on the *New York Times* bestseller chart, considered the most influential in the world. How long a book spent on this list was one of the promotional tools available to studios, such as MGM for *Where Eagles Dare* (from the Elliott Kastner Archive, courtesy of Dillon Kastner).

if she loves Smith; the movie has no time for such frankness. Screenplay and book take a different route to Smith and Schaffer's escape after their arrest at the inn. Originally, Smith dupes the Germans, and leaves them tied up. But the film takes a more brutal approach, killing them.

There's a minor subplot the film now avoids. To convince the Germans they are dead, Smith throws his cap into the river after the car, a point later developed. Hutton ignores this detail completely, assuming, more logically, that after the car has tumbled hundreds of feet into the river, the Germans believe nobody could have survived. There's another diversion from the film when they hide out in the ladies' toilet. MacLean specifically mentions Operation Overlord in his screenplay-book but the film is more discreet, limiting mention of D-Day to opening up a Second Front. Though by and large the bulk of the violence is perpetrated by the Hutton rewrite, MacLean originally had a very creepy scene of German matron Anne-Marie in the castle carrying out a brutal body search of Mary. Col. Kramer's annoyance at this shows him up as a "good German." The rewrite takes a different approach, Mary untouched, but Kramer and Von Hapen going head to head in a verbal battle for superiority. When Mary's confidence flags, Heidi remains convinced that Smith can overcome any obstacle; but again, the audience doesn't require that information since they can see for themselves how resourceful the major is. The film skips another revelation: that Heidi knew of the mission two weeks ago.

It's never entirely explained why Schaffer is on the mission. In the film, when that opportunity arises, at the inn, the camera shifts away and whatever explanation Smith gives fades out. In fact, at one point in the later version of the screenplay, it's because the American is a mechanic, hence him lifting the bonnet hood of the snowplow and fiddling around to ensure that it can start. That appears to be a Hutton invention because MacLean just has Smith turning keys left in the ignition. Despite MacLean's mania for authenticity, he falls short when the pair jump from cable car onto parapet, allowing them to gain a handhold by using a knife. More sensibly, the film furnishes them with ice axes. It's Hutton, too, who invents Smith leaving Schaffer to huff and puff his way up to Mary's room and for Schaffer to be disgruntled when he arrives. Again, MacLean is more courteous in his dealings with the enemy, leaving the soldiers in the telephone exchange bound and gagged rather than dead. But since cutting the telephone wires involves another climb outside, this complication is ignored in the film. MacLean also has the Germans aware Smith and Schaffer are inside the castle. At the big reveal between Smith and the Germans, the major claims the Gestapo officer is their inside man, another complication the movie disregards. Mary's Dusseldorf error is Hutton's invention, but has its roots in later line by the Gestapo man that she knows "precious little" about her supposed hometown. In the MacLean version the German's suspicions are alerted when he spots disturbed snow on a window ledge.

There's a wonderful twist in the MacLean version that Hutton passes up. Matronly Anne-Marie takes Mary into another room. There is the sound of blows, a crash, cries of pain—but it is Mary who emerges triumphant. Probably just too much at this stage of the game. Hutton also takes the violent way out, all the Germans shot, whereas MacLean opted for the ironic and less brutal solution, drugging them with scopolamine. However, MacLean's diversionary explosions, utilizing, as in the author's unique invention, CO_2 canisters, and subsequent fires are less powerful than Hutton achieved on film. MacLean has Smith substantially physically limited after being shot in the hand. Mary tries to prevent him leaping onto the cable car containing the escaping traitors. Jones attempts to play the hero but Smith drags him into the cable car. MacLean cuts to the waiting airplane—there's a 25-minute deadline—while Hutton remains with the quartet and omits the deadline. MacLean has a tank blocking their escape route, Hutton has not, and there's some more deceit of the Germans which again Hutton ignores. Pursuers are halted by broken glass from bottles rather than trees downed by booby traps placed earlier. But they do booby trap the bridge. It's Hutton who invents the disguised Mosquito requesting permission to land and for the snowplow to destroy stationary aircraft whereas MacLean makes it much easier. Hutton cuts down on the final confrontation with the traitor, but the gist is the same. MacLean has a more romantic ending, Smith telling Rolland he wants to marry Mary, Schaffer showing similar inclination towards Heidi, and the final line is another Schaffer Montana joke. But, essentially, Hutton follows the MacLean model almost to the letter, eliminating unnecessary complications in favor of drawing out the climactic chase.

It must have been tempting for MacLean just to go through the motions in turning his screenplay into a novel. And for an author with a noted distaste for the act of writing, it must have appeared an unnecessary encumbrance. In fact, it's beautifully written, arguably MacLean's best book. The set-up so clever, every piece of dramatic action matched by another piece of the mystery, leavened by humor—the "What a disguise" line in the novel brilliantly delivered by Burton in the film—and understated romance, and a nonchalant hero who takes everything in his stride and is far from flawed. But some of his descriptions are just superb. Witness a dilapidated village railway station possessing the "odd pessimistically-expectant air of waiting for someone to come along and finish it off." A treat.

Chapter Seven

When Eight Bells Toll (1971)

Alistair MacLean was now the world's highest-paid screenwriter, pocketing $550,000 (equivalent to $17.2 million today) for three features, the $250,000 alone paid for *Fear Is the Key* matching the record amount paid to William Rose for *Guess Who's Coming to Dinner* (1967). For the three pictures following this, he would earn more than star and director, unheard-of in the business.

For *When Eight Bells Toll*, the deal was somewhat different, structured to give MacLean a maximum share of profits, providing him with an equal share of everything the movie brought in once it was sold.[1] And it was partly this arrangement that allowed Elliott Kastner to keep down spending on *When Eight Bells Toll*; it had the lowest budget of the four movies Winkast made in 1969[2] and an unknown star compared to the marquee wattage of David Hemmings and Samantha Eggar for *The Walking Stick* (1970), Ava Gardner in *Tam Lin* and Lee Remick and Richard Attenborough for *A Severed Head* (1971).

MacLean bucked convention in other ways. This was the first time, for example, that he had written a character intended to be the first of a series. What would become *Force 10 from Navarone* was an afterthought, not the original intention. But with *When Eight Bells Toll*, MacLean planned to go down the sequel route of James Bond and Harry Palmer. At the time of publication in 1966, there had been only four of the former and one of the latter, while Derek Flint and Matt Helm were only beginning their screen adventures. In tandem with Kastner, MacLean aimed from the outset to turn his new espionage hero Philip Calvert into a series character, envisaging three, possibly four initial outings.[3]

The bigger question: why the film took over a year following completion to hit the cinemas. Normally when release takes an inordinately long time—or a film is "shelved," sitting in a vault somewhere until sold to television—it is down to a question of quality. With *When Eight Bells Toll*, the delay was deliberate. The reasons were various. The financial tsunami at the end of the 1960s had made studios "more hesitant about hitting the greenlit button"[4]; with studios cutting back severely on production, demand far outstripped supply; and Kastner wanted to capitalize on that as well as exerting greater control over his output. The product shortage had created a "demand in troubled times" for low-cost movies.[5] The 1969 crisis spurred producers to seek sources of finance outside the film industry. There had always been investors so dazzled by the business and so innocent of the financial realities that they could easily be persuaded to dip their toe in the waters for the sake of personal prestige and the chance to rub shoulders with stars at a premiere. And there was growing interest in the film industry being used as tax shelters. Kastner tapped into this "infectious trend." He explained, "I decided to structure a program of pictures, three to six, that did not depend on traditional financing. I wrote six letters to six rich men that I had read about in *Fortune* magazine" (five, apparently, gave a favorable response).[6] Kastner had a file (called "Rich Man's Letters"[7]) containing over two dozen names from which he sent missives requesting investment. He wrote to Howard Hughes.[8] He sought money from the Aga Khan.[9] Millionaire talent agency boss and former MCA colleague Jerry Perenchio was interested in investing up to $1.2 million.[10] Ivan Boesky of Threadneedle Capital believed that raising a "million dollars through my industry contacts should be doable."[11] Kastner was able to persuade investors that it was immaterial whether planned projects had a release outlet lined up because desperate distributors would form a queue and, without the interference of a major studio head office, producers would be left alone to do what they did best, which was to get the movie over the line in accordance with their initial vision. "Private coin" drove investment so substantially from 1969 that "scores of pictures from modest domestic contenders to major productions with class cast values" had gone before the camera without "distributor commitment or upfront bankroll [from a major studio]."[12] The emergence of the video cassette market provided another potential source.[13]

Kastner had always given the impression that his "Rich Man's Letters" had done the trick regarding funding for *When Eight Bells Toll* and that through this simple expediency he had acquired the funding from millionaire serial entrepreneur Menushan Riklis.[14] Israeli Riklis, born in Istanbul, was a conglomerate king, having finessed his Rapid-American Corporation into the Glen Alden Company; it owned the RKO-Stanley Warner cinema chain, Faberge, Playtex, Samsonite and the Riviera casino in Las Vegas. He was a pioneer of leveraged buyouts. In New York, Kastner pitched his idea to Leonard Lane, a Riklis associate, in February 1969:

> I made it clear it was fraught with danger. At the same time I sold the project on its merit: Alistair MacLean's name, Gershwin's clout, my clout, the respect we enjoyed in the industry, and told him it would be a good dice shot. I said I needed $1.8 million to make this Alistair MacLean project. And he heard me out and wrote the damn cheque.[15]

But that version of the funding story ignored the significant contribution of Kurt Unger (later producer of *Puppet on a Chain*—see Chapter Eight), an acquaintance of Kastner. When they met at the White Elephant restaurant in London on January 15, 1969, it turned out that Unger was an old school chum of Riklis and promised to put in a good word. And he wanted a reward for acting as an intermediary. Kastner had contractually agreed to pay him five percent of the profits from the English and Italian end of the deal.[16] In order to push the movie through, Kastner and MacLean both deferred their fees, as well as a substantial share of profits once the investors had been paid off; in lieu of a fee Kastner acquired U.K. and Italian distribution rights.[17] Had Kastner and MacLean taken their usual fees, the costs would have mushroomed as Kastner had been paid $400,000 for *Harper*, $500,000 for *Kaleidoscope* and $483,000 for *The Bobo*[18]; that trio, made in 1966, proved how

With so much of *When Eight Bells Toll* shot at sea, it wasn't surprising that its stars, dedicated anglers Anthony Hopkins and Robert Morley, took the opportunity to go deep sea fishing. According to a press release found in the Elliott Kastner Archive, Morley depended on the stronger Hopkins to haul the big fish into the boat (advertisement, *Independent Film Journal*, May 13, 1971).

lucrative producing could be (over $1.5 million for one year's work plus profit share). Belgian director Etienne Perier also deferred $15,000 of his fee.[19] Despite these deferrals, certain costs for office staff were set against the production, including salaries for associate producer Denis Holt and producer's assistant Marion Rosenberg.[20] Production of *When Eight Bells Toll* ran from August 1969 until February 1970 with both Kastner and Jay Kanter, his recently appointed partner, the designated producers.[21]

There was another problem to overcome: the potential opposition of the U.S. government. The fact that Glen Alden owned a cinema circuit attracted the attention of the government since, according to the 1948 Paramount Decree, exhibitors were barred from movie production. While the law, taking into account the shortage of product, had permitted NGC and ABC, one owning a cinema chain and the other a television network, to set up in film production, negotiations were delayed while federal court ruling was sought[22]—luckily in Glen Alden's favor.

In casting *When Eight Bells Toll*, Kastner embarked on a two-month search for a star. "I didn't want a star, I wanted a classical actor, a real actor," said the producer.[23] He screen-tested scores of young actors, hoping perhaps to turn the leading man into a marquee name that would carry the movie through the projected sequels.[24] Anthony Hopkins was not initially in the frame for the leading role and only second choice for the supporting role that went to Corin Redgrave. The leading contender for Calvert was Bryan Marshall[25] (*Mosquito Squadron*, 1969). Others in the running were John Castle (*The Lion in Winter*, 1968), John Stride (*Bitter Harvest*, 1963), Robin Hawden (*Zeta One*, 1969) and unknowns Gary Heyers and Drewe Henley[26] (*Puppet on a Chain*, 1970). While Nathalie Delon appeared to have nailed the female lead, the producers also listed as possibles Britt Ekland (*The Bobo*, 1966), Sylva Koscina (*A Lovely Way to Die*, 1968), Austrian Romy Scheider (*Otley*, 1969), Italian Silvana Mangano (*Theorem*, 1968) and Frenchwoman Geneviève Page (*Mayerling*, 1969). Orson Welles was the favorite for Skouras with Oscar Homolka (*Funeral in Berlin*, 1966) taking precedence over Jack Hawkins. Noël Coward (*The Italian Job*, 1969) and Alistair Sim (*A Christmas Carol*, 1951) were potential back-ups should Robert Morley turn down the role of Uncle Arthur.[27] Meanwhile, director Perier pushed for both rising star Michael Jayston (later top-billed in *Nicholas and Alexandra*, 1970) as the male lead and the legendary Orson Welles, insisting that each could "be clinched for $7500 maximum."[28] Kastner preferred Anthony Hopkins, best known at the time for a supporting role in *The Lion in Winter* (1968); Hopkins initially turned it down. His two-year marriage to actress Petronella Barker was in trouble and he was drinking heavily.[29] The actor was packed off to a health farm to lose weight[30] and then undergo a course of training with stunt arranger Bob Simmons.[31] There was no let-up in the fitness regime once shooting began. He completed a five-mile run every morning prior to filming and Simmons converted a table tennis room at their hotel into a small gym for evening sessions.[32] Hopkins was a pianist, "playing the piano very well from the age of seven," and studying music before moving into acting. He had done weight-lifting and some boxing. He was very interested in astronomy and his father, a former baker, owned a pub.[33] "I think it's a very good script and it's an interesting, attractive character," he said. "Calvert is more real than Bond … sex maniacs don't make good spies[34] … he is an unknown isolated man who does his job efficiently … [and] a stone-faced killer out for revenge. As the story progresses, Calvert comes out as slightly mad."[35] Kastner also ensured that his contract with Hopkins, which included the planned sequels, took precedence over the actor's existing deal with Columbia.[36]

The 16-week shoot began on September 16, 1969. But, even as the filming of establishing location shots got underway, the movie lacked a star. The female lead, Frenchwoman Nathalie Delon, was signed up before the top-billed male, a very odd state of affairs. "The male lead will be set before the company returns for interior filming in London," the producers blithely announced.[37] In the normal course of events, Delon should have received top billing. After all, she was being paid nearly three times as much as the denoted star Anthony Hopkins. Her salary was £20,800 (plus a living allowance of £390) while Hopkins was paid £7500 (and no living allowance, expenses, chauffeur or car).[38] Moroccan-born model-turned-actress Delon had made her acting debut in Jean-Pierre Melville's thriller *Le Samourai* (1967)[39] opposite husband Alain Delon (their five-year marriage ended before she was hired for this picture). This was her sixth movie and her English-speaking debut. She had previously only twice been top-billed, in *A Tender Moment* (1968) and *Sisters* (1969). She practiced yoga three times a week.[40]

There was some argument over Delon's remuneration following confusion over the date when she was due to report for work. The actress contended that she arrived in Scotland on September 20, 1969, at the "direct request" of the director. He denied this and her name was not recorded on the Call Sheet (which meant she was not expected to make herself available that day). Her name was on the Call Sheet for the next two working days (September 22 and September 23) but with the rider "to be advised" (which again meant she was not expected). This may simply have been miscommunication or misunderstanding, but nobody pays out on those principles. On September 23, she fell ill and was examined by a Dr. Clegg, who told her to stay in bed. The following day, according to the Call Sheet, she was instructed to "stand by at hotel" (which meant she was expected to work). However, as she was ill, she didn't report for duty.

She wasn't on the Call Sheet for September 25, and that created a second problem. If, technically, her employment was due to begin on September 24 and illness prevented her from working and she wasn't due to work anyway on September 25, it would suggest she shouldn't be paid until she physically stepped onto the set. The argument went that "her contract could not be deemed to have started" until September 28 when, again on standby at the hotel, she was called in for rehearsals. Not the best way to start a job.[41] In fact, if billing was judged purely on salary, then Robert Morley should have been billed above Hopkins. His salary was £18,000. All these figures would have been dwarfed, however, had Orson Welles agreed to play Skouras. Perier fell substantially short in his estimation that Welles was available for just £7500. In fact, the star demanded £40,000 for one week's work plus £5000 in expenses.[42] At one time, Jack Hawkins had been bigger than all of them, named #1 British star several years in a row in the 1950s thanks to hits such as *Angels One Five* (1952) and *The Cruel Sea* (1953). The budget for the entire cast was set at £62,505 (roughly equivalent to $150,000) but went over target by $3312. Corin Redgrave ended up with £400 more than his original £3300 fee. Maurice Roeves doubled his original £500. Oliver MacGreevy tripled his original £800. Hawkins was paid £3500 but savings were made on the salaries of Ferdy Mayne (£50 less), Peter Arne (£400 less), Martin Grace (£458 less) and Leon Collins (£360 less).[43]

Director Perier had been under contract to MGM for three years at the start of the 1960s and had *Lady L*[44] in preparation when his contract ended. He had known Kastner from the producer's MCA days. They were the same age. He had been lined up to direct one of Kastner's earliest projects, dating from 1962, *His Own Man*, to star Marlon Brando, based on a book by war correspondent Martha Gellhorn (Hemingway's third wife).[45] Once they fell out over Larry Cohen's screenplay, Perier asked to be "counted out."[46] By chance, encountering the producer in London, he was offered the director's job on *When Eight Bells Toll*. Kastner had successfully bet on the equally inexperienced Brian G. Hutton. Perier was best known for the inconsequential *Swordsman of Sienna* (1962) with Stewart Granger and *Hot Line* (1967) with Robert Taylor. "Alistair MacLean for me was not a big star," said the director. But he was attracted to the humor. "In this novel, more than the others, there are definite humorous trends."[47] The original script, delivered in May 1969, weighed in at 143 pages,[48] and then was reduced to 113 pages. Yet more was cut to meet a lean running time of 90 minutes.

Locations included the Isle of Mull, Tobermory, Duart Castle, the graveyard at Dervaig, Fingal's Cave on the Isle of Staffa, London docks and Malta. "You can't shoot underwater in Scotland," explained Perier, "because you can't see two feet ... there's not enough light coming through the top of the sea."[49] Although, as dictated by the script, anybody could fall into the waters off the west coast of Scotland, it was vital that nobody did in the River Thames. The scene intended to be shot at Southampton was transferred to the King Edward V Docks in London; a night shoot aboard the freighter *Port Auckland* involving Anthony Hopkins. Had he accidentally fallen into the water, the shoot would have been suspended because he would be subject to a compulsory three-week quarantine from risk of infection from the bugs in the river.[50]

Exposure to the elements was a feature of this picture. Corin Redgrave complained, "I seem to spend all my time in freezing cold water. They took a day to drown me on *David Copperfield* [1970], in *Oh, What a Lovely War!* [1969] I spent days in wet, muddy trenches. And here we go again."[51]

From the outset, the production team was determined to alter audience expectations of an espionage picture. Perier said, "James Bond is one-dimensional whereas Calvert could go off in any direction. I am convinced he could become a new kind of hero."[52] Bad weather and bad luck caused the movie to go £68,827 over budget. The biggest factor in the overages (the industry term for unbudgeted costs) was the £25,000 spent "because American underwater director Paul Stader transferred shooting from a large sea water tank in Malta to the open sea." There were mitigating factors: It was estimated that the extra footage required would have bumped up the costs of shooting in the tank—and an unexpected benefit as "it was most unlikely that so exciting a visual sequence would have been obtained in the tank." The underwater sequence ran for nine minutes as well as providing two minutes of material for the projected title sequence.

The underwater unit was hit by unseasonal weather, one set piece overturned while being floated to a location, and rough conditions on the surface preventing any shooting taking place. Extremely bad weather in Scotland meant that the second unit had to work an extra two weeks and three days. There was an extra £4330 for camera equipment due to extended stays in Scotland and Malta; travel costs in Scotland increased by £4251. Retaining Delon longer than anticipated added £300 to the bill for the dialogue coach. The boathouse set cost £4029 more and Malta location facilities another £7735. The camera crew cost an extra £6052 in part because the cameraman was changed after two weeks and his replacement was more expensive. There was an extra £1753 in labor costs to repair roads damaged by heavy transport plus £3000 on film and lab charges and a further £1753 in studio rental. Overages would have been around £30,000 higher had it not been for some savings in the budget and the expectation that the £11,400 lost on storm damage to the Malta underwater set could be recouped from insurance. Savings included: £5000 on stand-ins and doubles, £4750 on legal costs, £3500 on hotel costs when the ship's dock set was shifted from Southampton to London, £1000 on music, £500 on costumes, the same sum on a makeup assistant and £325 on power.[53]

Former child actor Bob Simmons was recognized as one of the top stuntmen in the business. He had doubled for Sean Connery in the tarantula scene in *Dr. No* (1962). In the takes with Connery, the tarantula was under a sheet of glass but, viewing the rushes, the producers noticed that reflections of the lights were showing. So the producers determined to re-do it with nothing between spider and human. A tarantula was borrowed from London Zoo. Simmons was under the misapprehension that it was a just a matter of snipping off the spider's poison bag, only to discover there was no such thing; the poison runs through its bloodstream. If bitten, he'd be paralyzed and/or die a horrible death. Two nurses and a doctor were on standby. He had to do it the scene twice. He was also called upon to swim through a tank of nine sharks in *Thunderball* (1965). He had to repeat that scene, too, because, understandably, he looked scared the first time.

In *When Eight Bells Toll*, rehearsals were the key to safety: "I have time to fully rehearse each piece long before the day we are shooting." The boathouse scene was choreographed "very carefully." The stunt where Simmons hung onto a helicopter undercarriage as it rose 200 feet and then climbed aboard before falling into the sea, shot in a Force 9 gale, was repeated four times. The first time, he grabbed the wrong side of the undercarriage and came up on the pilot's side of the helicopter. When he got it right, Perier called for more takes.[54] This feat made excellent copy for the media, but that particular press release was restricted to journalists working abroad "because of insurance problems."[55]

Getting the movie to market was not as simple as Kastner expected. Glen Alden lacked one vital piece of the Hollywood jigsaw. While now in the production and

Chapter Seven. When Eight Bells Toll *(1971)*

ALISTAIR MACLEAN

June 7, 1970

Dear Miss Muir,

It is with great pleasure that I introduce to you Philip Calvert, the new adventure hero I created in my recent novel, WHEN EIGHT BELLS TOLL, filmed recently by Winkast Film Productions.

You may be familiar with some of the other heroes from the film versions of my novels, ICE STATION ZEBRA, THE GUNS OF NAVARONE and WHERE EAGLES DARE. But Philip Calvert is a hero with a difference. No fast sports cars, no attache case full of gimmicks, no legions of bouncing beauties -- except for the luscious Nathalie Delon. Calvert does his own dirty work, and he does it with his own hands -- or, when the need arises, with his own two fists.

The producers of the film went to a great deal of trouble to find the right combination of acting talent and physical ability for the part of Philip Calvert. The choice of Anthony Hopkins is one which I would have made myself. An actor with a prestigious background in the National Theatre (in addition to winning wide acclaim for his film performances in THE LION IN WINTER and THE LOOKING GLASS WAR), Hopkins brings exactly the right touch of no-nonsense ruggedness to his portrayal of Calvert.

Needless to say, I am delighted with Winkast's film adaptation of my novel, which was directed by Etienne Perier. The way I saw it all happen in my mind, you will now be able to see in the movie theatre. For me, it is a personal thrill to share the experience. I know you will agree with me.

Most sincerely,

Alistair MacLean.

MacLean was intensely private and hated doing interviews, so the publicity world was stunned when, to promote *When Eight Bells Toll*, he agreed to write a letter to 300 American feature editors and columnists, introducing them to the film's protagonist Philip Calvert. According to a letter from Marion Rosenberg to MacLean dated June 1, 1970, MacLean's signature was forged by "Susan, in our office." The publicists made one error, sending this letter to the veteran journalist Florabel Muir, who had died the month previously (from the Elliott Kastner Archive, courtesy of Dillon Kastner).

exhibition business, it lacked an essential requisite: a distributor. Kastner was willing to keep *When Eight Bells Toll* on the shelf for "more than a year before it found a wholesaler and went to market."[56] Personnel changes were afoot at Winkast. The five-year partnership with Jerry Gershwin ended in 1970[57] and he was replaced by former MCA colleagues Alan Ladd, Jr., and Jay Kanter, previously head of European operations for Universal.[58] One of their first tasks was to prepare *Deakin* (aka *Breakheart Pass*) for production in 1970 while the company embarked on new production relationships with the fledgling Commonwealth United[59] and the more established Anglo-Amalgamated.[60] After *When Eight Bells Toll* was turned down for U.S. distribution by United Artists,[61] Kastner hawked it to Warner Brothers, Cinerama and Cinema Center. Simultaneously, he positioned it as the pilot for a proposed Philip Calvert TV series; both MacLean and Hopkins were signed up for three (possibly four) iterations of the character. "Let's see what we can do with a network before disposing of the domestic theatrical rights to the picture," said Kastner. "We can deliver MacLean for all the original stories and as story consultant."

Kastner headed off to Geneva to have MacLean "begin immediately on the three original storylines for the sequels."[62] He sought to secure $1 million for the U.S. TV rights. Also, since ABC owned Cinerama, he entertained the notion of the companies jointly ponying up $1.6 million for theatrical release and television.[63] Such a "shotgun approach" did not go down well in a "very strong buyer's market" in which movies, contrary to Kastner's expectations, were being sold on terms the "most favorable" to buyers in two decades. Cinerama was a bad bet because the "company position was very much on the low side" and Kastner might not get paid for two years. He was accused of being "completely disorganized in planning the sale."[64] Even MacLean grew frustrated, complaining in August 1970 of "no word of a distributor yet."[65] Finally, worldwide distribution rights for *When Eight Bells Toll*, excluding Britain and Italy, went to Cinerama on a 20-year deal.[66]

Attempts were made to get Nathalie Delon to pose nude for *Playboy* magazine on the grounds that this would not be the usual starlet-type glamor spread but focusing on her role in the film. Photos taken underwater "would, theoretically, illustrate how a spy works underwater. It would therefore be obvious that the nudity is obligatory within the framework of the film… [Y]ou can be confident … it would be done in extremely good taste."[67] At that point, "no great star has ever done a *Playboy* layout."[68]

A plan to involve MacLean in a 30-minute 16mm film aimed at TV audiences also failed to come off.[69] Maurice Silverstein, president of Commonwealth United, had been banging the drum about the movie in the Far East[70]; screenings were held in London in April 1970 for European distributors.[71] Possibly because of the rancor that had developed between Kastner and MacLean, the producer was in no hurry to show the author the finished film. "If you would like to see *When Eight Bells Toll*," Marion Rosenberg told MacLean two months after its general release in the U.K., "please give me a ring and I'll organize a screening for you."[72]

But the Rapid-American (the successor to RKO-Stanley Warner)-Unger-Kastner deal was not as straightforward as it had once appeared. In exchange for covering overages on the budget and the "very substantial" sums required to ensure Cinerama distributed the picture, Rapid-American had re-negotiated their agreement, resulting in Winkast handing over one-sixth of its profits from Britain and Italy. Unger had "got Alistair MacLean to make some kind of deal that nobody knew about." (Presumably, *Puppet on a Chain*; see Chapter Eight.) It was conceded that Unger was "due something" from the U.K. and Italy but how much depended on "what deductions we can get away with."[73] Rapid-American took Winkast to court in 1988, claiming that no accounts or payments had been processed since 1978; the company contended that it was due 50 percent of all U.K. revenues and 100 percent of Italy until it had recouped its entire investment plus a $150,000 "penalty."[74] MacLean was owed £18,894 in 1976[75] and received a check for £19,498 in 1977.[76] By the mid–1990s, Unger had become such an irritant that Kastner considered serving him with a writ.[77]

Kastner called on attorney Elwood A. Rickless for help. He suggested that Kastner undertake a "chain of title" investigation, following where labs were sending the films. He advised that "Kurt is likely to produce a perfectly innocent distribution agreement with some Riklis-dominated Panamanian company which is either illegally distributing in defiance of whatever was appointed for RKO" and explained that he had contacted Danny Unger, who "adamantly refuses to tell me where he got his rights."[78] And it appeared that, under the aegis of Roadshow Productions, deals were done on *When Eight Bells Toll* in Scandinavia[79] and possibly Japan, France and the Benelux.[80] Even MacLean felt let down by the financial situation surrounding the film. His lawyer David Bishop came up with an elegant solution. In exchange for Kastner cooperating with MacLean's biographer Jack Webster, he would wipe the debt clean,[81] there being no way Kastner could pay, having been declared bankrupt in 1988.[82] It was a sad end for the producer who had been instrumental in developing MacLean's second career as a screenwriter.

The Low-Budget Actioner

Pausing only long enough for judicious exposition, *When Eight Bells Toll* races along from set piece to set piece, danger lurking above and below the water, with a potential femme fatale thrown into the mix, and a driving score to keep the audience in high gear.

Like *Where Eagles Dare,* it begins in pitch darkness, in the sea this time, as a head pops out of the water and a frogman climbs aboard a ship and finds a gun pointed at him. It's strikingly done, a throwback to film noir, a strip of light illuminating the gunman's face. But he's dead. As we discover in flashback, he was a plant, part of an operation set up by espionage agent Calvert (Anthony Hopkins) to track hijacked ships transporting gold bullion. Calvert and mild-mannered sidekick Hunslett (Corin Redgrave) set themselves up as bait on a boat, the *Firecrest*, off Scotland's west coast. Sure enough, they attract attention: A fake Customs officer plants a transmitter on board, and thugs attack Calvert on the mainland. The local community is cut off, telephone wires severed, too many sudden deaths or disappearances for coincidence, people too frightened to talk. Calvert's interfering, bumptious boss Sir Arthur (Robert Morley) turns up in time to accept an invitation to visit the luxury yacht along with shipping magnate Sir Anthony Skouras (Jack Hawkins), his glamorous wife Charlotte (Nathalie Delon) and various business acquaintances, including Lavorski (Ferdy Mayne) and Arthur's high-class colleague Lord Charnley (Derek Bond). But this increases rather than allays suspicion, and in any case proves only a ploy to search the *Firecrest*. Commandeering a helicopter, Calvert, hunting for possible hiding places for the ship, comes across shark fishermen and fearful castle proprietor Lord Kirkside (Tom Chatto) and daughter Sue (Wendy Allnut). The helicopter is shot down, Calvert escaping into the sea. But now Hunslett is missing and, pleading for help and soaked from swimming, a desperate Charlotte arrives, seeking sanctuary, claiming to be held a prisoner, whip marks on her back testimony to brutal treatment. Hunslett is dead, dragged up on the anchor. So far, it's been an intriguing mystery, more gumshoe than derring-do, but now in a stroke of trademark MacLean genius, Calvert works out why nobody can find the missing ships. They've been sunk. And he reckons Skouras is operating a clandestine salvage operation from one of the remote islands. He thwarts an attack by Skouras' men to rescue Charlotte, who married Skouras a year after his first wife's sudden death. Calvert tests out his theory, enlisting the help of the fishermen, and discovers the lost bullion has been transported to caves beneath the castle. After a romantic interlude with Charlotte, Calvert scales the cliffs of the castle and, with Sue's help, disables guards holding people prisoners in the castle. Then he finds a secret entrance to the caves and waits until the fishermen-turned-mercenaries arrive at an appointed time for a shootout. Skouras is in the clear, a kidnapped wife forcing his cooperation. Charnley and Lavorksi are unveiled as the ringleaders, but you guessed that, so the only real twist is that Calvert not only lets Charlotte go but helps her on her way with a stolen bar of gold.

While Anthony Hopkins doesn't fit the brawny hero template, he's adept enough at dealing with villains, brings a shade more humanity to the role than predecessors in the espionage game, and certainly matches James Bond in romantic repartee. But he makes far greater use of the little gray cells since genuine mystery is rarely an element in this genre. And while he's a long way from the finished Oscar-worthy Hopkins—and bear in mind that it took decades for directors to work out how to use his stillness to advantage—there are certainly scenes showing a fine acting intelligence at work. In the opening sequence, for example, he works out that the gunman isn't alive by shifting gently to the side and noting that the gunman's eyes aren't following him. In his initial scene with Sir Arthur, before answering some query, he gives a half-glance to Hunslett as if making up his mind how he will reply. And while hardly radiating sexual charisma, he oozes self-deprecating charm, especially in the throwaway line "I'll even take my boots off." Charlotte's remark, "You've been a long time at sea, haven't you?" is all the sexuality this couple needs, this female, unlike the general Bond-Flint-Helm generation, not required to flaunt cleavage. Generally, innuendo here is gently done, and you are meant to laugh at innocent Sue's awkward attempt at seducing the castle guard ("Is your gun loaded?").

But female clumsiness, rather than the usual confidence, is the order of the day, and Nathalie Delon plays Charlotte in a manner than reveals her inner tensions and renders Calvert's suspicions understandable. The whip marks are physical proof of bad treatment, but the callous way in which Skouras orders his second wife to fetch a photograph of his beloved first wife verges on psychological torture. And there's certainly more humor than you might expect, mostly at the expense of the ever-hungry, somewhat buffoonish Sir Arthur. I'm not convinced this was good casting. Morley had played these types before, and his characterization doesn't leave much room for audience surprise. While the Civil Service in general might be stuffed full of such high-class public-school buffers, you would imagine the Secret Service, with its demand for ruthless application, would be free of them.

The low budget didn't allow for many high-powered action scenes: Notice that the caves' wooden gates, when rammed by the ship, merely splinter rather than being blown apart by the force of the collision. But the underwater sequences, while acceptable enough in the context, pale in comparison to *Thunderball*; and the above-water sequences can't compare to *Ice Station Zebra*. The various fistfights and shoot-outs are up to snuff but, like *Where Eagles Dare*, the action is largely subservient to the mystery.

In that regard, audiences certainly get their money's worth. Directorially, apart from the film noir–ish sequence, there's little that's worth mentioning. Etienne Perier is at its best in the tension-filled scenes between Calvert and Charlotte. The Walter Stott score comes into play whenever the pace showed signs of slowing.[83] All in all, though, the film is a good example of a screen translation of a MacLean thriller.

Book into Film

If you were of the generation that believed a .357 Magnum was the most powerful handgun in the world and could "blow your head clean off" (*Dirty Harry*, 1971), you weren't keeping abreast of Alistair MacLean. He opens *When Eight Bells Toll* with a disquisition on the Colt Peacemaker, the weapon staring Calvert in the face when he boards the gold bullion ship. Director Perier decided to concentrate on the gunman's eyes rather than the weapon and so missed a cinematic trick. But MacLean steals the thriller crown jewels with this opening scene. Other elements of the novel are skated over in the movie. In the novel Calvert is much more human, guilty about the colleagues he sent to their deaths, blaming himself for not preventing Hunslett's demise, given to perorations on his profession ("I wasn't supposed to have any feelings") and whether he can justify the killing, not thoughts that would trouble James Bond or even the ambiguous heroes of John le Carré. Also ignored are his scarred face and widower-hood, both the result of the accident that killed his wife. You also wouldn't recognize Charlotte, here a former actress a good decade older than in the film and "eyes a thousand years old." Sir Arthur is tougher than the plummy Robert Morley, still with a gourmand's sensibility but less of the master-and-servant mentality.

The flashback introducing Sir Arthur is inventive, following cinematic convention of introducing major characters in person earlier rather than later. In the book, it suffices to keep him at the end of a telephone and his appearance is more structural necessity than anything. With Hunslett out of the way, Calvert needs a figure he can trust to help dupe the enemy. He can't—and with good reason, as it transpires more pointedly in the book—trust Charlotte. Readers might suspect MacLean of pulling a fast one by using the whipped-back routine from *The Guns of Navarone*, seeding the idea in the book lover's mind that somehow these marks were false. In the film, Charlotte winces when Calvert touches her book. Critically, in the book, she doesn't; Calvert finds needle marks on her back, surmising that she was unconscious when the whip was applied. But she is also given more leeway in the book, even after Calvert's suspicions prove correct, for it turns out she is cousin to Skouras' missing wife and forced to play a role. It's in the interests of having a romantically unfettered hero—remember, this was to be the opening gambit in a series—that Calvert turns her loose at the end. The book, written before the idea of a threequel was mentioned, had a happier ending. "Very self-willed she was," muses Calvert in the final paragraph, "and I could see that was going to cause trouble in the years to come." In the film, Lavorski is steely-eyed and mirthless, in the film twinkle-eyed with a booming laugh, but I guess there was sufficient joviality in the movie with Robert Morley around. As well as the whip motif, MacLean monkeys around with another of his hallmarks: the deadline. Initially, Calvert has 48 hours to complete his mission. So, first of all, he fails to meet the deadline. Instead of chewing him out, Sir Arthur comes to the rescue.

Understandably, the film removes some of the complications. Far too many characters to fit into a film are in the thrall of the bullion robbers. And there are long sections of exposition, often explaining the motivations of the bad guys, the slump in personal fortunes that persuaded them to resolve financial problems through criminal enterprise. But in a movie, that's irrelevant. Point out the bad guys and get on with it. Some elements changed from book to movie out of a need to exemplify character or add tension. In the book, the helicopter is at Calvert's command; in the film, he commandeers it. In the book, the isolation of the village through the cutting of telephone wires occurs off-screen; in the film, Calvert's investigation triggers an attack by thugs. In the film, Calvert surprises Sir Arthur; in the book, it's the other way around. In the book, Hunslett is found dead in a secret compartment in the *Firecrest* engine room, though it's admittedly more dramatic to have him hauled up on the anchor chain. Dialogue from the book moves around. Sir Arthur's character assassination of Calvert in their first scene has been taken from much later in the book but preceded by praise: "the best agent in Europe." Although Sir Arthur is less of a semi-comedic fixture in the book, he is still given to such upper-class quips as "Made a fearful mess of the carpet."

The class warfare sniping is the film's invention. Much of the dialogue in the film is more carefully honed, especially the repartee between Calvert and Charlotte, and serves to keep tension high and perspective more evenly balanced, whereas in the book we see all the action from Calvert's point of view. The one element of the film that did seem unlikely was recruiting the fishermen as mercenaries. While Calvert in the book does enlist their help and promise them a share of the salvage reward money, to storm the cave he calls in the Marines. While the film ends on a romantic note, the book does so in more humorous fashion with Calvert imagining the reunion of a minor character with his kidnapped wife. "I hoped to God old Donald MacEachern had remembered to change his shirt."

Chapter Eight

Puppet on a Chain (1971)[1]

The 1969 *Variety* headline said it all: "Film Production Slump No Problem for Alistair MacLean."[2] Hollywood was facing financial crisis as overspending on big-budget roadshows and star-driven features took its toll. Prestigious productions were cancelled. Only the biggest stars could be sure of being offered work. As studios headed for potential bankruptcy, this wasn't the time to be worrying about how screenwriters or bestselling authors were coping.

But MacLean was worth talking about because the author appeared immune to the disaster enveloping Hollywood. He had hit the mother lode in unprecedented fashion. Six years after apparently giving up writing forever, he was the toast of the movie business. At a time when the industry was on its knees, *Variety* hailed MacLean as being in a class of his own. *Variety* announced, "You can sell a picture on the basis of his name,"[3] the true test of marquee power. Elliott Kastner concurred: "We have now reached the stage where we have a writer who is as important as the stars."[4] He was a "one-man industry." And it wasn't just Kastner queuing up to buy his work. He had become a major attraction for a wide variety of Hollywood, British and independent producers. By 1969, all 14 of his published novels (up to *Puppet on a Chain*) had been bought for the movies, five already released, nine on various slates.[5] Some were on a second option; for example, Martin Ransohoff picked up the rights the previous year to *The Golden Rendezvous* (published in 1962), lining up MacLean for screenwriting duties.[6] But to meet demand, MacLean had furnished the industry with another six properties. In the history of everything, no author had ever been in the position of 20 movies potentially being made from his books in around a decade and a half. Kastner at Winkast was at the forefront of investment, taking on *When Eight Bells Toll* (published in 1966) and projected sequels—the idea being to start a series to rival James Bond—as well as purchasing original screenplays *Deakin* (later re-titled *Breakheart Pass*) and the pirate adventure *Caribbean*. Winkast also took out an option out on *Fear Is the Key* (published in 1961) (see Chapter Nine) and was in the frame to produce the *Guns of Navarone* sequel (see Chapter Thirteen). *Caravan to Vaccarès* had been snapped up by ex–Columbia executive Maxwell Setton; Kurt Unger was set to produce *Puppet on a Chain,* and the rights to *H.M.S. Ulysses* had been transferred to Italian independent Count Volpi.[7] MacLean appeared untouched by the vagaries of the business. Winkast was also touting the notion that *When Eight Bells Toll* would be advertised as *Alistair*

Chapter Eight. Puppet on a Chain (1971)

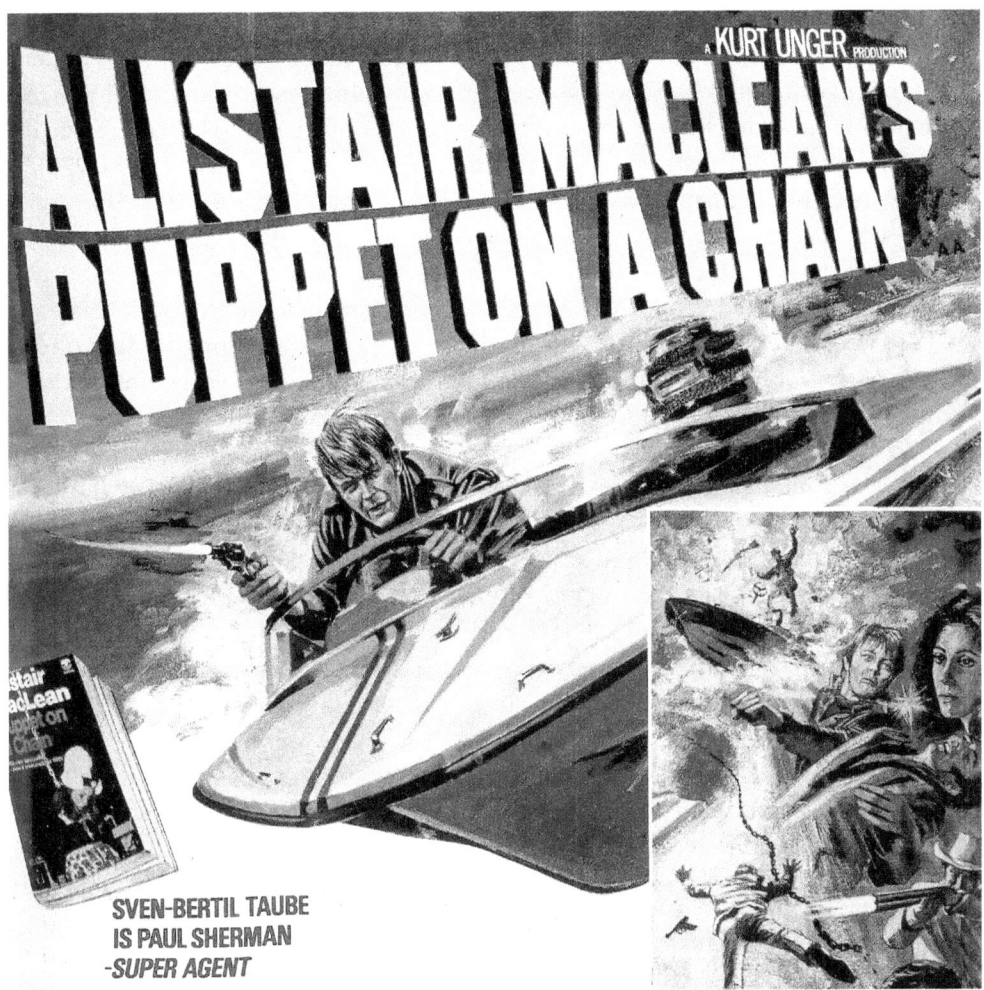

The value of MacLean's name to a movie in promotional terms was no better demonstrated than by *Puppet on a Chain*. Generally, only the biggest stars and directors had their name above the title. Even Ian Fleming, author of the massively successful James Bond novels, was not accorded that kind of credit (advertisement, *Kine Weekly*, August 7, 1971).

MacLean's When Eight Bells Toll, that kind of credit above the title normally the preserve of stars.[8]

And the author also planned to take more control over the films of his books, in part to guarantee greater financial reward, in part to ensure they remained faithful to his vision. He set up Trio Productions with Geoffrey Reeve, a highly rated director of commercials and promotional films for industry,[9] involved in the sequel to *The Guns of Navarone*, and high-flying wine retailer Lewis Jenkins. Jenkins had come across details of the author's deal for *Ice Station Zebra* (1968) and felt that MacLean was being underpaid.[10] Horrified at the state of the author's financial affairs,[11] he put MacLean in touch with international tax lawyer Dr. John Heyting, who in turn handed him over to David Bishop. One of Bishop's first tasks was to upbraid Carl Foreman over his temerity in jumping the gun on the

Navarone sequel and excluding the author. The triumvirate set about attracting finance from Columbia but were soon dealing with a much bigger fish. David Lean (*Doctor Zhivago*, 1965) had expressed considerable interest in turning the threesome into a foursome. But the tantalizing possibility of a Lean-MacLean movie fell at the first hurdle as the director was tied up developing *Ryan's Daughter* (1970).[12]

The idea for *Puppet on a Chain* originated from a trip to Amsterdam with Reeve, who had mooted the notion of a thriller with a drugs background; during the trip, by chance, MacLean spotted the image that sparked the title.[13] *Puppet on a Chain* was published in 1969 to commercial and critical acclaim; now it was up to Reeve to negotiate a deal with a major studio. And it says something for the solidity of their partnership that *Puppet on a Chain* hit the screens two years later, quicker than *When Eight Bells Toll* which took five years to be turned into a film.

Most critics failed to notice that *Puppet on a Chain* represented a subtle evolution. "It was a change of style from the earlier books. If I went on writing the same stuff, I'd be guying myself," MacLean said. But the *New York Times* noticed and in a lengthy review elevated him to stand comparison with Graham Greene and Eric Ambler, the doyens of the literary thriller. "It's a top-drawer effort," commented critic Thomas Lask "If you have any red corpuscles in your blood, you will find your heart pumping triple time…. The writing is as crisp as a sunny winter morning and MacLean has provided a travelog for a part of Amsterdam the ordinary tourist is not likely to go."[14]

At one point, Elliott Kastner was involved in the project—going to so far as to submit the script to Samuel Z. Arkoff of American International Pictures, who turned it down.[15] British studio Associated British Picture Corporation, owner of the country's largest cinema circuit, was interested,[16] hardly surprising since, in the interests of getting the fledgling production company off the ground, Trio only asked for $60,000 in total for the screenplay and Reeve's directorial fee.[17] ABPC boss Robert Clark hesitated over Reeve, insisting he be replaced if the rushes were deemed of insufficient quality. Clark sought to offset costs by involving an American partner, sending MGM's Maurice "Red" Silverstein a rough script. Despite the success of *Where Eagles Dare*, Silverstein was not impressed.[18] But MacLean still held considerable sway and the project attracted the attention of another independent producer, Kurt Unger, former United Artists European production chief,[19] who had been instrumental in raising finance for *When Eight Bells Toll* (see Chapter Seven). Prior to entering production, his biggest claim to fame was persuading United Artists to back Harry Saltzman and Cubby Broccoli for their proposed production of *Dr. No* (1962).[20] Now Unger was seeking a follow-up to his debut effort *Judith* (1966), starring Sophia Loren and Jack Hawkins, and *The Best House in London* (1969), starring David Hemmings, a feminist comedy set in a brothel.

"After *The Guns of Navarone* and *Where Eagles Dare*," noted Daniel Unger, the producer's son, "MacLean was top of the pops."[21] Kurt Unger's old Tel Aviv school chum Meshulam Riklis provided the $1 million budget.[22] Lack of finance limited the talent available. There was no possibility of approaching a Richard Burton, much less a Clint Eastwood. And it's more likely that Swede Sven-Bertil Taube was approved as

Chapter Eight. **Puppet on a Chain** *(1971)* 83

MacLean stares out of an Amsterdam window at a puppet on a chain. During a visit to the city, he had spotted a dangling puppet being used for advertising purposes and appropriated the image to chilling effect (courtesy of Daniel Unger, Roadshow Productions Ltd.).

a name with European appeal and following *The Buttercup Chain* (1970) could easily be sold as the next big thing in America, bearing in mind that espionage had paved the way in the previous decade for stars like Sean Connery and James Coburn.

Barbara Parkins (*Valley of the Dolls*, 1967) helped attract audience interest in the U.S. Rising British star Suzanna Leigh (*The Lost Continent*, 1968) was also on board, but her scenes were not included in the final cut. Supposedly, she played a villain, but it's more likely she was hired for the role of Belinda, one of the hero's sidekicks in the book. While hardly a big name, Brit Patrick Allen (*The Devil Rides Out,* 1968) brought dependable support and was sufficiently well-known in the home market. Pole Vladek Sheybal (*Women in Love*, 1969) was always good copy, having twice escaped World War II concentration camps. Another Pole, Ania Larson, was making her movie debut and is still working; you might have caught her in the mini-series *The Witcher* (2021). It was the maiden movie outing for Greek actress Penny Casdagli—and also her last.

MacLean's lawyer David Bishop knew Piet Cleverings, Amsterdam's police chief, so permission for use of locales and, more importantly, the city's extensive canals was granted.[23] Filming was due to start in early March 1970, but was postponed until April 15.[24] Unusually, and presumably due to his backing of the partnership, MacLean intended to spend time in Amsterdam observing the filming. He brought over quite a party, including his brother and sister-in-law, publisher Ian Chapman and wife plus Bishop. But any sense of triumph at his role in putting the picture together was dashed by the news that his protégé Geoffrey Reeve had been replaced. "It was Geoff Reeve's first film on this scale," reported Kurt Unger, "and there some things not right. We brought in Don Sharp as a second unit director responsible for such scenes as the motorboat chases."[25] According to Daniel Unger, director Don Sharp was brought in "to do the additional shooting to get to the final product."[26] Kurt Unger had already taken steps to reshape the script, calling on TV writer Paul Wheeler and Sharp to add an extra dimension. In the producer's view, MacLean "was a good writer but he was not a screenwriter. And what he wrote as a screenplay for *Puppet on a Chain*, I'm afraid, had to be rewritten."[27]

Understandably, MacLean was incandescent with rage at this "rubbishy travesty of what I wrote." You could almost feel his spleen dripping onto the page as he wrote to Unger,

> If [Wheeler] can improve on practically everything I write and is clearly of the opinion that he is so much the better writer, why is it I've never heard of him? …I feel like a doctor who has been called in after a group of myopic first-year medical students with hacksaws have completely misdiagnosed and performed major surgery on a previously healthy patient.[28]

It was a poor introduction to the role of co-producer, although clearly MacLean didn't think he had to protect his screenplay in the way that someone like Foreman would. If surrendering the rights for a low price furnished him with any power, he didn't know how to use it.

Sharp was an unusual addition. Rather than being a go-to second unit director, he was an experienced director in his own right, a favorite of Hammer (*The Devil-Ship Pirates*, 1964) and independent producer Harry Alan Towers (*Our Man in Marrakesh* aka *Bang! Bang! You're Dead*, 1966). Unfortunately, his movie career had turned turtle, film work drying up after *The Violent Enemy* (1967). Helming episodes of *The Avengers* and *Champion* in 1968 paid the bills but the lackluster *Taste of Excitement* (1969) hampered his career. (Aside from *Puppet on a Chain*, he remained in movie limbo for another four years.) Sharp argued that the script for the boat chase was "not good enough," especially if it was to be the film's highlight. "I chose the location," recalled Sharp, "I talked to the police, got the boats and worked with a wonderful bloke there called Wim Wagenaar, who ran a restaurant." As well as driving one of the boats, Wagenaar orchestrated jumping the boats in the canal. Sharp:

> We sketched out a whole sequence and, some of the things, other boatmen said, you can't do. I wanted his boat to run up on to the back of another boat and push it along. They said it won't…. I said, all right, let's try it. And it did work. And we ran into bridges and came spinning round the corner. One time we had to wait for a little while because I had broken, I think it was, four boat hulls and smashed about eight Mercury engines. And they couldn't get another one, they had to fly them in from Canada. It got a bit expensive.[29]

Part of what made the chase so thrilling was the unusual manner in which it was shot. Rather than shooting it in small sections and then editing it together, Sharp took the advice of camera operator Skeets Kelly, who wanted it done all it one shot. According to Sharp,

> I had considered doing it in a couple of cuts, and Skeets talked me out of it. He said no, there's so much more impact if you don't because the audiences are very intelligent these days, so *au fait* with cinema, that they will know.… But to go and do it in the one [shot], it's absolutely for real.[30]

Four weeks were allocated for the boat chase. Once it was complete, Sharp received another call from Unger, who was dissatisfied with the Reeve version. Sharp met with Unger and Lenny Lane, Risklis' associate. Lane's opinion was: "Bit of a mess." Unger was more forthright: "We've either got to spend more money and fix it or we've got to cut our losses and not release it." Sharp thought it would be "a great shame" to shelve the movie because thought the boat chase was good and that there were some good things in it. "So, I said, first of all, give me a couple of days in the cutting room with it, to look at it and make some notes, then I'll tell you whether I think you can save it."

After spending time in the cutting room, Sharp drew up a list of amendments. Unger talked to the financiers, sorted out the extra cash and commissioned Sharp to reshoot certain sequences, alter the plot and change the ending. Working with a Moviola of the original footage, Sharp was able to ensure that new footage matched old. He complained that Reeve "didn't have a story sense then, as a director ... and each set-up ... looked like part of a television commercial and wasn't there for the drama of it or just to let the audience know what was going on." For example, Sharp had to re-edit and re-film parts of the nightclub sequence. "Seventy-five percent of it was fine.... I did have to go and reshoot it because to shoot a couple of really good, important dialogue lines [were heard] in a shot between the legs of a dancer ... done for a visual effect" (rather than to tell the story).[31] In his defense, Reeve's son Tom, producer of *The Way to Dusty Death* (1995), argued that much of the history was written after the event by those who sought to diminish his father's considerable input.[32] And it's worth noting that even Sharp agrees that three-quarters of the movie was "fine." Tom Reeve has also acted as second unit director, and therefore is more familiar than most with that position within the framework of a production operation; he pointed out, "The second unit directors must do what is asked of them by the main unit director," so is not necessarily as independent as Sharp's comments would suggest. "The famous boat chase was designed and choreographed by [camera operator] Fred Tammes and my father," Tom Reeve added.[33]

Location manager Colin Leighton could possibly claim more credit for the boat chase sequence than anyone since he said he was responsible for persuading the Dutch harbormaster to raise the normal speed limit from six kilometers per hour to 60.[34]

Various sequences were added to the MacLean original. These included: the assistant manager on the phone giving out Sherman's room number; Sherman seeing photos of the dead people in California and the needles in the clocks; his pursuit by the Man in Grey; Morgenstern warning the Man in Grey not to underestimate Sherman; Belinda and Maggie in the hotel; a key sequence where Sherman reprimands Belinda for not removing giveaway dry cleaning tags from her clothes; Sherman finding the diary with the note about the *Marianne;* the corpse falling out of the elevator; the discovery of the boat in Barge City; Morgenstern and Astrid in the nightclub; Belinda left behind in the room; the fight on the boat, and Sherman finding Maggie's body.[35] Bond producers Broccoli and Saltzman had more to thank Unger for than giving them a leg up in the first place: The boat chase here inspired their boat chase in *Live and Let Die* (1973). Explained Sharp, "When [*Puppet on a Chain*] came out, Harry Saltzman and Cubby Broccoli asked Unger, 'How did you do that boat chase?' Because they'd never thought of one… [T]hey spent on the boat chase in *Live and Let Die* more than we spent on the whole film, both units and the reshoots."36

The Film: It Takes Two to Tango

The spy genre was dying on its feet, with even James Bond slipping into spoof territory. It was left to MacLean to revive the genre with believable heroes and settings not chosen just for their scenic potential, fitting somewhere between the gritty *policiers* of *Bullitt* (1968) and *The French Connection* (1971) and with an emphasis on violence that Sam Peckinpah would admire. Stylish bullet-ridden opening, crackerjack climax sums up *Puppet on a Chain*. In between, depicting Amsterdam scenery and depravity side by side, come betrayal, duplicity, drugs, heinous deaths and plenty action. As much as *Bullitt* reinvented the car chase, *Puppet* did the same for speedboats.

Tracking camera point-of-view follows an assassin into a house where he kills three people and removes something from the pendulums of clocks. U.S. narcotics agent Sherman (Sven-Bertil Taube) flies to Amsterdam but before his colleague

On the *Puppet on a Chain* set, left to right: producer Kurt Unger, financier Leonard Lane and director Geoff Reeve. (Photo courtesy of Daniel Unger, Roadshow Productions Ltd.).

Chapter Eight. Puppet on a Chain *(1971)*

Duclos can hand over vital information, he is murdered. Top Dutch cops Col. De Graaf (Alexander Knox) and Inspector Van Gelder (Patrick Allen) are unable to stop the growing heroin traffic. Van Gelder, with addicted niece Trudi (Penny Casdagli), knows only too well the personal cost. The police force is riddled with leaks, the heroin gang out to stop Sherman from the get-go. But Sherman hands out beatings and death to those who get in his way. He is helped by colleague Maggie (Barbara Parkins) and, inadvertently, by Duclos' girlfriend Astrid (Ania Lemay). The trail leads to the Morgenstern warehouse, which stocks all sizes of puppets, and a church run by shady pastor Meegeren (Vladek Sheybal) which has re-purposed Bibles. Sherman has no sooner escaped one attempt on his life than he encounters another, so the action never lets up. Clues lead him to a boat in the harbor and he discovers how the heroin is being shipped. Maggie, on hand to offer romantic consolation, shares his tough assignment but questions his methods.

The trail isn't that hard to follow but the obstacles are considerable. Meegeren and pals take hanging to the extreme, strangling victims with steel chains, dangling them high as a warning to others. So, mostly, leavened, depending on your point of view, by the titillation available for a price in the Dutch capital and a sexy dance troupe that would put Bob Fosse to shame, it is fist- and gunfights all the way. Except for his dalliance with Maggie, a romance that has to be kept under wraps, Sherman fits the tough MacLean template of loner with a ruthless streak wide enough to have won plaudits from the *Where Eagles Dare* team. He gets a good dousing in the sea and is an unwilling candidate for a brainwashing technique that combines tradition with a personalized version of the sonic boom.

The highlight without doubt is the high-speed speedboat chase, beginning in the Zuider Zee before reaching the narrow, twisty Dutch canals. For the Dutch Tourist Board, it was a game of two halves, organ music a-plenty, cobbles and canals, and people dressed in traditional garb promoting the city as a desirable destination but the unsightly addicts and the sex trade as likely to put overseas visitors off. It was rare at this point, in a polished Hollywood-style picture, to dig so deeply into the seamy side of a city, but *Puppet* pulls no punches, nitty-gritty winning out over gloss. Where *Easy Rider* (1969) canonized drugs, this favored grim consequence,

It seemed particularly difficult to cast the right leading man for a MacLean movie of the lone wolf variety. The all-star war pictures had no trouble attracting major players—and if you turned up your nose at Richard Widmark in *The Secret Ways* (1961) and George Maharis in *The Satan Bug* (1965), you might find fault with Swede Sven-Bertil Taube. He makes a fairly decent stab at the author's standard dour character, although as Daniel Unger observed, "Sven didn't have the necessary presence to carry it."[37] Barbara Parkins, way out of her comfort zone, does well as the tough woman with a soft center. On the upside, casting relative unknowns prevented audiences arriving with preconceptions. In her only movie, Penny Cadagli is the pick of the support, especially as her role in the movie is to play a role. Not only plenty of bang for your buck, but a riveting chase and one of the first sightings of heroin supply as the key driver of the narrative.

Book into Film

In the MacLean book, there's no speedboat chase. There's not one female assistant but two, Maggie (Barbara Parkins in the film) joined by a Parisian, Belinda (played by Suzanna Leigh, except her part was cut), on her debut assignment. The espionage newcomer's role in the book is to question the actions of boss Paul Sherman (Sven-Bertil Taube), provide more of an outsider's perspective on his character, since, as his lover, Maggie is much more accepting of his behavior. I can see why Belinda never made it into the film; the movie's emotional heart, little as it is, comes from Sherman's relationship with Maggie. In the book, Sherman and Maggie are British, not American. Amsterdam cop Inspector Van Gelder (Patrick Allen) doesn't have a heroin-addicted niece but an adopted daughter. In the book, he is far closer to her than in the film, to the extent of conducting an illicit affair. It's always fascinating to note the changes from book to film, especially since, as in this case, MacLean receives a screenplay credit, and that, from *Where Eagles Dare* (1968) onwards, he tended to write his books with movies in mind.

Like many MacLean characters, Sherman has a physical disability, the two sides of his face not matching following plastic surgery after a plane crash. So that's the first element from the narrative of the novel (it appears on the opening two pages) excised from the novel. Nor does the book begin with an anonymous assassin gunning down three addicts. Instead, it starts at the airport where Sherman sees a colleague murdered. Maggie doesn't meet him in Amsterdam (as in the film) but is his companion on the plane along with Belinda. The novel sees Sherman attempting to prevent the shooting of his colleague Duclos rather than being a mere observer to the airport slaying. And again, rather than keeping out of the way to safeguard his anonymity, he pursues the killer and in so doing knocks over Astrid Lemay (Ania Marson). On leaving his hotel (via the roof as in the movie), Sherman dodges his follower by nipping into a restaurant, not (as in the film) a sex worker's room.

His pursuer is old, not young. Sherman follows him on the subway, not by foot. But when the tables are turned and Sherman is the pursuer, the man does enter the Morgenstern premises (trimmed from the book's more unwieldy Morgenstern & Mugganthaler and with only one owner rather than two partners). The man he finds in his room is not the assassin but the hotel floor-waiter, an addict. After a fight, Sherman dangles him over the balustrade before killing him. Sherman's first meeting with Colonel de Graf (Alexander Knox) is in the latter's office, not the more scenic canal boat as in the film. Understandably, the movie attempts to cash in on both Amsterdam's tourist areas as well as the more sordid elements. The nightclub is tamer in the book, little more than an old-fashioned bait-and-switch type of strip club, and certainly lacking the panache of the film version's topless waitresses and sexy dance routines worthy of a Bob Fosse or at least Pan's People.[38]

But Morgenstern isn't one of the club's customers in the book, and neither does Astrid reject his advances. In fact, one of the book's subplots is that Astrid makes herself scarce, flying out of Amsterdam. Obviously, a book can invest more in characters. Trudi is introduced as having "the nicest voice for speaking bad English I'd

Chapter Eight. **Puppet on a Chain** *(1971)* 89

come across in a long time"; but rather than, as with the film, just speaking of her addiction, Sherman simply leans over and rolls up her sleeves. With two female assistants rather than one, the job of tailing various characters can be split, so it's Belinda who follows Astrid from the church. Although the notion of the puppet dangling on a chain is a major theme, it's not the way Maggie dies, as in the film. Instead, she is pitchforked to death by a bunch of women in what initially appears, in true Hitchcock fashion, to be little more than a harmless pagan rite. And the impotent Sherman gets to watch rather than just discovering the corpse, as in the movie.

That's about the most horrific scene in the book but it's closely matched by Sherman locking two recalcitrant villains, the nightclub owner and a slimy associate, in a safe until they agree to spill the beans. These two guys form a subplot the movie doesn't have time for. The purpose of having a pair of girls in the book is to heighten the tension when Maggie dies, leaving Belinda, betrayed and captured, ready to endure hanging by hook. MacLean is clearly a student of heinous ways to die, topping hanging and murder by pitchfork with torture by the high-pitched amplified sound of chiming clocks. Why a villain sophisticated enough to dream up such means of death would tie a captive up with electrical wire is anybody's guess. You couldn't expect a criminal to imagine that his opponent would have the brainpower to consider sticking the exposed wires in a plug, thus shorting the power supply and ending the torture. But film follows book in anointing this unlikely escape.

Once free, there's no thought in Sherman's head, as in the film, of making use of a speedboat and pursuing the villain through the canals. He merely takes the more normal route back to the puppet premises. When Sherman is trying to find the boat, *Marianne*, in the film he takes to the water, in the book he remains on shore and locates it via binoculars. The scenes of Sherman getting aboard the barge and the

When Eight Bells Toll and *Puppet on a Chain* were reissued as a double bill to cash in on the trend to speedily bring hits back to theaters, rather than waiting seven years or longer as had been the custom (Hannan collection).

clandestine collection of contraband from the sea are largely lifted entirely from the book, although there's no helicopter involved as in the film. In the climax of the film and the book, it's revealed that Trudi is not an addict, and Van Gelder is trapped on the hauling chain. Shame they left out the wonderful MacLean line, "Her mental age is not eight, it's older than sin itself."

CHAPTER NINE

Fear Is the Key (1972)

You might wonder why this movie took so long to be made—not hitting screens until more than a decade after publication. It was ideal material for the likes of Steve McQueen, who demonstrated the thrills you could achieve with a motorbike in *The Great Escape* (1963), and had been for several years trying to set up what ultimately became *Le Mans* (1970). Admittedly, car chases were not big box office until, McQueen again, *Bullitt* (1968). His screen persona would have been ideal for a trademark MacLean loner. Presumably, after *The French Connection* (1971) and *Vanishing Point* (1971) showed that speed was not going to be a short-lived trend, *Fear Is the Key* popped up to the top of the pile. By this point, however, MacLean was disillusioned with the film game. "I have become so leery of film people," he told Elliott Kastner in 1970, complaining that *Golden Rendezvous*, *Caravan to Vaccarès* and *Force 10 from Navarone* had been the "victim of internal power politics ... [or] stresses" (all these projects had stalled) and that *Deakin* and *Caribbean* were "firmly earth-bound," and concluding that if he had concentrated on writing novels and selling the film rights he would be a "million bucks better off."[1]

Meanwhile, Kastner's production outfit had benefited from a major shift in the British movie business. Hit hard by the financial crisis at the end of the previous decade, the industry was fighting back. In 1969, Associated British Picture Corporation—which had purchased *H.M.S. Ulysses* on publication—relaunched, following a takeover by EMI, as a major production entity, aiming to provide increased programming for its own 270-strong ABC cinema chain as well as targeting the export market. Chairman Bernard Delfont set up two parallel production strategies, director Bryan Forbes (*King Rat*, 1965) appointed production chief of ABPC[2] while Nat Cohen, as head of subsidiary Anglo-Amalgamated, augmented that effort. ABPC was allocated a total budget of £36 million to make 28 pictures, with Forbes' outfit taking the lion's share, leaving Cohen only $7 million to make 13 movies.[3] The Forbes project didn't go according to plan with flops like *Hoffman* (1970), *And Now the Darkness* (1970) and *The Man Who Haunted Himself* (1970). *The Railway Children* (1971) was the only hit. Forbes fared better when MGM tied up with EMI, creating MGM-EMI, which produced the hits *The Go-Between* (1971) and *Get Carter* (1971). But by 1971, he had had enough and Cohen took over the entire operation, enjoying success with the sex-change comedy *Percy* (1971) and big-screen versions of the British television comedies *On the Buses* (1971) and *Up*

Pompeii (1971). By 1972, he had 18 pictures set for American release through a variety of distributors.[4]

Kastner had persuaded MGM-EMI to invest in *Villain* (1971)[5] with Richard Burton and *Fear Is the Key* (1972).[6] Initial casting for *Fear Is the Key* was on the same ambitious level as *Where Eagles Dare*, the producers eyeballing Paul Newman,[7] one of the top three or four male stars of the period. With *Harper* (1966), Kastner had revived the actor's career, which was going through a fallow period with misfires like *What a Way to Go* (1964), *The Outrage* (1964) and *Lady L* (1965). Despite the gigantic success of *Butch Cassidy and the Sundance Kid* (1969), Newman's career had slipped into another trough following the flops *WUSA* (1970) and *Sometimes a Great Notion* (1971). An action picture looked like a possible cure. Newman didn't bite.[8]

That another Newman, Barry Newman, ended up as the lead was the result of his pushy agent Robert H. Solo of William Morris, who argued that his client was "very hot right now and is moving rapidly up; he is the right age and would be a marvelous idea." He added a kicker: "[Q]uite possibly … Fox, which is very high on him, might even co-finance it if he were in it."[9] In fact, Fox had rejected the idea three

A star's work was not done on the completion of shooting. As part of their contracts, stars were committed to post-production, re-recording dialogue and/or re-shooting scenes. Astonishingly, Barry Newman on *Fear Is the Key* was not remunerated for such work. According to agreements found in the Elliot Kastner Archive, Newman had to agree to provide the producers with "two free weeks." Co-star Suzy Kendall had to be available for three weeks (Hannan collection).

years previously.[10] New Fox boss Gordon Stulberg, less dismissive, had one quibble. "I do have an interest.... I like the script because it has action and several unique situations [but it is] a shade too long."[11] Kastner was convinced that below-the-line costs could be limited to $707,000 for ten weeks shooting plus $255,000 for the car chase in addition to fees for actors, crew and screenplay. But keeping the budget under a million dollars was only achieved by the producers deferring $50,000 of their fee[12] and MacLean and Barry Newman each deferring $25,000.[13]

The original chase outline envisaged a Corvette rather than a Gran Torino, tearing along "corduroy roads" (planks atop muddy swampland), just missing a head-on collision with a lumber truck, passing an oil refinery (to establish a thematic background), leaping a gap in the middle of a wooden bridge, a "ballet" involving dune buggies and more.[14] Richard Fleischer (*Fantastic Voyage*, 1966) expressed an interest in directing the movie, and after filming *10 Rillington Place* (1970) in London was "most anxious to return"[15] (to the British capital). Alf Joint (*Villain*, 1971) was proposed as second unit director.[16] The scheduling of *The Poseidon Adventure* (1972) ruled out stuntman Paul Stader.[17] Composer Elmer Bernstein (*The Magnificent Seven*, 1960) came into the frame as a possible contender for the music.[18]

Work on the Robert Carrington screenplay stalled in September 1971 until a major star and a director were in place.[19] Despite the involvement of MGM in the British venture, there was no guarantee the Hollywood company would handle U.S. distribution and that proved the case with *Fear Is the Key*. Instead, EMI promised to fund the movie in full, the producers negotiating $100,000 as a production fee and half the profits. But the door was left open for a third partner.[20]

Barry Newman was a relative newcomer. He had started out as a jazz saxophonist; the first character he played on stage, in the Broadway production of Herman Wouk's *Nature's Way* (1957), was a musician. He was nearly 40 when he made his movie debut in *The Lawyer* (1969). He attracted more attention as the cool driver in *Vanishing Point* (1971). That picture's surprising success turned its maker Twentieth Century–Fox into the initial front runner for *Fear Is the Key*. But a deal foundered when studio president and chief operating officer Gordon Stulberg, previously instrumental in setting up Cinema Center for CBS,[21] demanded 90 percent of the distribution fees in return for providing half the costs,[22] although he was willing to cut its normal distribution fee from 40 percent to 27.5 percent.[23] While Columbia had offered $1.2 million,[24] Anglo EMI struck a deal with Paramount to split the costs with both having the "right to cut and edit the film" (which, presumably, could lead to two different versions).[25] Kastner, having signed a two-picture deal with United Artists to make *Cops and Robbers* and *The Long Goodbye*,[26] handed the producing reins to partner Jay Kanter, an American. The Winkast name was dropped, and this went out as a K-L-K (Kastner-Ladd-Kanter)[27] production.[28] While that operation still sought financing outside the studio system, such as for *The Nightcomers* (1972),[29] it would increasingly rely on the majors.[30]

Despite the credits on *Fear Is the Key* boasting that it was shot entirely on location in Louisiana, that was far from the truth. Shooting began in the Bayou State on May 1, 1972, but only for three weeks[31]; then the moviemakers repaired to Britain for interiors and to transform Binfield Manor in Berkshire, built in 1754, into a Southern mansion. Shooting ended in mid–July.[32] The Louisiana backdrop was primarily used to film the car chase, the vehicles driven by stunt drivers Joie and Tim Chitwood, whose family had been in this business since the 1940s. "Half the battle," observed Tim, "is doing a stunt in a confined space. …Everything has to be exactly planned." Six drivers worked on the movie. "The only way we'll work is if we have all our own drivers in all the vehicles involved."

According to Tim, "We only had two cars to work with but made it look like ten. We kept wrecking them and repairing them, staying up all night fixing them and painting them for the next day's scenes."[33] But not everything went according to plan; Newman recalled:

> I almost lost the car in one scene. We were on these roads, and we were using walkie-talkies on a quarter of a mile run…. They had forgotten to stop the traffic or something. I was driving pretty fast because I wasn't expecting anything to be on the road and this car came straight at me. I went off roadside and almost crashed.[34]

The actor added,

> To me, *Fear Is the Key* is more than a James Bond–ish action thriller. The character I play has real motivation…. Talbot is a totally believable guy…. He is vulnerable while Bond is never shown in this way, MacLean is known for his action thrillers but in *Fear Is the Key* he gives a more sympathetic than usual central character.[35]

Production executive Denis Holt had reservations about the screenplay. He wasn't keen on an extended sequence on a tanker—"a bad red herring in the book"—and felt the "underwater stuff can be made more exciting than creeping around a tanker's decks." (That advice was taken.) He complained that the oil magnate (known as the Brigadier in the first version of the screenplay) was too submissive to the villain (known as Phillips at this point) and also that the father-son relationship between Phillips and Larry should be spelled out in the film as it was in the book. One last suggestion: "I know it isn't in the MacLean routine but don't you think that the hero might get the girl for a change."[36]

British actress Suzy Kendall had appeared in several pictures, top-billed in five including *Up the Junction* (1969) and *Fraulein Doktor* (1969), and Canadian John Vernon specialized in playing heavies, including *Point Blank* (1967). *Fear Is the Key* marked the debut of Ben Kingsley (*Gandhi*, 1982) and was the third movie produced by Jay Kanter. MacLean was due £75,000 for the "assignment of rights" to the novel.[37] Robert Carrington, "approved by both parties,"[38] was assisted in the screenplay by the film's German-born director Michael Tuchner and, uncredited, Ian La Fresnais (*Villain*),[39] in the "rewriting, changing and polishing."[40] The final screenplay was still "one beat too long." Eliminated were the elderly beachcomber featured in the chase "ballet" and the night trip to the oil rig; the radio shack fight was shortened "in order not to dissipater the later fight sequence" and more scenes with Sarah (at this point known as Vicki) were to be added.[41]

Barry Newman was paid $90,000 for ten weeks plus "two free weeks." He was

Chapter Nine. Fear Is the Key (1972)

entitled to $9000 a week if the movie ran over schedule or one-fifth of that amount per day for studio work or one-sixth if on location (studio weeks ran to five days, while location work was six days). He received first-class air travel, a car for his use and a chauffeur.[42] There would be a trailer on location and the "star dressing room" in the studio.[43] Tuchner received £2000 for his work on the screenplay and £7000 in his role as director, the last £1000 of that payable on delivery of the answer print. He was contracted for 22 weeks, the first seven in pre-production. While he didn't have the final word on casting, technicians and composer, he would be consulted and had the contractual right to the first cut (but not final cut).[44] The producers encountered difficulties hiring American actor Dolph Sweet to play Jablonsky; the British government[45] favored domestic actors or Canadian actors domiciled in England. The Department of Employment proved so obdurate that casting director Mary Selway was reduced to claiming that Jablonsky was "the second most important part" in the picture, which would have come as news to Suzy Kendall and John Vernon.[46] So K-L-K had to find reasons to discard around 30 actors as "not tall enough" (Shane Rimmer) or "too young" or "too good-looking." It was argued that Sweet in his previous pictures *The New Centurions* and *The Lost Man* had played "a role identical to that required." He worked three weeks for a salary of $350 per week plus expenses.[47]

Tuchner, dispatched on a Florida location recce on January 29, 1972,[48] ran out of funds so the equivalent of $300 in cash was quickly deposited in an American bank by EMI.[49] Gavrik Losey, son of director Joseph, was hired as assistant producer for £200 per week on a 25-week contract beginning January 31, 1972,[50] with the proviso that should EMI require him for the proposed *My Family and Other Animals*, they would take precedence.[51] Joining him at various other points were production secretary Veronica Welton at £35 per week, casting director Mary Selway for a flat fee of £800, production designer Sidney Gain (£150 per week), Colin Beaver (£125 per week) and location manager (then first assistant and draftsman) Fred Hole (£60 per week), whose task was to bring "set drawings up to standard for pricing."[52]

There was a wrangle over production office space. An initial proposal to rent space from Pathé Equipment, part of EMI, in Wardour Street was rejected in favor of rooms in Bayswater.[53] A dispute arose over the music. Paul Fishman had supplied, free of charge, "Bayou Blues" and "Loulou Ferry," heard on the radio in the picture.[54] Roy Budd had composed only 24 minutes of music, "insufficient to provide a commercial (soundtrack) album." Adding Fishman's nine minutes plus another track from Budd made it feasible. However, EMI disagreed, turning down distribution. Pye stepped in with Coronado taking on the U.S. rights, but Fishman, though reimbursed his $1500 costs, denied the American company publishing rights[55]—and it was never released there[56]—while producer Kanter had to chase up the synchronization license.[57] The producers were furious being billed $2900 by J. Walter Thompson for a Gran Torino Sports Coupe, admittedly totalled during filming, but which, thanks to the 16-minute car chase, had provided an "incredible promotion campaign" for the car manufacturer.[58]

The Film

Shocking opening, thrilling car chase and terrifying claustrophobic climax make this the most satisfying adaptation to date of a MacLean novel outside of *Where Eagles Dare*. With mystery to the forefront, the exposition that often threatened to clog up screen versions of MacLean novels is minimal. On a deserted low-rent airfield, Talbot (Barry Newman) waits by the radio trying to get in touch with airborne colleague and his (Talbot's) wife and child. As interference limits communication, the pilot indicates he has thwarted an attempt to blow up the plane which is carrying a precious cargo out of a war-torn region. When Talbot finally speaks to his wife, the plane is attacked. The last noise Talbot hears is the plane falling out of control. We cut to Talbot, driving a battered vehicle, stopping at a gas station in a remote part of Louisiana. Refused a drink on a Sunday, he leaps over the bar to help himself. Cops are called, a fight breaks out, Talbot is arrested. Turns out he has quite a history: fugitive from justice, former salvage diver, "a man of violence." Before the judge can pass sentence, Talbot steals a guard's gun and takes hostage Sarah (Suzy Kendall), an innocent bystander. Hijacking a car, he takes off, causing mayhem, racing out of the town, pursued along the main and dirt roads by the cops, temporarily escaping capture with a death-defying leap across the water onto a ferry. More hard-driving cops await him on the other side. It's breathtaking stuff, the vehicle at an angle as it races along levees.

Talbot holes up with crooked cop Jablonsky (Dolph Sweet) but his buddy double-crosses him, handing him over to Sarah's oil magnate father Alexander (Ray McAnally) for the reward money. Bodyguards are not required, what with menacing business associate Vyland (John Vernon) and all-around thug Royale (Ben Kingsley). Coincidentally, Talbot is in the right place at the right time, since the business partners are on the lookout for a salvage expert. With Jablonsky's assistance, Talbot sneaks out at night, making his way to a nearby oil rig, where he hears something untoward in one leg of the rig.

It's beginning to blow up a storm so much of what follows takes place in blinding rain. On his return, he finds Royale digging a grave. The corpse is Jablonsky. Sneaking back in via Sarah's bedroom, he explains to her his charade: He's working undercover. Worried that her father is in over his head in some unsavory deal, she agrees to help out. Back at the rig, Talbot realizes his suspicions are correct: Vyland, having stolen an experimental bathyscaphe, is on a deep-sea treasure hunt. Talbot evades his guard and with the assistance of Sarah puts in a radio call to his agency. Submerged in the vessel with Vyland and Royale, he sabotages the air supply and reveals that he knows the treasure they seek is the gold his colleague was transporting when their plane was shot down. "Killers and victims all together in the end," muses Talbot as they slowly suffocate, staring at the skeletons in the plane wreck. Naturally, the villains confess.

Directed at a high pitch of intensity, *Fear Is the Key* hits the button. It has three stand-out sequences, and Barry Newman is up to the challenge of conveying a sense of desolation at the start and satisfaction—almost personal peace—at the end. In between, he snarls his way through the action. The storm heightens the drama. Dramatically, this scores high by maintaining the element of mystery. Not just who Talbot is and what he wants but also concerning the villains' intentions. And then how are they going to achieve their aims and, as brilliantly worked out, how Talbot is going to thwart them. It's rare for the author's technical knowledge, so integral to many of his books, to be given an airing on screen. That the revenge element is downplayed helps. The car chase adds the same high-octane thrills as *Puppet on a Chain*'s boat chase, but that was already in the book, not a creation of the screenwriter. Suzy Kendall doesn't have a great deal to do: scream and look terrified in the first section, transition from fear to confusion to acceptance in the bedroom scene and thereafter play a more physical part. The director avoids the temptation to lob in some romance. John Vernon exudes menace while Ben Kingsley has the steely stare of a killer. *Fear Is the Key* is the movie equivalent of a rattling good read.

Book into Film

In terms of narrative, Robert Carrington changed little. He retains the structure. Whereas, following the prologue, the book begins in court, the movie takes time out to show the disgruntled Talbot being arrested. And the screenwriter contributed the leap across the water. Carrington drops one minor character, Kennedy the Ruthven chauffeur, who has a soft spot for Sarah, and the writer also dispenses with the needling between the villains.

You can't adequately capture the MacLean essence in a film. Readers just adore those sections where, for example, in this book, Talbot explains how, escaping from the police, he knew the fuel drums were empty before he aimed the car at them and that, to keep Sarah on edge and maintain the charade, he was responsible for shooting out the windscreen rather than the pursuing cops. Much of the dialogue comes wholesale from the book, the "man of violence" line and "killers and victims together." Talbot is not the type to unburden himself, he's denied such opportunity in the book, and Carrington sticks to that approach. It does lay a lot on the actor, of course, to convey that state of mind through facial expression, but Newman just about achieves that though he doesn't really need to, since the audience can register for itself what he must be going through hearing the plane shot down. The aural and visual template laid down by MacLean is all that's required.

CHAPTER TEN

Caravan to Vaccarès (1974)

Roy Scheider, about to hit the box office heights with *Jaws* (1975), signed on to star. Unfortunately, he slipped a disc on Steven Spielberg's paean to sharks and was out of action for eight months.[1]

That kind of bad luck plagued *Caravan to Vaccarès* from the outset. This should have been a major Hollywood studio release rather than a lower-budgeted indie. Initially, the prospects were highly favorable. Another studio heavyweight, this time Maxwell Setton, the former head of European production for Columbia, had gone out on his own, but with a three-picture deal with his old company in his pocket. *Caravan to Vaccarès*, published in 1970, was planned as his debut, filming to begin in spring that year.[2] Columbia had remained bullish at the end of the 1960s. While other studios pulled in their horns, Columbia stuck to a 24-picture production schedule including both *Caravan to Vaccarès* and *Force 10 from Navarone*.[3] However, when Columbia hit the financial buffers, Setton was axed. With Trio long since defunct, Geoffrey Reeve, who had suggested the idea to MacLean for *Caravan to Vaccarès*,[4] re-entered the frame. He might have remained on the periphery of the Kastner-MacLean operation, for contracts for both *Deakin* and *Caribbean* stipulated Reeve receive an "associate producer" credit and a $25,000 fee.[5] Reeve was not short of work, being in high demand for commercials.[6] The MacLean name was still a lure, marquee power proven by European box office for *Puppet on a Chain*. So, although this was Reeve's sophomore movie, he was regarded as having delivered a MacLean hit (see Appendix: Box Office).

Reeve was friends with British entrepreneur Richard Morris-Adams,[7] with whom at one point he had come close to setting up *Puppet on a Chain* as an independent venture outside of Kurt Unger. Morris-Adams had provided informal assistance on *Puppet on a Chain* through Dutch business connections.[8] As joint producer with former English international rugby player Larry Webb,[9] he entered into a co-production deal[10] with French production house S.N. Prodis. The latter had dipped its toe into home-grown production with *Angelique* (1967) and its sequels, and was now investing in Hollywood pictures (*Little Big Man*, 1970, and *The Getaway*, 1972). "Reeve more or less came up with the storyline and presented it to Alistair MacLean," recalled Morris-Adams. Reeve was instrumental in installing MacLean "for some considerable time" in a hotel in the Camargue until the screenplay was written.[11] It's not unusual for a writer to find that ideas that work well in a novel do not fly when transferred to the screen, and this was somewhat different to the normal MacLean thriller. So, Reeve called on screenwriter Paul

Chapter Ten. Caravan to Vaccarès *(1974)* 99

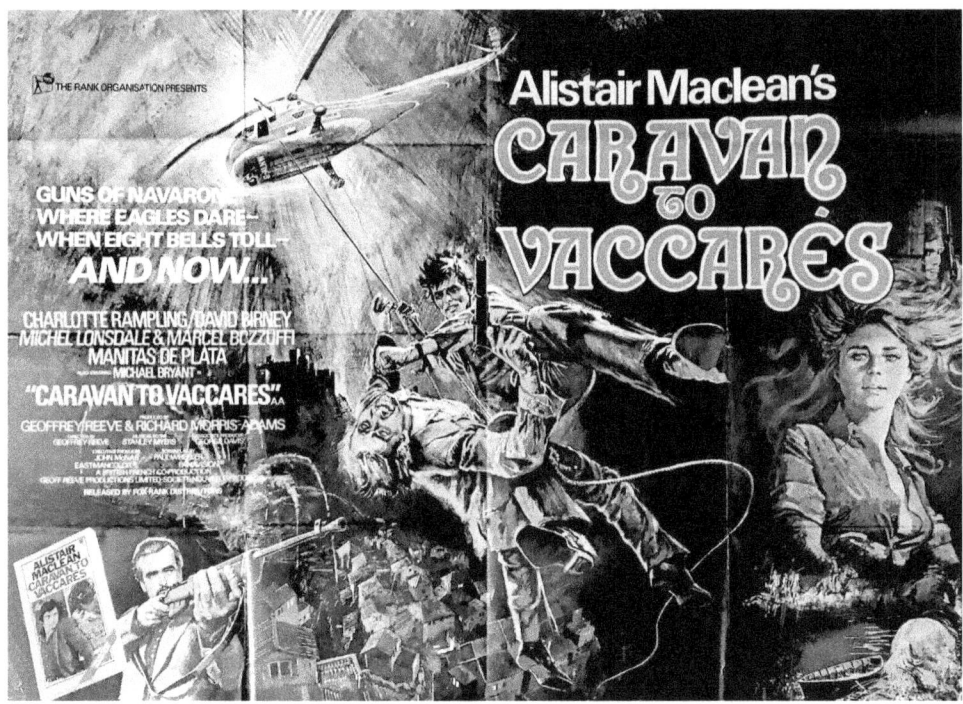

In a key scene in *Caravan to Vaccarès,* the main character (David Birney) was seen in an upmarket restaurant, ordering a burger with ketchup. This was at the suggestion of director Geoffrey Reeve's son Tom, a teenager at the time. Tom later produced *The Way to Dusty Death* (1995) and *Air Force One Is Down* (Hannan collection).

Wheeler (*Puppet on a Chain*) and neophyte Joseph Forest[12] to knock it into shape.[13] (The later *Floodgate* was Forest's idea.)

Reeve and Morris-Adams flew to Paris to interview rising star Charlotte Rampling, who was coming off *The Night Porter* (1974). "She was just making waves," remembered Morris-Adams. They secured her services for $25,000. Despite being Sean Connery's leading lady in *Zardoz* (1973) and one of the few successful MTAs, Rampling[14] was better known as an arthouse darling following *The Damned* (1970) and would probably have remained so except *The Night Porter* burst out of its arthouse confines and became, possibly because of the sexuality and controversial setting, a genuine crossover box office hit.

One month before principal photography, Reeve flew to New York to meet Roy Scheider, only to be met at the airport by his agent bearing the news that the actor had been hospitalized and was unable to participate. The agent suggested as a replacement his client David Birney, promoted as the next young superstar. With a production deadline imminent and conscious that an unknown had played the male lead in *Puppet on a Chain* and *When Eight Bells Toll*, Reeve accepted. The movie debutant was best known for the TV series *Bridget Loves Bernie* (1972–73) opposite Meredith Baxter, whom he later married. Appeal to French audiences was guaranteed by casting character actors—brought in by Prodis—who had memorable roles in American movies: Michael Lonsdale (*The Day of the Jackal*, 1973),

Marcel Bozzuffi (*The French Connection*, 1971) and Serge Marquand (*Barbarella*, 1968). Morris-Adams' introduction to the movie business proved dicey after he was arrested by French customs. He had acquired the Rolls-Royce that was to be used in the film, and drove it himself over the English Channel, carrying with him the expensive cameras supplied by Leica for Rampling in her role as a photographer as well as all her costumes. He was detained by French customs for two days until he could verify his bona fides.[15]

Trade reports at the time set the budget at $1.6 million,[16] rising to $1.75 million to comply with French overtime and weekend working regulations.[17] However, those figures may have been inflated or misinterpreted. Geoff's son Tom Reeve recalled the budget as being around the $750,000 mark,[18] the lowest budget afforded any MacLean picture so far. It was filmed in Provence, the arena at Arles doubling for the bullfight, and L'Oustau de Baumanière in Les Baux, the area specified in the novel, standing in for the hotel. The eight-week shoot commenced in October 1973.[19]

A small new independent couldn't hope for the clout of the Kastner operation so Geoff Reeve and Richard Morris-Adams handed distribution to ITC World Sales.[20] Rank snapped up the British rights and, prior to the completion of filming, over half the budget had been covered by sales to Italy, Latin America and Japan.[21] The American market proved tougher to crack, David Birney a drawback in attracting a buyer. No distribution deal was struck until a year after the movie's Royal Charity World Premiere in London on August 8, 1974. The U.S. distributor was a newcomer, Bryanston.[22] Formed in 1972 and making its name on the back of exploitative fare like *The Texas Chain Saw Massacre* (1974), Bryanston held back release further to piggyback on *Breakheart Pass* (1976).[23]

The Film

Hitman Ferenc (Serge Marquand) kills two people in quick succession. The first is sitting in a car with binoculars trained on the road. The second is the youth who led him to the observer. The driver is shot in his car, the young man in the limestone caverns. Meanwhile, American tourist Bowman (David Birney) picks up freelance photographer Lila (Charlotte Rampling) hitchhiking to the gypsy festival in the Camargue. Ferenc forces a car towing a caravan to crash, but before he can reach the wreck, Bowman turns up. Gypsy caravanners, Stella (Françoise Brion) and her husband, refuse offers of help. There is an altercation with Ferenc before Bowman disarms him.

Bowman heads for a high-class hotel to meet his mysterious employer, the Duc the Croyter (Michael Lonsdale), and his friend Czerda (Marcel Bozzuffi). De Croyter has hired Bowman to transport an unnamed person to New York. Czerda invites the pair to his ranch. Ferenc attacks Bowman in his room. Bowman meets with Stella, who is hiding Hungarian scientist Zuger (Michael Bryant), who has a secret formula for solar energy smuggled out from the Iron Curtain by the gypsies. But when Bowman collects him, they are attacked by Ferenc and a gang of cowboys. The pair hides out with the duke's assistant Cecile (Marianne Eggerickx); the duke's daughter is later whipped to death. Czerda wants to sell the scientist to the highest bidder.

When Lila is kidnapped, Bowman arranges to swap the scientist for her but the plan goes awry and Czerda takes both captive. Bowman re-rescues both, then sets off with Zuger to an appointed rendezvous. They are attacked by Ferenc, shooting from a helicopter. The car crashes. Bowman, wearing the scientist's hat in an attempt to dupe Ferenc, escapes on horseback through marshland but is trapped in quicksand. He is rescued by a helicopter (piloted by racing driver Graham Hill) but when the killer realizes he has the wrong man, they fight on the hoist. Ferenc falls to his death. Bowman, trapped on the hoist, is dumped in a bullring where Czerda on horseback drives him towards a bull. Czerda is gored by the bull and Bowman is saved by the duke, who is no slouch with a high-powered rifle.

As it stands, it''s not a bad adventure. The solar energy is an interesting touch, and non-stop action, chase, capture, repeat, helicopter assault, quicksand and bullfight. Bowman is characterized as independent, standing up to his snobbish employer, but then guilty because doing it his way has resulted in the death of Cecile and the kidnapping of Lila and Zuger. The bullfight is well done and cowboys rampage like refugees from the American West. Some of the gypsy material, such as masterly guitar-playing (by Manitas de Plata), adds atmosphere. But other times, it's standard stuff. Czerda is a polished villain. Lila plays an active part in various ploys. Rampling and especially Lonsdale excel but Birney is out of his depth and no amount of smug grins can provide him with charisma and the necessary spark to make romance with Rampling believable.

The Book: Missed Opportunity?

This is one of these instances where book and screenplay were on divergent tracks. Geoff Reeve believed the tone of the book wouldn't work on film. And he may have been correct. After all, the general moviegoer wouldn't have Alistair MacLean down as a master of the romantic thriller. Yes, there is occasional romance in his books, but generally only in snippets, and never core to the tale. Romance in *The Guns of Navarone* is a filmic invention; in *Where Eagles Dare* where Smith's girlfriend Mary is part of the gang assaulting the castle, there's a wonderfully intimate scene of him (in the novel) tucking her up in her sleeping bed on a freezing cold mountain; Calvert develops feelings for fugitive Charlotte in *When Eight Bells Toll*; and in *Fear Is the Key*, Talbot shows more romantic interest in the woman he takes hostage in the book than the film. But here it's full-blown romance of the will-she-or-won't-she kind, assuming Cecile (Lila in the film) can spare the time for romance while trying to keep her wits about her. From the outset, while in mostly in joking terms, there's a constant refrain of marriage, Bowman musing about the hows and whys of their wedding. You may remember *Pirates of the Caribbean: Curse of the Black Pearl* (2003) and the unspoken love of servant Will Turner for his mistress Elizabeth Swann: Despite her entreaties, he keeps his distance and refuses to call her anything except Miss Swann. Many critics thought that was the most romantic thing they'd heard in ages. Guess what? MacLean beat them to it, and nobody noticed. Here Cecile constantly calls him Bowman, ignoring his pleas to call him Neil, until in a moment of supreme danger she screams his Christian name. In the book, Cecile is not a freelance photographer, a hitchhiker or a duke's daughter. On the other hand, the Duc de Croyter is a world expert on gypsies, hence his reason for being in the Camargue for the festival. Quite why Bowman is there is left unexplained. He's certainly not in the employ of the duke. In fact, the duke's mysterious ways make him a more likely candidate for criminal gypsy mastermind Gaiese Strome.

In the prologue, Ferenc and three men chase a youth, Alexandre, through the limestone caves, killing him and burying him there. The caves are key to the MacLean vision, and we return there twice more, including the climax.

Ferenc's not intent on ambushing a caravan with a mysterious guest. He's part of the gang smuggling scientists out from behind the Iron Curtain. Cecile is a secretary on holiday with her friend Lila (why the screenwriter changed the names around is anybody's guess) and Lila has attracted the attention of the duke. Cecile dines with Bowman, an English playboy of no fixed abode or obvious means. The mystery of who Bowman is and what he's doing is retained for most of the book, rather than, as in the film, given away at the start as if the tension-giving aspects of mystery are of little use in this thriller. Gradually, he infiltrates the gypsy community, making contact with those lamenting the missing Alexandre, including his mother Countess Marie and his fiancée Tina. Bowman is more protagonist in book than film, privy to a secret agenda (like Major Smith in *Where Eagles Dare* and Jones/Carpenter in *Ice Station Zebra*). He is on the trail, we finally discover, of Russian rocket scientists. The duke appears in league with gypsies led by Czerda and may even be the dreaded Gaiese Strome. As you might expect, there are umpteen complications, secret codes, missing stashes of money, pursuit, rescue. Attackers end up in the river, crushed to death with boulders, shot or simply put out of commission by lethal fists. A clever disguise backfires and halfway through Bowman is thrown into a bullring. Tina is whipped, but not killed, for asking too many questions. And that incident provides a different emotional twist: It puts Cecile, who has previously doubted Bowman, firmly on his side. Inevitably, there's a deadline involved. And hostages: Alexandre's mother and Tina's father. There are three scientists rather than one, their specialty rocket fuel, not solar energy, headed for China, not the U.S. When Bowman mounts a horse, it's not for some unexplained attempt at embarrassing him. He does need rescue from quicksand. The shoot-out is instigated by Bowman, not from a helicopter but from the duke's Rolls-Royce, and he commandeers a fishing boat to prevent Czerda and the duke escaping with the scientists and hostages. MacLean's books always require a Poirot-style scene where the villains are tricked into confessing, and this is cleverly engineered to take place where the novel began: in the caves.

Bowman is Secret Service. But not only is the duke his boss but Cecile and Lila also belong to some secret oversight department, sent by the Admiralty to keep an eye on Bowman and the duke on the grounds that one of them was under suspicion. There's a distinctly happy ending, marriage proposals in the air.

The book appears to me more thematically of a piece, closely following the template of the romantic thriller, the badinage and repartee between Bowman and Cecile very entertaining. Some of the movie choices just seemed odd. Why take Bowman back to the bullring when from a helicopter hundreds of feet in the air you could as easily drop him into the sea? And why turn Bowman into an employee when, like Talbot in *Fear Is the Key*, there was greater mileage in him mounting an undercover operation? The middle scene in the cave is the greatest loss from the book, the tone having been set from the opening sequence that there is no escape and that the pursuers have the advantage of knowing the territory, so Bowman turning the tables is exceptionally well done. The final scene, in the same setting, rounds off matters. One of the MacLean hallmarks was the traitor inside the camp so ideal that readers had suspicions about the duke, a marvelous character, whose predilection for food makes Sir Arthur in *When Eight Bells Tolls* appear to be on a starvation diet.

It may have been that the producers wanted to try something fresh and believed several of the book's complications required ironing out. But even so, the film seems to take too savage an approach. If you've never read the book, you might be happy with the film, a good action thriller in its own right, although David Birney is a weak point. But if you are familiar with the book, you might come away, like me, thinking "What a shame," because this is one of MacLean's finest novels, unusual in his portfolio in having a central believable romance in the vein of *North by Northwest* (1959), *Charade* (1963) and *Arabesque* (1966).

CHAPTER ELEVEN

Breakheart Pass (1976)

Originally tabbed "Western," this was key to the author's initial pact with producer Elliott Kastner. According to the scheduling of their joint projects, the screenplay was written by March 1968, with the novel to follow by the end of the year.[1] "I wanted a Western and I wanted Alistair to write it," recalled the producer, "with a lot of zigs and zags." It was later known as *Deakin,* after the main character; Kastner claimed credit for the final title. Despite promptings from MacLean and his lawyer David Bishop, this was forever "inching forward."[2] It's more than likely that it required publication, and the bestseller status that conferred, to make Hollywood sit up. And most likely MacLean's publishers balked at the author moving away from his established territory, a Western considered a lesser genre for a bestselling writer.[3]

The book was published in 1974. Readers didn't appear to worry that MacLean was outside his comfort zone. By the time of the film tie-in paperback edition from Fawcett, there were 800,000 copies in print in the U.S.[4] The first draft of the MacLean screenplay ran to 135 pages, the second 107 pages.[5] Although MacLean received full credit on screen, he was, in fact, assisted by Lorenzo Semple Jr. (*Three Days of the Condor,* 1975), whose name is attached to two joint screenplays, one running 125 pages, the other 119.[6] Kastner, meanwhile, had abandoned the idea of finding money from financiers and was back at the beating heart of the industry. This was the fifth picture he planned to make for United Artists, following *Cops and Robbers* (1973), *The Long Goodbye* (1973), *11 Harrowhouse* (1974) and *Rancho Deluxe* (1975). For the first three, the producer was in line for a total fee of $525,000 plus a $75,000 contribution to his overhead and a share of the profits.[7] Former partner Jerry Gershwin, who had "more or less dropped out of the picture business for a spell," returned to act as the line producer here to shepherd this one home at the same time as setting up two further pictures with Kastner.[8] An executive producer credit went to Kastner.

Star Charles Bronson was an anomaly. He was 50 before he made any impact with domestic audiences. By the late 1960s, he had already had three stabs at stardom, twice on television via *Man with a Camera* (1958–1960) and *The Travels of Jamie McPheeters* (1963–1964), and in supporting roles in the highly popular *The Magnificent Seven* (1960), *The Great Escape* (1963) and *The Dirty Dozen* (1967). But even this trio did not make Hollywood any more inclined to turn an aging actor into a star. Like Clint Eastwood, he had to head abroad to find acceptance of his marquee value; *unlike* Eastwood, he found that domestic audiences remained uninterested in those ventures: *Farewell, Friend* (1968), *Rider on the Rain* (1970), *Cold Sweat* (1970)

Chapter Eleven. **Breakheart Pass *(1976)***

and *Someone Behind the Door* (1971). His Italian movies fared no better in the U.S. *Once Upon a Time in the West* (1969) was a colossal flop, *Violent City* (1970) scarcely registered, and even the bigger-budgeted *You Can't Win 'Em All* (1970) and *Red Sun* (1972) did no better.

But Bronson had a secret. In one vital aspect, he reflected Eastwood. Foreign audiences loved his pictures. His movies regularly scored three times the box office abroad that they did in the U.S. and that made him eminently bankable. Before his U.S. breakthrough with *Death Wish* (1974), three of his previous movies, taking worldwide revenues rather than domestic as the touchstone, had done very well indeed, especially as his pictures were cheaply made. *The Mechanic* (1972) cost only $1.89 million, *Chato's Land* $1.51 million and *Mr. Majestyk* $2.12 million. Their domestic tallies were nothing to write home about—$2.6 million in rentals for the first, $1.27 million for the second, $3.7 million for the third—but they were hits abroad. Outside America, *The Mechanic* hauled in $7 million, *Chato's Land* $4.4 million and *Mr. Majestyk* $6.5 million, figures that denoted a true star.[9]

When *Death Wish* proved a box office hit in the U.S. as well as around the world, Bronson was on a roll. Columbia was so convinced that Bronson had finally arrived, it opened *Breakout* (1975) on a record 1400 U.S. screens.[10]

But Bronson was not Kastner's choice. "I was never a fan of his, never wanted to work with him … [but] Charlie was a big star, you could finance a movie with him at that point." Nor was Kastner a fan of director Tom Gries, best known for his Westerns *Will Penny* (1968) and *100 Rifles* (1969) and for *Breakout*. "So if [Bronson] wanted Tom, who was a mediocre director, I'm not going to argue."[11]

Others in the cast: Western stalwart Ben Johnson, an unexpected Oscar winner for *The Last Picture Show* (1971), Richard Crenna (*The Man Called Noon*, 1973), Charles Durning (*Dog Day Afternoon*, 1975) and Ed Lauter

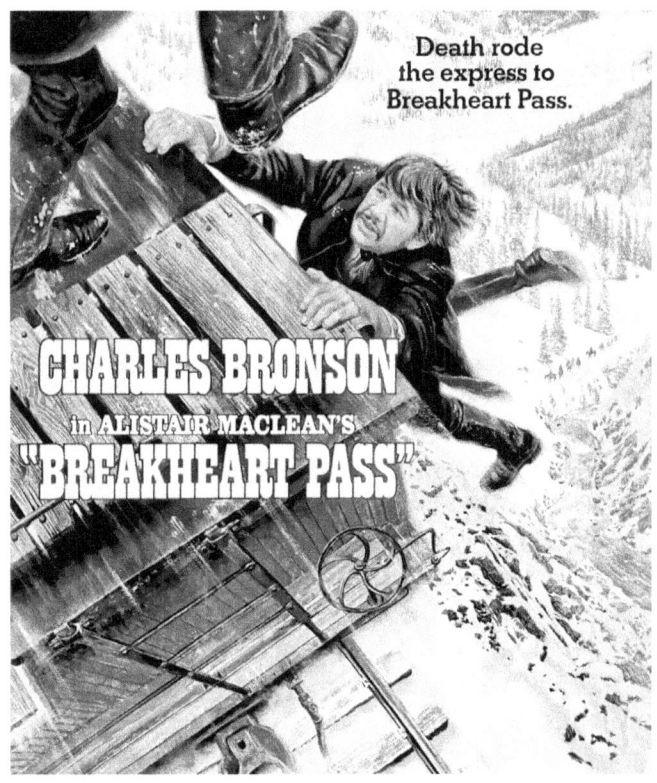

Husband-and-wife Charles Bronson and Jill Ireland, the stars of *Breakheart Pass*, made 16 pictures together, double the total of famous screen pair Spencer Tracy and Katharine Hepburn (Hannan collection).

(*The Longest Yard*, 1974) plus Jill Ireland (*Breakout*), Bronson's wife, as the leading lady, and a cameo by boxer Archie Moore.

Moore recalled Bronson's physical strength. After four hours atop the railroad car, and required then to fall over the side, Moore said, "I pulled myself up with both arms but I saw Bronson do a one-arm pull that astonished me."[12]

Counted as a bonus was a rousing, hummable,score by multiple Oscar nominee Jerry Goldsmith (*Chinatown*, 1975).Bronson was hired for $1 million plus ten percent of the gross—a new high for the star—for ten weeks plus "four free weeks" and entitled to $100,000 a week overtime. He had approval of two co-stars and the script, although the producer "had the right to make further alterations in the script with Bronson's approval" provided they didn't change the basic storyline, Bronson's role "in any material way" or his character in relation to other characters. Although his name would be above the title, its size would be limited to 30 percent of the title.[13]

Lorenzo Semple, Jr., stuck pretty close to the MacLean template, his 109-page script departing from the original MacLean screenplay in relatively small ways. It starts not in a rundown hotel but in a town of tents, the sex workers in one tent, the poker game in another. We first see Deakin in long johns, not a fur coat. Some information passed to the audience is more overt: Fairchild works out that Peabody is Deakin's partner, and Deakin and Marica embrace twice. When he hides in her compartment, it's under the blankets, suggesting greater though perhaps risky intimacy, rather than under the bed. By the end, romance is established.[14]

The revised draft began, as in the book, at the Imperial Hotel. While the town is more established, there is visual reference to a gold strike. Deakin appears in the second shot. The train isn't due for two weeks, Marshall Pearce bums a match from Deakin, and the telegraph office receives a message in code. Deakin still hides under the blankets. But there's no reunion with her father at the end. Instead, while she is clearly intent on pursuing romance with Deakin, he deliberately walks away from her.[15]

The initial budget was $4.97 million—$2.63 million below-the-line—allowing for 35 days location shooting in Lewiston, Idaho (standing in for Nevada) and 24 days in the studio. The locations chosen were remote. Depending on the weather, it could take three to four hours a day to travel to and from locations. Allowing for breaks and other issues, actual filming was restricted to six and a half hours a day. The Great Western Railway Steam Locomotive No 75 (number changed to "9" in the movie) being used as a set was required, on the Camas Prairie Railroad single line track, to shunt into a siding to permit normal traffic. After three days shooting at the titular location, heavy wind and rain "caused two feet of snow to vanish overnight" and, with a further nine days' work still required at that particular site, the producers considered moving (incurring further delay and loss of time) or bringing in artificial snow. Gershwin and Gries planned to move to the High Country where there was still sufficient snow. To keep the budget down, they asked 79-year-old second unit director Yakima Canutt (on his final assignment, with his son working as a stuntman) to get pickup shots, shoot background plates, complete scenes such as the Fort Humboldt exterior sequences, shift scenes originally planned for other locations to the studio and move onto the train as many scripted-for-outdoors scenes as possible.[16] Six cameras filmed the train derailing at Halfmoon Trestle but there were no "casualties" since the dummies didn't fall out. (Even the wreckage showed no sign of corpses.) Sixteen Native American extras, mostly from the Nez Perce tribe, walked out in a strike over pay, claiming that at $30 a day they were underpaid.[17] The final budget jumped to $5.52 million.[18] Gershwin summed up the film's travails: "The picture moves forward at the same rate as an 1888 train climbing a steep hill."[19]

Kastner had made 34 pictures in nine years with another $30 million invested in forthcoming product.[20] "Guys of limited imagination commit the folly of saying Westerns and pirate plots are obsolete," he said challengingly. The success of *Murder on the Orient Express* (1974) put train movies back in fashion, with *Silver Streak* (1976), *The Cassandra Crossing* (1976) and *The Great Train Robbery* (1978) on current studio slates.[21] Although UA did not splurge on the number of *Breakheart Pass* prints—just 254 in the opening salvo[22]—it proved a natural for promotion with cinemas combining standard Western shoot-outs with train paraphernalia.[23]

The Film—Charles Bronson: The Epitome of the MacLean Hero?

It might be heresy to suggest that the sullen, monosyllabic Charles Bronson could epitomize the MacLean hero. Casting flaws in MacLean movies tended to revolve around leading men who lacked that quiet air of authority essential to the author's characterization. Gregory Peck, Richard Burton and Clint Eastwood had it in spades, other leading men, even Anthony Hopkins (who would later acquire it), less so. Bronson was playing against type. Audiences who had enjoyed watching him leading villains to the slaughter in *The Mechanic*, *Chato's Land* and *Death Wish* might balk at accepting a character described as "not a man of violence." (Deliberate irony given that Talbot in *Fear Is the Key* is accused of being "a man of violence.") Had the movie been made soon after MacLean had written the original script, it might have proved an antidote to the excesses of *The Wild Bunch* (1969) and *Soldier Blue* (1970) and the revisionist tone ("There are better ways of dealing with Indians than shooting holes in them") would have pre-empted *Little Big Man* (1971), *Chato's Land* and the like. And it goes against all preconceptions about the Western where, generally, the plot is plainly stated at the start. Genuine mystery has little place in this genre.[24] This was not just "murder on the Western express" but presented as its central character a sleuth who was as much an enigma as Hercule Poirot.

A troop train, plus Governor Fairchild (Richard Crenna) and his fiancée Marica (Jill Ireland), is headed for Fort Humboldt in Nevada. It makes a stop at the dirt-poor town of Myrtle. This is far from a standard Western municipality, more an outpost, houses built on stilts, none of the rambunctiousness you would associate with a saloon, though there are sex workers on call. Marshall Pearce (Ben Johnson) wants to hitch a lift to bring back desperado Calhoun (Robert Tessier). A stranger, Deakin

(Charles Bronson), caught cheating at cards, turns out to be a fugitive, wanted for murder and arson. His presence provides Pearce with the excuse to warrant a passage. The initial mystery centers on the military mission; commanding officer Major Claremont (Ed Lauter) is kept in the dark. Ordinarily, the sudden disappearance of two soldiers would have been grounds for investigation but there's no time to wait because Fort Humboldt has been decimated by a diphtheria epidemic and the soldiers are required to bolster the garrison. Marica is the only one to show pity for the chained outlaw. She later gives him some whisky and unties his legs, not realizing he has already freed his hands. But he doesn't attempt to take her hostage.

Meanwhile, in Fort Humboldt, Calhoun has escaped and taken control. On the train, Dr. Molyneux (David Huddleston) is found dead. Deakin, a qualified doctor, finds a puncture mark on the body and concludes that he was murdered. The triple mystery is set; what's awaiting them at their destination? Who's the murderer on board? And just who the heck is Deakin, who now hides the soldier's spare telegraph transmitter? The train's fireman falls to his death; the car carrying the bulk of the soldiers is detached and starts hurtling backward down the track. Cue panic in the coach. The brakeman has been murdered. The carriage derails, killing all on board.

We discover that Calhoun is in league with Native Americans. As punishment for speaking his mind, Deakin is sent to stoke the engine, and finds the bodies of two missing soldiers. Under cover of darkness, he sends a telegraph message to Fort Humboldt saying the plot to wreck the troop carriage has failed. Now Rev Peabody (Bill McKinney) has gone missing. Deakin has such an air of mystery that Marica asks, "Who are you? What are you?" An exasperated Fairchild mutters, "He's told us what he's not, but not what he is."

The train reaches higher ground, the land covered in snow. Deakin finds dynamite in medicine boxes and guns in coffins intended to transport epidemic victims. Caught snooping, he is chased onto the carriage roof by the cook (Archie Moore). Yakima Canutt and his stunt team are in their element here as an impressive fight ensues. O'Brien, Fairchild's aide, discovers that the coffins have been tampered with and tracks down Deakin, who finds refuge in Marica's room after explaining that he's not a killer, but a Secret Service agent on the trail of her corrupt lover.

Native Americans plan to attack the train. Deakin explains to the major that the train is not carrying medical supplies but 400 rifles for the Native Americans. The shocked Marica overhears the governor instructing the marshal to kill both Deakin and the major. It's also revealed that Peabody was Deakin's partner and that the missing soldiers were killed because they saw too much; the fireman was murdered after he found their corpses. After the death of the driver, Deakin takes over his role and explains the crux of the plot, that Fairchild and his gang plan to hijack bullion at Fort Humboldt and bring it back in the coffins nobody would bother to examine. Calhoun is in on the deal, weaponry the reward for Native Americans. At Breakheart Pass, Native Americans, posing a splendid threat across the snow, begin their attack. Deakin and Claremont blow up the track. Calhoun arrives and takes Marica hostage but is shot by Fairchild. In a saber duel, the corrupt politician is slashed to death by the major. Tables are turned when a cavalry troop races to the rescue. Marica is reunited with her father, held hostage in Fort Humboldt. The movie ends with a superb overhead long shot as Deakin, job done, walks away from the father-daughter reunion.

All in all, it's not just a rewarding Western but a very satisfying adaptation of a MacLean novel, the narrative kept virtually intact, the moviemakers avoiding the obvious temptation to add romance or make more of the heist. Train fans would be in ecstasy as the shots of the locomotive puffing up the hills, rounding mountainous bends, crossing vertiginous bridges, adds color to the picture. There are excellent performances all around, undercurrents of hostility between the various members explored mostly in glances, the heaping of mystery upon mystery well-maintained. By remaining patient, never losing his temper, never raising his voice, Charles Bronson gives the ideal impression of the MacLean hero, who is not just always in control but one jump ahead. He wears, as MacLean puts it, "a habitual mask of impassivity."

Book into Film—Play It as It Lays

MacLean's Reese City becomes Myrtle. The past-its-prime but still substantial Imperial Hotel makes way for a nondescript, unnamed saloon. Colonel Claremont is demoted to major and the epidemic switches from cholera to diphtheria. More importantly, Marica becomes Fairchild's lover rather than his niece. As you might expect, with MacLean's interest in technical know-how, the reader learns a great deal about the running of locomotives, marvelous details proving that the author has done his homework—something that can easily be discarded for a movie. As can the various introductions, the whys and wherefores of Rev Peabody and Dr. Molyneux being permitted on the train, the bond between old soldiers O'Brien and Pearce. While the movie simplifies the details about Deakin via a wanted ad in a newspaper, there's still really no justification to transport him to Fort Humboldt on a special military train. The movie leaves out the reason: Deakin blew up a U.S. Army supply train, so that makes it military business. In truth, the movie doesn't need that detail. He's a bad guy and he's going to jail. However, that would also make Deakin an anomaly. Pearce is going up to Fort Humboldt to bring back Calhoun—and if he's escorting him down, what's he taking Deakin up there for? (Imprisoning him in a military jail beset by epidemic doesn't make sense.) Such niceties don't need to be explained in movies, apparently. But in the book, it's the major who decides not to continue with the hunt for his missing soldiers. Deakin is unable to free himself in the book, so Marica, a bit feistier than in the film, unties him. Calhoun isn't instantly a man of violence, doesn't kill the telegraph operator in his first scene, but that murder indicates his brutality better than dialogue. In the book, Deakin descends by rope to see the fallen man, and brings him back up, but in the film he walks down; and in the book, the fireman's death is construed as a drunken accident. The film eliminates Pearce beating up Deakin. It won't do in a film for Deakin to reveal his identity to Marica by handing her his business card as he does in the book, so that gets spelled out.

Claremont knows exactly who he is, his fame having preceded him. There's a stand-off in the book, Deakin, Claremont and Marica at the engine, the bad guys in the rest of the train. MacLean's weapons are the newest type: repeaters (none in commercial use yet, but stolen from the factory) rather than ordinary rifles. But MacLean's ending is completely different to the film. Claremont stampedes the horses, and once they are off on the speeding train, Marica saves Deakin from Pearce. Deakin rides to the fort, taking Marica and Claremont as purported hostages, then apprehends Calhoun and mines the bridge outside the fort, blowing up the train. Pearce, O'Brien and White Hand escape but not for long. Deakin is stuck in the fort, though with a hint of burgeoning romance.

CHAPTER TWELVE

Golden Rendezvous (1977)

Golden Rendezvous went way over budget, required extensive reshoots and, after parting company with the producer, was finished by the completion bond guarantee company. And although the novel, published in 1962[1] and based on a hijacking a few years previously, had ushered in the new seagoing action subgenre far removed from the normal war cliché, by the time the movie appeared, it was the tail end of a disaster cycle that had already exploited the hijacking of ship (*Juggernaut*, 1974) and train (*The Cassandra Crossing*, 1976). And both of them happened to star, as here, Richard Harris!

MacLean sold the film rights for $250,000 to yet another actor, Laurence Harvey (*BUtterfield 8*, 1960), nursing an ambition to direct, although, oddly, he viewed the thriller as an "oceangoing comedy-suspense."[2] This would not be his directing debut, as he had already helmed *The Ceremony* (1963). Setting himself up as star and with Danny Angel, behind the proposed filming of *South by Java Head*, carrying out producing chores, shooting was scheduled for the Bahamas in 1964.[3] Harvey later expanded his slate to include three other films,[4] but none of the quartet made it across the line.

In 1968, Martin Ransohoff of Filmways planned to follow up *Ice Station Zebra* with *Golden Rendezvous*, again in league with MGM,[5] handing MacLean another $200,000 for rights and screenplay.[6] MGM forked over $6500 to John Gay in 1973 for a revised script.[7] South African André Pieterse, head of MGM's European production division, planned "to match the company's *Where Eagles Dare* and Columbia's *The Guns of Navarone* in large-scale size and large-scale grosses."[8] But when MGM proved risk-averse, Pieterse turned into another high-flying studio executive who believed MacLean could provide the banker for an independent producing career. Having broken his duck with *Forever Young, Forever Free* (1975) starring Jose Ferrer, Pieterse's company Film Trust Overseas acquired the rights from his former employer for just one dollar[9] and spent two years on the script and raising funds, initial financing coming from himself and Milton Okun,[10] John Denver's music publisher. The budget was set at $4.12 million though later reports put it at $4.5 million.[11] "This was all our own money," said Pieterse, "no tax shelter here."[12]

That wasn't strictly true. There was a loan of $800,000 from the South African government and another from the Chemical Bank in New York. Pieterse deferred his own producer's fee of $173,000 while advances from distributors made up the rest, including $850,000 from United Artists for the U.S. rights,[13] $500,000 from Rank for Britain and Australia,[14] and another $977,000 from around the world.[15] However, it was correct that Pieterse did not seek all the financing from Hollywood sources. The decision not to involve a major studio was deliberate. Clearly, he had not taken note of Kastner's experience in making *When Eight Bells Toll* without securing in advance a U.S. distribution deal. "I don't know any other way of doing it," Pieterse admitted. "You lose your independence when a major is involved. Nothing is more exciting than putting your own money into a property—and it is a success."[16] Five hands were involved in the screenplay: MacLean, Gay, the team of Allan Scott and Chris Bryant (*Don't Look Now*, 1973) and finally Stanley Price (*Arabesque*, 1966).[17]

A more important consideration was the cast. "The difficult thing is, do you cast it for the U.S. or Europe or the rest of the world? So we made it with an international cast,"[18] explained Pieterse. Richard Harris, costing $500,000 for 60 days, was the headliner.[19] Though still a marquee attraction, his last big hit was *A Man Called Horse* (1970). Oscar-nominated character actor Burgess Meredith was suddenly a box office name again after the surprise success of *Rocky* (1976). David Janssen (*The Swiss Conspiracy*, 1976) was beginning to slip down the credits. With a worldwide following from his horror roles, Christopher Lee (*The Three Musketeers*, 1974) essayed the villain. Leigh Lawson (*Brother Sun, Sister Moon*, 1972) was a rising British star, Dorothy Malone (*The Tarnished Angels*, 1957) and John Carradine (*House of Dracula*, 1947) American veterans. Other roles were played by British television actors Gordon Jackson (*Upstairs, Downstairs*, 1971–1975) and Robert Flemyng (*Compact*, 1963–1964). Female lead Ann Turkel (*The Cassandra Crossing*), another model-turned-actress, was best known as Richard Harris' wife. *Golden Rendezvous* didn't have the stellar line-up of a *Towering Inferno* (1974) or *Earthquake* (1974), but acceptable enough in global markets by the all-star–cast standards of the day. South African director Ashley Lazarus (*Forever Young, Forever Free*) cost $60,000.[20]

The 49-day shoot commenced on February 28, 1977.[21] The moviemakers were almost immediately behind schedule due to Christopher Lee being fired (replaced by John Vernon [*Fear Is the Key*]), script changes, including Harris demanding Turkel's role be enhanced, and technical issues. By May 19, it was $600,000 over budget and the key pre-credit sequence showing the theft of the nuclear warhead had still not been filmed. Due to overtime, Harris was now owed an additional $150,000.[22] Composer Jeff Wayne, some decades away from his *War of the Worlds* phenomenon, sued for $73,000 in unpaid fees.[23] The director was fired and completion bond guarantor Film Finance assumed responsibility for the production. Distributors were within their rights to decline a movie if the completed film strayed from the screenplay on which they had based their investment, and the absence of the planned theft sequence in the final edit raised concerns. Minus that sequence, the movie was savaged in the trades. To offset that problem, Film Finance, at a cost of $24,000, hired British director Freddie Francis and his son Kevin to oversee that six-minute section, which overran its allocated two-day shoot by four days.[24] Rank appeared content with the outcome and added the sequence to the movie in time for its U.K. general release.[25] United Artists were not content and pulled out of its distribution deal.[26] While released internationally with no further rancor, the lack of a U.S. distributor

Chapter Twelve. Golden Rendezvous (1977) 113

The troubles besetting *The Golden Rendezvous* did not end when filming was completed. Afterwards, star Richard Harris was arrested and sued for around $1 million by producer André Pieterse on the grounds that his drinking and breach of contract added $750,000 to the budget. In addition, Pieterse was accused of fraud (Hannan collection).

proved a sore point, especially given the problems that would create in recovering negative costs. Hemdale,[27] originally a British independent which had expanded into the U.S., made an attempt to find a buyer but the film was rejected by all the major studios as well as those mini-majors who occasionally ran short of product. As a fallback, hoping to snag a "Movie of the Week" slot, Hemdale tried the three networks with no luck.[28] Sales efforts were not helped by a savage *Variety* review which tabbed it the "phoniest and least exciting Alistair MacLean adaptation to date."[29] It was re-edited into a television feature; 14 minutes were cut, including the theft sequence.[30] The shorter version appeared to do some sort of trick because United Artists re-entered the frame, planning to sell it to a network for $1.5 million. Finally sold to Time-Life, it received its U.S. premiere on Home Box Office.[31] Canadian distributor Mutual attempted to revive it under a new title, *Nuclear Terror*, and it was screened at the Sitges Festival in 1981.[32] Shown by the U.S. network ABC on June 27, 1982, it placed 100th in the rankings that year for movies shown on television.[33]

The Film

It's difficult to see what UA was so exercised about, especially given the paltry amount it was paying for the U.S. rights, and it's equally hard to understand the viciously dismissive *Variety* review. For sure, the market had long been saturated by disaster pictures and this hybrid heist with an overabundance of characters and a weak leading lady would not have necessarily lent itself to an extremely positive assessment. One of the problems of adapting MacLean is that the author's narrative energy and command of his subject matter can easily dissipate in the face of apparent complication. What comes across as control on the page can become unwieldy on the screen. The real difficulty is that it's a murder mystery that later transitions into a straightforward heist drama, one billion dollars in gold bullion, and from there into potential nuclear calamity of disaster cycle proportions. And the climactic switcheroo—the villains, in snatching the gold from another ship, leave on it the nuclear device—results in audiences scratching their heads. The countdown to disaster had already been done to death in *Juggernaut* without throwing a complex switch and heist into the mix.

But structurally, it works smoothly. The opening section introduces S.S. *Campari*'s Chief Officer Carter (Richard Harris), new arrivals hoity-toity beauty Susan (Ann Turkel) and her older alcoholic lover Conway (David Janssen), Carreras (John Vernon) and the severely ill Dr. Taubman (Robert Beatty). A couple of coffins hold up departure. Passengers already on board include inveterate gamblers Van Heurden (Burgess Meredith) and Fairweather (John Carradine), lonely Mrs. Skinner (Dorothy Malone), arrogant Cerdan (Leigh Lawson), incompetent ship's surgeon Dr. Marston (Gordon Jackson) and grumpy Capt. Bullen (Robert Flemyng). Most are only glimpsed in passing and the initial thrust is Susan engaging in mild flirting and Conway getting drunk. But then crew members start getting killed off. When the new purser Benson (Michael Howard) goes missing, Carter organizes a search of passenger cabins, irritating the easily annoyed Susan. He becomes suspicious of the ill passenger and his nurses. Just as Carter begins to round up likely suspects, a gang of mercenaries crashes through the upper windows, firing a fusillade of bullets, killing and wounding indiscriminately.

Act Two: Carreras has smuggled on board, in the coffins, a nuclear warhead, and the sick passenger turns out to be the doped-up kidnapped scientist required to arm it. Carreras plans to use the missile to hold up a ship carrying gold bullion and escape by blowing it up, eliminating all evidence by killing all the passengers and crew who he aims to transfer to it. Act Three: Carter must defuse the bomb, alert the other ship, prevent further slaughter, stop Carreras and, with limited access to weaponry, disable the *Campari* and prevent the villains getting away with the gold. By this point, Susan has proved less frivolous than she initially appeared, Dr. Marston less incompetent, but Conway more culpable. The weather takes a turn for the worse. The derring-do is left to Carter, slung over the side, dunked in the ocean, scrambling up the ship's sides, swimming between vessels and generally facing one impossible situation after another. Final twists are thick on the ground until the avuncular Van Heurden is revealed as the mastermind.

There are interesting character touches. Susan dumps Carreras' intrusive camera in a bowl of punch, Van Heurden wears a bowler hat and continues to play roulette in the midst of chaos, Fairweather's arthritis is so bad he can't cut meat, a steward nips the tip off his cigarette. But the movie tries to cram in too many storylines: Conway is Susan's father, not her lover, hitting the bottle to get over a divorce, and the ship owner to boot, thus explaining sightings of him on the bridge with Carreras. Though Richard Harris' hair is too long for a ship's officer, he's at home with the action, the mild romance given extra charge since he and Turkel were an item. John Vernon has been here before and his restrained villain is a fresh twist on the more intemperate of the species. Ann Turkel is no more than passable, but then her role doesn't call on her to do much.

Perhaps the bigger problem for audiences was expectation. Viewers didn't know whether they were being sold a seabound version of *Murder on the Orient Express* or *Breakheart Pass*, a heist picture exhibiting little of the usual criminal ingenuity on which the genre depended, or a countdown thriller in which they had invested time getting to know and sympathize with the individuals in peril. Once the action kicks off, the members of the all-star cast are mostly sidelined, leaving no one, except the obvious hero, to root for. It might have been better, though possible heresy, to delete one of the parallel stories, opt for either heist or disaster; this would have allowed more time for character development. *Die Hard* (1988) showed how these movies should be made: focus entirely on the duel between good guy and bad guy, provide personal pathos for the hero and allow the villain to go over the top. *Under Siege* (1992), while not in the *Die Hard* league, shows how easy it is to construct an effective thriller with minimal exposure to subsidiary characters.

But you can't blame Ashley Lazarus for not inventing a screen subgenre commensurate with what MacLean had already achieved on the page. You wonder just what would have happened to the MacLean movie had the likes of John McTiernan been around to strip the story down to basics and pump up the volume.

Book into Film: The All-Star Mistake

There was no reason for the all-star cast. The characters played by Burgess Meredith, John Carradine and Dorothy Malone didn't exist in the book. The David Janssen character did, but he was not divorced and using booze as a salve. This wasn't the kind of ship, either, boasting a roulette wheel. Nor did Carter require various incidental characters to appear at critical moments to save the day.

MacLean had come up with the perfect ending—strike that, two perfect endings—demonstrating once again (as with *Fear Is the Key*) that he was the master of the devilishly ironic climax. So the producers padded out a lean tale for the sole purpose of acquiring some marquee names to facilitate the selling of the picture, rather than stopping to consider how much simpler it might be to re-cast Burgess Meredith, David Janssen *et al.* in more important parts. Yet again, screenwriters had determined that, despite MacLean's proven credentials, that they could improve on his work. It's not impossible to find a screen correlation for MacLean's style—*Where Eagles Dare* managed it—but Hollywood made a greater consistent effort with Dickens and Raymond Chandler and it paid off, all movies relating to those worlds coming with a distinct visual or verbal aura that recreated the original work.

I guess it would have been too onerous for the cinemagoer to consider MacLean's genius in dreaming up this particular kind of ship. In the movie, its oddities are unexplained. It's not a liner in the usual sense nor a cruise ship, and although tramp steamers did occasionally carry passengers, it was hardly at that level of luxury. MacLean invented the notion that a shipping magnate had created the ultimate rich person's travel adventure, a no-expense-spared mystery cruise, the passengers given no clue where the ship might be headed because destination was determined by cargo. Limiting the number of passengers ensured an enormous waiting list as the wealthy stood in line to be allowed to pay to participate. Oddly, it plays a critical element in the story because people jumping the queue (i.e., Carreras and the sick man) is the reason the radio transmitters are put out of action.

Apart from Meredith, Malone and Carradine, the passengers are straightforward: a fading Hollywood actress, a penniless duke, the happily married Beresfords and their daughter. In *Caravan to Vaccarès*, the heroine refuses to call the hero by his first name as a means of keeping him at bay. Here, Susan implores Carter to do the opposite, but he cannot comply simply because it would be a breach of protocol for a ship's officer to fraternize with a passenger.

The movie misses a trick by deviating from MacLean's portrayal of Susan. Once the criminals take over in the book, she plays a very active part. It's her rather than (as in the film) Dr. Marston who creates the diversion to allow Carter to investigate the sick man. In fact, she's the one who has spotted something out of the ordinary. And it's her instead of (as in the film) the scientist who accompanies Carter into the hold to check out the coffins. In fact, Carter is too stricken with pain to reach the coffins and it's Susan who finds them. And it's her who attacks Carreras Jr. to save Carter. The idea that Burgess Meredith had been effectively clowning his way through the picture in order (surprise, surprise) to be revealed as the *eminence grise* was the kind of tacked-on twist that audiences generally gave the cold shoulder. More logically, MacLean places the all-important key in the pocket of Carreras Sr.

But it's criminal the way the screenwriters ignored the genius of MacLean's triple ending. First, by a stroke of ingenuity, Carter ensured that the thieves absconded with the wrong (bullion-free) containers. Secondly, Carter removed the nuclear weapon from the coffin so that it was not on board the other ship but was still primed and ready to go off. So, thirdly, in sailing away in her tramp steamer minus any gold and still carrying the weapon, Carreras was "his own executioner." This is such a beautifully written book, with a plot well worked out and characters you root for. It's a shame that the producers wantonly went down a completely different route. Another missed opportunity.

Chapter Thirteen

Force 10 from Navarone (1978)

It would be standard these days for a studio or producer to own the characters in a film, allowing him to make a sequel or a remake. The reason Ross MacDonald's private eye, for example, was renamed Harper for the 1966 movie *Harper*[1] was that the author refused to surrender the rights to his series character Lew Archer to producer Elliott Kastner. After producing *The Guns of Navarone*, producer Carl Foreman automatically assumed that he had the rights to a sequel and so in 1967 blithely announced he was embarking on *After Navarone* with production scheduled for spring 1969.[2] The movie seemed a sure thing after Foreman enticed back original stars Gregory Peck, David Niven and Anthony Quinn, director J. Lee Thompson and even composer Dimitri Tiomkin. That didn't go down well with MacLean, who believed he had not given Foreman permission to make a sequel. Once their differences were ironed out, Foreman claimed he wrote the basic outline on which MacLean based first his screenplay and then his novel,[3] an instant bestseller when it was published in 1968. But that very much depended on your definition of "basic story." Foreman did come up with a version—an eight-page outline[4]—of what was eventually used; the credits scene harking back to the original; bringing back Mallory and Miller, retired from active duty,[5] and Andrea; and introducing the idea of the traitor in Yugoslavia and the "conflict between youth and middle-age,"[6] within the new team. But he didn't invent the blowing-up of the dam or sketch out the new characters. The traitor aspect was "the kick-off to the actual story" but he didn't flesh out what happened next beyond that they "will be involved in something even more important and exciting."[7]

Shortly after the initial announcement, the title was changed to *High Dam* in reference to the explosive climax.[8] As before, Foreman's name was to the forefront.[9] MacLean declined to play the game the Foreman way, refusing to follow the producer's dictate of "doing the book first, then the screenplay."[10] Presumably, this was because it ensured that the author would be paid twice, as with *Where Eagles Dare*, rather than being forced, according to standard contracts, to share movie rights with his publisher. Foreman was credited with the screenplay and, in his capacity as producer, considered filming it in Cinerama[11] (as he would do for 1969's *Mackenna's Gold*). However, with six projects on the go for Columbia,[12] Foreman decided against proceeding personally with the MacLean movie. After the author delivered a screenplay, he farmed it out in 1968 to Winkast's Elliott Kastner,[13] with whom he was on good terms.[14]

In the foreword to his adaptation, Foreman explained:

> [T]he idea for the sequel was conceived by this writer [Foreman] and upon which Alistair MacLean was engaged to write the screenplay and novel. Unfortunately, MacLean saw fit to depart from the original premise to such an extent that ... the story and screenplay ... were not considered a practical basis for such a film.[15]

Foreman had hired Kastner "to prepare a new script based on the novel and the original premises." But he had no better luck than with MacLean. "Unfortunately," he grumbled, "the screenplay written under Winkast's supervision went even further astray and has been discarded in toto."[16] Columbia had agreed to finance and distribute the Winkast movie[17] after taking out a three-year option on March 13, 1968,[18] for $60,000 plus ten percent of the net profits.[19] Foreman reiterated his claim that he, not MacLean, "contributed the basic idea upon which the screenplay and novel are based" and he had a "sketchy" agreement[20] with Geoffrey Reeve as associate producer.[21] The Winkast picture would be made on location, "including studio work," in Yugoslavia[22] on a budget of five or six million,[23] including $290,000 in Winkast fees.[24] Jerry Gershwin, who had shifted to Cinema Center,[25] still retained close enough links with his old company to offer advice[26] on the Winkast screenplay by John T. Kelley (*A Rage to Live,* 1965),[27] which dumped Mallory, Andrea and Miller in favor of two new teams, one younger and one older. Gershwin expressed concern that the screenplay lacked the "exceptional action sequences" of *Where Eagles Dare.* To compensate, urged Gershwin, "The action it does have must be heightened via suspense ... with the accent on the people involved."[28] The more experienced team is led by Compton, the younger by Nichols. Compton, an American, has "nothing to lose," having gotten away with killing his unfaithful wife.[29]

According to a *Screen International* article from December 1977, *Force 10 from Navarone* switched locations, to Jersey from Yugoslavia, because the former was a tax haven acceptable to British tax exiles Robert Shaw and Guy Hamilton (advertisement, *Box Office,* January 30, 1978).

Chapter Thirteen. Force 10 from Navarone (1978)

Nichols vents antipathy to authority through sports. Norwegian earth mother Maria watched Germans slaughter her family. Italian Santini "finds himself ... in a fight between himself and his love/hate of his country." Ronald is a well-bred Englishman and Shanahan a Chicago cop. Gerald dies at some point and his death "only serves to drive Compton and Nichols closer together."

Foreman envisaged saving money by shooting the entire film in the U.K. with some model work in Malta. The U.K. location would be tweaked to double up for both the partisan and pro–German camps. Despite his later grand announcement to reassemble the original cast, Forman had initially concluded it would be "better for costs" if the *Guns of Navarone* stars were not involved.[30] In his version, Mallory and Miller were retired from active duty, and Mallory was not redeployed (as in the finished film) in some kind of managerial capacity. The two men were called back into action because only they could identify Nicolai, the traitor from the previous film, who was now hindering prospects for the Allied invasion of Yugoslavia. Major Sessler, also from the previous picture, worked with Nicolai. The task force envisaged by Foreman did not include Americans. The ploy of smuggling penicillin was employed, but Marica (Maritza in the finished film) was "obviously Sessler's mistress." The notion of Miller and Mallory being forced to spy for the Germans came into play, as did the bandaged faces of the pro–German Slavs, the Zenica Cage, and Mallory opting to destroy a dam rather than a bridge. Also included: Marica, a partisan spy, being interrogated in the remote blockhouse (as in the book) by Sessler and Droshny, and subsequently being rescued; also, Mallory's double bluff. The dam is destroyed (as in the book) by the RAF dropping torpedoes into the dam reservoir for Miller and Mallory to activate.[31]

But by 1970, Foreman, interest revived, reclaimed *Force 10 from Navarone*,[32] "talked into taking it back" within the Columbia fold,[33] still with the original cast in mind.[34] He informed Gregory Peck that he was "getting ready to write the screenplay," planning a summer 1971 release.[35] Despite announcements that it would "roll soon" in 1973,[36] it remained in limbo. In part, this was due to a falling-out between producer and Columbia after the failure of *Young Winston* (1972) and Foreman being wooed by independents Run Run Shaw and John Woolf and majors Warner Brothers and Universal.[37] Foreman's eye was taken off the ball as he negotiated in 1975 to make the $12 million *Tai Pan* for Run Run Shaw.[38] For Warners, he was writing *The Day the World Ended*.[39] With Columbia balking at the budget, deeming it "too expensive,"[40] Foreman took advantage of a new financial development in the industry—the co-production—as exemplified by *The Towering Inferno* (1974) by which Warner Brothers and Twentieth Century–Fox shared costs and distribution rights. In October 1976, he engineered a deal between his own company and the German firm Mondo GmbH to buy the rights from Columbia[41] with MacLean paid $300,000.[42] Oliver Unger, former boss of Commonwealth United which had funded Kastner's *Tam Lin*, and had held a production position in Foreman's company, had managed to interest Mondo in a $40 million investment in two movies, including *Back to Navarone*, to be filmed in Greece.[43] Unger claimed: "The project was the easiest I've ever been associated with to finance."[44]

Unger also said, "We live in the year of the anti-hero, and we've had to shape Mallory and Miller accordingly."[45] Uncharacteristically, Foreman took a back seat, credited only as executive producer.[46] Mondo was viewed as putting up the "end money." There was a reason for Foreman easing into the background: He had signed an exclusive deal with Universal that would have prohibited involvement elsewhere.[47] Geoff Reeve (*Caravan to Vaccarès*) was announced as line producer.[48] Budget was set at $10 million—with $600,000 set aside for the dam scene—and a January 1977 start, 24-week schedule, British director and $1 million each for three stars.[49] Initially, taking the Kastner route with *When Eight Bells Toll* and that of Pieterse with *Golden Rendezvous*, Unger sought to "hold off on any distribution deals so as to maintain complete control."[50]

In fact, to cover the substantial budget, he sold the North American distribution rights to mini-major AIP[51] and the rest of the world to Columbia,[52] though it had originally reserved the right to "first refusal" on U.S. distribution.[53] In fact, Columbia was now delighted to be associated. Its output had diminished; this was only its eighth movie in 1977 compared to 14 from WB, 13 from Paramount and 15 from UA.[54] So now it was, effectively, a five-way co-production between Columbia, AIP, Navarone Productions, Mondo Film 78 and Open Road (Foreman's other company). AIP ponied up $2.1 million, Columbia a total of $4 million, Mondo $1 million and ABC $1.8 million for TV rights, with the remainder coming from a Yugoslavian production company and, to cover the overages, some finance from the completion bond company.[55]

AIP was the most bizarre home to date for a MacLean movie. Since its inception in 1953 by James H. Nicholson, the company had specialized in low-budget exploitation, majoring on horror, biker and Beach Party pictures. Come the 1970s, AIP attempted to join the mainstream with upmarket fare such as *Julius Caesar* (1971), *Wuthering Heights* (1971) and *Kidnapped*. It also concluded a deal with Unger's Commonwealth United. The expansion failed and AIP returned to its roots until 1975 when, as part of a renewed attempt at diversification, it funded movies like the political thriller *Hennessey* (1975), produced by Peter Snell, the arthouse drama *The Wild Party* (1975), the sci-fi *The Land That Time Forgot* (1976), the comedy Western *The Great Scout and Cathouse Thursday* (1976) and the musical *A Matter of Time* (1976). *Force 10 from Navarone* and the $16 million *Meteor* starring Sean Connery were key to its 25th anniversary in 1978. Originally, the war film was viewed as ideal summer fare.[56]

Incidentally, this wasn't AIP's first brush with Alistair MacLean. The company had turned down the chance to back *Puppet on a Chain*[57] and, in the years following *Force 10 from Navarone*, had *The Way to Dusty Death*[58] and *River of Death* in its sights. AIP offset its costs on *Force 10 to Navarone* by selling cable rights to HBO and TV rights to ABC; they both ran it in early 1980.[59]

Initially, the movie was going to have the strongest cast since *Where Eagles Dare* with both Clint Eastwood and James Caan sought.[60] Robert Bolt (*Doctor Zhivago*, 1965) was approached for the screenplay, but he turned down the job and it went to Robin Chapman, an odd choice for such a substantial enterprise. Chapman had

Chapter Thirteen. Force 10 from Navarone (1978)

According to a February 1980 article in *Fongoria*, Caroline Munro (*The Spy Who Loved Me*, 1977) was the first choice for the female lead in *Force 10 from Navarone*. She turned it down on account of the nudity, clearing the path for Barbara Bach. An April 1977 article in *Hollywood Reporter* revealed that Rod Steiger was briefly in the running for the role of the partisan leader (Hannan collection).

written only one screenplay, the lower-budgeted *The Triple Echo* (1972),[61] with a bit of uncredited assistance from George MacDonald Fraser (*The Three Musketeers*, 1973). Guy Hamilton (*The Battle of Britain*, 1969) was a shoo-in for the director's chair. Despite Gregory Peck's box office resurgence in *The Omen* (1976), he was considered too old, as were Quinn and Niven. A few years earlier, Robert Shaw would have been a dubious choice for top billing. Although briefly considered matinee idol material after *Custer of the West* (1967), the British actor was better known for playing villainous characters in *The Sting* (1973) and *The Taking of Pelham One Two Three* (1974); even his curmudgeonly Quint in *Jaws* (1975) was not far off that mark. Universal for *Swashbuckler* (1976) and Paramount for *Black Sunday* (1977) had called on him to play the hero; he was the villain again in *The Deep* (1977). He was clearly considered box office, otherwise he wouldn't have pulled in $750,000. With a huge hit—$51 million in global rentals[62]—his asking price rose to $1 million. "If an actor is in *Black Sunday* or *The Deep* for six months and *Jaws* for eight months he is entitled to his million," he argued.[63] Five hits in five years was proof of marquee value. However, he conceded that at his age, "it was a bit ridiculous to be running round a mountain."[64]

There was a fair chance *Force 10 from Navarone* could also cash in on new star Harrison Ford, riding on the success of *Star Wars* (1977); Ford wanted to "avoid being stereotyped as a science fiction type."[65] British star Edward Fox, best known for *The Day of the Jackal* (1973), was coming off *A Bridge Too Far* (1977) while Barbara Bach had been the love interest in the box office smash *The Spy Who Loved Me* (1977). Franco Nero (*The Virgin and the Gypsy*, 1970) was well regarded in European markets. Add Carl Weathers (*Rocky*, 1976) to the mix and it was a powerful line-up.

Pakistan and Greece were considered as locations before Unger and Hamilton settled on Yugoslavia and Malta.[66] Despite doing all the reconnaissance in Yugoslavia, Reeve was replaced as producer and assigned another role within the Foreman organization.[67] The schedule, once trimmed to 16 weeks, added another fortnight.[68] The biggest chunk of the shoot—nine weeks—was spent in Yugoslavia, locations including Durdevica Tara Bridge in Montenegro and the Jablanica Dam in Bosnia and Herzegovina. Six weeks at Shepperton on four sound stages involved the construction of a full-sized interior of a World War II Lancaster bomber, the bridge and deck of a destroyer, and military encampments. The three weeks at the Mediterranean Film Studios in Malta were given over to the destruction of the scale models of bridge and dam.[69] Other scenes were filmed on Jersey and in the Royal Naval Dockyard in Plymouth. The initial start date of September 19, 1977, was pushed back to October 10.[70] The movie—its budget already risen to $11 million—added another $300,000 due to bad weather.[71]

Despite the big budget and presumably the fees received, the principals were uncomfortable in their roles. Shaw complained, "I'm appalled at some of the lines. I'm not at ease in the film."[72] Ford confessed that he was "lost," arguing, "[T]here was no reason for my character being there."[73] According to Edward Fox, "[T]he characters were stick figures. We had to dress them up and make the lines fit as we went along."[74]

The movie was sold to journalists attending a junket in the Caribbean as a "continuation" of *The Guns of Navarone*[75] and screened for the U.S. First Family over Thanksgiving at Camp David.[76] Release was shifted to December 22[77] on an initial salvo of 475 screens.[78] But there was a major setback: Robert Shaw died at age 51.[79] And there were other worries. The Christmas period was "overloaded" with product[80] and it was going head to head with a different kind of war picture, *The Deer Hunter*.

The Film—A Twist a Minute

We begin with a recap of the climax of *The Guns of Navarone* and cut to the figures of Mallory (Robert Shaw) and Miller (Edward Fox) sitting bedraggled on the deck of a destroyer. They are reunited an indeterminate period of time later at a military training camp, Mallory having acquired a limp (not from the previous picture). Also deployed there: Miller, promoted to sergeant, an explosives expert fresh from Winston Churchill's dirty tricks department. They face a new mission, to flush out a traitor, Captain Lescovar (known to Mallory from a previous encounter), who has infiltrated the Yugoslavian partisans. They are dispatched under the wing of American commando Lt. Col. Barnsby (Harrison Ford), heading up a team engaged in a separate secret endeavor. Due to leaks in the Allied command, they must steal a plane, along the way accidentally collecting insubordinate American prisoner

Chapter Thirteen. Force 10 from Navarone (1978)

Weaver (Carl Weathers). When their plane is attacked, these four plus Lt. Reynolds (Angus MacInnes), the only survivors, parachute into enemy territory. Weaver immediately earns his stripes by saving Miller from a German. They are met by a troop of Chetnik Yugoslavs, led by the giant Capt. Drazak (Richard Kiel); these men turn out to be on the side of the Germans. Interrogated by German Major Schroeder, Mallory spins a yarn about them being deserters peddling stolen penicillin packed in Miller's suitcase. Maritza (Barbara Bach), the German commander's lover, urges him to kill them but he checks out their story and when he saves them from a firing squad, the suitcase is revealed to contain only firewood. Mallory and Miller, escorted by Maritza and a bunch of Chetniks, head for the spot where the penicillin is supposedly buried. Maritza shoots her comrade and sets the Brits free. Escaping to hunt down Lescovar, they kill a pair of pursuing Chetniks with faces bandaged to disguise wounds caused by flame-throwers. The Brits reach the partisan hideout. But when they inform partisan leader Major Petrovic (Alan Badel) of their mission, he laughs in their faces, explaining that Lescovar died long ago. Despite recognizing Petrovic's German confederate Col. Von Ingolsleben (Franco Nero) as Lescovar, Mallory can do nothing. The Yugoslavs are trapped: Battalions of Germans are ready to cross a bridge to wipe them out. The bridge itself is impervious to bombing missions and explosives. Using partisans disguised as bandaged Chetniks, Mallory and Miller return to the Chetnik camp to free Barnsby, Weaver and Reynolds. As they do so, Drazak returns with the corpses and beats up Maritza as a traitor. After the team escapes, Barnsby divulges his real mission is to blow up the bridge. When Miller explains it's

Force 10 from Navarone was originally planned as a summer picture. When it was released in the U.S. at Christmas 1978, it entered a marketplace that was "overloaded" with top product, according to *Variety*, as 19 new movies competed against perennial holiday favorites and November holdovers. Its opening week in New York was considered "decent" but in Los Angeles it was rated "slim." (advertisement, *Variety*, November 15, 1978).

indestructible, Mallory suggests destroying the dam at the top of the valley. "It's like having an enormous bath," explains Miller. "All you've got to do is pull out the plug." Another Lescovar betrayal results in a massacre of the partisans and the death of Maritza.

Descending on the nearest town to steal German explosives, Lescovar unwittingly gives away his true allegiance and is killed. As the Germans begin their final assault on the bridge, Barnsby and Mallory mine the dam and Weaver kills Drazak in a knife fight. The resulting dam burst washes away the bridge and saves the partisans.

The picture is cleverly and often subtly done. There is ongoing tension between Barnsby and Mallory, the American feeling smugly superior, resenting having to accommodate the infirm Brit, with Weaver smarting from racist abuse. The narrative thrives on twists, the giant Slav being the enemy, the German believing Mallory's penicillin tale, the suitcase switch, Maritza revealed as an Allied agent, the "death" of Lescovar, the use of the bandaged men, Lescovar's further treachery, the surprising murder of Maritza (whom tradition dictates should escape, possibly having formed romantic attachment to Barnsby), both missions effectively thwarted, and then, through inspiration, suddenly workable. Except for the double agents, characterization is straightforward apart from Weaver, who has a fabulous part, an outsider, abused by friend and enemy alike over the color of his skin, forced to earn his keep by repeatedly saving his comrades (Miller twice) and providing the equivalent of the shoot-out finale in his knife duel with Drazak. The bandaged men do quadruple duty: They appear first as fearsome faces, then as fearsome pursuers, then as devices to permit Mallory and Miller re-entry into the Chetnik stronghold and finally as visual signs that the trick has not worked. The Chetniks are on horseback, allowing them speed of maneuver, ensuring they should win any chase. Miller is as laidback as in the previous film, nonchalantly tossing an explosive into the airplane as they jump out so that it explodes in mid-air, convincing any observers that nobody escaped alive. As nonchalantly, he creates an explosive ambush for Drazak and finally as tension mounts at the dam he lies back on the hillside awaiting the outcome.

Maritza performs roles similar to both the feisty partisan and the seductive traitor in *The Guns of Navarone*. Except as hampered hero, it's difficult to work out why Mallory has a limp (though Robert Shaw was similarly encumbered in *The Sting*), but it does limit his involvement in action, more the brains of the operation. You wouldn't say Mallory and Barnsby bond, but they do know how to work together, especially when, improvising wildly, the American backs up the penicillin gag. Mission pictures are not intended to be so twisty. Usually, the target is stated upfront, a large section devoted to exploring tensions between the characters before they finally bond, the mission itself a fitting conclusion to the build-up. Here, we're mostly kept in the dark. Even Mallory doesn't know what Barnsby is up to. Both heroes are confounded in their initial quests.

The movie didn't take off at the box office for a number of reasons, possibly key being the death of the star. But, also, it was a summer picture, not a winter one, a popcorn movie not intended to provoke thought. So it was unfortunate to come up against the critically acclaimed *The Deer Hunter* which asked its audience a different set of questions. For the seasoned MacLean fan, accustomed to twists and a stunning climax, it was still a rewarding experience.

Book into Film—Carl Foreman Strikes Again

You can see why the producers wanted to change some elements of the original, though the reasons for other alterations (the usual name switches, for example) are less obvious. The book centers on bluff and double bluff. Building on the idea of duping the enemy into believing the penicillin smuggling notion the Germans counter by engaging in their own duplicity. For a start, to ensure that Mallory is indeed a deserter and willing to assist the Germans, the German commander Capt. Neufeld (not Major Schroeder) enlists him to spy on the partisans. That permits Mallory to retail falsehoods that back up a myth the British have been trying to perpetuate: that an Allied attack is imminent, and that the British and Americans wish to invade Yugoslavia and set up a second front, forcing the Germans to commit massive numbers of troops that otherwise could be sent to Italy. The Germans have their own ploy, positioning 200 false tanks at a different place along the river to fool the Slavs into thinking that's where the attack on them will begin. Then Mallory sets out to find and free the four leaders of the previous missions (mentioned only in passing in the film) who had disappeared in Yugoslavia. Only then does he turn his attention to destroying the dam.

In the book, there is never any intention of targeting the bridge per se. However, MacLean cleverly keeps from the audience details of this plan (it's not mentioned until page 188 of the 254-page paperback). But MacLean would scoff at the screenwriter's ideas about how to blow up such a massive dam, with a few bits and pieces from Miller's suitcase. Mallory & Co. can't get to the dam earlier because they are adhering to a specific timetable. The RAF will drop into the water of the dam 3000 pounds of high explosive (*that* sounds much more likely to complete the job) encased in three canisters which Mallory and Miller simply have to prime rather than ramming the equivalent of a few sticks of dynamite against the dam wall. The screenwriter goes for the simpler option.

Setting aside these complications and adding more of their own (the raid on the German supply dump, for example), the producers take much of MacLean's original material and switch it around. For example, there are two Chetniks with terribly scarred faces. But they are easily identified in the book by their false beards whereas in the film their distinctive (and initially scary) white bandages become a clever visual motif. In the book we find Reynolds, an insubordinate, grumpy British soldier constantly challenging the officers and complaining of being left out of things; the movie counterpart is the American Weaver (Carl Weathers), whose antipathy to all concerned is understandable given the racism he endures (an element that would not apply to the book). But while Reynolds loses his fight with the giant Chetnik Droshny in the book, Weaver wins his against the giant Chetnik Drazak (another name change) in the film. In the film, Maritza (Maria in the book) is shot at the plateau by Lescovar. There is no Lescovar in the book and Mallory is not being sent to find him—that's the film's invention. And Maria in the book doesn't die, although her true identity becomes known to the Germans, resulting in her need to be rescued. And that does allow her to be involved in MacLean's more complicated, more action-packed climax. In the book, she has a brother, a blind guitarist who turns out to be neither blind nor a relative but her husband, and she doesn't seduce a German. The brother is eliminated from the film and, instead, she takes the German officer as a lover, permitting the last item any reader would expect to find in a MacLean book, a sex scene.

There are no Americans in the book. Barnsby and his cohorts are the film's invention, though, oddly enough from the audience perspective, Mallory has switched nationality, from the American Gregory Peck to the British Robert Shaw. In the book, there's no need to replace Andrea (the Anthony Quinn *Guns of Navarone* character) because he's very much alive. But Mallory isn't sent to England to recuperate. There is no time. His boss, Commander Jensen, already has an extremely urgent job for him. So, only allowing a brief respite for Andrea to be married, the three men are packed off to Yugoslavia via Italy with another three British soldiers, each of whom plays an important subsidiary role in the book.

Reynolds is an exceptionally clever creation from the narrative point of view, not only overtly questioning Mallory but suspecting him of treason, and constantly annoyed at being kept in the dark, and allows the reader to voice similar concerns. When parachuting from the plane, Miller is caught up in the tree in the book for the sole purpose of introducing Weaver as a man of action. In the book, he lands safely, and no action is required to avoid marauding Germans because no Germans are marauding. The scene where Drashak appears to try to shave Weaver's skin is taken from Droshny running his knife along Andrea's skin. Since there's no Barnsby in the book, he's not required to back up Mallory's drug-running tale, which he spins out on his own, without the presence of either Miller or Andrea. In the book Miller isn't carrying a suitcase of *any*thing, neither penicillin nor explosives, because Miller doesn't have to prove the existence of the drugs: His story is backed up by a phone call to Italy, so there's no need for Maria-Maritza to fill the suitcase with wood or for the Allied pair to be sent back to recover it from its hiding place. The badly injured Chetniks are killed and Andrea distrusts Maria-Maritza early on. But there's no need to rescue the rest of the Allied gang because everyone goes along to meet the partisans and everyone comes back. Mallory comes across the locomotive and uses it to reach the dam, and that idea inspires the hitching the ride on the train in the book. The clearing of the plateau comes from the book but there the plane lands safely and there's no massacre. At the finale, MacLean injects overtones of the anti-war elements that he included in *The Guns of Navarone*. The three young British soldiers are dead, casualties of war.

I have to agree it would have been impossible to film the MacLean book as it stood: The implausibility factor, the disbelief that a reader happily suspends when caught in the thrill of the writing, is too much, the constant bluff and double bluff would wear an audience out. In *Where Eagles Dare*, the bluffing was limited to the scene in the castle, but here it's ongoing, and from both sides. An audience couldn't keep up with the twists, fun though they are in the book. And you can see why Maria-Maritza has lost her brother and been given a new narrative arc. Nor are audiences going to question how much explosive is required to blow up a dam, so the film gets away with that as well. The invention of Lescovar both simplifies the storyline and adds another layer of tension. And an American star of the caliber of Harrison Ford (Carl Weathers is a bonus) would be a necessity for raising finance. Certainly, a very good attempt at keeping the more easily adapted elements of a MacLean story while developing the core material in interesting fashion and overcoming the author's tendency to complication.

Chapter Fourteen

Bear Island (1979)

Kastner's serial efforts had failed to solve the problem of establishing the Alistair MacLean brand in a manner similar to that of Ian Fleming's James Bond. Unlike 007, there was no controlling interest, no Harry Saltzman-Cubby Broccoli-type overseers who ensured that every couple of years there would be a new adventure. While the MacLean movie output exceeded that of Ian Fleming—12 MacLean pictures from 1961 to 1978 compared to ten Bonds from 1962 to 1977—there was no single entity in overall charge who could direct marketing and tie-in operations and build the brand. Of course, Fleming had a repeat character while each MacLean tale introduced a new hero. Setting aside that MacLean would have been smart enough to follow in the footsteps of Ross Macdonald and not sell off his series character, creating interlinked movies featuring one character should not have been beyond the producers. Why could Mallory not have been called in before or after his Navarone adventure to rescue the American officer held in Schloss Adler in Germany? His mountaineering skills would have come in handy for scaling the castle, dangling over the precipice, etc. There was no ostensible reason for Talbot not to be a secret agent tasked with investigating villains as far apart as the North Pole, the west coast of Scotland, Hungary, France or Amsterdam; geographical limitation was not imposed on James Bond. To some extent, Kastner had attempted to blend together the disparate elements of the MacLean machine. So it was no surprise that someone else thought there was a simpler solution to this puzzle, which these days would be accepted as revolving around brand-name or a MacLean-verse. Canadian producer Peter Snell, recognizing that MacLean had been badly served by such a haphazard approach to translating his work onto screen, concluded that the author required a concerted effort from one outfit to ensure that the books were developed in a consistent manner. So he began buying up published and unpublished works alike. Oddly enough, he had a competitor in this venture. Kastner, possibly encouraged by *Breakheart Pass*' initial box office returns, had the same idea: In 1976, he enquired of MacLean's editor which of the author's titles were still available for filming. Five novels had not reached the screen. The rights to *H.M.S. Ulysses* were now in the hands of an Italian sports car manufacturer, Count Volpi, *South by Java Head* was with Danny Angel–Twentieth Century–Fox and *Night Without End* with Paramount.[1] Kastner did not realize that *The Last Frontier* (the original British title) had already been filmed as *The Secret Ways*. The only title still unsold was *The Dark Crusader* (1961), the other novel written under the Ian Stuart pseudonym.[2] While all the titles lying dormant would surely have been available for purchase, Kastner took the matter no further, possibly with enough on his plate seeing through his biggest film to date, *The Missouri Breaks* (1976) with Jack Nicholson and Marlon Brando.

In terms of production experience, Snell was in the Kastner league. He was the former chief executive of British Lion; under his leadership, 1973's *Don't Look Now* and *The Wicker Man* were released.[3] His independent ventures had taken him into Shakespeare territory with *Julius Caesar* (1970) and *Antony and Cleopatra* (1972), both starring Charlton Heston; they added a certain prestige to his operation. Now he owned three television stations in Canada and was itching to return to the movie business. With Kastner falling by the wayside, Snell had a clear field. In fact, he acquired the rights to *Bear Island* from an unusual source. For several years, MacLean's wife Marcelle had owned the screenplay and, fancying herself a movie producer, had planned to make it in 1972 with Peter Hunt (*On Her Majesty's Secret Service*, 1969) at the helm.[4] She had commissioned a screenplay from David Butler (*Voyage of the Damned*, 1976). Delivered in May 1972, the 138-page first draft retained much of the movie background of the original novel. But rather than being a doctor, Marlowe is the stunt director and Hedi a stunt double. The script opens with a character being scythed down on the island by a SnoCat before shifting to the *Morning Rose* where funeral rites are being administered for the movie's murdered art director, whose girlfriend Anne is continuity girl for the World War II picture *The Hidden Enemy*. Two others are dead before they disembark. The scientific camp is empty. The island was a notorious U-boat hiding place. They find dead Norwegians from the war. Smith and his lover, the film's star, Mary,

Bear Island was at the forefront of a booming Canadian film industry. Around $34 million went into 12 movies made in Canada in 1978 alone compared to a total of $60 million for the entire previous decade. In the 35 years from 1924, 22 movies were made in British Columbia; in the 1960s, 11; and in the 1970s, over 50 (advertisement, *Hollywood Reporter*, November 6, 1979).

go down into the U-boat base for privacy. The radio mast blows up. Marlowe chases a hooded figure who turns out to be Hedi, who works for Norwegian security, as did the man killed by the SnoCat. A stunt is sabotaged and Marlowe nearly dies. Smithy is killed. In an ambush scene from the film, the bullets are live and Marlowe again narrowly escapes death. Lechinski (a film investor here) is revealed as being in the S.S. during the war. Hedi and Marlowe become romantically involved. They are attacked (as in the film) by a SnoCat. Marlowe finds Nazi gold painted gray in the U-boat pen. Smithy turns out not to be dead but in league with Gerran (here also an investor). Marlowe and Smithy fight but the latter escapes. Lechinski is still trying to revive the Nazis. Marlowe uses the amphibious qualities of the SnoCat to attack the boat on which his enemies are escaping. As with *When Eight Bells Toll*, the principals help themselves to some gold, although Marlowe is determined to continue with Hedi rather than abandon her.[5]

When the rights became available after reverting to MacLean in 1977 as part of his final divorce settlement,[6] Snell pounced and became integral to the second attempt to properly develop the MacLean brand. Said Snell, "MacLean complained of having no continuity because of 12 different productions on various other projects that have been made from his books which have sales of 60 million worldwide. His books were just bought, and he was invited to premieres. He wanted more than that."[7] Snell maintained regular telephone contact with MacLean in Geneva. The writer must have trusted Snell implicitly because the producer was suggesting dramatic changes to *Bear Island*. But Snell was in a terrific position to relaunch the author as a movie powerhouse. As well as the novel *Bear Island* (sales topping 8,000,000 copies[8]), Snell was in possession of the rights to *The Way to Dusty Death*, *Goodbye California* and *El Dorado* (aka *River of Death*). *The Way to Dusty Death* could not be filmed until 1980 because it required racing footage. Snell also bought *Night Without End* from MGM and was working with MacLean on a seven-year

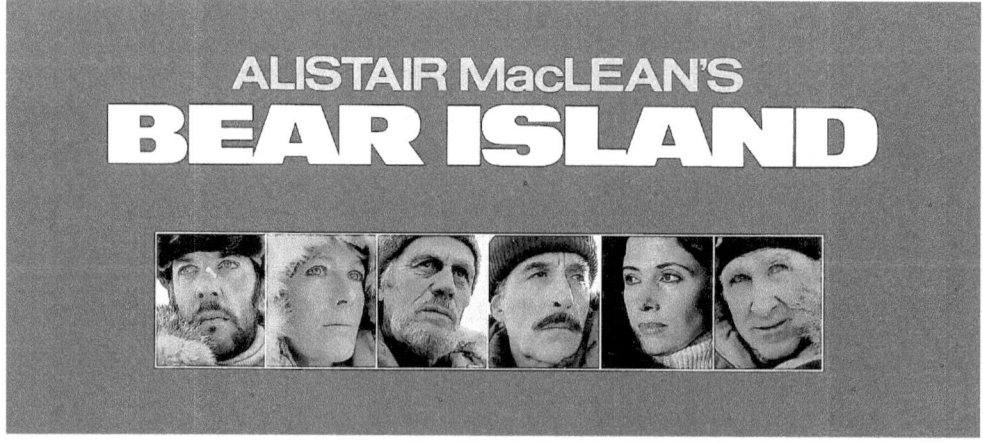

The notion that stars on location are housed in fancy hotels is often far from true. For *Bear Island*, the stars were accommodated on board a ship, which created a problem for Christopher Lee. The bunks were too short to accommodate his frame. According to Lee's memoir, *Tall, Dark and Gruesome*, a carpenter was summoned to add a two-foot extension (advertisement, *Hollywood Reporter*, November 6, 1979).

program of adventure pictures—to be released once a year at Christmas—the kind of continuity that emulated the Bond mold, and able to be sold as a package to television.[9] *Athabasca*, based on an idea by Snell, was in the planning stage but the author had sold *The Golden Gate* to Sir Lew Grade's outfit. Snell's enthusiasm was based on the hard evidence of a "central core of people who turn out to see MacLean yarns." That put Snell in control of six of the nine available MacLean properties (Irwin Allen had *Circus* and Columbia had *Seawitch*).[10]

Originally, *Bear Island* was budgeted at $7 million and backed by Snell's Selkirk communications group, based in Toronto, which owned TV stations and a cable and record company. Max Youngstein, long associated with United Artists, was also involved, recommending "script changes, casting and directors."[11] Don Sharp had been the top choice as director since the project was first mooted by Kurt Unger, producer of *Puppet on a Chain*, in 1970. "When I was in the final days of shooting *Puppet on a Chain*, Kurt Unger asked me to read the galley proofs of Alistair MacLean's new book," said Sharp. But he gave it the thumbs-down. "Films about film units aren't convincing and particularly in the kind of plot Alistair had. It was just incredible." So Karl Unger passed.[12] When a later screenplay moved away from the book, Sharp's interest was piqued. In 1976, Warners became interested so Sharp worked on a screenplay with David Butler. "It's much more logical. I mean, why would a film crew go to Bear Island to make a film? They'd probably go just outside Oslo."[13] (Though, in point of fact, Snell found out the reason: As a location, Norway was too expensive.) "A scientific unit was saner and more rational than a film crew," was Sharp's argument.[14] But Warners changed its mind.

Snell found a better financial solution: "During 1977, it became apparent to the CFDC [Canadian Film Development Corporation] that I was still walking around with a Canadian passport in my pocket. So Mike Spencer of CFDC asked me to explore the possibility of doing the MacLean series I was talking about." To access the location he required, he had to "go across the border to Alaska to get the ice and snow we needed at sea level."

The price tag soon rose to $9.3 million—at that point, the breakdown was $3.3 million from Columbia's U.K. division, $3 million from Selkirk Film holdings, $1.2 million from Toronto Dominion bank and $1.2 million from the Bank of Montreal.[15] The Canadian Film Development Corporation had put up $100,000 in seed money—paid back when Snell secured other investors—in return for 0.5 percent of the gross receipts.[16] But the budget soon rose to $12 million with an increased contribution of $5 million from Columbia.[17] Snell was in pole MacLean position and already setting out his planned production schedule as by 1979 he had scooped up the rights to all remaining MacLean novels. Next up on the schedule was *Goodbye California*, to be followed by *The Way to Dusty Death*, *Dark Crusader/Black Shrike*, *Night Without End* and *Athabasca*.[18]

For the casting, Snell was "anxious to get as many movie names for *Bear Island* as I could. But for *Dusty Death* I plan to use unknown Canadian actors."[19] He attracted a stellar cast, one of the biggest collections of marquee names to grace a MacLean production. He was clearly able to call on past association in recruiting fellow Canadian Donald Sutherland (*Don't Look Now*) and Christopher Lee. Richard Widmark was already familiar with the MacLean world through *The Secret Ways*, as was Barbara Parkins via *Puppet on a Chain*. Lloyd Bridges was a Hollywood veteran and Bruce Greenwood and Patricia Collins the rising stars. Sutherland was the big catch, a genuine star with a cult following after *The Dirty Dozen* (1967) and *M*A*S*H* (1970), entering the Hollywood mainstream as an unlikely matinee idol with *Klute* (1971). He was appreciated by the arthouse cognoscenti after appearing in Bernardo Bertolucci's *1900* (1976) and Fellini's *Casanova* (1976). Sutherland was quite versatile at a time when stars were increasingly sticking to the tried and tested; the actor flitted easily between a variety of genres: comedy (*Start the Revolution Without Me*, 1971, and *S*P*Y*S*, 1974), thriller (*Lady Ice*, 1973, and *The Great Train Robbery*, 1978), war (*The Eagle Has Landed*, 1976) and even sci-fi (*Invasion of the Body Snatchers*, 1978). His easygoing screen persona had widespread appeal and those devilish eyebrows worked wonders with the female audience.

An Oscar winner for *Julia* (1977), portrayer of the eponymous role in *Agatha* (1978), Vanessa Redgrave got her career back on track after a mid–1970s lull when she appeared out of favor. She was well-known for an earlier string of critical and commercial hits such as *Blow-Up* (1966), *Camelot* (1967) and *Mary, Queen of Scots* (1971).[20] A top star in the 1950s and '60s, Richard Widmark's last top-billed role was *To the Devil a Daughter* (1976)—which also featured Christopher Lee—but mostly now he was an all-purpose addition to all-star casts: *The Domino Principle* (1977), *Rollercoaster* (1978) and *The Swarm* (1978). Christopher Lee had already had a bad experience with MacLean, fired from *Golden Rendezvous*. While best known for his horror portfolio, he was appreciated by the mainstream for character parts in *Airport '77* (1977), *Caravans* (1978) and *Arabian Adventure* (1979). Though more recently active in television, Barbara Parkins retained a certain marquee appeal after holding her own against Lee Marvin and Roger Moore in *Shout at the Devil* (1976); audiences remembered her from *Valley of the Dolls* (1967) and *Puppet on a Chain*. Lloyd Bridges' movie career dated back to the 1940s and he had only just been seen on the big screen in a pivotal role in *The Fifth Musketeer* (1979).

Certainly, this was a more impressive ensemble than was seen in *Golden Rendezvous*.

The MacLean connection obviously came in handy in selecting Tasmanian director Don Sharp, who had helmed the political thriller *Hennessey* (1975) for Snell. In the adventure vein, he had recently completed the remake of *The Thirty-Nine Steps* (1978). Said Snell, "[MacLean's] books work in foreign areas no matter where they're set but to work in in the U.S. you need an American character."[21] (Widmark was American but Sutherland was Canadian.) Sharp said,

> We've chosen names because if it's a reasonably large budget, you need names to support it. The overriding factor was realism ... you can believe in Dick Widmark in a place like this. And you can believe in Donald. And you can believe in Vanessa—boy, you can believe in Vanessa—in a place like this.[22]

Like André Pieterse and Elliott Kastner before him, Snell made a point of not acquiring a global distributor at the outset. "I've been there before," he explained.

Chapter Fourteen. Bear Island (1979)

"With major studios having the world rights you don't win. And with inflationary dollars as television and cable rights you could get far more in the end if you don't make a deal."[23] Though presumably Columbia would have some territories in return for its investment, Snell targeted a Christmas 1979 release.[24] As was now becoming the norm, MacLean movies represented an opportunity for an independent distributor to make a big splash and this was taken up for the U.S. by Taft Industries,[25] with United Artists picking up the Canadian rights.[26]

A key location was at the foot of the Granduc mine at the Leduc glacier.[27] Snell wanted to use a Canadian ship but they were all in dry dock and demanding $20,000 a day compared to a Russian operator happy to settle for $6000.[28] The vessel carried 101 staff including 66 women. While the vessel's crew had to toe the party line, with a political officer on board to ensure they did so, they were also happy to sell a bottle of cognac for $8, caviar at $10 a tin and fur hats at $40.[29] On board was a complement of 103 actors, but nobody was allowed to leave the ship due to the uncertain weather. The vessel carried 50 tons of water. An acupuncturist treated director of photography Alan Hulme after he lost feeling in his hands. Shooting began in Vancouver on November 20, 1978, with location work in Alaska—Norway had originally been considered but proved too expensive—and other studio work in England.

Work began with seven weeks location work in the Stewart area, but the production was hit by a snowstorm and icy conditions 58 degrees below zero. The actual maritime location of the ship was vital: If they went too far north, they would be limited to two or three hours of daylight in wintry conditions, but the chosen seagoing location ensured at least four or five hours. Glacier Bay was a protected wilderness, so they had to be careful not to damage the environment. Using the Bay required the posting of a $200,000 bond and there was an outcry over the proposed use of a mechanized vehicle. So only a few vehicles could be employed to ferry the crew and actors from the set of a few huts close to the shore; to allay environmental fears, the hydrocopters used in the film were employed.[30] Despite these precautions, Sharp and crew, hit by a whiteout, were stranded on the glacier for four days[31] while carrying out preliminary lensing and trying out the hydrocopter on the glacier. The hydrocopter wouldn't start and they were trapped.[32] Snell described the hydrocopter chase as "our version of the road chase through the streets of San Francisco in *Bullitt*." A helicopter pilot died transporting equipment. Christopher Lee said, "Two helicopters carried the Canadian crew and equipment. On a terrible day, the weary pilot of the second helicopter, returning, failed to notice the first already squatting on the pad and landed on top. The ghastly experience affected the whole team." Lee suggested that the accident was the reason "the ingredients failed to come together."[33]

In January, the production shifted to a Russian liner for a month (one week more than originally planned) and then over to Pinewood for a month of interiors. Filming wrapped two weeks behind schedule.[34] "Everything has to be as realistic as possible," explained Sharp, "So in the avalanche sequence there's no beautiful skiing to get away from it. They are simply trying to stay on their feet to save their lives. If they fell ... I didn't cut it. I told them to get up and keep going."[35] Vanessa Redgrave recalled, "It was very difficult work. Although the location work always seemed to carry problems, I think what you gain is absolutely invaluable. Any actor … prefers it … it's an extremely exciting project."[36]

Proof of MacLean's marquee name came in a survey in which 25 percent of respondents said that the author was the chief reason for seeing the film, compared to only nine percent who deemed Donald Sutherland the main attraction.[37] Possibly to cement the relationship with Snell, the media-shy author agreed to do a book tour to promote the film.[38] "I don't suppose there are many homes in the English-speaking world that don't have a MacLean paperback somewhere," said Snell.[39] But just as *Golden Rendezvous* came at the end of a cycle the book could fairly make a claim to have started, so did *Bear Island*. It was the first Nazi-themed bestseller of the 1970s. But, although appearing in 1971, it was beaten into the cinema by *The Odessa File* (film 1974, book 1972), *Marathon Man* (film 1976, book 1974), *The Boys from Brazil* (film 1978, book 1976) and *Brass Target* (1978, book 1974).

The Film

It was sabotage from the outset. Where director Don Sharp had added a thrilling boat chase through the canals of Amsterdam in *Puppet on a Chain*, here he begins with malevolence in the extreme. After treating us to fabulous views of the hostile Arctic, with pillars of ice stretching into the sky, Sharp gets immediately down to business. A skier, racing down a glacier, sends a garbled message to the passenger ship *Morning Rose* before he is mowed down by a speeding snowmobile. There's hardly time for the audience to settle into the narrative—rather virtue-signaling for a MacLean venture, sees a multi-national team of scientists combating climate change (a more contemporary note now than it was then)—before the arrival by helicopter of German-born Frank Lansing (Donald Sutherland) nearly ends in disaster, the newcomer rescued from the sea by Smithy (Lloyd Bridges). In the meantime, various hostilities and old relationships are sketched out. Team leader German Otto Gerran (Richard Widmark) reads the riot act to squabbling American Judith Rubin (Barbara Parkins) and Pole Lechinski (Christopher Lee). Rubin is keen to re-start a romantic liaison with Lansing, who has eyes for Swedish psychiatrist Heddi Lindquist (Vanessa Redgrave). A skyline populated by crosses marking the graves of U-boat crews who died here during the Second World War adds a menacing note and it turns out that Lansing's father, a submarine commander on the German side, was one of the casualties. Tension is further raised when his belongings are searched. Gerran needs to know whether Lansing speaks German, as if he might overhear something untoward. But the first order of business is to try to find the missing scientist. When Lansing and Rubin set out to help, she is killed in an avalanche triggered by persons unknown. Lindquist reveals that the missing man worked for the Norwegian government, as does she. For no apparent reason, Lansing dons a frogman's outfit and swims underwater and finds the U-boat cave. The docked submarine is the U351, his father's command. Inside he finds his father's skeleton chained to the ceiling. The snowmobile transporting Lansing and Smithy explodes, but they avoid injury. After discovering a hidden message, Lindquist begins

Chapter Fourteen. Bear Island (1979)

her own enquiries, and in alliance with Lansing discovers that Jungbeck (Nicholas Cortland) and Heyter (Michael J. Reynolds) are pure Aryan, born on a Nazi "baby farm." The message makes reference to "Zelda," clearly the mysterious criminal chief. Lansing finds an easier way into the U-boat pen, descending from a hole in the roof rather than underwater. With Lindquist, he discovers that boxes of explosive contain gold ingots, the fabled Nazi gold. It turns out that's what Gerran is also seeking. Though cleared of accusations of being a war criminal, as an act of contrition, Gerran wants to return the gold to Norway. Catastrophe strikes again, the radio mast collapsing after sabotage and badly injuring Lechinski, who also mutters about "Zelda." An explosion starts a fire and Lansing and Lindquist determine to seek help. The saboteurs—Jungbeck and Heyter—pursue them in snowmobiles. Managing to defeat the enemy, Lansing heads for the open water where Smithy and Hartman are escaping with the gold. As the snowmobile is amphibious, Lansing chases the boat across the water. Both thieves die in a shootout.

Bear Island is pretty much an all-action film, chases and fights interrupted by explosions, fire and avalanche. The Nazi gold narrative just about holds the picture together. But there are several plot holes and we are told twice that Lansing's father was a German U-boat commander. You have to wonder how the saboteur knew Lansing and Lindquist would divert from their agreed route to put them in harm's way and whether the saboteur had planted the explosive device in the ice and just planned to hang around in the hope of disposing of these two. Given that the saboteur was skillful enough to hit the explosive device from some distance with a high-powered rifle, you would have thought it easier just to shoot the pair of them and dispose of the bodies.

Also, Lansing's arrival is never satisfactorily explained.

Bear Island star Vanessa Redgrave had a secondary reason for signing up for a movie that played out in the Arctic: She was in discussions to shoot a movie about a woman in an Arctic (Russian) prison camp, so she took the opportunity to Hoover up any information that might be useful, studying maps and talking to experts. The prison camp movie was never made (Hannan collection).

And the screenwriters are very slack in setting fire to the cabins. In the book, MacLean very specifically explained that huts were always set some distance apart from each other for the purpose of limiting damage should one catch fire. I'm not sure I went for the contrition notion either. Nobody treats Gerran as if he's a leper and this part of his past only pops up at a convenient moment. More importantly, where the speedboats added thrills within the narrow confines of the Amsterdam canals in *Puppet on a Chain*, the wide-open spaces of the Arctic hinder rather than enhance the tension. One snow slope is very much like another, and skiers might just as well be in Klosters as racing along Bear Island. The constant fallback on action destroys the mystery. Not interested in the various deaths, Lansing is more focused on the U-boat pen. Quite how he knew where to go is never explained.

Book into Film

MacLean had written an exquisite mystery, one of which Agatha Christie would be proud, in which the Nazi gold element was almost incidental. Don Sharp and the screenwriters David Butler and Murray Smith (*Die Screaming Marianne*, 1971) pivoted the tale on the Nazi treasure, discarding most of the book in the process, and ignoring one of the most fiendish murder plots imaginable. The whole Arctic scientist ecology notion had no place in the original book. You can imagine that since MacLean had already gone down the Arctic scientist route in *Ice Station Zebra* and *Night Without End* that he was determined not to repeat himself. The idea of focusing on a movie crew could be interpreted as MacLean's revenge, having felt duped by too many producers' promises. Equally, if you made movies for a living, as Sharp and Peter Snell did, and were aware how drab that reality was and didn't want to emulate the sensationalism of *The Carpetbaggers* (1964) or *Valley of the Dolls* (1967), you could see why it was more appealing to ignore that background altogether. And you can also imagine that the filmmakers wanted to get away from the claustrophobia of the seagoing vessel—*Ice Station Zebra* and *Golden Rendezvous*—in favor of wide-open spaces filled with equal menace. I'm presuming that MacLean, hoping this would spur a whole series of movies based on his books, went along with the Sharp-Snell notion.

I wish MacLean had stuck to his guns. The book is the nautical equivalent of *Murder on the Orient Express*, far better than its cowboy equivalent *Breakheart Pass* or the previous nautical outing *Golden Rendezvous*, with both forensic investigation way ahead of its time and an examination of the serial killer mentality, which except for factual cases like *In Cold Blood* (1967) and *The Boston Strangler* (1968) was not yet the trope it would become.

There is a smidgeon of science, but the idea that the film crew is headed for Bear Island in an ornithological-geophysical capacity is merely a ruse to gain access to a restricted area. Bear Island itself is more of a metaphorical location, in World War II known as "The Gate." Passing through it, "boys grew up" overnight and middle-aged men "grew old." It was "the graveyard of the Arctic" (a theme which the film visually expresses with the row of crosses on the cliffs) and "If you passed through the Gate and came back again, you were a lucky man." Dr. Marlowe is the ship's surgeon on the former trawler *Morning Rose*, transporting a film crew to the remote island. There is an Otto Gerran in the book—and a Smithy, and a Judith and Heyter and Jungbeck—but there's nothing scientific about any of them. While Smithy retains the same job description (ship's mate), Gerran is a Viennese film producer, reputed to have been a Russian spy during the war, Judith an aging actress and the other two mostly in the background. Three people are killed and four seriously ill from food poisoning, and in his best Poirot manner Marlowe determines that this is the deliberate result of sprinkling food with the root of aconite (wolf's bane), frequently mistaken for horseradish. Marlowe avoids succumbing to poisoned whisky but the death toll mounts when someone else drinks it. Naturally, Marlowe is attacked and he grows suspicious that the unexpected overture from one of the actresses is a ploy to keep him off the scent.

Of course, Marlowe is more than a doctor, he's a British Treasury agent, on the trail of Nazi treasure, and has identified Heissman, a partner in the production company, as the worldwide criminal authority on that subject. Smithy is also an undercover agent. But out of 22 actors, production team and crew, by the time they land on Bear Island, Marlowe has only eliminated 13 people from his enquiries. More digging reveals that several members are linked to a tragic incident two decades before. There are red herrings a-plenty and, as ever, the reader is pulled in by the authoritativeness of the background, whether it be history, geography, the special predisposition of the Arctic storm or the insights into the movie business and its financial chicanery.

On land, the deaths continue, and a lethal dose of morphine is stolen from Marlowe's medical supplies. You won't be surprised to learn there's nothing so obvious as a U-boat pen nor that Nazi gold is not actually the most valuable item on the island. Securities, worth three or four times the price of gold, are what is being sought. The final scenes of Marlowe delivering his thesis and explaining how and, more importantly, why the killings took place, is a masterpiece of detection. Since Agatha Christie was already anointed the Queen of Crime, it seemed rather greedy for the King of the Thrillers to try to steal her crown as well. But that's exactly what MacLean did. A mystery with an all-star cast might well have appealed more, especially in the wake of *Murder on the Orient Express* (1974) and *Death on the Nile* (1978). I can certainly see the attraction of spinning an entirely different tale out of the original material and I can understand a producer and director believing that they had a better idea of what would attract an audience than a mere writer. But it still seems to me that another mistake has been made.

Chapter Fifteen

The Last Movie Hurrah

The Hostage Tower *(1980)* and
River of Death *(1989)*

The Hostage Tower

It should have come as no surprise that MacLean—a novelist ahead of his time when it came to translating his books into other media—eventually alighted on television. The initial nudge came from Peter Snell, who introduced him to TV impresario Jerry Leider, now switching to movies and prepping *The Jazz Singer* (1979). Excited by the challenge, MacLean produced an 87-page teleplay called *Air Force One Is Down*. Leider sent colleague Burt Nodella to meet him.[1] Previously a TV writer and agent for stars Lee Marvin and Charles Bronson, and a double Emmy-winning producer for *Get Smart* (1967–1969), he had joined Leider in 1978, producing the small-screen movies *And I Alone Survived* (1978) and *Willa* (1979). Nodella spent two weeks with MacLean in Cannes and another in Geneva. "We just talked and talked about story ideas," he recalled. "The great thing about MacLean is, he knows about the specialist tools of the espionage trade and however extravagant his tales may seem, there is always a real element of plausibility in them."[2]

MacLean invented UNACO (United Nations Anti-Crime Organisation), a team of dedicated experts called in to deal with international situations, and proposed eight outlines.[3] CBS, which had embarked on an $80 million TV movie spree,[4] was sold on the idea but opted to debut with *The Hostage Tower* rather than *Air Force One Is Down* and ponied up half the $4.2 million budget.

The resulting movies premiered on TV in the U.S. and sold for cinema screening in the rest of the world. MacLean received $25,000 for each script and a further $25,000 if the movies were shown theatrically. And, as usual, he retained the publishing rights.[5]

The story was primarily set at the Eiffel Tower and the producers pulled off something of a coup in persuading the landmark's operators to permit access (admittedly, during the off-season). *Willa* director Claudio Guzmán was set to make his sophomore picture (after *Linda Lovelace for President*, 1975) from a screenplay by old MacLean hand Robert Carrington (*Fear Is the Key*). One of the casting tactics appeared to be wooing back to the big screen stars who had been missing for several years. Among those touted for leading roles were Italian star Gina Lollobrigida (*Come September*, 1963),[6] off-screen for seven years, Constance Cummings (*Blithe Spirit*, 1945),[7] off-screen for 17, and Elsa Lanchester (*Bride of Frankenstein*, 1935), first movie in four years.[8] Douglas Fairbanks, Jr. (*The Prisoner of Zenda*, 1937) and Celia Johnson (*Brief Encounter*, 1945) took the comeback publicity plaudits, the former out of Hollywood employment for nearly a quarter of a century, the latter for over a decade. Jennifer O'Neill,[9] although in more regular demand, had dropped down the marquee rankings since her career highpoints *Rio Lobo* (1970) and *Summer of '42* (1971). Peter Fonda, his name above the title, had seen his career sag since the success of *Easy Rider* (1969); *Dirty Mary, Crazy Larry* (1974); and *Futureworld* (1976). More recently, he had turned to direction but *Wanda Nevada* (1979) with Brooke Shields was a flop. Billy Dee Wil-

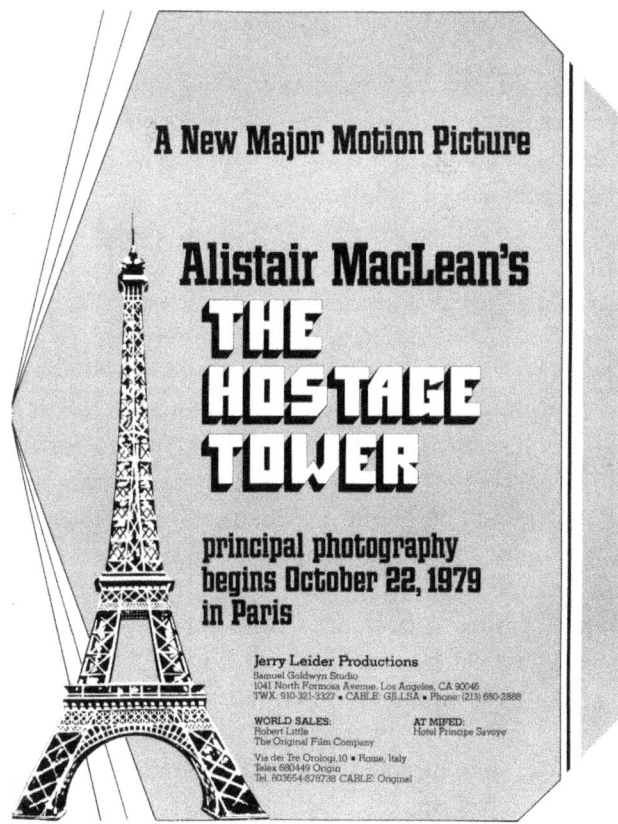

"Paris hadn't changed much since [Warren] Oates and I rolled through in '71," recalled Peter Fonda, star of *The Hostage Tower*, in his memoir. "I worked all over the Eiffel Tower; I even had to jump in the Seine River" (advertisement, *Screen International*, October 20, 1979).

liams had worked in TV for the previous three years after relative success in the movies *The Take* (1974) and *Mahogany* (1976). Maud Adams' most recent role was top billing in David Hamilton's dubious *Laura* (1979), a step-up perhaps after a string of TV parts but a comedown from the big-budget *Rollerball* (1975) and the second female lead in *The Man with the Golden Gun* (1974).[10]

After *2001: A Space Odyssey* (1968), Keir Dullea was in regular employment. In movies he was generally the second-billed male lead in low-budget fare (*Black Christmas*, 1973, *Leopard in the Snow*, 1978). This was his fourth successive TV movie. Britt Ekland was still best known to contemporary audiences for *The Man with the Golden Gun* and, although she had made a splash as the top-billed star of *Slavers* (1977),[11] she was either in TV or played supporting roles in movies. None of the 11 French actors were marquee names.[12] In a more practical vein, Europe's top stuntman Remy Julienne was hired.[13]

The six-week Eiffel Tower shoot began on October 22, 1979.[14] Weather-wise, it proved to be "consistently cold, wet and windy."[15] Another hiccup was a lawsuit by

French screenwriter Jean Max Brand, suing for $122,000, claiming the plot was similar to a 200-page screenplay—originally an un-filmable 428-page tome—called *Eiffel Encounter* which he said had been shopped around various studios. His argument was refuted by producer Nodella, who explained, "I was with Alistair MacLean in Canada two years ago when he came up with a whole series of story ideas including this one which CBS chose."[16]

Other scenes were shot on the River Seine and at the Pompidou Center and Chateau de Neville, home to notorious serial killer Landru ("the Bluebeard of Gambais"). In the U.S., the Goldwyn Studios were utilized.

"The Tower was an extraordinary set," enthused Nodella, "like being in a strange airship invented by H.G. Wells and landed somewhere in 2001."[17] There were high hopes for the cinematic release. Robert Little of Original Films, previously sales chief for the Italian outfit Titanus, drummed up considerable expectation, mostly based on the MacLean name, selling the picture, on the strength of the script and before filming had commenced, into Norway, Sweden,[18] Denmark[19] and Finland.[20] Further testament to MacLean's marquee name on the international stage came from Swedish distributor Bourne, which acquired rights to Scandinavia, Spain and Holland. Commented Peter B. Trymen, "MacLean is very big in Scandinavia as he is throughout Europe."[21] CBS snapped up the TV rights in February 1980[22] and an advert announcing the 9 p.m. screening of *The Hostage Tower* on CBS on May 13, 1980, also carried a plug for the "in preparation" *Air Force One Is Down*, to be directed by Claudio Guzmán, with a Leigh Vance screenplay.[23] *The Hostage Tower* was released theatrically in Europe by Columbia-EMI-Warner in 23 territories including the United Kingdom[24] plus South Africa[25] in 1980 and via Filmways in Australia,[26] Shaw Bros. in Hong Kong[27] and Singapore[28] and Tony Blanco in Venezuela.[29]

High Flying Action—The Movie

The movie opens with an aerial shot of the titular tower. The camera pans over Paris to a chateau where master criminal Smith (Keir Dullea) frolics in a hot tub with mistress Leah (Britt Ekland). Three short sequences set up his confederates. Cat burglar Clarence Whitlock (Billy Dee Williams)—a.k.a. C.W.—breaks into a museum in a skyscraper. Sabrina Carver (Maud Adams), dressed entirely in black, breaks out of a high-security diamond vault in Amsterdam and speeds off on roller skates with her haul, easily evading police. In Germany, ex–C.I.A. weapons expert Mike Graham (Peter Fonda), masquerading as a high-ranking U.S. Army officer, makes off in a helicopter with a cache of top-secret laser weaponry.

All undergo rigorous training which includes firing the lasers. At UNACO headquarters, operations chief Malcolm Philpott (Douglas Fairbanks, Jr.) and secretary Sonya (Rachel Roberts) are called in when Smith's team invades the Eiffel Tower and takes as hostage Mrs. Wheeler (Celia Johnson), mother of the U.S. president. They demand a $30 million ransom. Much of the initial action takes place on the high girders of the tower, as Smith's team sets up their defense perimeter and plants bombs.

Tension arises from two different strands. How on Earth, in broad daylight, and in the full glare of the world's media, does Smith hope to get away with his loot? And how soon will he realize that his team has been penetrated by UNACO agents C.W. and Carver? Use of the lasers is certainly original, as is how his team will avoid being harmed in the crossfire. It does appear that Smith is outnumbered, but he's not the world's best master criminal for nothing and his getaway plan is superb. While the locale and the stuntmen take center stage, C.W. has most to do up top, in rescuing Mrs. Wheeler and carrying her, over his shoulder, to safety. This is quite a refreshing take on the cops-and-robbers scenario or even James Bond with the secret agents not in the infallible 007 bracket when it comes to physicality or sexuality, although Carver, scarcely a simpering Bond girl,[30] is more likely to exert her superiority over adoring men. Graham tangles with Smith at the climax, coming off second best in a tussle on a helicopter ladder dangling above the Seine. But there's a sting in the tail. When Smith climbs the ladder to what he imagines is safety, he finds Philpott and Sonya in command of the helicopter.

By and large, *The Hostage Tower* is well done. The gentle romantic banter between Philpott and Sonya does not make up for lack of expected sizzle between Graham and Carver.

As with the best MacLean pictures, the movie fairly twists and turns. Tension escalates not just from the dizzying heights scaled by the performers, but by four separate narrative threads. Firstly, there is the possibility of Smith discovering that his operation has been infiltrated by UNACO. Then there's the problem of rescuing Mrs. Wheeler. Carver is tasked with defusing the bombs, on a ticking countdown, helped in the latter stages by C.W. It is left to Graham to prevent Smith from escaping with the money. There is also the side issue of whether Graham recognizes Carver, who has attended one of his C.I.A. courses, and where, exactly, Graham fits into the schematic. Why he has joined up is only revealed at the end: He's seeking revenge for the death of his wife.

Throughout, *Hostage Tower* is marked with MacLean notes. The kidnappers avoid being killed by the lasers by wearing a computer-coded safety tag. But that tag can be used to deflect light to send coded messages to UNACO while ripping said tag off an adversary will result in his death. From an incident involving a small explosion, C.W. realizes how Smith will make his escape. Likely narrative necessity demands Smith kill Leah for otherwise Graham would be unable to steal her wetsuit and oxygen mask and pursue Smith through the tower's water mains. The movie does set up the tantalizing notion that those attracted to the business of the super-spy are unlikely to be angels, although it's not explained what hold Philpott has over operatives who appear to indulge in criminality.

It's interesting that MacLean opted for a team, as with *The Guns of Navarone* and *Where Eagles Dare*, rather than the lone operative of *When Eight Bells Toll* and *Fear Is the Key*. As Bruce Willis later proved in *Die Hard* (1988), an individual foiling thieves in a tower is a lot more exciting than dividing up the various jobs between three people. One of the film's failings is that most of the characters are underwritten, the exceptions being Carver and Smith. But, given the short running time, barely 100 minutes, roughly 50 minutes shy of *The Guns of Navarone* and *Where Eagles Dare*, it's a sufficiently thrilling enough ride.

Source Material—The Book

MacLean didn't write the book which was, in effect, a novelization of the script. John Denis, assigned the task, presumably also had access to the MacLean outline, and I do not know how much, beyond dialogue, Carrington added to the source material. Generally speaking, judging from the novel, the movie narrative sticks relatively close to the original MacLean storyline. The book expands on character history and weaponry detail, but the film occasionally jettisons characters and scenes. The book, for example, has a middleman, Lorenz van Beck, who works both sides, acting as recruitment agent for Smith while at the same time passing on information to Philpott. Readers interested to know how Carver came to be inside the airless vault find answers in the book. Unusually for an MacLean novel, there is a sex scene between Smith and Leah. Who added that is an interesting question.

River of Death (1989)

The genesis of this novel took place much earlier than previously supposed, and it may have originated as a screenplay. In the early 1970s, studio executive Gerry Blattner (*The Sundowners*, 1960), looking to achieve independence through MacLean, was joint owner with Erwin Hillier of a property known as *The Lost City*. Blattner in 1973 sought Gregory Peck for the lead. Peck conceded that it was a "potential blockbuster" but complained that it "seems something of a ponderous venture" in "another of

From the October 25, 1986, *Screen International*, an early advert for *River of Death*. Christopher Walken (pictured) was slated to star, but when production stalled, he left the project in favor of the starring role in *Witness in a War Zone* (1987).

Chapter Fifteen. The Last Movie Hurrah

those hellish locations." Eventually rejecting the project, he advised, "You have a very fine story which needs the attention of a first-rate screenwriter."[31] Hillier remained involved until the end of the decade, when he had a spat with Peter Snell over the work, now entitled *El Dorado* and described as a kind of *Treasure of the Sierra Madre* set in Brazil. As part of his multi-picture pact with MacLean, Snell claimed ownership[32] but that was disputed by Hillier.[33] When the movie finally appeared a decade later, Hillier was credited as associate producer.

Alistair MacLean's sudden heart attack death in 1987, aged just 64, put a temporary end to the movie boom. At that point, virtually all his unfilmed works had been optioned for the movies, some with significant budgets, and in the hands of major players (see Chapter Eighteen). These days, the death of a bestselling author proves only a minor hindrance to the publishing business, and we are accustomed to seeing books being marketed under the names of Wilbur Smith and Victoria Andrews long after their demise. While Collins continued to publish MacLean books written by John Denis and Alistair MacNeill, it encountered public resistance to what was seen as passing-off—it even lost a court case—and so the name of Alistair MacLean lost much of its luster. Movie output, already crimped after *Bear Island*, petered out. In large part, his name continued to be used for television vehicles (see Chapter Sixteen).

The final theatrical movie made from his books should have appeared shortly before his death. Another mini-major, Cannon, added MacLean's *River of Death* to its considerable slate of projects. Cannon was originally set up by Americans Dennis Friedland and Christopher C. Dewey in 1967 to import Swedish soft porn pictures such as *Inga*, augmenting their output with a surprise mainstream hit (director John G. Avildsen's *Joe*, 1970), horror pictures including *I, Monster* (1971) and kung fu movies. But *The Happy Hooker* (1975) could not save the company from financial disintegration and in 1979 they sold out to Israeli duo Menahem Golan and Yoram Golus, whose films, notably the teen drama *Lemon Popsicle* (1978), it had distributed in the U.S. An association with Charles Bronson, beginning with *Death Wish II* (1982), provided Golan-Globus with a solid footing in the U.S. and soon they were churning out movies in a variety of genres. Occasionally these featured a marquee name: Sylvester Stallone (*Cobra*, 1986), Brooke Shields (*Sahara*, 1983), Roger Moore (*The Naked Face*, 1984), Donald Sutherland (*Ordeal by Innocence*, 1984), Bo Derek (*Bolero*, 1984), Katharine Hepburn (*Grace Quigley*, 1985), Kim Basinger (*Fool for Love*, 1985) and Robert Mitchum (*The Ambassador*, 1984). They also employed name directors such as J. Lee Thompson, Robert Altman, Roman Polanski, Michael Winner, John Frankenheimer and Andrew V. McLaglen. Though most of its output was in the lower budget bracket, some connected sufficiently with audiences—*Revenge of the Ninja* (1983), *Missing in Action* (1984) and *Breakin'* (1984)—to generate sequels. By the time *River of Death* appeared, an ill-fated production of *Superman IV—The Quest for Peace* (1987), coupled with poor box office for other films and investigation by U.S. authorities for financial irregularities, led to Cannon's sale to Pathé Communications.

In 1985, J. Lee Thompson (*The Guns of Navarone*) was first choice to direct *River of Death*.[34] He dropped out, and a year later Peter Medak (*The Changeling*, 1980) was assigned to the Christopher Walken-starring film[35] from a screenplay by Stanley Mann.[36] Then *that* fell through. It was revived two years later: Director Steve Carver (*Lone Wolf McQuade*, 1983), handed a $3 million budget[37] (Carver disputed that there was any proper budget[38]), helmed the movie with Michael Dudikoff (*American Ninja*, 1985). There was strong support from veterans Donald Pleasence (*The Great Escape*, 1963), Robert Vaughn (*The Magnificent Seven*, 1960) and Herbert Lom (*The Pink Panther Strikes Again*, 1976).

Due to its South American setting, Carver initially sought to use production facilities in Sao Paulo, Brazil, with location work in the Amazon. But the prospect of American moviemakers setting off explosions in the rain forest didn't sit well with Brazilian authorities and the difficulty of receiving permits caused the movie to shut down. Six weeks later, Carver was dispatched to the tiny town of Port St. Johns in South Africa, where *Shout at the Devil* (1976) had been filmed. Port St. Johns was a four-hour drive along dirt roads from Durban and on the edge of the Indian Ocean.[39] Filming began there in August 1988.[40]

The production was fraught with difficulties. Due to apartheid, Carver was officially barred by the Directors Guild of America from participating; as a result, he incurred a $5000 fine.[41] He was not impressed with the existing screenplay. "The screenplay had been written overnight, it seemed," said Carver. Unlike, for example, *The Guns of Navarone*, it did not "really have a beginning, middle and end." In part, the problem lay with the source material, the MacLean novel, in which it was difficult to know who were the good guys and who were the bad guys. Deciding to "make something more current with the times," Carver and screenwriter Andrew Deutsch updated the story to include an AIDS-like contagious disease and brought in a character similar to Nazi Josef Mengele, with whom the audience would be familiar.[42]

Fittingly, the production company employed "the one man cannon"[43] a.k.a. Harry Alan Towers, a prolific producer of both low-budget productions of the horror (*Brides of Fu Manchu*, 1966) and exploitation variety (*99 Women*, 1969) and better-funded but not quite top-end all-star movies. Having fallen foul of U.S. authorities, Towers was a perennial peripatetic, one of his regular ports of call being South Africa. His relationship with Golan-Globus went back years. Regarding *River of Death*, he recalled, "I spent a considerable amount of time during this production commuting between the bank in Rotterdam and Cannon in Los Angeles to ensure the money kept flowing down the river to Port Saint John."[44]

Importing gunpowder to South Africa was forbidden, so the special effects team relied on nitroglycerin, which was very volatile, and shooting live rounds. The explosives were so unpredictable that at one point when they failed to go off, someone had to swim out to the boat and fix them. Shooting in a genuine jungle made things look great onscreen, but that environment was unforgiving. "Everything that crawled was poisonous, everything was contaminated," said Steve Carver. Star Dudikoff fell ill simply by touching his face with his hands, which were somehow contaminated. His illness meant restructuring a shoot that was already under budgetary pressure. Two weeks were lopped off the schedule. Veterans Vaughn, Pleasence and Lom understood the pressure the director was under and helped out, at times lugging heavy camera cases

Chapter Fifteen. The Last Movie Hurrah

River of Death star Michael Dudikoff did double duty in South Africa where the film was shot: Under contract to Cannon, he was ordered to stay on and make *Platoon Leader* (1988). Given that movie was set in Vietnam, it was an unusual choice of location (advertisement, *Screen International*, October 19, 1985).

two miles uphill into the jungle to reach the next location. At one point, for lack of sufficient German uniforms, it looked like Carver would have to excessively trim the opening sequence, but in the basement of a local hotel they found an abundance of Nazi flags and uniforms.

Carver managed to get hold of one of the two remaining canvas planes in the world for the scene in which Robert Vaughn's character makes his escape. It was pure luck that during the filming of that scene, it happened to be raining. Lack of cash inspired the director to dream up visually interesting scenes.[45]

River of Death on Screen

Nazi gold, Nazi hunters, a fabled lost city, cannibals, the search for a cure for a rare disease and biological warfare are tossed together in a plot that fuses action and derring-do with duplicity a-plenty. It kicks off with betrayal. At the end of the Second World War, Dr. Manteufel (Robert Vaughn), a Mengele disciple carrying out human experiments on concentration camp inmates, and high-ranking German officer Col. Spaatz (Donald Pleasence), with a horde of stolen treasure, plan their escape as the Allies close in. Manteufel shoots his colleague and flies away in a plane. Cut to 1965 and adventurer Hamilton (Michael Dudikoff) leads Dr. Blakesley (Victor Melleny) and his daughter Anna (Sarah Maur Ward) through the Amazon jungle. The doctor is seeking a cure for a plague that afflicts only natives. Captured by tribesmen, Hamilton finds a way out of their rudimentary prison, but after he makes it to Romano, a small town, the doctor is shot and his daughter re-captured.

Using a map to the lost city as lure, Hamilton assembles a crew of interested parties, recruiting mercenary Hiller (L.Q. Jones), millionaire Smith (Spaatz in disguise) and blonde girlfriend Maria (Cynthia Erland), Nazi hunters Dalia (Foziah Davidson) and Pare (Rufus Stewart), newspaperman Fanjul (Gordon Mulholland), security chief Tracy (Norman Anstey) and tribal expert Serrano (Alain Woolf). They are pursued by Diaz (Herbert Lom), a corrupt police chief. Marooned after their helicopter engine fails, they are attacked by river pirates but, thanks to Dalia's skill with explosives, they blow up the pirate HQ and steal their boat. Smith spins Hamilton a tale about being a Jew and seeing his son killed in Dachau and wife murdered by Manteufel, whom he believes is hiding out in the lost city. Under another native assault, the boat is blown up. By now, fed information by Pare, Hamilton doubts Smith's story. Their destination is inhabited by cannibals. "We may be all right," says Serrano, with no trace of irony. "Traditionally, they only eat their enemies." Col. Diaz arrives in the nick of time and in the firefight, Dalia and Pare are killed. To everyone's surprise, Diaz knows the way to the lost city, leading them to Manteufel's lab replete with swastika. Hamilton is reunited with Anna, who has succumbed to the mysterious illness. Assisted by a witch doctor, Hamilton escapes. Smith reveals himself as Manteufel's former colleague but before he can exact retribution, Maria takes over: She seeks vengeance for the death of her father, a German soldier. Hamilton is the only one to get out alive.

River of Death is kept moving by sporadic action without sufficient mystery to sustain the required tension. It's a poor last hurrah for the MacLean movie cycle. Too many characters harbor secret ambitions and most of the characters are underwritten. Hamilton is attracted to both Anna—a tryst interrupted by her father—and Maria, but opportunity for genuine romance goes begging. While Hamilton is kept in the dark about Smith's real identity, the audience isn't, so there's no mystery. Only Diaz is a surprise when revealed as an ex-Nazi. Budget cuts outlined above contribute to a limp ending. While Michael Dudikoff is not in the Charles Bronson-Richard Widmark-Richard Harris tough guy league, his growling voiceover is reminiscent of Martin Sheen's in *Apocalypse Now* (1979), as are shots of the mist-laden river and eruptions of action from the shore. The veteran triumvirate of Pleasence, Vaughn and Lom provide a touch of class the movie hardly deserves.

River of Death would have passed muster as a direct-to-video actioner, but as a theatrical venture it lacks the Alistair MacLean imprimatur.

Additions and Subtractions from the Original Novel

As mentioned above, the biological warfare element was added by the screenwriters. They held onto the prologue escape of Von Manteufel with Nazi gold and his betrayal of Col. Spaatz. The book opens with a bloodied Hamilton and his companions, twins Ramon and Novarro, who turn out to be police detectives, plus Hiller and Serrano, landing at Romano. Hamilton returns with one bag of rough-cut diamonds and another of gold Greek coins. Hiller and Serrano burgle his hotel room. Hiller, a journalist working for multi-millionaire newspaper magnate Smith, believes that Hamilton has found the lost city. Meeting with Smith, his secretary Maria, manager Tracy, Hiller and Serrano, Hamilton demands $250,000 to take the millionaire to the lost city. Diaz, a good guy in this version, provides Hamilton with information on the secretive Smith. Hamilton is a typical MacLean hero, widowed, wife murdered, secret agent of sorts rather than adventurer, and with a good deal more cunning than his movie namesake. On the way, during a helicopter ride, Hamilton kills one of Smith's thugs, Heffner, just as he discovers Hamilton's true occupation. With their helicopter disabled, they land on an island where they are attacked by the Chapati tribe. They steal an old, abandoned boat and some canoes, negotiate a waterfall, and make their way to a hovercraft, placed there for this purpose, before clearing rapids and sustaining an attack from the Horena tribe. In addition, they encounter wild boar, piranhas, alligators and an anaconda and finally, purportedly, cannibals. But that's a fiction, invented by explorer Dr. Huston, who discovered them. He wishes to prevent the more curious of the civilized world from infecting them with disease. Finally, upon arrival at the lost city, they find it's inhabited by ex–Nazis including Von Manteufal. Hamilton introduces him to Smith-Spaatz. Maria is Israeli intelligence. Serrano also turns out to be a good guy. Von Manteufel's men get the drop on the visitors. The prisoners don't have to do much as the author invokes a *deus ex machina*, having Diaz drop napalm on the Germans. But Hamilton does discover an El Dorado and reveals that Manteufel killed his wife, Huston's daughter.

Chapter Sixteen

Television Endgame

Death Train *(1993)*,[1] The Way to Dusty Death *(1995)*, Night Watch *(1995)*,[2] Air Force One Is Down *(2013)*

Except in exceptional circumstances—Steven Spielberg's *Duel* (1971) and Michael Mann's *The Jericho Mile* (1971), for example—you can't compare TV movies to those intended for the big screen. The former are just dwarfed—in scale, scope, size (cinema screen vs. even the largest television screen, no contest) and, just as important, stars and directors. Even were you able to hang some major stars upon the frameworks of the television movies, you forget that what marquee power brings most of all is endless extra work, the polishing of the script, the fine tuning of the character arc and development of relationships, the director, assisted by the finest of cinematographers, framing the material in distinctive fashion. Virtually every frame of every television movie would be completely different if made for the movies. So it's an invidious task to compare small screen MacLean with the big screen. Yet, the author's name carries such expectation, especially if you're a fan of *Where Eagles Dare* or *Puppet on a Chain* or *Fear Is the Key*, that it's easy for viewers to feel let down, perhaps even duped. Taken on their own merits, however, accepting the limits of budget and time, it's a different story, and, perhaps surprisingly, some of these come across as top notch in one way or another.

Death Train

The reboot was not yet part of Hollywood parlance, but changes made to UNACO characters—not just wholesale replacement of the actors—more than a decade after *The Hostage Tower* pre-empted the revolutionary changes in sequels that would later become standard. The alterations were so substantial they amounted to complete overhaul. Here, the criminality of the three major characters—Sabrina Carver, Mike Graham and C.W.—was completely excised, Graham reinvented as a former SAS associate of team leader Malcolm Philpott, Carver now a markswoman and linguist and C.W. a physicist.

Nor had the trio previously met. Graham was rebranded as a sexist sparking tension with feminist Carver. As was by now par for the course, a new company used MacLean as a launch pad, this time on television. USA Pictures, an offshoot of cable[3] company USA Network, specialized in made-for-TV movies. The new venture intended to double or even quadruple existing $2.5 million budgets[4] to ensure "larger productions with increased star values for international theatrical release."[5] *Death Train* was its debut. Co-financing came from British Lion, Yorkshire International Films[6] (Peter Snell, instrumental in both, acted as producer) and the Croatian studio Jadran Film. The new UNACO line-up comprised a pre–James Bond Pierce Brosnan (*Remington Steele* 1982–87, *The Lawnmower Man,* 1992), Patrick Stewart (*Star Trek: The Next Generation*, 1987–94) and Alexandra Paul (*Baywatch* 1992–97) and TV regular Clarke Peters. Christopher Lee (*Bear Island*) essayed the villain.[7] Writer-director David Jackson's experience was limited to U.S. television and the straight-to-video *Death Merchants* (1991). As he did with *The Hostage Tower*, MacLean provided a screen treatment; the novel, published in 1989, was written in this instance by Alistair MacNeill.[8] Six years after MacLean's death, he remained a major selling point. The film was shot in Slovenia from May 4, 1992, to June 15. "It's everything I've ever wanted to do," commented Brosnan, "run along the top of trains, shoot guns and climb in and out of helicopters."[9] It was his first project since the premature death of wife Cassandra in December 1991. Brosnan did the stunt of hanging out of a helicopter 350 feet up without a safety net. According to the actor, "We traveled through a bombed-out town and that was chilling ... you could smell the war."[10] The train tunnel shootout lasted four days. "It was suffocating. They would crank up the engine and you would see this smoke billowing up and rolling down the walls… [A]t the mouth was a quarry where they were mining so here there was a white film of dust and noise constantly."[11]

The Film Version

It has an atmospheric opening, but mostly the concentration is on action and twists. Voiceover (by Malcolm Philpott) informs us that renegade Russian General Benin (Christopher Lee) has employed German scientist Leitzig (John Abineri) to make a nuclear weapon. Benin's henchman Tierney (Ted Levine) and crew hijack a German train, taking a bomb aboard. On a motorcycle track, Mike Graham (Pierce Brosnan) is in training for the annual Daytona meet. UNACO chief Philpott (Patrick Stewart) is alerted to the danger, by Sabrina Carver (Alexandra Paul) on his backroom staff. Graham initially turns down Philpott, until agreeing with the cryptic line, "After this, we're even on Laos." Whitlock (Clarke Peters), stands guard over Leitzig, hospitalized after radiation burns. Graham opposes Carver's involvement even after she proves her marksmanship by firing a gas canister through the window of the speeding train. The terrorists foil this ploy, so Graham lands on the train by helicopter but is thrown off. Philpott plans an ambush in the Tirnano Tunnel in Italy. Despite a barrage of firepower, the train escapes. As Carver and Graham recover from their ordeal, he continues to belittle her. In a marvelous scene, she takes him down a peg by delivering a retort in Italian which he doesn't understand but everyone else does. Whitlock discovers there's another bomb elsewhere. Instead of UNACO infiltrating the villain's set-up as in *The Hostage Tower*, it's the other way around, Carver uncovering team member Rodenko (Nic D'Avirro) reporting to Benin.

The train heads for Iraq as Benin seeks to goad Russia into responding in a manner that would restore its former military glory. Carver and Graham find a way on board the train, Carver shooting Tierney and Graham defusing the bomb. Following Carver's instinct, they decamp to a private airfield to find a second bomb. Carver shoots Benin while Graham defuses the bomb, only to discover in an ironic twist that it's a fake.

Not only is *Death Train* pretty solid stuff with some excellent action, especially the scenes involving the helicopter, but it marks Carver's ascendancy. She takes out both bad guys and works out the enemy plans.

This Ain't the Novel

Beyond its basic nuclear terrorist threat plot, this isn't the novel nor, presumably, the MacLean outline. The book is more of a detective story as Carver, Graham and Whitlock—collectively known as Strike Force Three—investigate why a homeless guy has died from radiation burns. The trail leads to Strasbourg, Mainz, Switzerland and Italy. Carver has a shoot-out with two assassins. But there's no freight train. The nuclear device—one bomb, not two—is placed on a passenger train, Carver and Graham boarding in normal fashion. Alistair MacNeill does a terrific job not only in replicating MacLean's ratatat style, but building up tension and fleshing out characters. Carver, terrified of rats, owes her job to a powerful father, not the polyamorous seducer of *The Hostage Tower*, and has given up fast cars after coming a-cropper in a saloon race at Le Mans. Conversely, Graham, apart from endless bickering with Carver, still blames himself, as in *The Hostage Tower*, for the death of wife and child.[12] But he's no longer a motorbike racer, living now in solitude on a mountain. Whitlock, suspecting Leitzig who works in a German nuclear plant, avoids seduction by femme fatale Karen. Leitzig isn't incapacitated, instead blackmailed into helping the Russians. Interest in the train, however, is fleeting, the dangerous cargo being redirected to Libya. Carver's marksmanship forces Graham to reassess her professional qualities. There's also more of the technical research MacLean fans loved: the difference between a newspaper "stringer" and a correspondent and between "diversion" and "MUF"—both involving stealing nuclear components—and how to accrete plutonium gram by gram in the post-processing period. Characters are introduced according to preferred weaponry. Graham's Beretta clip carries seven more bullets than his beloved Colt. Benin isn't a renegade but heads up a secret branch of the KGB. A standout scene between Graham and Benin accomplice Hendrique revolves around playing chicken with volts of electricity. Whitlock gets most of the best lines. Graham's inherent misogyny softens, especially after Carver turns up disguised as a nun. However, there's no national alarm about a nuclear bomb racing across Europe on a hijacked train, none of the palaver in a railway HQ, no terrorist driver, and it's only in the last fifth of the book that the terrorist plot begins to grip. The climax is speedboat vs. seaplane. The movie producer has taken the nugget of bomb on a train in a post-*glasnost* Russia and run with that.

* * *

The Way to Dusty Death

With this film, the MacLean torch was passed from father Geoff Reeve to son Tom Reeve.

In writing the novel, published in 1973, MacLean had imagined his Scottish compatriot racing driver Jackie Stewart in the leading role. At one point, J. Lee Thompson (*The Guns of Navarone*) planned to direct.[13] Peter Snell and the author's ex-wife Marcelle MacLean planned to start shooting *The Way to Dusty Death* "with a name cast" in summer 1975 for AIP[14]—long before its involvement with *Force 10 from Navarone*.[15]

To make the cars used in *The Way to Dusty Death* appear authentic, there had to be advertisements on them. In an interview with the author, producer Tom Reeve shared that they applied to Coca-Cola for permission to use their colors; that request was rejected, but the beverage company offered them Sprite (advertisement, *Variety*, May 7, 1975).

It remained on the mini-major's schedule for another two years[16] with Peter Fonda (*The Hostage Tower*) as star.[17] Don Sharp (*Bear Island*) was a prospective director with a script by John Gay (*Golden Rendezvous*).[18] However, Marcelle gave up her rights as part of her final divorce settlement with MacLean.[19] Following the failure of Snell's ambitious plans to regenerate the MacLean brand, when the rights became available in 1981,[20] Elliott Kastner, offered the opportunity, "was not interested in picking it up."[21] That left the way open for another television heavyweight, CLT, the Luxembourg-based owner of the RTL network, whose production outfit Delux stitched up a deal with Britain's

Grafton Media, initially planning to spend $8.5 million on a four-hour mini-series[22] (the budget was later reduced to $6.1 million)[23] directed by Geoffrey Reeve (his third MacLean venture after *Puppet on a Chain* and *Caravan to Vaccarès*). The writers were Paul Wheeler (*Caravan to Vaccarès*) and Christopher Wicking (*To the Devil a Daughter*, 1976). The cast was international, top billing accorded American Linda Hamilton[24] (*The Terminator*, 1984) and Brit Simon MacCorkindale, a TV regular whose last movie was *Jaws 3D* (1983); Uwe Ochsenknecht (*All Out*, 1990) was virtually unknown outside the German market. By now Geoffrey Reeve had established his reputation as a producer, switching with ease between polished cinematic drama (*The Shooting Party*, 1985, with James Mason and Edward Fox), television (*The Far Pavilions*, 1984) and two pictures starring Michael Caine, *Half Moon Street* (1986) and *The Whistle Blower* (1986).[25] That marked the producer debut of his son Tom Reeve,[26] who carried out the same function on *The Way to Dusty Death* as well as handling the second unit.

Tom Reeve had moved from TV production in the U.S.[27] to setting up a studio in Luxembourg. The country had introduced a 30 percent tax credit scheme but after his company was bought, he formed a new production unit with the aim of producing mini-series. On calling MacLean's lawyer David Bishop to find out if there were any MacLean projects available, he was offered *The Way to Dusty Death*. The racing theme immediately appealed to Tom, who was a keen amateur driver. In fact, the notion of motor racing as front for a drug smuggling came from Tom's experience of buying a British Touring Car Championship BMW sports car from Vic Lee, who was later convicted of smuggling drugs in their transporters. With his background in the sport, Tom was able to recruit professional drivers who covered their own crew and car costs.[28] He shot racing scenes at Brands Hatch and the Mallory Park Racing Circuit in England and Zandvoort in the Netherlands. Cameras followed the world championship that year, snatching footage at various races. Two cars were hired with Tom using his own vehicle for the third. The organizers of the Formula Opel race at Zaandvoort permitted the producers to film during an 90-minute lunch break, using the real track and with a grandstand packed with spectators.[29] For the sequence when two Coronado cars crash, Tom was driving one and Dave Brunston the other. Tom said that, after they did three laps,

> Brunston hit me. My car slid across the gravel. Having hit the tire wall I was winded. But, as in the script, I ran over to attack Dave, we were pulled apart by racetrack fire marshals in orange suits who hadn't been listening to the instructions issued over the loudspeaker and thought our fight was for real.[30]

Tom added, "I hit it off with Simon [MacCorkindale] after he came to me in Luxembourg with a couple of projects."[31] Reeve had met Tom Burlinson while working in Los Angeles; the actor was then part of an Australian acting Mafia that also included Nicole Kidman and Deborra Lee-Furness, later the wife of Hugh Jackman.[32] The U.K.–German co-production was heavily tax-funded. Given the budget, Tom Reeve "tried to make it not about racing but about the characters and the drug storyline."[33]

Chapter Sixteen. Television Endgame

The Film

One-time champion racing driver Johnny Harlow (Simon MacCorkindale) is now an alcoholic ex-jailbird; he did time for manslaughter after being involved in a fatal accident. He is brought out of retirement by under-pressure James MacAlpine (Anthony Valentine), boss of a racing outfit. Having taken the pledge, Harlow shapes up but his comeback is marred by an accident involving teammate Ike (Tom Burlinson). Mysterious Russian reporter Alexis (Serena Scott-Thomas) suggests it was sabotage. When MacAlpine dies from a heart attack on his boat, his wife Beth (Linda Hamilton) takes over the business, turning down an offer from sponsor Paul Vincennes (Christopher Cazenove) to buy her out. While Beth uncovers a payment of $5 million in the accounts, Johnny grows suspicious of charismatic gambling addict teammate Gerhard Tracchia (Owe Ochsenknecht) and hires private investigator Tom Hagen (Hidde Maas). Alexis pops up from time to time, either to exact revenge on villains or in seductive mode; in a very effective slow-burn scene, Johnny cleans her face and body of oil. An equally mysterious fellow with a dog also seems to be around when cars blow up. With the help of Alexis, who turns out to be working for a South African diamond cartel, Johnny discovers a diamond smuggling-money laundering scheme involving the racing outfit's transporters. There's snooping a-plenty, car chases and shoot-outs, but the various plot elements take a while to coalesce. Despite often speaking in a whisper, MacCorkindale doesn't come close to suggesting the quintessential MacLean hero. The women, Linda Hamilton and especially Serena Scott-Thomas, better capture the camera's attention. Racing scenes are remarkably authentic given the budget. I only saw the movie version which I enjoyed.

The Book

This is an old-fashioned detective tale with champion racing driver Harlow—a quintessential MacLean tough guy—masquerading as an alcoholic in order to cover his investigation into sabotage. It begins with Harlow being blamed for the death of colleague Ike in a Grand Prix race, but Coronado's chief engineer Jacobsen can find no flaw with the car. Despite being officially cleared, Harlow's confidence is apparently shattered (whisky bottles are found in his room). In subsequent races, he fares badly. Clouding his life is the recent death of his racing driver brother in an accident on the track. Teammate Nicolo Tracchia and rival Austrian racing driver Neubauer create trouble. Boss MacAlpine's daughter Mary, in love with Harlow, has her ankle pulverized by his accident. MacLean keeps most of the goings-on from the reader for quite some time, as Harlow maintains his pretense while carrying out clandestine sleuthing. The Alexis here is not a female Russian but a male Englishman, but he, too, is operating under a guise and working for Interpol. Eventually, with alcohol driving him to the edge, Harlow quits his profession but is employed as driver of the company's transporter, excuse enough to head to Marseilles where he finds proof of a Mafia drug smuggling enterprise funded by the racing car sabotage, overseen by Jacobsen: By gambling on race results, Tracchia and Neubauer make fortunes. The author falls back on a previous trope, of the husband being blackmailed by villains who have kidnapped his wife.

The climax is a superb car chase. Actual fisticuffs and shoot-outs are delayed until the latter stages of the book, but Harlow is ruthless in the MacLean vein. Standout scene: He forces villains to divulge information by ramming a cyanide pill into one of their mouths and taping it shut so that his victim can't tell the others the pill is a fake. Gentle romantic banter between Harlow and Mary offsets the dangers inherent in motor racing. Having befriended Scottish racing ace Jackie Stewart, MacLean's research has a stamp of authority. The book was published in 1973, so coming at the material two decades later, the lone investigator and the drugs business must have appeared old hat. With Tom Reeve's personal experience, it's no surprise about the changes. The novel is a satisfying read but you can see the problems of translating it, as it stood, onto the screen.

* * *

Night Watch

Peter Snell produced the third in the UNACO series, a sequel of sorts to *Death Train*. Writer-director David Jackson, Pierce Brosnan and Alexandra Paul returned but Patrick Stewart was replaced by William Devane (*Rolling Thunder*, 1977). A U.S. independent outfit, J&M Entertainment, co-funded with British Lion and Jadran Film. Filming began on August 8, 1994, and ran until September 14 on locations in Amsterdam, Hong Kong, Zagreb and at Jadran Film Studios in Zagreb, Croatia.

Film–UNACO Reboot #3

Tech millionaire Schraeder (Michael Shannon) has a sideline: forging classic paintings. His plan to fit every phone and computer in the world with a computer chip controlled by North Korea might not have attracted the attention of UNACO, where another reboot has taken place. Whitlock and Philpott are gone, the former's cat-burgling climbing skills appropriated by Graham, the latter replaced by Caldwell (William Devane). Graham (Pierce Brosnan) is grieving once more, this time for a colleague lost in the action-packed opening rescue of a diplomat's family from North Africa. Gone, too, is the motorbike enthusiast of *Death Train*. In his place we find a floppy-haired dude complete with Van Dyke mustache and a nibble of beard. Quite why the forging of Rembrandt's "The Night Watch" should require the involvement of UNACO is never explained.

This time around, Carver (Alexandra Paul) is in charge. There's a canal chase that isn't a patch on *Puppet on a Chain*. The pair's investigation leads them to Hong Kong and a tech conspiracy. There the picture shifts from action-driven film to romantic thriller as Graham and Carver pretend to be honeymooners. Fiction gives way to a closer relationship after a kiss instigated as part of the charade turns more serious. In an excellent casino scene, Brosnan gives notice of his James Bond aspirations. The background (technology in meltdown if control is in the wrong hands) will resonate more strongly today given the various outages inflicted by computing pirates. While there's a full complement of chases and fights, twists are limited. Graham's bomb defusing skills, a highlight of *Death Train*, fails him. Location shots are spoiled by passersby staring fixedly at the camera, though nobody runs for cover when the shooting begins. The picture ends with Caldwell taking part in an assault on a freighter. Narrative thrust places the movie more in James Bond territory, cyberterrorism having been a feature of both *Tomorrow Never Dies* (1997) and *Spectre* (2015). The romantic element, setting it apart from the previous entries, makes for a more satisfactory viewing.

The Book

The film is an improvement on the book. Alistair MacNeill, working from a three-page outline,[34] sets the initial discovery of forgery in New York, the final destination of a five-country tour of the famous painting. UNACO is brought in because it has multi-country jurisdiction. However, there's no cyberterrorism in the book and, after initial sleuthing in Amsterdam, Graham, Carver and Whitlock head for Rio de Janeiro in pursuit of ex–chemical weapons dealer Schrader, whose sidekick Drago has a drug-running sideline. The fake marriage here is devoid of romantic undercurrent. However, the casino scene is lifted from the book. A subplot involving a hunt for a double agent seems as out of place as the commentary on Brazil's social inequalities. And while there's the usual quotient of action, both principals battling their way out of trouble, and a hang-gliding scene, it lacks the save-the-world impact of *Death Train*. I would hazard that Hong Kong is implicitly no more exotic than Rio, but the harnessing of cyberterrorism to romance makes the film better than the book.

* * *

Air Force One Is Down[35]

Always intended for television, *Air Force One Is Down* was originally lined up as a direct sequel to *The Hostage Tower*, based on a 120-page MacLean outline. (Trade posters for *The Hostage Tower* flagged this up.) In 1980, Don Sharp signed on to direct with Warner Bros. supplying the finance. Sharp had gone so far as scouting locations in Yugoslavia before the project was dropped.[36] It sat on the shelf for decades before being revived. In the meantime, *Air Force One* (1997) starring Harrison Ford as a U.S. president foiling the hijacking of a presidential jet had been a major hit. But sufficient time had elapsed for a similar storyline, and in the less critical environs of television, to take shape.

However, in essence, this was the final attempt to revive the MacLean brand following the Peter Snell playbook. Now Justin Bodle of Power TV took on the mantle. Originally, there were going to be three mini-series, each running four hours: *Air Force Once Is Down* to be followed by *Dark Crusader*—a fundamental change to the script saw the philanthropist less intent on eradicating diseases (as in the novel) than de-populate an over-populated planet—and a *Puppet on a Chain* remake. Like Snell and Elliott Kastner, the investors were experienced, but in the television sector. Bodle had a longstanding relationship with RHI, created in 1979 by Robert Halmi, Sr., and Jr.,[37] specializing in the television mini-series, including *Lonesome Dove* (1989) and its sequels, *Merlin* (1998), *The Rules of Marriage* (1982) and *The Ten Commandments* (2005). When Tom Reeve became involved, he introduced the package to TeleMunchen. British-based Power TV had produced quality content like *Archangel* (2005), *Henry VIII* (2003), *Flood* (2007), *Mary Bryant* (2005–07) and *Crusoe* (2008–2009), plus an occasional foray into the movies such as *Casanova* (2005) with Heath Ledger.

Reeve (*The Way to Dusty Death*) was hired to produce this as a two-part mini-series to premiere on U.S. TV with subsequent worldwide DVD release. The eight-week schedule "was tough since it involved a lot of locations and a big cast," he said, but it was also "one of the most fun shoots since we were left alone."[38] It cost EU 8.5 million (about $11.3 million), the backing coming from Lynx Productions and Film Fund Luxembourg. Peter Snell was credited as executive producer, and the telemovie was made in association with British Lion.

For casting, RHI provided a list of actors currently hot in TV. Linda Hamilton (*The Way to Dusty Death*) offered the only genuine star wattage but her role is actually a cameo. Jeremy Sisto (*Law and Order*, 2007–10) takes the leading role with Jamie Thomas King (*Tower Block*, 2012) as his sidekick and Emilie de Ravin (TV's *Lost*, 2004–10) as the woman who comes between them. Rupert Graves was a British TV regular while German Ken Duken (*Robin Hood*, 2013) was a relative unknown. Niall Leonard (*Fifty Shades Freed*, 2017), married to E.L. James, wrote the script—"he was adamant the final scene was core to the movie," said Tom Reeve.[39] Director Cilla Ware had a decade of British TV experience. According to Reeve, "The only major location away from Luxembourg was Rome, with bits over the border in France and Belgium."[40] Drawing on his racing background and his second unit skills, Tom rode the motorbike on the cobbled streets outside the Vatican and his son Jordan was on the pillion with a camera. The scene was shot at 4:20 a.m. Filming around the Vatican was strictly controlled so Tom took the precaution of applying for a permit a few days before so if he got stopped by cops, he could show the paperwork. And Tom has kept up the family tradition of inculcating love of movies in the family. "The scene at the end of *Air Force One Is Down* when the motorbike arrives and misses a little girl … that's my daughter Darci, now a makeup and prosthetics artist."[41]

Film–UNACO Reboot No 4

Despite being written as part of the UNACO series, that organization is eliminated, as is all mention of Mike Graham, Sabrina Carver, Whitlock and Malcolm

Chapter Sixteen. Television Endgame

Philpott. Unrelated to the previous films, it is set in the aftermath of the Balkan conflict. Rogue U.N. Peacekeeper Fergus Markey (Jeremy Sisto)—"allergic to orders"—has captured Serbian warlord Dragutin (Rupert Graves). While Markey pursues Dragutin's cigar-chomping deputy Petrovic (Ken Duken), Dragutin, from within a prison, organizes the hijack of Air Force One. On board is U.S. President Harriet Rowntree (Linda Hamilton), various high-ranking politicians and journalist Francesca (Emilie de Ravin). Markey, foiled in his attempt to capture Petrovic in Serbia, complains about a traitor to British Consul Steven Featherstone (Jamie Thomas King), banished to this wilderness for an indiscretion at home. When the consulate is attacked, the bickering pair become unlikely allies. By electronic interception, Petrovic takes control of the plane. The passengers are knocked out by gas pumped through the emergency oxygen system—all except Francesca who, realizing what was happening, didn't don her mask. Markey and Featherstone end up at the airfield where the plane lands and follow the disembarked kidnapped president and journalist. Remote control takes the plane back up into the air long enough for U.S. fighter jets to see it come crashing down.

The president is held captive in a ruined castle while Petrovic orders Francesca's execution. The journalist overcomes her guard and escape. She rescues Harriet, and Markey rescues them. All are recaptured except Markey. Unless Dragutin is released, Harriet will be raped and killed live on camera. From a house in the woods, Markey telephones Featherstone's boss Gillian Barry (Amanda Donohoe), but is dismisses as a crank. With some astonishing acrobatics and a lock-pick ("standard journalist equipment"), Francesca frees herself and Featherstone. Francesca turns out to be C.I.A. Released, Dragutin is flown to Serbia. Francesca and Featherstone find Harriet in a booby-trapped house. Having reached safety, Dragutin cuts out of his arm a transponder device. Harriet dies, and the other three are recaptured. Dragutin reveals that Francesca is a double agent, a Russian working for the FSB. Harriet and Featherstone are locked nearly naked in a pit of freezing water. Dragutin locks the transponder around Markey's neck and sets him free. Americans launch a rocket at a target they presume is Dragutin. The warlord sees it explode but doesn't realize Markey has escaped down a narrow crevice.

Dragutin intercepts a Russian stealth plane on a bombing exercise, brings it down on Serbian soil and boards it with a pilot, aiming to launch missiles at Moscow and London. The drowning pair are rescued by Markey. Harriet, as you might expect, is not dead. Using the phone in the wood, Francesca contacts the FSB, gives them the plane's position, announces that her cover has been blown and that Defense Minister Kozinski (Carsten Norgaard) is in danger. Despite the perils they have faced together, and the times she has saved his life, and his undoubted attraction to her, Featherstone is faced with the choice of exposing her as a spy—and also whoever got her a job in TV news in the first place and a spot on Air Force One. Assaulting the castle, the trio free Mackenzie, the Brit computer geek forced to take charge of the electronic controls, and persuade him to alter the plane's course so that it crashes into a mountain with Dragutin on board. They are recaptured by Petrovic but freed by a U.S. squad.

After 135 minutes, you'd think the story was done, but there's still a half-hour to go. Francesca (known as Nadia at home) is awarded a medal in Russia and the person who betrayed her to Dragutin is unmasked. Featherstone receives a medal from Harriet on board a new Air Force One and is reassigned to the British consulate in Rome. Markey is made redundant—he was working, it turns out, for a war crimes tribunal task force in the Netherlands—but smells a rat. Featherstone has not given Francesca up to the authorities and they meet in Rome. Markey tells them that Dragutin is still alive. The warlord wanted the Americans to believe he was on the plane so it could be shot down and he could disappear. From a glimpse of a photo of the Sistine Chapel at the warlord's stronghold, Markey deduces that Dragutin has kept one warhead and is targeting Rome to avenge the NATO bombing of Belgrade 20 years ago tonight. At his trial, he blamed the Catholic Church as well as various countries. Since the Vatican is impregnable and heavily guarded, Francesca expects the bomb to be planted underground. In a shoot-out in the catacombs, Francesca takes a bullet protecting Markey. Featherstone temporarily gets the drop on Dragutin before being captured. But Markey has the remote detonator—hence the re-titling of the picture for DVD and the connection with *Death Train*. Dragutin holds the other two hostage. In the swap, Markey tricks Dragutin, who blows himself up. Back in Russia, Francesca fingers Kozinski as the real traitor and in London Featherstone has his boss arrested for the same reason. There's a cute ending as Francesca avoids committing to either of her prospective lovers.

This was easily the best of the made-for-TV adaptations, filled with interesting touches. A repeated montage showing kids playing in Serbia is revealed as the trigger for Markey's personal animosity towards Dragutin. Visually, there's an outstanding graveyard scene. Featherstone is exceptionally well-written, developing from disgraced incompetent civil servant into the "best useless Brit I've ever worked with"—take that as a compliment from the surly Markey. Jamie Thomas King steals the show. Emilie de Ravin is very convincing in her transition from hapless journalist to competent spy and the way she plays both guys is just brilliant. The potential love triangle making the ending a treat, one of the best twists ever. In prison, Dragutin plays chess with himself and conducts an imaginary orchestra as, in another country, his men move into position. Rupert Graves brings a fresh approach to the villain. Observed Tom Reeve, "He was better than the role."

There's some discreet stuff. The computer geek's fingertips are bandaged and eventually we guess that his nails have been pulled out. Yes, the capture-escape trope seems to be in overload but that's the nature of the espionage action beast. I saw the full four-hour show for this one and was thoroughly entertained, especially by the acting. The clever final twist, I imagined, would open the door for a sequel.

Book—*Hostage Tower*: The Sequel

Published in 1981—"soon to be a major film," claimed the paperback cover—and intended as a direct sequel to *The Hostage Tower*, based on a 120-page MacLean outline, it was novelized by John Denis. It is still a genuine UNACO operation, though only Sabrina Carver and Malcolm Philpott are retained. Mike Graham is replaced by Joe McCafferty, but C.W. is no longer involved. Master criminal Mr. Smith, who held the Eiffel Tower ransom, escapes from high security incarceration and organizes the hijack of Air Force One, carrying not the president but the Secretary of State and Saudi oil moguls. Employing almost futuristic levels of cosmetic surgery and re-voicing, Smith arranges for a duplicate (Cody Jagger) to replicate McCafferty, head of onboard security. Carver is a stewardess, but unaware of McCafferty's real role. Also aboard is highly intelligent child Faisal, suffering from diabetes. Despite thorough training, Jagger, while familiar with McCafferty's previous lovers, doesn't know the real McCafferty has made a date with Sabrina, raising suspicions when he tries to chat up another stewardess. Another basic error jeopardizes the original plan of hijacking the plane. Using computer infiltration, Smith takes command of the plane, landing it in Yugoslavia. He takes the politicians and moguls hostage, killing all other passengers. He intends to take savage revenge on Sabrina for her part in foiling the Eiffel Tower plot. To create confusion, Smith blows up a dummy Air Force One in midair. The Russians, who occupy the territory, permit the landing in exchange for McCafferty. Smith demands a ransom of $50 million ($170 million today). The real McCafferty manages to escape and contact Philpott. Sabrina, having saved the diabetic's life, is imprisoned with the others in an ancient castle. Just as Sabrina is about to be raped by her enraged captor, she is saved by McCafferty. Philpott is injured in direct confrontation with Smith, who appears victorious. However, hostages rescued, there is a final twist: Smith kidnapped by Russians to prevent such criminal talent rotting away in another U.S. jail.

This is a pretty competent imitation of MacLean's style but lacking the master's gift for tension and I do wonder if, as with the *Hostage Tower* movie, the sexual elements were added, since MacLean wasn't one for explicit threat of rape. But the detail is typical MacLean, including that the plane is only Air Force One when the president is on board and Air Force Two when it's the Secretary of State. But what was original when initially published would appear as little more than a low-budget, pale imitation of Harrison Ford's big-budget *Air Force One* and the producers clearly sought to strike a more contemporary note.

CHAPTER SEVENTEEN

The Final Mystery
What Happened to Caribbean?

In his initial deal with Elliott Kastner in 1966,[1] Alistair MacLean went far outside his comfort zone to tee up a movie harking back to the golden age of the swashbuckler.[2] His fee was $150,000 plus half the profits.[3] MacLean delivered his first draft, untitled but referred to as *Caribbean*, in September 1967.[4] At 197 pages, it was way too long.[5] Winkast's Denis Holt pointed out, "[S]ome good action early in the picture would be useful," intimating that a sequence involving capturing a ship would achieve that goal. He made four suggestions: that villain Macafferty "should be a bona fide criminal pirate"; that the audience should know sooner "what [the hero Quennell] is all about"; that heroine Jane goes "too easily to begin with" to Quennell; and that the sought-after treasure "emerald mines or gold should be made more important."[6] Holt noted that "for an action picture, everyone is inclined to talk too much" and that "too much has been explained too soon." He suggested cutting 30 scenes entirely to make room for "another two or three blood-curdling hand to hand battles."[7]

MacLean clearly took this advice. The revised draft for what was now known as *The Swashbuckler*, dated August 1969, was reduced to 153 pages.[8] Kastner anticipated that MGM would pay $500,000 for the MacLean screenplay and his services as a producer.[9] Richard Burton was mooted as star.[10]

But by mid-1969, MGM was no longer interested.[11] Still, attempts were made to find suitable locations in Greece[12] or Sardinia. The project Kastner pitched to the Aga Khan and Howard Hughes was this: "Believe timing propitious," wrote Kastner in a telegram to the former, "for beginning of motion picture industry in Sardinia … we plan a major spectacular *The Swashbuckler* with potential location Sardinia."[13] To Howard Hughes, he proposed "one subject that is quite spectacular,"[14] the terminology suggesting it was the same picture. Twentieth Century–Fox, shown the first version of the screenplay, turned it down.[15]

By mid-1970, the project was reported as "inching forward."[16] Major effort had gone into getting the project underway by September 1971. The 153-page script still needed to be "pruned very drastically," according to Holt, with the number of ships involved "strictly controlled." Holt decreed that the screenplay needed to be cut to 130 pages and $200,000 added to the proposed $1.5 million budget for a 12-week shooting schedule. What with finding the right ships and two-thirds location work (in Spain), he was inclined to believe it would be impossible to get it all done in 12 weeks.[17]

Why MacLean departed the project is not known. David Bishop intimated that Kastner's option ran out as early as 1969.[18] Exactly when Kastner started again is also not known. But it was without MacLean. Two new screenwriters entered the frame, future bestselling thriller writer Robert Ludlum[19] (creator of Jason Bourne) and Paul Wheeler (*Puppet on a Chain*).[20] Ludlum had written a work called *Satan's Ribbon*. In August 1972, Kastner told Ludlum, "You're a beautiful writer."[21] At this point, the *Satan's Ribbon* screenplay consisted of 63 pages and while Kastner was confident that Ludlum would soon get the hang of writing screenplays, he complained that the "introduction of character is too time-consuming."

The Jerry Gershwin–Elliott Kastner operation was not as productive as it could have been. All production entities regularly ran adverts promoting films they were putting together. From this ad, not one of this quartet received the green light—including the MacLean-scripted *Caribbean* (from the Elliott Kastner Archive, courtesy of Dillon Kastner).

Ludlum's screenplay was written with actor Burt Reynolds in mind.[22] His tale revolved around the real-life Anne Bonney, an Irish pirate who moved to Nassau and became the lover of Calico Jack, on whose ship she disguised herself as a man. She was captured in 1720; her death sentence was lifted due to her pregnancy. Ludlum turned her into a revolutionary.

With Paul Wheeler's involvement in 1973, the title changed to *The Buccaneers*. Kastner preferred this screenplay to *Satan's Ribbon*, whose beginning was "too bloody" and "used a very exploited subject typical of *Where Eagles Dare*, *The Dirty Dozen* and *The Magnificent Seven*." Wheeler was contracted for £9,000 in November 1973[23] to "write a screenplay from Ludlum's novel."[24] Kastner had reservations about Wheeler's screenplay, complaining that since Anne (Wheeler's heroine) is "a lady," she would not stoop to kicking someone in the groin. He saw the hero (renamed Roberts) as caring for "the little people," returning to them money he stole from the money lender. "However, he believed Anne required more motivation regarding the money and that the pirates needed to be seen planning their attack on the ship."[25] While Wheeler was better at dialogue, he had made use of four key Ludlum points, so Kastner advised him to be "clear in your rights to use Ludlum's work."[26] Despite discarding the bulk of Ludlum's screenplay,[27] Kastner intended holding onto novelization rights,[28] incorporating elements of Ludlum's work.[29]

In December 1973, the project was rejected by United Artists as not working "as a straight dramatic vehicle."[30] British Lion also rejected it.[31] Warner Brothers offered a different perspective and it was "recommended" internally to studio president Frank Wells, but the notion of an "exciting well-written adventure" with a central female role that worked "remarkably well" did not trigger a deal.[32]

For his most ambitious picture since *Where Eagles Dare*, Kastner in 1974 targeted top star Jack Nicholson, hot enough after *Easy Rider* (1969), *Carnal Knowledge* (1971) and *The Last Detail* (1973) but now molten with the impending release of *Chinatown* (1974). Aware that the actor was interested in "a swashbuckler along the lines of Tyrone Power and Errol Flynn, and that his devilish demeanor would be ideal for the part," Kastner told Nicholson that the "time was propitious to do a real meat-and-potatoes pirate movie."[33] Nat Cohen of EMI agreed to provide half the finance and Paramount seemed certain to provide the rest.[34]

When Nicholson passed, Kastner eyed a potentially greater prize, teaming Albert Finney (*Murder on the Orient Express*, 1974) with Raquel Welch (*100 Rifles*, 1969). Paramount was set to provide funding, conditional on Bryan Forbes (*Deadfall*, 1968) directing, and with another $2 million added to the pot from "the Canadians" or Nat Cohen of EMI.[35] A new "firm" start date was set (February 1975) with shooting split between the Bahamas and Pinewood, England.[36] Instead of Welch, Goldie Hawn and "even Jane Fonda" were mooted if the female part "became predominant to make a starring vehicle."[37] But Forbes pulled out after receiving "an offer I could not refuse": $350,000 to direct *The Slipper and the Rose* (1976).[38]

Other directors considered included a pre–*Jaws* Steven Spielberg, Jules Dassin (*Topkapi*, 1964), Sam Peckinpah (*The Wild Bunch*, 1969), Michael Winner (*The Mechanic*, 1972) and Clint Eastwood (*Play Misty for Me*, 1971).[39] Raquel Welch put forward Sidney J. Furie (*The Ipcress File*, 1965) and Peter Hall (*Perfect Friday*, 1970).[40] Michael Apted (*Stardust*, 1974) was later added to the list. "I almost had [Norman] Jewison—for about 16 days," lamented Kastner.[41] Welch's money for a co-star was on Donald Sutherland (*Klute*, 1971).[42]

Initial casting focused on such mainstream stars as Robert Redford (*The Way We Were*, 1973),[43] Jon Voight (*Midnight Cowboy*, 1969), Anthony Hopkins (*When Eight Bells Toll*), Stacy Keach (*Fat City*, 1972), Richard Chamberlain (*The Three Musketeers*, 1973),[44] Roger Moore (*Live and Let Die*, 1973), Sean Connery (*Diamonds Are Forever*, 1971), Michael Caine (*Sleuth*, 1972), Ryan O'Neal (*Love Story*, 1970), Clint Eastwood (*Dirty Harry*, 1971) and Charles Bronson (*The Mechanic*).[45] Valerie Perrine (*Lenny*, 1974), Barbra Streisand (*What's Up, Doc?*, 1972), Ali McGraw (*The Getaway*, 1972) and Candice Bergen (*The Hunting Party*, 1971) were other potential female leads.[46] But in reality, Kastner had gone deep into left field from the outset, pitching the movie to Italian producer Fernando Ghia (*The Red Tent*, 1969) in the hope of snaring the anarchic duo Terence Hill and Bud Spencer (*They Call Me Trinity*, 1970) under the direction of John Sturges, Brian Hutton or J. Lee Thompson, with filming to start in late 1974.[47] All these negotiations took place without a final screenplay. Jeffrey Bloom was second choice after Nicholas Meyer, an odd decision given that by this point Bloom's only screen credit was *Invasion of the Bee Girls* (1973). Bloom did not deliver a first draft of his take on the script until February 8, 1975; his total remuneration over $30,000.[48]

Anxious to secure funding for a project that would soon enter its second decade, Kastner pursued Jennings Lang of Universal, with whom he was good terms.[49] Lang was red-hot after *Airport '75* (1974), *Earthquake* (1974) and the comedy *The Front Page* (1974). Kastner still aimed for a spring 1975 start,[50] expecting to clear for himself $200,000 plus 22.5 percent in profit share from a movie he predicted would hit $30 million worldwide.[51]

But his remuneration package was too high and in January 1975 he settled for $100,000 and 25 percent of net profits, with shooting to begin in September that year.[52] "Never in my life have I agreed to take less on a picture," complained Kastner. He told Jennings Lang,

> You did not see fit ... to reimburse me for monies I had expended for the acquisition and development of the material to date.... This has indeed resulted in aborted screenplay fees for writing that are not charged to your picture. All this, until I came up with a do-able screenplay that I presented to you.[53]

Lang decided on Kastner's credit, producer or executive producer,[54] the former more prestigious. The compromise they reached presented the picture as a Jennings Lang–Elliott Kastner Production, with Kastner credited as executive producer. The screenplay went through various drafts—from 131 pages cut down to 114 pages[55]—and the final script was credited to Jeffrey Bloom (his first draft was called *The Buccaneers*), who had by now written the hit heist picture *11 Harrowhouse* (1974) and the flop *Dog Pound Shuffle* (1975, which he also directed) for Kastner.[56] Paul Wheeler objected to losing a screenplay credit, even though it was his efforts that had "sold the project in the first place."[57] Eventually he accepted a "story by" credit.[58] While the title reverted back to *Swashbuckler*, Alistair MacLean did not receive a mention.

Budgeted at $7.2 million, it was Kastner's third-biggest production after *The Missouri Breaks* (1976) and *Where Eagles Dare*. Kastner was not convinced that Robert Shaw had sufficient marquee status given that he was billed second in *Jaws* (1975) and third in *The Sting* (1973). The replica of Sir Francis Drake's *The Golden Hinde*, built just a few years before, doubled as both pirate ship and the pursuing British ship-of-the-line. The replica 16th century warship was turned into the pirate vessel *The Blarney Cock* by the movie's art department at Berth 177 in Wilmington. After being presented to the media, it sailed for Puerto Vallarta, Mexico, arriving on October 12, 1975, to begin filming. Four weeks later, it returned to Los Angeles where it was converted to the Ship-of-Line for a further week's night-for-night shooting in Los Angeles Harbor.[59]

The MacLean Version—First Draft

At a court-martial in the Admiralty in London, Lt. Quennell, accused of turning pirate, is deported to Nova Esperanto in the West Indies on the *Amethyst* (along with his sidekick Macafferty). There he is whipped, yoked and starved by Capt. Naismith.

Captain Fairfax, something of a hero having escaped capture by the French, looks forward to a ball with Lady Jane, 30-year-old daughter of the governor; he is quarantined with an infectious disease, Guadeloupe Fever. Britain and France are at peace; two French ships are in the harbor, waiting to escort sugar galleons home. On the other side of the island is Horseshoe Harbor, home to Fer De Lance, a fearsome pirate.

Deputizing for her father, Lady Jane welcomes Naismith, who fancies her, but she is so appalled at the state of Quennell that she orders him taken to the naval sick bay rather than prison. Lady Jane's younger sister has recently died. After telling Naismith that the treasure he stole is buried nearby, Quennell overcomes Naismith, steals his clothing and wig, joins the ball and dances with Jane, who finds him "not so stuffy as before." Later, breaking into the governor's room, he finds it empty. Surprising Jane in her room, he tells her he doesn't believe her sister drowned: He knows that both father and sister are being held hostage by Fer De Lance. With Jane's help, he plans to rescue them. Dirtying her face, he disguises her as James, the governor's deaf-mute son. Quennell then frees imprisoned shipmates, including Macafferty. Meanwhile, Fer De Lance proposes attacking the *Amethyst* the next night when loaded with gold. Quennell details confederate Lovelace to take over the *Amethyst*, sends Macafferty to steal gunpowder from the armory and hides Naismith in a disused emerald mine. On the French frigate, Quennell discovers an unexpectedly large supply of guns and ammunition. He ties together the rudders of the French ships and steers the *Amethyst* out of the harbor. He explains to Jane that he is not a pirate but an admiralty agent, as are Macafferty, Lovelace and Masters.

While Jane's disguise is accepted by the sailors, Quennell makes continued jokes about her maintaining that disguise. Masters is sent ashore to find the hostages while the *Amethyst* sails into Horseshoe Harbor flying the white flag. Quennell proclaims that he has come to join the pirates. Fer De Lance is perturbed not to find the half-million in gold the *Amethyst* should be carrying. But he is appeased when it's revealed that the supposed cargo was a ploy to entice the pirate to attack the ship and then entrap him. Superstitious Fer De Lance steers clear of Jane-James when he's told that he-she has the "evil eye." To Quennell, Jane whispers, "Deaf, dumb, crazy and now the evil eye."

Invited to dinner with Fer De Lance, Quennell and his companion find dessert is the crucified Masters. Jane-James, next in line for crucifixion, reveals that she is not mute. After Quennell confesses that he is a spy, they are imprisoned ashore in separate houses. Using her female charms, Jane kills a guard and rescues Quennell. They swim to the *Amethyst* and free the crew. Quennell tells Jane that her father and sister are not on Horseshoe Bay. That was a trick to get her away from the town.

Meanwhile, Macafferty dynamites the bluffs above the harbor, raining boulders down on the pirates. Assuming that Quennell is still a pirate, the fort is preparing to fire on the returning *Amethyst* until Jane appears on deck dressed in a gown. His credentials respected, Quennell is welcomed ashore and his shipmates are pardoned.

But the pirate is not dead and in one final twist he appears with the hostages. But this being Alistair MacLean, there's no such thing as just one final twist. Fairfax is revealed as a traitor and spy for the French whose sugar galleons contain 200 soldiers intent on re-taking the town. Both Fer De Lance, shot by Jane, and Fairfax die at the climax while Naismith unwittingly stumbles upon the lost emeralds.

Clearly, this is less a traditional pirate adventure—almost nothing in the way of swordfights, for example—and more a typical MacLean tale of subterfuge and hidden agendas. But Quennell is a very likable hero and the narrative trips along on a cleverly constructed engine of mystery. Every time we think we know what's going on, Quennell changes track. Jane goes from unwilling to willing accomplice, and from spoiled lady to killer. Quennell and Jane have some repartee in the *Charade* "romantic thriller" mode; MacLean attempted this again with considerable success in the novel (though not the film) of *Caravan to Vaccarès*. Of course, at the end, the hero must return home. Here's how (an example of the quality of MacLean's dialogue) he presents that.

> **JANE:** I suppose nothing short of serious illness could prevent you from sailing.
> **QUENNELL:** Nothing less than that.
> **JANE:** Do you know, you don't look well at all?
> **QUENNELL:** No?
> **JANE:** No. there are so many mystery illnesses in the Indies.
> **QUENNELL:** Is that so?
> **JANE:** It is indeed. Take Guadeloupe fever now. Guadeloupe fever is very catching. Don't you think you might catch it?
> **QUENNELL:** Well, now, I believe I could if I tried.[60]

The MacLean Version—Second Draft

MacLean took on board Holt's complaints. The "revised draft" of what was now known as *Swashbuckler*, delivered in August 1969, begins with pirate Fer De Lance capturing *two* British ships. Quennell's court-martial is reduced to just a half-page of the judge reading out his crimes and sentence. There is the clarification requested by Holt—the sugar galleons and emerald mines are more upfront while Fer De Lance makes efforts to ensure that "nothing smaller than a rowing boat" can access Horseshoe Harbor. MacLean dispenses with the unlikely scene of Quennell duping Jane at the ball; now they first meet when he invades her bedroom. The narrative proceeds much as before. Quennell rather than Macafferty mines the bluffs above the pirate port and escapes, in best swashbuckling style, down a rope. At 153 pages, this would still be considered overlong and it does lack the single most important element of a swashbuckler—a swordfight. All that stands in the way of a shorter, more acceptable, screenplay is the elimination of a couple of unnecessary plot points and characters (a French geologist, for example) and some scenes could easily lose a few pages. What's left is a superb story of intrigue, Quennell going undercover to thwart a combined French-pirate force taking over the island and the rediscovery of the fabled lost emerald mines. The central relationship between Quennell and Jane is great stuff, following the romantic thriller template. While some of the supporting characters are less well-drawn, good casting would sort that out.

Swashbuckler (1976)–The Jennings Lang Version

This follows the premise of pirate Ned Lynch (Robert Shaw) turning into a freedom fighter to save the town from its acting governor, the dictatorial Englishman Lord Durant (Peter Boyle). Durant has imprisoned Lord High Justice Barnet, evicted his feisty daughter Jane (Geneviève Bujold) and plans to sail home with the island's accumulated treasure. Jane hires Ned to assassinate Durant. Jane, captured and sentenced to death, is rescued by Ned and his men, who kill Durant and restore the town to the proper authorities.

It wouldn't be such a bad premise if everyone took it seriously. But Bujold seems to be on a different planet than the other actors. She's serious while the rest look like they're in a spoof, hamming it up, constantly laughing their heads off, singing sea shanties and reciting dirty limericks. There is more swashbuckling, to be sure, but the highlight, a swordfight between Ned and Jane, the latter hindered by wearing a gown, results in her humiliation. And Jane gets to swim naked for no particular reason. Subtlety is in short supply.

It's full of supporting characters with odd characteristics: Durant undergoes wax treatment to remove hair from his back, one of his underlings is furnished with sharp metal claws for torture purposes, and most of the British soldiers are idiots, clichéd upper-class buffoons. *Swashbuckler* failed dismally at the box office and Alistair MacLean was probably delighted his name was nowhere to be seen on the credits.

Chapter Eighteen

Unmade, Sequels, Remakes

Almost all of Alistair MacLean's novels attracted interest from moviemakers. Below is an alphabetical list of how they fared, as well as a number of projected sequels.

Athabasca (published in 1980): This novel was acquired pre-publication by Peter Snell in 1979 as part of his MacLean portfolio,[1] but it was still available in 1981.[2] Elliott Kastner, when offered the opportunity, "was not interested in picking it up."[3]

Big Iron (1975): In 1975, Columbia acquired *Big Iron*, an original screenplay.[4] This may have been *Seawitch*.[5] A start date was set for July 1, 1976,[6] with John Kemeny and Henry Gellis producing.[7]

***Breakheart Pass* sequel**: In 1981, there was a resurgence of interest in a sequel to *Breakheart Pass*. As a result of an inquiry from Kastner's organization, David Bishop wrote: "I do not know what progress Alistair has yet made on a sequel to *Deakin* [the original title]. I think he will probably not get down to this until after summer as I know at present he is in the middle of another novel."[8]

***Caravan to Vaccarès* sequel**: It was reported in 1974 that Geoff Reeve was planning to make a sequel called *Death in Vaccarès* with David Birney.[9]

Circus (1975): Based on the original screenplay and pre-publication, independent producer Irwin Allen announced in 1973 a $6 million adaptation, in conjunction with Ringling Bros, for release at Christmas 1975 through Twentieth Century–Fox, which had backed *The Poseidon Adventure* (1972) and *The Towering Inferno* (1974).[10] The movie would incorporate a modernized 3D process; 18 cinemas would be fitted out at a cost of $18,000 each.[11] Featuring 11 major stars, *Circus* was reportedly going to revive the "hard ticket" roadshow, now out of fashion.[12]

***The Dark Crusader* (U.S. title *The Black Shrike*)** (1960): This was added to the Peter Snell portfolio in 1979,[13] then purchased by Simon Lewis in 1991.[14] Power TV bought the rights and hired Tom Reeve to produce a four-hour mini-series as a follow-up to *Air Force One Is Down* (2013). Caleb Ranson's screenplay changed the plot so that the philanthropist no longer wishes to eradicate disease but to rid the world of many of its inhabitants.[15]

***Fear Is the Key* remake**: In 2011, Cary Elwes wrote a 98-page screenplay for Cinema Seven Productions (Elliott Kastner's company, now run by his son Dillon). It is credited thus: "Alistair MacLean's *Fear Is the Key* by Robert Carrington. Revisions by Cary Elwes based on the novel by Alistair MacLean."

The story is updated. Talbot, a Virginia Tech engineering graduate, was deported from Haiti and served three prison sentences before working in salvage in Havana. The kidnapped girl is called Mary (as in the original novel), not Sarah (as in the film). An impending storm means everyone is moved to the rig. Mary's father has been sedated, courtesy of a supposed heart attack, but it's clear, though duped by Vyland, that he is in opposition to this salvage scheme. The rig cost $600 million and the submersible called The Fathom can descend to 13,000 feet. Except for the unexpected arrival of the FBI to take command of the rig once Talbot has gone undersea, the story plays out much as before.[16] In 2016, it appeared that Cassian Elwes was back on track for a remake after acquiring the rights from Studio Canal.[17]

Floodgate (1983): "Ex–J. Walter Thompson copywriter Joe Forest [*Caravan to Vaccarès*], a friend of Geoff Reeve, had written a story around the idea of the Netherlands being held to ransom by a gang threatening the canal network." Paul Wheeler wrote a screenplay based on that. "MacLean wrote his novel based on the screenplay and my father was down to direct," said Tom Reeve, who holds the rights.[18]

The Golden Gate (1975): Peter Snell held the original rights.[19] At one point, J. Lee Thompson (*The Guns of Navarone*) was the favorite to direct with Charles Bronson (*Breakheart Pass*) as star.[20] But Snell sold the rights to British producer and TV magnate Sir Lew Grade as part of his $97

The Golden Gate, from the Alistair MacLean bestseller, joined an ambitious slate from British producer Sir Lew Grade that included *The Boys from Brazil* starring Gregory Peck and Laurence Olivier, the calamitous *Raise the Titanic* and *The Cassandra Crossing* starring Sophia Loren and Richard Harris (advertisement, *Screen International*, April 8, 1978).

million slate for Grade's new shingle ITC.[21] Production was to begin in February 1978, directed by Jerry Jameson (*Airport '77*, 1977) with a screenplay by Marc Norman (*Breakout*, 1975). Norman later won an Oscar for 1998's *Shakespeare in Love*.[22] Stanford Whitmore reworked the screenplay in 1978 with a start date penciled in for summer of the following year.[23] The movie was still on the stocks in 1979.[24] Production switched to another newcomer, Rosemont, with production scheduled for 1980, funded by a total investment of $25 million to $30 million to make four pictures.[25] Argentina was listed as a possible location.[26] MacLean's marquee power was such that distributors took out trade ads boasting of their involvement long before filming was underway, as occurred with Minerva Films in Sweden for this.[27]

The Golden Girl (1978): As part of their divorce settlement, MacLean's wife Mary Marcelle MacLean received this original screenplay which was intended as a television series.[28] She attempted to recruit Farrah Fawcett-Majors for the lead.[29] But it clashed with *Goldengirl* (1979), produced by Elliott Kastner, starring Susan Anton and James Coburn, which appeared in 1979.

Goodbye California (1977): This was MacLean's biggest seller in the U.S., paperback sales topping two million.[30] Peter Snell acquired movie rights as part of his long-term MacLean project. It was going to follow *Bear Island* on the production line, fulfilling the annual quota required to create brand awareness similar to the Bond movies.[31] The $12 million budget covered six weeks shooting in San Francisco and six weeks at Pinewood. Snell explained: "I know it sounds mad to shoot American interiors in a British studio but if I did them in the United States the movie would cost $14 million."[32] Don Sharp (*Bear Island*) signed on as director and a start date of early 1980 was proposed.[33] The screenplay paired Allan Scott and Chris Bryant (*Golden Rendezvous*).

Goodbye California faltered on the starting grid and the rights were again available in 1981.[34] Kastner, when also offered the opportunity to take on this project, "was not interested in picking it up."[35]

Guns for Butter: In 1968, David Bishop told Elliott Kastner, "There is still interest in Amsterdam in the possibility of a co-production of *Guns for Butter* especially if it's a non–British quota using Dutch studio facilities. Has Sandy Mackendrick come up with anything yet?"[36]

The Guns of Suez (1970): Also known as *Wings Over Cairo*. It's hard to say if this was ever a genuine idea. MacLean, on a ten-day cruise around Haifa in the Middle East, was quoted as saying, "I am in search of material for a possible story to be filmed but I have no idea what the story will be about until I look around."[37] His trip could have been reconnaissance for the proposed *Puppet on a Chain* sequel.

H.M.S. Ulysses (published 1955): Robert Clark, managing director of a top studio, Associated British, had high hopes for this one, initially viewing it as a successor to the box office hit *The Dam Busters* (1955). He bought the rights pre-publication and was pictured with MacLean at a party to launch the book.[38] J. Lee Thompson (*The Guns of Navarone*) was a front runner to direct.[39] But financial issues stopped development. By 1969, the rights belonged to Count Volpi, son of the founder of the Venice Film Festival.[40] A racing driver himself, winner of the Sebring Trophy, he was now a manufacturer of speed cars.[41] Another movie neophyte, he planned, with director Hugh Hudson and a David Osborn screenplay, a biopic of Formula One legend Juan Fangio.[42] Meanwhile, British producer George H. Brown was announced in 1970 as "prepping" *H.M.S. Ulysses*, having received the green light from the Ministry of Defence which had shied away from the picture after the controversy surrounding PQ17.[43] Coincidentally, Osborn was commissioned to write the screenplay for *H.M.S. Ulysses*.

The movie fell into the abyss until 1980 when Rank announced the picture as part of a $50 million investment in ten films.[44] David Puttnam, about to begin production on *Chariots of Fire* (1981),[45] signed on as producer with Brown as executive producer, from a screenplay by Howard Barker.[46] Filming was scheduled for fall 1980.[47] *Bugsy Malone* and *Defence of the Realm* had been released through Rank, so Puttnam had enjoyed a "relationship of sorts"[48] with the studio. He described Volpi as a "complicated man, the classic wealthy son who didn't know what to do with his wealth."[49]

Initially, prospects appeared rosy, Rank, selling the picture at Cannes, reported "considerable interest … with a number of upfront guarantees."[50] Fred Turner, named Rank managing director the following year, sold the picture to a number of territories.[51] But such optimism proved misplaced and Rank abruptly cancelled all its production commitments.[52] Brown kept the project alive for a few years.[53]

Three decades after entering MacLean's orbit, Elliott Kastner was back, commissioning in 1998 a spec outline from screenwriter Robert Boris (*Electra Glide in Blue*, 1973),[54] intending to film in 1999 with an all-star cast.[55] Conscious of the need for a big Hollywood star, Boris created American war correspondent Lt. Stephan Poyer. The movie begins in 1942 with Poyer testifying before a British Admiralty Inquiry about the sinking of the ship to which he was assigned. Then we are into flashback with the 24-year-old "cynical and irreverent" journalist being hauled out of bed while enjoying rampant sex with a beautiful nurse. The ship is on the Arctic run to deliver much-needed supplies to Russia. However, the crew needs "to redeem themselves" after "being punished for what is perceived by High command as a 'mutiny' on the last cruise."

Through Poyer, we meet the crew "at emotional breaking point," including a very ill captain, a "comical extrovert," a Scandinavian who has lost his family in the war, the padre, vindictive junior officer Carslake and a violent ex-con who was the ringleader for the previous troubles. Poyer observes acts of courage as well as Carslake's attempt to electrocute a colleague. Punctuating the consistent action are punch-ups and a suicide. As the ship begins to sink, Poyer defiantly hoists the Union Jack.[56]

Ice Station Zebra Remake: In 2013, Christopher McQuarrie (*The Usual Suspects*, 1995) took on both writing and directing duties with Warner Bros. providing the funding.[57]

Incomplete Projects: MacLean undertook research into Gallipoli and for a novel set against the American Civil War.[58]

Night Without End (1960): In 1959, independent producers William Perlberg and George Seaton bought the rights (see Chapter Two). The project fell apart when Perlberg-Seaton dissolved their partnership. *Night Without End* was added to the Peter Snell portfolio in 1979[59] with Leon Griffiths (*The Grissom Gang*, 1971) writing the screenplay. To date, the only development has proved to be a BBC television (rather than radio) spoken word serialization in 1960.[60]

Partisans (1982): Never optioned that I could see.

Puppet on a Chain **Sequel**: In 1971, producer Kurt Unger planned to bring Sven-Bertil Taube back as a private eye in a sequel written by MacLean.[61] Kurt's son Daniel recalled, "We tried a few times. We paid for Alistair to go to Israel to try to come up with ideas. Don Sharp went a few times, too, but they couldn't lick a script. It was to be called *The Jack* with the main character based on the Paul Sherman character."[62]

Red Alert: Advertised as *Alistair MacLean's Red Alert*, this was listed as a "forthcoming production" from indie outfit J&M. it was to be directed by David S. Jackson (*Death Train*, 1993), a Peter Snell production re-teaming Alexandra Paul and William Devane from the UNACO series. Filming was set for August 1995.[63]

San Andreas (1984): Taft Industries inquired about rights to *San Andreas*, but that was as far as its interest went. In 2016, Dancing Ledge Productions in London, headed by Lawrence Bowen, signed a deal with HarperCollins to turn MacLean novels into an event television series. First up was to be *San Andreas*, written by Tony Marchant. Noted Bowen, "I doubt there are many bookshelves in the U.K. that don't have one Alistair MacLean thriller, so the opportunity to work with HarperCollins to adapt a number of them for the screen is incredibly exciting."[64]

Santorini (1986): I can find no reference to rights being sold.

Seawitch (1977): Owned by Columbia.[65]

The never-made film *Red Alert* was intended as the third UNACO movie, based on the MacLean idea. It was to feature William Devane (star of its predecessor *Night Watch*) and Alexandra Paul, who had appeared in both UNACO movies (advertisement, *Hollywood Reporter*, October 31, 1995).

South by Java Head (1958): British producer Daniel Angel (*Reach for the Sky*, 1956) purchased the rights pre-publication.[66] Daniel Fuchs (*Love Me or Leave Me*, 1955) was assigned to write the screenplay.[67] Angel had a deal with Twentieth Century–Fox to make this and *The Sheriff of Fractured Jaw* (1958), a comedy Western starring Kenneth More and Jayne Mansfield.[68]

Strike Force: In 1986, Peter Snell announced that British Lion would be putting into production the "first 13 episodes of Alistair MacLean's first television series," *Alistair MacLean's Strike Force*.[69]

Untitled: In 1978, it was reported that J. Lee Thompson was planning to follow *Cabo Blanco* with an original screenplay by MacLean, which was currently being converted into a novel.[70]

***When Eight Bells Toll* Sequels**: The Calvert thriller was originally planned as the first in a series, all to be filmed. Income would be split 50-50, Elliott Kastner sharing his producing fee, splitting revenues from the screenwriting fees and whatever percentage of profits was negotiated with a major studio.[71]

***Where Eagles Dare* Sequel** (1973): Prior to making his own MacLean splash with *Golden Rendezvous*, André Pieterse, in his capacity as MGM's European production chief, contacted Elliott Kastner after learning that Kastner was proposing a *Where Eagles Dare* sequel. "I'd like to make a picture with you," enthused Pieterse in March 1973.[72] Although contractually it was possible for Kastner and his partner to make a sequel five years after the original's release, such a proposal was "meaningless" because until MGM's investment in the original was totally recouped, the studio reserved the right, equally contractually, to make up any deficiencies from the shortfall in profit from not just *Where Eagles Dare* but also *The Walking Stick*, which had been collateralized alongside it..[73] It would be a deterrent to any potential investor to know that the first profits from a sequel would head into MGM's pockets.[74]

Conclusion

"Broadsword Calling Danny Boy" may not have the same ring to it as *Casablanca*'s "Here's looking at you, kid," but it has served as almost a password to an exclusive club of Alistair MacLean fans. Add action-packed sequences: cable car fight, submarine punching through the ice, shirt ripped from the back of a female traitor, speedboat chase through canals, car chase through dusty back roads, fistfight atop a speeding train. Inquisitions in German strongholds, shootouts in exotic locations, a Louisiana courtroom and prehistoric French caves, traitors unmasked by cool heroes in every corner of the globe, women taken hostage, ships, trains, iconic structures, the world, held to ransom.

Hard to believe this all emerged from the same fertile mind and that whether the films came to a satisfactory conclusion, in financial or critical terms, there was always an image or sequence or line that kept an audience gripped. I have my favorites: *Where Eagles Dare, Puppet on a Chain, Fear Is the Key, Breakheart Pass* and *The Guns of Navarone* seem to me to capture the essence of the author and at the same set a high bar in delivering on audience expectations. According to that standard, some fall just short: *When Eight Bells Toll, Ice Station Zebra* and *Force 10 from Navarone*. Some in obviating from the author's master plan or hampered by low budgets fail to do justice to the original material: *Caravan to Vaccarès, The Satan Bug, Bear Island, The Secret Ways* and *Golden Rendezvous*. *River of Death* is the odd one out, a clunky narrative not helped by the leading man or location. Of the made-for-television brigade, I was impressed most by *Air Force One Is Down* due to the character interplay, *Death Train* for the gradual demolition of our misogynist hero, and *Night Watch*, again for character development.

MacLean appeared to exert a magnetic hold on filmmakers. Elliott Kastner produced four films; Peter Snell, planning to make a half-dozen, managed only one; Geoff Reeve directed three; John Sturges and Don Sharp two; Kurt Unger was involved in a pair, as was Tom Reeve. Richard Widmark appeared in two. Had things worked out, Gregory Peck and David Niven would have, too, and Richard Burton. MacLean movies attracted the top stars of the day: Burton, Peck, Clint Eastwood, Anthony Quinn, Rock Hudson, Charles Bronson, Robert Shaw, Harrison Ford, Richard Harris, Donald Sutherland and Vanessa Redgrave. But they were just as likely to be populated by unknowns, rising stars in their first top-billed roles: Anthony Hopkins, George Maharis, Sven-Bertil Taube, Patrick McGoohan, Pierce Brosnan and David Birney. In some respects, it was quite astonishing that the movies attracted the experienced as much as the neophytes, no more so than on the producing side where every person that ever wanted to make a movie clearly saw the MacLean name as a guarantee. Of course, he was no more a guarantee of box office success than any other top Hollywood personage, but what was astounding was that, as a mere writer, he was considered as such. Just as John Wayne or Steve McQueen or Paul Newman (regardless of their flops) came with the assurance of audience appeal, a similar rule applied to MacLean. His name ranked high, if not at the very top, in the credits of his films, unlike most stars whose names slowly begin to tumble down the billing until they are mere supporting players. MacLean was never a supporting player. Even if films did not stick to his knitting, they represented a particular vision. No matter how often his original was tampered with, audiences would recognize his imprint.

Appendix: Box Office

Like Clint Eastwood and Charles Bronson,[1] Alistair MacLean was a much bigger name abroad than at the domestic U.S. market. Which was why his movies were greenlit with far greater alacrity than their U.S. box office would suggest. A phenomenon as far as his novels were concerned—in excess of 150 million sold[2] put him at the very top rank of all-time bestselling authors—MacLean was even more impressive in some countries in terms of his movies. In Scandinavia, where his novels sold in greater numbers per head of population than anywhere else in the world,[3] he was a colossus at the movie theaters. However, there was not the same access to global box office as there is now. Figures relating to movies outside the U.S. were often erratic, and generally only covered the top performers. Domestically, *Variety*, which produced an annual chart, only included movies whose rentals (the movie companies' share of the overall gross) reached $1 million. In compiling my own Alistair MacLean box office movie league, I've been able to draw on other sources, from private archives, for example, in the case of *Where Eagles Dare*, given access to MGM's "Profit Participation" figures whose distribution was severely restricted, and subsequent financial reports from Warner Brothers. However, I am not planning to discuss movie profitability (i.e., comparing cost to receipts) so in essence rentals here relate more to a picture's popularity. The more people who see a picture, the greater its income and hence its rentals, regardless of whether, as far as the studio was concerned, it made its money back or went into profit.

The "long tail" did not exist in the 1960s and 1970s; ancillary revenue at the time was limited to television sales[4] and reissues. However, as the ancillary markets grew, expanding into cable and then VHS, DVD, Blu-ray,[5] demand for old movies soared. Revenues from these areas were rarely included in box office figures made generally available. But if you took *Where Eagles Dare* as an example, then you could easily assume that every MacLean movie made substantial amounts as the VHS-DVD-Blu-ray-cable markets exploded.

The Eagle Soars

Where Eagles Dare was easily the pick of the box office, registering an astonishing $47.8 million in rentals,[6] far above what has commonly been claimed. While not matching expectations with just $7.2 million in rentals in the U.S., *Where Eagles Dare* was a box office colossus overseas, bringing in total cinema rentals of upwards of $30 million, making it one of the most successful movies of the 1960s. The initial thrust in the foreign markets came from the opening playoff in 70mm roadshows which by 1970 touched $7.6 million; Britain was the standout.[7] Opening in roadshow at the Empire in London's West End, the movie took £11,011 in the first week, the next week even better and didn't dip below £10,000 for the next five.[8] Kastner and Gershwin's share of the profits was reduced since it went to pay off debts accrued to MGM via *The Walking Stick*, which had been cross-collateralized with *Where Eagles Dare*.[9] But that had not affected MacLean,[10] a point emphasized by his lawyer.[11] However, the author underestimated the realities of Hollywood accounting and presumably had little notion that the film would have to garner in the region of $18 million in rentals (2.2 times cost) before it broke even. Small surprise, then, that in 1973, "Alistair is very annoyed not to have received any money by way of his share of the profits."[12]

Television played a surprisingly small role in worldwide revenues, by 1981 only amounting to $2.74 million—the U.S. providing the lion's share[13]—out of a total income at that point of $27.55 million.[14] By 1982, relations between MacLean and Kastner were so poor that the author's lawyer informed the producer, "Alistair tells me he is not willing to meet with you."[15]

However, there *was* a steady stream of revenue, mostly from residuals—share of profits amounting to $33,406 from Turner Entertainment in 1992, another $16,221 in 1996 and $5433 from Warner Brothers in 2001.[16] In the area of profit share, Richard Burton was the biggest winner, entitled to ten percent of the rentals (cinema only) above $10 million, which meant he would have earned over $2.6 million from the movie,[17] the largest amount paid to any star for one picture made during the 1960s, exceeding even his wife Elizabeth Taylor's earnings for *Cleopatra* (1963). He would have earned more if television had been included in his deal. MacLean also did very well, notching up $730,000 by the mid–1980s. By 1987, including $5 million from worldwide television, income had risen to $32.5 million, with foreign revenue at $20.2 million, far outstripping the domestic tally of $7.3 million.[18] The latest report, dated 2014,[19] showed non-theatrical as equally impressive at $13.4 million with free-to-air television contributing the lion's share with $8.7 million, home entertainment adding $1.83 million and Pay TV $1.3 million. Swelling the pot were sums from copyright royalties and showings on military bases.[20]

Had sales of the soundtrack album been included, and for that matter, had streaming been included, it might well be looking at $50 million in rentals, which would make it one of the most successful movies ever made.

Navarone Climbs a Box Office Mountain

Initial rentals for *The Guns of Navarone* were more equally divided between domestic ($13 million) and foreign ($12 million) but, by 1970, worldwide rentals topped $30 million.[21] Opening week salvos in London,[22] New York[23] and across America[24] and Britain[25] broke records and it set new highs in a huge number of first-run cinemas in across the globe.[26] In Paris, it enjoyed what would turn out to be the fourth best opening week—and the second–highest screen average—of the 1960s[27] and over 18 years registered 10.1 million admissions.[28] After its U.S. box office petered out, it was screened three times in five years on U.S. television.[29] Following a major mid–1960s reissue worldwide, it was revived in Britain in 1974 and ran for six weeks at the Dominion in London's West End where the second week improved on the first.[30] The same year, *The Exorcist* was shifted out of a prestigious location in Bangkok to accommodate the return of *The Guns of Navarone*.[31] It grossed 2.4 million kroner in a Swedish reissue in 1975.[32] Despite having been screened on U.S television, it warranted a big-screen return in 1977.[33] In 1981, RCA in the U.S. spent about $100,000 on videodisk rights[34] while Video-Express in Sweden brought out the video.[35]

Breakheart Pass Steams Home

The combination of MacLean and Charles Bronson proved a winner. While total rentals hit $15.6 million,[36] there was a considerable discrepancy between U.S. ($2.27 million) and foreign ($5.13 million). Italy was the top performer with $581,000 in rentals, followed by West Germany with $547,000, France with $483,000, Japan with $420,000, with the U.K. lagging way behind with $251,000.

Although the movie opened in the U.K. at the Odeon Leicester Square in London's West End, it only lasted three weeks, the figures disappointing.[37] It received a Rank circuit release. However, the growing power of ancillary was no better demonstrated.[38] *Breakheart Pass* generated a better financial result from U.S. TV showings ($3 million) than from theaters. The remainder of the revenue came from foreign television. But the bonus came from abroad: $5.74 million from foreign cinemas. Italy again led in overseas TV sales with $448,000, followed by Japan ($405,000), France ($261,000) and Britain ($121,000). Proof of the growing ancillary tail could be seen in $400,000 from "basic" cable, $385,000 from pay cable, $279,000 from videodisk, $227,000 from video and $186,000 from in-flight.[39] By 1996, net proceeds (i.e., profits) were put at $6.1 million with Bronson earning $455,000 from his percentage share, in addition to his original million dollar fee.[40]

Foreign Saves *Force 10*

Released in the U.S. during an "overloaded" Christmas season,[41] the *Navarone* sequel managed only $3.2 million in rentals, light years behind *Superman* ($81 million), *Every Which Way But Loose* ($48 million), *Rocky II* ($43 million) and *Alien* ($40 million). It was the wrong year for the old-fashioned war picture when it went up against *The Deer Hunter* ($26 million) and *Apocalypse Now* ($22 million).[42] Overseas saved the day with $9 million—the same as the critically acclaimed *Midnight Express*.[43] Aiming for a big splash, it opened at both the Odeon Leicester Square and Odeon Marble Arch, four weeks in the former, eight in the latter,[44] and it was ranked tenth for the year in the U.K. with £381,000 (about $700,000) in rentals and placed #11 in the Swedish annual league with $1.14 million.[45] To compensate for the poor showing Stateside, it was virtually whisked onto television, screening on ABC on March 16, 1980.[46]

Ice Station Zebra

Tabbed an "admitted failure" in the U.S. with rentals of $4.7 million, *Ice Station Zebra* in 70mm Cinerama lacked the anticipated pull at the box office, with studio executives wondering whether it would have been better to have opted for a general release where it appeared to pick up some lost ground.[47] In Britain, it followed *Where Eagles Dare* into the marketplace rather than the other way around as in the States, opening at the Casino Cinerama in roadshow in London's West End. Given the seeming tradition of foreign audiences to more warmly embrace MacLean movies, I am assuming it did at least as much abroad. An estimated $10 million global take would not be excessive.

The Problem with the *Variety* Annual Chart

Movies that didn't meet the standard—$1 million in rentals—for entry in the *Variety* Annual Chart were immediately classed as flops, regardless of whether they did better overseas or whether their budgets were so low that break-even figure was also comparatively small. A goodly number of MacLean films fell into the U.S. flop category and yet their foreign figures—Sweden a classic example—pointed to success, or at least not outright failure. You could point to a mismatch between what U.S, moviegoers looked for in the action thriller and the rest of the world, though U.S. exhibitors were inclined to argue that overseas customers were less discriminating and likely to accept inferior product. As we have seen, sometimes the fault lay with a poor distributor or with an over-ambitious producer. However, for the series to continue for long as it did in the face of sometimes poor results in the American arena suggests that producers took a more global view and believed that low box office in the U.S. would be more than compensated from income elsewhere. The movies listed below failed to be selected for the *Variety* Annual Chart.

When Eight Bells Toll

When Eight Bells Toll premiered at the Odeon Leicester Square in London's West End as a replacement for *Love Story*, withdrawn due to a distributor dispute.[48] It ran for four weeks after clocking up £13,900 for the opener.[49] In many cities in first run, it was retained for a second week and was generally considered a success. It placed tenth in Sweden over a box office chart covering a two-year period above such huge U.S. hits as *Last Tango in Paris* (1972), Steve McQueen's *Le Mans* (1971) and *The Getaway* (1972), *Deliverance* (1972), *The Day of the Jackal* (1973), *The French Connection* (1971), *High Plains Drifter* (1973) and the James Bond blockbuster *Live and Let Die* (1973).[50] In the U.K. in 1973, it was reissued in an Odeon circuit release double-bill with *Puppet on a Chain*[51] and turned up again in London's West End in 1976.[52] In the U.S., exhibitor confidence failed to match distributor exuberance. In New York, it went straight into a one-week showcase (wide) release, the resulting $229,000 from 37 houses deemed "fine" by *Variety* with the Penthouse in Manhattan closest to Broadway first run.[53] Apart from a "good" $22,000 in Toronto and a "loud" $6000 in Pittsburgh, little hit the mark, "mild" or "fair" or "soft" the consensus.[54] *Variety* reckoned that rentals were in the region of $500,000 to $749,000.[55]

However, *When Eight Bells Tolls* was a long-term beneficiary of the ancillary tail. Worldwide distribution rights, excluding Britain and Italy, originally in the hands of Cinerama,[56] shifted to Orion in 1976[57]; when the deal expired in 1985, Orion proposed an upfront $75,000 against 50 percent of video and 65 percent of anything else.[58] In the 1990s, when various video distributors came calling, Kastner believed his movie could be worth $500,000 in a single market.[59] In Britain, it was especially attractive as it was not available on video, and TV showings had been minimal.[60] So when Rank's deal expired in March 1985,[61] he was confident the picture "could continue to earn money." Asking for £175,000,[62] Kastner settled for £70,000 in 1989.[63] Even so, in other markets, the double-bill remained potent. Daniel Unger, acting for the investors, remembered high demand for the program in Scandinavia.[64]

Puppet on a Chain

Britain had a double dose of MacLean a few months apart in 1971. But *Puppet on a Chain* was very much a surprise package, opening in August at the Pavilion in London's West End, enjoying the best opening week since *Midnight Cowboy* (1969),[65] and a seven-week run,[66] and then transferring to three cinemas for "robust figures"[67] and the smaller Cinecenta where it remained for the rest of the year,[68] even after the ABC circuit release on October 31.

The picture didn't reach America until the following year. Again, Toronto was the first booking; there it broke the house record.[69] But then it suffered from haphazard distribution, often straight into the suburbs and, if first run, in smaller units. The high spot was $160,000 from 29 houses in New York followed by a second week of $82,000 from 15.[70] There was a "good" take in Cleveland and a "neat" in Boston but mostly nothing to write home about. In Detroit, it was double-billed with *When Eight Bells Toll*.[71] As mentioned above, it was reissued in the U.K. with *When Eight Bells Toll* in 1973. It did well in Sweden, 27th over the same two-year period as *When Eight Bells Toll*, its grosses topping those of the big Stateside winners *The Poseidon Adventure* (1972), *Klute* (1971), *Jeremiah Johnson* (1972) and *Joe Kidd* (1972).

Fear Is the Key

Another strong opening in Britain in London's West End, where it ran for seven weeks followed by an ABC circuit release again with many holdovers.[72] It had a poor showing in the U.S., the New York "showcase" a disappointing $100,000 from 45 (*Shamus*, opening the same week, earned $320,000 from 92),[73] a "lame" $39,000 from 13 in Los Angeles, just $12,000 in Toronto and a "thin" $11,000 from 11 in Kansas City.[74] Again, Sweden came to the rescue, one place behind *When Eight Bells Toll* for the same two-year period.[75]

The Secret Ways

Getting the jump on *The Guns of Navarone* but with little of the publicity that might have been attendant in bringing the first MacLean novel to the screen, *The Secret Ways* initially bypassed first run: In April 1961, it launched wide in 28 neighborhood (not city center) houses in Detroit.[76] Conversely, it hit a "boffo" $17,000 in first run in Philadelphia.

But that was its best result, and thereafter, first-run receipts in major cities were noted in *Variety* as "fair" or "modest" or "dullish." Even a brief sojourn in first run in New York was deemed just "okay" with the movie yanked after two weeks, none of this filling future exhibitors with the excitement required to turn a movie into a hit never mind providing the momentum essential to just getting it over the line.[77] In the U.K., *The Secret Ways* was afforded a premiere on June 8, 1961, at the Odeon Marble Arch where it made a "promising start" despite "uncomplimentary reviews."[78] "They used bullets, bombs and blondes," ran the tagline.[79] Supported by the Audie Murphy Western *Posse from Hell* (1961), it went out on the Rank circuit as an alternative to the main choice, *Spare the Rod*, a British drama starring singer Max Bygraves.[80] Producer-star Richard Widmark undertook a small promotional tour that saw him visit Glasgow.[81] Competition from *The Guns of Navarone* hindered its box office prospects.[82]

The Satan Bug

The Satan Bug fitted into what would become the standard MacLean business model: better receipts abroad than at home. Like *The Secret Ways*, it followed a haphazard release plan, first-run in some cities, straight into wide release in others. New York set the tone. A "showcase" (wide) release from 23 cinemas earned $145,000 but that included $14,400 at the first-run Victoria on Broadway and $6600 from the arthouse Trans-Lux on 52nd Street. *Variety* expressed disappointment at the results— "slow" or "sad" or "okay."[83] In the U.K. it opened "strongly" at the Leicester Square Theatre in London's West End in May 1965, knocking up £3,500 in the first four days,[84] but the second full week disappointed with just £2,200.[85] The London general release, however, "lacked general appeal and wound up on the wrong side of average."[86] It went out on the Rank circuit supported by the British low-budgeter *Never Mention Murder* (1965).[87] Foreign rentals amounted to $1.75 million compared to just $850,000 in the U.S.[88]

Caravan to Vaccarès

The power of the MacLean name ensured a Royal Premiere in August 1974 in the U.K. and a "fine" opening at the Odeon Leicester Square where it experienced marginal drop-offs during a four-week run before going out on the Rank circuit.[89] Although it received a code rating in the U.S. in September 1975,[90] distributor Bryanston didn't get it into the North American market until March 1976, and then only to poor results.[91] It's as good as example as any of the MacLean attraction to Swedish moviegoers. Hardly arriving decked in box office glory, nonetheless it performed well above average. Among non–Swedish films screened over an 18-month period from July 1974 it placed 26th, its 1.99 million kroner gross[92] was good enough to outpoint Clint Eastwood thriller *The Eiger Sanction* (1975), the Charles Bronson trio of *Breakout* (1975), *The Streetfighter* (1975) and *Breakheart Pass* (1976), and just above the reissue of *The Guns of Navarone*.[93]

Golden Rendezvous

It says much for MacLean's ongoing appeal that this was the #1 film in London's West End for the first two weeks of release in December 1977. In keeping with distribution developments, it opened at three West End sites, the ABC1, Warner West End and Scene 2, where it made an "okay" $23,900 from three houses and ran for three weeks with surprisingly small drop-offs.[94] A re-edited version (see Chapter Twelve) was sent out on general release via Rank in March. Overall, it earned $420,000 in nine situations in London in its first 28 days and $136,000 from six in Japan in its opening two days.[95] It was scheduled to open in France and Germany in February, Italy in March and Spain in April. Mutual had the Canadian distribution rights, though not for the U.S.[96] While results in the opening salvo in Paris were "leaden,"[97] in Sweden it ranked 22nd out of foreign imports for the period 1977–78, beating *Force 10 from Navarone* and *Marathon Man* (1976) as well as Clint Eastwood's *The Gauntlet* (1977), *The Outlaw Josey Wales* (1976) and *The Enforcer* (1976); the three Eastwoods had soared high at the American box office.[98] *Golden Rendezvous* was the fourth most watched program of the week on its television debut on Britain's ITV in September 1982, collecting 11.4 million viewers.[99]

Bear Island

At the start of the 1980s, there appeared to be the prospect of a MacLean picture turning the box office corner in the U.S. when *Bear Island* took a "bullish" $452,000 from 58 Los Angeles houses.[100] But Chicago was less welcoming, just $154,000 from 38[101] and thereafter response was tepid.[102] It was no better in London and an "unimpressive" opening of $30,000 at the Odeon Leicester Square.[103] Though ranked 19th for the year in the U.K., its total rentals of $323,000 were a far cry from leader *Alien*'s $5.7 million.[104]

There was better news elsewhere: $200,000 gross in three weeks in Tokyo,[105] ranked 25th for the year in Spain with $336,000[106] and 18th among the non–Swedish films in Sweden over two years with a take of $1.13 million, above Clint Eastwood's *Escape from Alcatraz* (1979) and *Every Which Way But Loose* (1978) as well as *Rocky II* (1979).[107]

River of Death

Box office was exceptionally poor, posting in 1989 a screen average as low as $652 in its opening week in 23 New York cinemas.[108] In San Jose, it hauled in just $12,000 from seven berths.[109]

Made-for-Television

Although all the U.S. made-for-TV films were designed to be shown in cinemas overseas, I can find little evidence of that occurring. But since *Variety*, the main source of such information, generally only carried box office figures relating to top performers, it would be no surprise if these chugged away without attracting much attention. Movies made with the intention of attracting tax credits in the U.K. were required to produce a shortened movie-length version. Proof that this was done did not come from actual cinema showings, sufficient to submit it for registration and censorship to the British Board of Film Censors. Sometimes, these films were submitted by a video company, indicating where their future release prospects lay.

The Hostage Tower

Timing is as vital to a television release as to a movie. Had the showing of *The Hostage Tower* been delayed beyond its May 13, 1980, premiere on CBS, in the 9–11 p.m. slot, it might well have benefited from public response to Billy Dee Williams, star of *The Empire Strikes Back* (1980) which opened a month later. The producers were so confident of success that trade adverts positioned *Air Force One Is Down* as a prospective sequel, with Guzman again directing from a script Leigh Vance.[110] As it was, *Hostage Tower* performed so poorly—128th in the annual standings in its category[111]—that CBS dropped its option on any sequels. In Britain, it was given a regional try-out in the Midlands Television area beginning on September 6, 1980; it appears *not* to have received a London West End opening.[112] It flopped in Finland where previously MacLean offerings had done well.[113] It may have come into its own on video, straight in at #13 on the wholesalers chart in the U.K. in January 1985, ahead of the VHS debuts of more theatrically successful *An Officer and a Gentleman* (1982) and *Terms of Endearment* (1983).[114]

Death Train

It was shown on cable in the U.S. on April 14, 1993. There's little sign of it appearing in foreign cinemas, although I did find a Japanese poster for the movie, and it was more likely shown on video. It was classified as a "15" by the British Board of Film Censors (now known as the British Board of Film Classification) but submitted by the Entertainment in Video operation. So it appears to have gone straight to video.

Night Watch

Night Watch didn't receive a cinema release in Britain. It was classified "15" by the BBFC on April 12, 1996, for Home entertainment, i.e., straight to video.

The Way to Dusty Death

This has no BBFC classification so it was not released in cinemas or on video.

Air Force One Is Down

This wasn't classified by the BBFC until June 6, 2017, and in its shortened form (110 minutes), and again for home entertainment only.

Chapter Notes

Introduction

1. Iain Johnston, "Author Says He's Businessman," *Los Angeles Times*, December 24, 1972.

2. There were five films in the 1960s and eight in the 1970s so, effectively, they were arriving at the rate of at least one every two years.

3. By comparison James Michener's major novels tended to be turned into television mini-series, only *Hawaii* and *Caravans* (unsuccessfully) making it onto the big screen. Michener's career divided into two. Prior to *Hawaii*, he was a moderate-selling novelist whose books were turned into films—*Sayonara*, *The Bridges at Toko-Ri*, *South Pacific*—at a greater rate than when he started producing novels whose page counts topped the 700–800 mark. From the Arthur Hailey blockbuster portfolio only *Hotel* and *Airport*—and its sequels—were filmed, the rest of his output again feeding the maw of television. Harold Robbins came closest to matching Alistair MacLean. Eleven of his novels ended up on the big screen—although two of these were before he hit his bestseller stride and one was a prequel—with another three being made for television.

4. Hollywood had a nasty habit when purchasing a novel to also take the rights to all the characters. That meant that Ian Fleming, for example, except in one instance, could not hawk his books individually to Hollywood since James Bond was owned by producers Cubby Broccoli and Harry Saltzman. When the likes of Ross Macdonald sold his private eye novels to Hollywood he made a point of not selling the character, hence Lew Archer was renamed *Harper* (1966), but outings for Travis McGee, the John D. MacDonald investigator, were limited after *Darker than Amber* (1970) put him center stage. And although various actors have reinvented James Bond over the years—as also occurred with Sherlock Holmes and Tarzan—that has not applied so much to more recent series characters. *Force Ten from Navarone*, though retaining the Mallory and Miller characters from the original novel, was produced by a different studio with the parts played by Gregory Peck and David Niven now taken by Robert Shaw and Edward Fox.

5. Press release, Elliott Kastner Archive (EKA).

6. Colin Vaines, "Sharp Steers Course to Proven Success," *Screen International*, March 10, 1979, 40.

7. In Europe and the rest of the world *Where Eagles Dare* was road-shown but in the U.S. it went straight into general release. *Ice Station Zebra* was a global roadshow.

8. Barry Didcock, "The Untold Story Behind Alistair MacLean," *The Herald*, December 4, 2021. MacLean had first achieved recognition after winning in 1954 a short story competition in the *Glasgow Herald* which had attracted over 900 entries. The first prize of £100 was the equivalent of four months wages for the author, a teacher at Gallowflat School in Rutherglen. The winning entry was *The Dileas*, "a story of exciting action… in which the simple emotions of courage and affection are treated with undemonstrative conviction."

9. This was over a period of six months. Hardback books did not race off the shelves so fast. A typical hardback bestseller, over the two years before a paperback reprint, accounted for 60,000 copies. By comparison, *Gone with the Wind* only sold 176,000 copies in its first year (Lynn Andriani, "*Gone with the Wind* Still Going Strong at 75," *Publishers Weekly*, April 25, 2011").

10. *H.M.S. Ulysses* was purchased by Associated British, which also owned the ABC cinema circuit. Ultimately, it was never made.

11. The book had been published in Britain as *The Last Frontier*. American publishers changed the title to *The Secret Ways*.

12. Out of the 36 movies with which he was associated only six of Goldman's books were filmed.

13. This would certainly have appealed to MacLean's sense of righteousness. The normal situation was that a publisher sold the movie rights and took half of the purchase price. This new MacLean deal eliminated the publisher from any share in the movie monies, and with the movie going into production shortly after ensured that a movie tie-in paperback would prove beneficial to all concerned. Georges Simenon in France in the 1930s also insisted on holding to the entire movie rights.

14. *When Eight Bells Toll*, *Fear Is the Key* and *Breakheart Pass*.

15. But he did get a rave from the *New York*

Times for *Where Eagles Dare*: "splendid audacity…a real dazzler of a thriller, fine set pieces of suspense, and a virtuoso display of startling plot twists."

16. Nicholas Montserrat's novel following sailors in the Battle of the Atlantic was a huge success on publication in 1951 and the film in 1953 was one of the biggest of the year in Britain.

17. Austin Thompson, "USC Pen Pals," *Hollywood Reporter*, March 11, 1996, 8.

Chapter One

1. *Harper/The Moving Target* (1966), for example, starring Paul Newman, cost producer Elliott Kastner only $1,000 to acquire the movie rights from Ross Macdonald.

2. Of the 1962 contingent, six were filmed within three years. Of the class of 1963—composed of *The Shoes of the Fisherman* (released in 1968), *The Group* (1966), *Caravans* (1978), *The Sand Pebbles* (1966) and *The Battle of the Villa Florita* (1965)—only one took longer than five years to be filmed, and even then *Caravans* was on MGM's production schedule for most of the decade. Three from the 1965 Top Ten were promptly filmed—*Up the Down Staircase* (1967), *The Green Berets* (1968) and Arthur Hailey's *Hotel* (1966). Three others took longer—John le Carré's *The Looking Glass War* (1970), Ian Fleming's *The Man with the Golden Gun* (1974) and Morris West's *The Ambassador* (1984). Of course, a bestseller was not guaranteed fabulous box office. Number one bestsellers—*Advise and Consent* (filmed in 1962), *The Agony and the Ecstasy* and *The Shoes of the Fisherman*—were flops. On the other hand, *Valley of the Dolls* (1968) and *Airport* (1970) were massive hits.

3. "Commercial Tie-Ups Back After Slump," *Variety*, December 27, 1961, 7.

4. "Paperback-Film Tandems Zowie," *Variety*, February 3, 1960, 5. A massive sales increase of 23 percent over the previous year had been "largely due" to movie tie-ins with *Anatomy of a Murder* topping three million copies sold and *The Horse Soldiers*, *The Earth Is Mine* and *Ben-Hur* notable performers.

5. William C. Engel, "Big Stake in Publishing's 280,000,000 Annual Sale," *Variety*, January 4, 1961, 25.

6. "Big Hike in Film Tie-Ins Noted by Bantam Books," *Box Office*, November 27, 1961, A3.

7. "Columbia's Book Bally Budget," *Variety*, September 21, 1960, 24.

8. "Commercial Tie-Ups."

9. "To Issue Paperback Books on 10 United Artists Films," *Box Office*, August 28, 1961, 9.

10. "Dell Paperback Tie-Ins," *Variety*, January 13, 1965, 22.

11. "Ten Books in Paperback Promote MGM Releases," *Box Office*, May 31, 1965, E4

12. "Paperback Books Arranged for 9 Paramount Films," *Box Office*, August 15, 1966, E5.

13. "Scholastic to Publish Disney Properties," *Box Office*, May 2, 1966, A1.

14. "12 Publishers Print Books on 20th-Fox Productions," *Box Office*, February 26, 1968, A1.

15. "Tenth Year for Tie-Up with Library Week," *Box Office*, May 5, 1969, 6.

16. "Bantam Books Plans Film Fest Tie-In," *Box Office*, November 10, 1969, 10.

17. Patricia Johnson, "Ego, Yes, Indecision Often, But Love That Hollywood," *Variety*, January 10, 1962, 42.

18. *Ibid*.

19. "Anti-Brush-Off of Writers," *Variety*, November 16, 1966, 11.

20. "Book Notes," *Hollywood Reporter*, January 17, 1962, 7.

21. "Book Notes," *Hollywood Reporter*, December 5, 1961, 11.

22. "Inside Stuff—Pictures," *Variety*, August 10, 1966, 24.

23. "Sci Fi Award Goes to 20th-Fox for *Voyage*," *Box Office*, September 26, 1966, SW2

24. "*How the West Was Won* with L'Amour," *Hollywood Reporter*, January 26, 1962, 10.

25. "Book Notes," *Hollywood Reporter*, October 27, 1961, 9.

26. "3-Yr Advance Campaign for *King of Kings*," *Hollywood Reporter*, July 5, 1961, 2.

27. "*The Undefeated* Is Now Available in Paperback," *Box Office*, November 3, 1969, A2.

28. "Book Notes," *Hollywood Reporter*, August 15, 1962, 7.

29. "*Crossbow* Books Tie In with Picture Release," *Box Office*, May 31, 1965, A2.

30. "Signet Print Paperback of Cinerama *Khartoum*," *Box Office*, June 13, 1966, A1.

31. "Gold Medal Books to Print *Alvarez Kelly* Paperback," *Box Office*, September 12, 1966, A1.

32. "Four Paperbacks Are Set on New Universal Films," *Box Office*, September 19, 1967, A2.

33. "*Divorce American Style* Film and Book Tie-Up," *Box Office*, June 20, 1966, 12.

34. Advertisement, *Krakatoa East of Java*, *Box Office*, November 17, 1969, 13–18.

35. "*Stagecoach* Screenplay to Become Paperback," *Box Office*, March 14, 1966, A1.

36. "*Paint Your Wagon* Set for Novelization," *Box Office*, October 6, 1969, A2; "*Wagon* Tie-In into Second Printing," *Box Office*, December 1, 1969, A2.

37. "Paperback Film Tie Ups Multiplying—They're Novelty to British," *Variety*, September 23, 1959, 23; "*Guns of Navarone* Set in 15 Languages," *Box Office*, September 1, 1960, 5. A global bestseller was harder to achieve than you might think. A good many of the U.S. and U.K. bestsellers were considered parochial in their subject matter and not ideal for translation. *The Guns of Navarone*, translated into so many languages, had hit a publishing and movie marketing mother lode.

38. It's worth noting how potent a marketing tool the movie tie-in was by exhibitors. *Box Office* magazine, which targeted exhibitors more than

Variety, ran news stories in the context of marketing whenever a movie tie-in appeared, usually on the back of encouraging cinema owners to arrange their own tie-up with a local bookstore, window displays coinciding with movie's showing in the picture house.

39. A "dump-bin" was a lot grander than it sounds. It was a custom-made cardboard self-standing arrangement with slots for about a dozen books, and it stood in the middle of a bookshop, in a prime spot close to the door rather than among the books set out on the shelves.

Chapter Two

1. Photo, *Daily Film Renter*, October 4, 1955, 6.
2. "A Sequel to *Dam Busters*," *Daily Film Renter*, September 26, 1955, 1.
3. "Article," *Kine Weekly*, November 21, 1957, 22.
4. Peter Noble, "On the Floor," *Daily Film Renter*, May 30, 1957, 4.
5. "London," *Hollywood Reporter*, February 20, 1958, 3.
6. "Angel Here to Cast 20th's British *Java*," *Hollywood Reporter*, January 15, 1959, 1.
7. The book was published in Britain in 1959 as *The Last Frontier*. In America the same year Doubleday renamed it *The Secret Ways*. There was a Victor Mature western called *The Last Frontier* in 1955—and the title had also been used in 1932 and 1939—so unless Richard Widmark had purchased the film rights prior to American publication and announced a name change, then I have no idea why the book title changed.
8. "London," *Hollywood Reporter*, January 6, 1959, 3.
9. "Perlberg-Seaton Buy *Night Without End*," *Hollywood Reporter*, August 8, 1959, 3.
10. "$3,500,000 Budget on *Night Without End*," *Hollywood Reporter*, November 18, 1959, 3.
11. "Eric Ambler Reports," *Box Office*, November 23, 1960, 2.
12. "Widmark Sold on Producing U.S. Pix O'Seas," *Variety*, January 7, 1961, 14
13. Richard Widmark, "Creating Without Compromise," *Films and Filming*, October 1961, 7–8.
14. "Widmark to Star Self in *Secret Ways*," *Hollywood Reporter*, March 20, 1959, 18.
15. "Widmark Projects Three Heath Prod'ns Next Year," *Hollywood Reporter*, November 11, 1959, 2.
16. "Widmark Indie Unit in Two-Film Deal with U-I," *Hollywood Reporter*, August 10, 1959, 2.
17. "Widmark Projects."
18. Widmark, "Creating Without Compromise."
19. "Widmark to Star Self."
20. "Viertel *Secret* Plotter," *Hollywood Reporter*, October 2, 1959, 1.
21. "Bill Templeton Plots *Secret Ways* for U-I," *Hollywood Reporter*, December 17, 1959, 1.
22. "Widmark Signs Fem Lead," *Hollywood Reporter*, July 11, 1960, 2.
23. "Viennese Actress Set," *Hollywood Reporter*, August 9, 1960, 3.
24. "Austrian Sex Bomb," *Variety*, April 26, 1961, 154. Rather ungallantly Widmark expressed his surprise that you could find women as beautiful as his two leading ladies in Austria.
25. "Phil Karlson Will Direct Widmark *Secret Ways*," *Hollywood Reporter*, May 18, 1960, 2.
26. "Widmark Sold."
27. "Widmark Film Rolls," *Hollywood Reporter*, August 1, 1960, 3.
28. "Widmark Sold."
29. ."Widmark Reports," *Hollywood Reporter*, October 11, 1960, 3.
30. "Crew Hazards Under Red Guns as Documentary for U's *Secret Ways*," *Variety*, March 1, 1961, 19.
31. Widmark, "Creating Without Compromise."
32. "Phil Karlson Resumes," *Hollywood Reporter*, September 6, 1960, 2.
33. "Karlson Exits Widmark Picture Over Different Endings," *Hollywood Reporter*, September 22, 1960, 1. It's unknown what ending the director preferred.
34. "Widmark Back to U-I," *Hollywood Reporter*, December 15, 1960, 2.
35. Widmark, "Creating Without Compromise."
36. "New Role for Sonja," *Box Office*, May 8, 1961, W2.

Chapter Three

1. Foreman at this point should have been an Oscar-winning screenwriter on account of his contribution to *Bridge on the River Kwai* (1957). Since he was on the Hollywood blacklist he was not included, though that exclusion was rectified later. But at the time he was given the task of producing *The Guns of Navarone* that Oscar had not been handed out.
2. "Foreman to Make Four Pictures for Col in England," *Hollywood Reporter*, March 11, 1957, 2; "Columbia-Foreman British Film Deal," *Kine Weekly*, March 14, 1957, 8. The producer had an ever-evolving slate. At various times prior to the release of *The Guns of Navarone* he was associated with *The Key*, *The Mouse That Roared* and *The Human Kind*—which were all made, the latter as *The Victors* (1964)—plus *The League of Gentleman*, whose rights he later sold, *Insurrection* based on the Liam O'Flaherty novel and *Holiday* from the Constance Fitzgibbon book which was never made. He had also contracted with British author Stephen Potter ("Foreman Signs Author," *Hollywood Reporter*, June 7, 1957, 4) to make a series of films from his books and had purchased an original screenplay ("Foreman Gets *Debut*," *Hollywood Reporter*, May 16, 1957, 2) by Jane Byrd. But these weren't made either.
3. "Columbia Buys Novel," *Hollywood Reporter*, February 22, 1957, 3; "Columbia to Produce *Navarone* in England," *Hollywood Reporter*, March

4, 1957, 2; "Another Columbia Best Seller," *Hollywood Reporter*, March 26, 1957, 12. An immediate best seller in the U.K., the book had entered the U.S. Top Ten hardback chart and was serialized in the *Saturday Evening Post*.

4. "British Works Used for Many Columbia Films," *Variety*, May 8, 1957, 12; "Columbia to Produce 14 British Pix in Yr," *Variety*, December 10, 1958, 10. Other pictures being mooted were *Suddenly, Last Summer*, *Once More with Feeling* and an abortive attempt to film *Lord of the Flies* directed by Carol Reed and starring Alec Guinness. The studio had also gobbled up a huge number of British books as potential sources of movies. "Columbia to Prod 40 Feat: Half of Them Double A Heft," *Variety*, December 23, 1957, 13. Added to the A-pictures and B-pictures was a new category—Double A denoting big-budget pictures with multiple stars as part of an industry-wide campaign to win back audiences lost to television. Columbia was committed to making around a third of its annual output in Britain. "Novelists as Kings of Screen," *Variety*, August 20, 1958, 5. Hollywood was gobbling up books pre-publication. *The Guns of Navarone* was one of 49 that studios had purchased pre-publication. Columbia had 12, Fox 11 and the titles included *Exodus*, *Anatomy of a Murder*, *Ice Palace*, *Peyton Place*, *Lady L* and *The Bramble Bush*, all except one made within the next few years.

5. "13 Films About Three Wars," *Variety*, August 3, 1960, 3. By the time the movie came out, cinemas were awash with war pictures even though no movie in the genre except *The Young Lions* (1958) had made it big since *Bridge on the River Kwai* in 1957.

6. Brian Hannan, *The Making of* The Guns of Navarone (Baroliant, 2015), 16–18, 25–27; Carl Foreman Collection, British Film Institute. He had been called before the House Un-American Activities Committee but refused to name names. He fled to the United Kingdom, but was far from destitute. He took with him $250,000 from selling his share in the company he part-owned to partner Stanley Kramer. He was feted in London in part because he was seen as a fugitive from unfair American justice, in part because London was in awe of a Hollywood name and in part because he enjoyed the kind of living that opened doors to high society.

7. "Carl Foreman Forms His Own Company," *Hollywood Reporter*, October 27, 1951, 1.

8. Under a pseudonym or uncredited altogether he worked on *Sleeping Tiger* (1954), *Born for Trouble* (1955), *A Hatful of Rain* (1956) and *Heaven Knows, Mr. Allison* (1957).

9. "Foreman Setting Up Bette Davis Picture," *Hollywood Reporter*, February 4, 1952, 1. Foreman was to be writer-producer on *The Innocent* to be shot in London. "Foreman Scripts *Widow* for London Productions," *Hollywood Reporter*, August 5, 1952, 2. This was to be shot in London and France and star Marlene Dietrich, with whom Foreman was having an affair. "Rank Signs Foreman for Three Pictures," *Hollywood Reporter*, January 12, 1953, 2—this was only as a screenwriter.

10. Mike Connolly, "Rambling Reporter," *Hollywood Reporter*, November 8, 1956, 2; "Ask for Full Testimony in Carl Foreman Case," *Hollywood Reporter*, April 16, 1957, 2; "Carl Foreman's Rep Rehabilitated Set for Four Columbia Scripts," *Variety*, March 1957, 12. When he was officially in the clear, Columbia threw a huge party for him at Claridges Hotel in London ("London," *Hollywood Reporter*, March 29, 1957, 3) inviting over 200 guests.

11. "Columbia Bets $5m on Foreman's *Navarone*," *Variety*, September 24, 1958, 3.

12. "Carl Foreman to Percenters," *Variety*, November 12, 1958, 3. At the outset Foreman foresaw five top roles to be played by two American actors, two British and one European.

13. Mike Connolly, "Rambling Reporter," *Hollywood Reporter*, September 26, 1958, 2.

14. With Alexander Korda, he had owned the rights to *Bridge on the River Kwai* and wrote the first version of the screenplay which was discarded by David Lean.

15. "*Kwai* and *Key* Set the Columbia Pattern," *Hollywood Reporter*, June 19, 1958, 80; "London," *Hollywood Reporter*, July 25, 1958, 3; Mike Connolly, "Rambling Reporter," *Hollywood Reporter*, October 7, 1958, 2. Grant wanted $500,000 upfront, a 10 percent share of the gross and ownership of the negative after seven years.

16. "Burt Lancaster Up for *Navarone* Role," *Hollywood Reporter*, October 7, 1958, 1; Mike Connolly, "Rambling Reporter," *Hollywood Reporter*, July 15, 1959, 2; "Mason Draws *Guns*," *Hollywood Reporter*, November 6, 1959, 3; "Offer Palance *Guns*," *Hollywood Reporter*, November 5, 1958, 1; "Poise Brian Keith for *Guns*," *Hollywood Reporter*, November 10, 1958, 2; Mike Connolly, "Rambling Reporter," *Hollywood Reporter*, December 1, 1958, 2.

17. Hannan, *Making of* The Guns of Navarone, 69.

18. Hannan, *Making of* The Guns of Navarone. Howard had starred in Foreman's debut *The Key* (1958).

19. Kenneth More, *More or Less* (Hodder and Stoughton, London, 1978).

20. "Peck Out of Love with Marilyn Draws *Guns* for Columbia," *Hollywood Reporter*, November 19, 1959, 2.

21. Anthony Quayle and David Niven served in World War II.

22. "Chatter," *Variety*, December 17, 1958, 78; "Carl Foreman to Percenters," *Variety*, November 12, 1958, 3. Somewhat ambitiously, given the limitations of the role, he was on the lookout for a new Ingrid Bergman, Sophia Loren or Jennifer Jones.

23. "Globe Trotting Indie Film Rep Not Sorry for Self—But His Wife," *Variety*, April 29, 1959, 22.

24. "London," *Hollywood Reporter*, January 19, 1959. Trevor Howard acted opposite her for the screen-test which was directed by her lover French director Roger Vadim. Foreman was so confident

of his choice he invited the media to watch and persuaded the BBC to screen the test on its *Monitor* program.

25. "Dickering Callas for *Guns of Navarone*," *Hollywood Reporter*, August 5, 1959, 1; Hannan, *Making of* The Guns of Navarone, 62–63, 73.

26. British films were notoriously unpopular in America. Ealing comedies and Alec Guinness and Laurence Olivier had some success on the arthouse scene but only a handful (literally) of British movies featured on the *Variety* Annual List of Top Grossers (movies that had accumulated rentals of at least $1 million—rentals being the amount studios received from box office receipts once cinemas had taken their share). The war genre, so buoyant in Britain in the mid-1950s, was no better received.

27. "London," *Hollywood Reporter*, December 5, 1958, 3.

28. "Sees *Key* Likely Get $7m Gross," *Variety*, June 24, 1959, 67. The movie had done poorly in the U.S, grossing only $2m, but the $5m earned overseas meant it was "heading for real profit."

29. "London" *Box Office*, July 25, 1958, 3. One possibility was Orbetello on the west coast.

30. "Col Co-Prod Deal in Belgrade Looms," *Variety*, May 13, 1959, 12.

31. "Foreman May Train *Guns* on Grecian Locales from First Seagoing Studio," *Hollywood Reporter*, October 30, 1958, 6. Planning to convert a ship from the Greek Line, Foreman envisaged not just a floating studio, and accommodation for actors and crew, but a vessel to transport equipment and supply constant power for lights and camera. It would be complete with make-up and costume departments, an editing suite and a projection room.

32. "Columbia Adds *Holiday* to Foreman Slate," *Hollywood Reporter*, March 27, 1959, 6.

33. Best-known for his novel *The Mask of Dimitrios* and other thrillers in the Graham Greene class, he had written screenplays for *The Passionate Friends* (1949) for David Lean, Ronald Neame's *The Card* (1952), *The Cruel Sea* (1953), *The Purple Plain* (1954) starring Gregory Peck, *A Night to Remember* (1958), and Michael Anderson's *The Yangtse Incident* (1957). He was also scriptwriter on MacLean's *Night Without End*.

34. "U.S. British Writers Evolve Plan of Action," *Variety*, September 17, 1959, 23.

35. Carl Foreman, "Words Lose their Meaning," *Beaver County Times*, July 11, 1961.

36. "London," *Hollywood Reporter*, December 18, 1958, 3. The screenplay was only 118 pages. The standard calculation was one page equaled one minute of screen time. Foreman's rewrite ran to 158 minutes.

37. "Greeks: Hey Yanks, No Income Tax," *Variety*, December 16, 1959, 5; Halsey Raines, "Revolution in Rhodes," *Variety*, March 16, 1960, 24. The company would be absolved of all taxes and no duty applied to equipment.

38. Halsey Raines, "Producer Carl Foreman Hunch Kept *Navarone* Out of Strife-torn Cyprus," *Variety*, May 18, 1960, 12. "To justify my hunch, I had to prove I could make a better deal elsewhere. So I made a rush trip to Greece and looked at the island of Rhodes for a second time and it seemed to have all the ingredients I required. It turned out to be the luckiest of breaks."

39. Halsey Raines, "Producer Carl Foreman," *Variety*. Although *Variety* was old-school in its approach, it occasionally permitted articles that were written from a particular perspective. Halsey Raines was, in fact, the movie's unit publicist.

40. "British Navarone Seen Strike-Safe," *Variety*, March 2, 1960, 15.

41. "Mackendrick Backs Out," *Variety*, March 9, 1960, 21.

42. *Ibid*.

43. "Lee Thompson New *Navarone* Director," *Variety*, March 16, 1960, 19. The situation was also complicated by Peck having director approval. The choice came down to Thompson or Anderson. Thompson had a Cannes Palme D'Or to his credit and Peck admired Thompson's action work on *Flame Over India/North West Frontier* (1959). It was a pure stroke of luck he was free thanks (Hannan, *The Making of* The Guns of Navarone, 79) to the last-minute postponement of *A Dream of Troy* and the director pulling out of *Fire Over Etna* due to start filming in April. Thompson had worked with Quayle on *Ice Cold in Alex* and with Scala on *I Aim for the Stars* (1959).

44. "The Guns of Navarone," *After the Battle* Issue No. 177, 2017, 46–54.

45. Hannan. *The Making of* The Guns of Navarone, 64–65. Turnbull was for thirteen years the commanding officer of the raiding forces in the Aegean, carrying out 381 raids on German forces and subsequently honored by the Greek government. Bayerlein served with Rommel in Africa and had been technical adviser on *The Desert Fox* (1951) and *The Desert Rats* (1953) while Commander G.W. Stedman was captain of the U.S. Coast Guard ship *Courier* stationed at Rhodes since 1952.

46. "Filming *The Guns of Navarone*," *After the Battle* magazine No 177.

47. *Ibid*.

48. *Ibid*.

49. "Filming *The Guns of Navarone*," *After the Battle* magazine No 177.

50. "*Navarone* Tests Niven," *Spokesman-Review*, August 31, 1961.

51. "*Navarone* Star Competes with No One but Himself," *Telegraph-Herald*, September 7, 1961.

52. "Bill Hunt Interviews Director J. Lee Thompson," *The Digital Bits*, June 6, 2020. The repercussions were substantial. The Greek captain of the vessel was court-martialled. The navy, and thereafter the government, was furious with Foreman. The navy withdrew its cooperation. Although the captain was later reprieved, it was an ugly time, not something easily brushed under the carpet.

53. *Ibid*.

54. "King and Queen Watch Film Shooting," *Montreal Gazette*, July 2, 1960

55. Hannan, *The Making of* The Guns of Navarone, pp. 85–86; *After the Battle*; *The Digital Bits*.
56. Peck biography. Quinn biography. Peck was used to injury: on *The World in His Arms* he had lacerated his scalp, while production on *The Snows of Kilimanjaro* had shut down for nine days after he tore ligaments and ruptured blood vessels in his leg.
57. Pressbook, *The Guns of Navarone*.
58. Hannan, *Making of* The Guns of Navarone, 88–90.
59. *Ibid.*
60. *Ibid.*
61. Hannan, *Making of* The Guns of Navarone, 91. A new attempt was made to set up *Holiday*, this time with Lee Remick and Anthony Quinn. Foreman pursued film rights to Brecht's *The Three Penny Opera* and bought the rights to *Roar Like a Dove*, a Broadway show with over 1,000 performances and set David Niven as star. MGM dangled a writing-producing-directing gig for *40 Days of Musa Dagh* by Franz Werfel. And he wanted to capitalize on the success of his second production *The Mouse That Roared*, designed to beat the box office hoodoo that beset many British film releases in the U.S. Costing only $400,000, it had so far taken in $2.5 million, the bulk of it in the States. At the 495-seater Carnegie in Chicago, it had the longest run—20 weeks—of any film in a decade. His Columbia pact extended to six films including *Double Crossing* starring William Holden and Shirley MacLaine, *Trial of Strength* and *I Was Khrushchev's Double*.
62. Columbia's roadshow reticence was influenced by the flop of so many big-budget pictures on hard-ticket release the previous year including *The Alamo*, *Can-Can*, *Sunrise at Campobello*, *Pepe* and *Cimarron*.
63. Foreman's travels resulted in a record number of European royal premieres.
64. Pressbook; Hannan, *The Making of* The Guns of Navarone, 153–154.
65. "1961: Rentals & Potential," *Variety*, January 10, 1962, 13.

Chapter Four

1. He used the name Evan Hunter for more serious novels like *The Blackboard Jungle*, *Strangers When We Meet* and *Buddwing*—all filmed—and also went by the name of Richard Marsten, and Hunt Collins. All told, he produced over 100 novels.
2. Creasey wrote *The Toff* series under his own name; was J.J. Marric for the *Gideon* books and Anthony Morton for the *The Baron* series; and employed different names for his westerns, science fiction and romances. He published over 600 novels.
3. Jack Webster, *Alistair MacLean* (Chapmans Publishing, London: 1991), 94, 113. Milton Waldman was MacLean's chief tormentor, advising the author to abandon war stories.
4. Webster, *MacLean*, 89–90.
5. F. Scott Fitzgerald famously couldn't spell and his original title for *The Great Gatsby* was viewed as idiotic. T.S. Eliot's poem *The Waste Land* only emerged after copious editing and it was claimed, more recently, that the minimalist style of the critically acclaimed Raymond Carver was also the work of an editor.
6. Webster, *Alistair MacLean*, 112. Waldman was heavily critical of this effort, complaining it overstepped the bounds of probability so badly it would lose the reader.
7. *Ibid.*, 114.
8. *Ibid.*, 116.
9. "Book Notes," *Hollywood Reporter*, July 24, 1962, 6.
10. Glenn Lovell, *Escape Artist: The Life and Times of John Sturges* (University of Wisconsin Press, Madison, 2008), 244. A hard enough sell without the MacLean name attached, it was viewed in some quarters as no more than a "pulp detective novel."
11. "Sturges in 4-Picture Deal with the Mirisch Corp.," *Box Office*, April 15, 1963, 20.
12. Walter Mirisch, *I Thought We Were Making Movies, Not History* (University of Wisconsin Press, Madison, 2008), 211. "John was getting impatient to get back to work," said Mirisch. Sturges hadn't made a film in two years.
13. "High on John Sturges, Pin Him for Four," *Variety*, April 10, 1963, 15.
14. Lovell, *Escape Artist*, 244.
15. *Ibid.*
16. *Ibid.*, 243. "I'm no message director," said Sturges, "[but] this story is within the realm of possibility."
17. Charlton Heston, *An Actor's Life, Journals 1956–1976* (Penguin, London, 1983), 181.
18. Mirisch, *I Thought*, 211. "I had felt the subject required a major action-adventure star," he said.
19. *Ibid.* 212. Hackett was fired after two weeks.
20. Lovell, *Escape Artist*, 245.
21. *Ibid.*, 246.
22. *Ibid.*, 247.

Chapter Five

1. Webster, *Alistair MacLean*, 123. He admitted to *Sunday Express* journalist Robert Pitman: "I'm not a born writer. I know it and you know it…in Switzerland I wrote each book in thirty-five days flat…I just wanted to get the darn thing over." In fact, speed did not equate necessarily to poor quality. Georges Simenon wrote his books much faster. And MacLean glossed over the pressure of being a bestselling author, the need to produce a book a year. Not only that, but an author was also generally working on three books at once. Answering queries and correcting proofs and dealing with marketing issues on one book while writing the next and beginning to think about a third. "Alistair thought of his novel writing as a formula.

I think that's to diminish his ability," said Ian Chapman, son of Ian Chapman who discovered MacLean. "He never thought of himself as a good writer. On occasion he said he would prefer to write in Gaelic or even Spanish than in English. He didn't feel his English was good enough, which is clearly nonsense." Murray Scougal, "The Adventures of Alistair MacLean—The Scots Author Who Invented the Thriller," *Sunday Post*, December 27, 2021.

2. Webster, *Alistair MacLean*, 120. At the same time, he purchased two other operations, Bank House at Worcester and the Bean Bridge Hotel in Somerset.

3. Until the arrival of James Bond, it was the best-ever British release at the U.S. box office.

4. "Richard Wilson Directs Final P-S Pic at Para," *Hollywood Reporter*, December 8, 1961, 1.

5. "Harvey Huddles with Maugham on Bondage," *Variety*, May 15, 1963, 25.

6. "Filmways 3-Month Income," *Box Office*, February 1, 1965, S2.

7. "Hollywood Report," *Box Office*, May 11, 1964, 8.

8. "Hollywood Report," *Box Office*, October 12, 1964, 20.

9. *Ice Station Zebra* Files, Margaret Herrick Library.

10. "Ransohoff-Metro Prep *Zebra* Via Chayefsky," *Variety*, January 20, 1965, 5; "Hollywood Report," *Box Office*, February 1, 1965, 11.

11. "Novelist, Producer, Meet on *Ice Station Zebra*," *Box Office*, April 5, 1965, NE2.

12. Phil Kellogg of Wm Morris to Peck, May 11, 1965. Margaret Herrick Library, File 401, *Ice Station Zebra*, ID Number 71485932.

13. Cable, David Miller to Peck, May 6, 1965. Margaret Herrick Library, File 401, *Ice Station Zebra*, ID Number 71485932.

14. Margaret Herrick Library, File 401, *Ice Station Zebra*, ID Number 71485932.

15. Sturges to Peck, June 14, 1965. Margaret Herrick Library, File 401, *Ice Station Zebra*, ID Number 71485932.

16. Charlton Heston, *The Actor's Life, Journals 1956–1976* (Penguin, 1980), 222.

17. Kellogg to Peck, July 23, 1965. Margaret Herrick Library, File 401, Ice Station Zebra, ID Number 71485932.

18. Cable, Seymour Sommer to Peck, July 26, 1965. Margaret Herrick Library, File 401, *Ice Station Zebra*, ID Number 71485932.

19. "Hollywood Report," *Box Office*, December 6, 1965, 18.

20. Kellock to Peck, May 27, 1965. Margaret Herrick Library, File 401, *Ice Station Zebra*, ID Number 71485932.

21. Lovell, *Escape Artist*, 264.

22. "*Ice Station Zebra* Slated as MGM-Cinerama Film," *Box Office*, May 15, 1967, 16.

23. "Filmways Production Slate Hits New High with 11 Features Set," *Motion Picture Exhibitor*, July 20, 1966, 13.

24. "*Eagles*, MGM, to Star Richard Burton," *Box Office*, May 22, 1967, 10.

25. "Hollywood Report," *Box Office*, June 21, 1965, 12.

26. Lovell, *Escape Artist*, 264. This put him among the top-earning directors as well as being on a par with many big-name stars.

27. "Incomplete Composite Screenplay," September 20, 1965, Margaret Herrick Library.

28. "Outline by John Sturges," April 20, 1967, Margaret Herrick Library.

29. Lovell, *Escape Artist*, 264.

30. Ibid., 267.

31. Peck to Dee Pollock (an actor), November 1, 1966.

32. Ibid., 265.

33. Ibid.

34. Advertisement, *Variety*, June 21, 1967, 8–9.

35. William Kirtz, "Out to Beat Bond," *New York Times*, June 23, 1966, 109.

36. "*Ice Station* Finishes Production After 19 Weeks," *Box Office*, November 13, 1967, W3.

37. Dave Worrall, "*Ice Station Zebra*, Film in Focus," *Cinema Retro*, Volume 17, Issue 51, 23–24.

38. Lovell, *Escape Artist*, 265.

39. Worrall, *Cinema Retro*.

40. "*Ice Station Zebra* in World Premiere," *Box Office*, October 28, 1968, W1.

41. "Record Number of Prints Ordered for *Ice Station Zebra*," *Box Office*, November 4, 1968, 8.

42. "15 Major City Openings Set for *Station Zebra*," *Box Office*, November 11, 1968, 13.

43. "*Ice Station Zebra* Frozen Out; No N.Y. Cinerama Booking," *Variety*, October 23, 1968, 12; "No Zebra Shootout in N.Y., Gets *2001* Niche, Latter Grinds," *Variety*, October 30, 1968, 3 "*Zebra* Opens Dec 20 At Cinerama Theater," *Box Office*, November 11, 1968, E9.The problem was the city had, after the closure of Loew's Capitol, only one cinema capable of screening Cinerama films. While the new Ziegfield had that capability, it wasn't due to open until spring 1969 and was already committed to Columbia's *Mackenna's Gold*, ironically a Carl Foreman production. At one point, it looked as though *Ice Station Zebra* would be locked out of New York until March 1969 at the earliest.

Chapter Six

1. You might be surprised that so many independent producers pop up in MacLean's career. But the era of Hollywood studios running their own substantial production departments was long over. Instead, they tied up long-term deals with significant independent producers who, in return for finance and distribution, would feed movies on a regular basis into the studio supply chain.

2. "Kastner Joins Writer Mann," *Box Office*, February 19, 1962, 3; "Mann-Kastner Picks De Sica for Sanchez," *Box Office*, April 9, 1962, C3; "Kastner and Mann Sign Sophia Loren for Film," *Box Office*, July 30, 1962, 10.

3. "Mann-Kastner Buy Rights to *Light in August*," *Box Office*, May 7, 1962, 15.

4. "Elliott Kastner to Produce ECA-Beatty Production," *Box Office*, June 28, 1963, E4. The connection with Beatty paid off as in 1966 Beatty starred in *Kaleidoscope*.

5. "Hollywood Report," *Box Office*, June 25, 1962, 16; "To Film *Tropic of Cancer* for Embassy Pictures," *Box Office*, January 7, 1963, 15.

6. Kastner fell foul of writer William Inge, a Pulitzer Prize-winning playwright, who demanded his name be taken off the credits after disagreeing with the producer's alterations.

7. Worth pointing out how cheap movie rights and screenwriters could be, if either author or screenwriter lacked status and was looking for a breakthrough. The work of Ross Macdonald offered an upscale version of the pulp fiction that had flourished in the 1950s, novels with lurid covers that went straight into paperback. His Lew Archer private eye had appeared in over a dozen books before *The Moving Target* was purchased and Macdonald was being hailed as a natural successor to Raymond Chandler. But he hadn't cracked Hollywood. Goldman, while a best-selling novelist, had no standing as a screenwriter, and was seeking Hollywood redemption after being fired from his first movie gig *Masquerade* (1965).

8. Webster, *Alistair MacLean*, 128.

9. Contract signed by Beatty and Kastner, October 9, 1965. EKA.

10. "G-K Productions; 5 to WB; 9 More Pend," *Variety*, November 30, 1966, 3; "G-K Set for 14 Films in Two Years," *Box Office*, December 5, 1966, 6.

11. Letter, Denis Holt to Jack King, March 14, 1968; Letter, Kastner to MacLean, November 3, 1965. EKA. "I enjoyed our talk and your analysis very much," wrote Kastner to MacLean, and, moving the discussion along more professional lines, put his attorney in touch with the author.

12. "Kastner, Gershwin Sued by MacLean," *Hollywood Reporter*, February 16, 1982, 4. Originally, the deal had been assumed (Webster, *Alistair MacLean*, 130) to be worth $100,000 but that was intended as a down payment with the same again later. Letter Norman R. Tyre (of Gang, Tyre & Brown) to Gershwin, October 12, 1970. EKA. A dispute arose about whether this had been paid in full at the time of signing the contract with MacLean or whether half the sum was to be deferred. At first, as seen in this letter, it was assumed it had all be paid, but this later transpired not to be the case, creating bad feeling between author and producer. Letter, G.H. Ornstein to Kastner, February 7, 1967. EKA.

13. Webster, *Alistair MacLean*, 130. Screenplays by William Goldman and Robert Carrington, so presumably, respectively, *The Moving Target* and *Kaleidoscope*. Carrington would later be credited for *Fear Is the Key*.

14. Webster, *Alistair MacLean*, 130.

15. Webster, *Alistair MacLean*, 126. MacLean proved less astute as a hotelier than a writer. The hotels had not worked out and were eventually sold off.

16. Contract agreement signed by MacLean, January 20, 1966. EKA. Some observers have dated this five days earlier, working from, presumably, a verbal agreement made (Webster, *Alistair MacLean*, 130).

17. Webster, *Alistair MacLean*, 130.

18. Letter, G.H. Ornstein to Kastner, February 7, 1967. EKA.

19. "Calling Kastner," *Where Eagles Dare*, Movie Classic Special Edition (Revised Version) No 1, *Cinema Retro*, 56–57.

20. Telegram, Kastner to Burton, August 1966. EKA

21. Telegram, Kastner to Gershwin, May 2, 1967. EKA. Burton's agent had demanded 10 percent of the gross. Letter, Aaron R. Froch of Atlantic Programmes to MGM, February 25, 1970 (EKA) pointed out that, according to Richard Burton's contract once grosses had reached $14.5 million the star was due 10 percent of the gross over $10 million. Ironically, Burton's deal had been negotiated when the budget sat around $4.7 million so that, according to the standard 2.2 times budget break-even point, his percentage deal would be activated around the $10 million mark. "Producer/Participant Statement," MGM, November 20, 1969 (EKA) showed that to date Burton was entitled to $290,000 as the movie had by that point grossed $12.9 million. His $1 million upfront was an advance against his percentage. His deal was stepped—upwards. He remained on 10 percent until the profits reached 2.7 times the negative, went up to 12.5 percent when profits equalled 3.2 times the negative, increased again to 15% until profits touched 3.5 percent after which point Burton was entitled to a ceiling of 17.5 percent. (EKA)

22. "*Eagles*, MGM, to Star Richard Burton," *Box Office*, May 22, 1967, 10. "Solomon and Finger Examination of Accounts," November 12, 1971 (EKA) held up to scrutiny MGM's accounting, calling into the question the amount the studio allocated to *Where Eagles Dare* after it sold a block of four pictures to television for $6 million. And it also questioned a reissue double bill with *Ice Station Zebra*, arguing that proceeds should not be shared equally between the two pictures but that the war film should receive more.

23. Telegram, Kastner to Red Silverstein of MGM, November 1, 1967. EKA.

24. Memo, Maurice ("Red") Silverstein to Kastner, undated. EKA.

25. "Casting Suggestions" Folder, internal document, Winkast, August 1967. EKA.

26. Letter, Jerry Gershwin to Kastner, September 15, 1966, enclosing a copy of a telegram from Denis Selinger, September 14, 1966. EKA.

27. Telegram, Kastner to David Picker, 1967. EKA. Kastner said Brando would commit to the picture after completing *Reflections in a Golden Eye* (1967).

Notes—Chapter Six

28. Internal memo, undated. EKA.
29. Undated sheet. EKA.
30. The list entitled "Where Eagles Dare" and undated was typed on *The Bobo* letterhead. EKA. Cast salaries were set at $1.55 million, director at $250,000 with producers and screenplay expected to cost $450,000.
31. Internal memo, undated. EKA.
32. Letter, Brian Hutton to Kastner, August 7, 1967. EKA.
33. Telegram, Kastner to Red Silverstein of MGM, November 1, 1967. EKA.
34. *Ibid.*
35. "Casting Suggestions" Folder, internal document, Winkast, August 1967. EKA.
36. Letter, Brian Hutton to Kastner, August 7, 1967. EKA.
37. "Casting Suggestions" Folder, internal document, Winkast, August 1967. EKA.
38. At the time of these initial discussions, this character still went, as in the first draft screenplay, by the name of Torrance-Smythe. EKA.
39. Also considered for Schaffer according to Kastner's telegram to Picker. EKA.
40. "Casting Suggestions" Folder, internal document, Winkast, August 1967. EKA.
41. *Ibid.*
42. *Ibid.*
43. Memo from Bridge Drury, July 15, 1967. EKA.
44. Telegram, Kastner to Paul Kohner (Bronson's agent), October 11, 1967. EKA.
45. Telegram, Kastner to Red Silverstein of MGM, November 1, 1967. EKA.
46. Letter, Jack King to Denis Holt, March 26, 1968. EKA.
47. Contract, October 23, 1968, 1968. EKA.
48. Letter, Jack King to Denis Holt, March 26, 1968. EKA.
49. MGM Form 531. EKA.
50. Lee Pfeiffer, "Brian G. Hutton in Conversation," *Cinema Retro Special*, 53.
51. Letter, Jack King to Denis Holt, March 26, 1968. EKA.
52. Letter, Cymbeline (MacLean's company) to Gershwin and Kastner, August 4, 1967. EKA.
53. Letter, Denis Holt to Jack Foster, October 3, 1967. EKA.
54. Letter, Georges Lourau to Kastner, August 21, 1967. EKA.
55. Telegram, Kastner to Gershwin, May 2, 1967. EKA.
56. Telegram, Kastner to Red Silverstein of MGM, November 1, 1967. EKA.
57. *Ibid.*
58. *Ibid.*
59. Richard McWhorter had been executive producer of *The Taming of the Shrew* (1967) and would be associate producer on later Burton vehicle *Anne of the Thousand Days* (1969).
60. "Calling Kastner." However, I noted from examining the Kastner Archive that various versions of the script ran to 154 pages, 138 pages and 132 pages.
61. Letter, Gershwin to Kastner, April 1, 1966. EKA. He also called for "more depth of character for Smith," and "an intensified love story for Smith and Mary."
62. Telegram, Kastner to Red Silverstein of MGM, November 1, 1967. EKA.
63. Letter MacLean to Holt, May 27, 1967. EKA. MacLean wrote: "I think Yakima Canutt's suggestion that the cable car should cross this very dicey-sounding river is an excellent one; I should have thought of something along those lines myself!"
64. This is based on the "Denis Holt script." EKA. There was an anomaly here. The general rule-of-thumb was that each page of a screenplay was equivalent to one minute of screen time. So, theoretically, that should have resulted in a movie running of 132 minutes. But that didn't take into account so much of the action which was not detailed on the page.
65. Letter, Geoffrey Shurlock to Robert Vogel of MGM, November 20, 1967. EKA. The final decision on the official rating would be forthcoming after viewing the finished picture.
66. Letter, John Trevelyan to Kastner, August 9, 1968. EKA. That decision of course depended on seeing the final cut. The film went out as an "A," the British equivalent of a PG-13.
67. Letter, Jules Dassin to Kastner, May 23, 1966. EKA. Dassin wrote, "I am embarrassed not to share your enthusiasm for *Where Eagles Dare*."
68. "Believe can deliver Lean," Kastner told Picker in his 1967 telegram. EKA.
69. Memo referencing *The Bobo*, the Peter Sellers film dated 1966. EKA.
70. "Calling Kastner." The producer misremembered the budget. He put it at $6.2 million even though it cost two million more.
71. "Brian Hutton's Selling Out as Tie to Time, Mood," *Variety*, July 8, 1970, 22.
72. Internal memo, 1966. EKA. *The Violent Land* was on a list of planned projects headed by *Kaleidoscope* and *The Bobo* (both 1966). Some movies on the list were not made till later—*Sweet November* (1968), *The Long Goodbye* (1973), *The Bank Shot* (1974). Other projects on the list not making it onto the screen were *The Children of Sanchez*, *Flight into Camden* from the David Storey novel and an adaptation of William Goldman bestseller *Boys and Girls Together*.
73. Memo, Kastner to Gershwin, 1965. EKA. At that point *The Violent Land* with which Hutton was later involved was ascribed on the Kastner project list to the novel's author William Jacobs.
74. "Brian Hutton's Selling Out."
75. Letter, Hutton to Kastner, August 7, 1967. EKA.
76. *Ibid.* On this issue, he sought advice from Kastner.
77. Press release, "Hutton Hailed as Successor to Sturges."
78. Lee Pfeiffer, "Brian G. Hutton in Conversation," *Cinema Retro Special*, 53.

79. Letter, Sophie Vargas to Denis Holt, October 30, 1967. EKA. Canutt was born Enos Edward Canutt. He would be aged 74 by the time filming began.
80. Letter, Wm Meiklejohn Associates (Canutt's agent) to Kastner, April 26, 1967. EKA.
81. Letter, Jerry Gershwin to Ben Melnicker of MGM, May 1, 1967. EKA.
82. Austria was currently popular as a location with Rock Hudson-Gina Lollobrigida heist thriller *The Quiet Couple* (aka *A Fine Pair*), Maximilian Schell in *The Castle* and Omar Sharif in Terence Young's *Mayerling* all before the camera.
83. "Richard Burton," *Kine Weekly*, June 3, 1967, 12.
84. Letter, Holt to MacLean, May 24, 1967. EKA.
85. Schloss Hohenwerfen was built by Archbishop Gebbhard. It was in use at the time as a police training school.
86. Telegram, Kastner to Red Silverstein of MGM, November 1, 1967. EKA.
87. "Filming a Fortress," *Cinema Retro* Special Edition, 20.
88. "Austrian Not-So-Hideaway," *Cinema Retro* Special Edition, 28.
89. "Cable Car Capers," *Cinema Retro* Special Edition, 40.
90. "Leap of Faith," *Cinema Retro* Special Edition, 70.
91. "Stunts in the Studio," *Cinema Retro* Special Edition, 74.
92. "Cable Car Capers," *Cinema Retro* Special Edition, 40.
93. "Elevated *Eagles*," *Kine Weekly*, February 3, 1968, 16.
94. Letter, Silverstein to Kastner, April 2, 1968. EKA.
95. Memo, Gershwin to Holt, September 23, 1969. EKA. This lists a total of 12 areas including hairdressing and make-up that incurred cost overages.
96. Documentary accompanying the DVD.
97. "In Conversation," *Cinema Retro* Special Edition, 53.
98. Internal Memo, Kastner to Holt, February 15, 1968. EKA.
99. Memo, Kastner to Arvid Griffin, March 12, 1968. EKA. The first 13 scenes were shortened; dialogue cuts "agreed" to in the next six; for scenes 104–106 "Brian has worked out a shooting method to shorten scenes"; scene 154 was cut entirely; and dialogue was "trimmed" in scenes 157–160.
100. Memo to Jerry Gershwin, October 13, 1969. EKA. This looks as though it was actually sent by Denis Holt to Gershwin.
101. "*Where Eagles Dare*: Details of Negative Cost." EKA.
102. Invoice, "Americans Abroad Estate Office," September 26, 1967. EKA. The apartment was rented from September 27 to December 26, 1967, with a further four weeks added at the rate of £73.10pw.
103. Letter, Holt to Bishop, May 18, 1976. EKA.

104. Letter, Bill Edwards to Bayley Silleck, October 14, 1968. EKA.
105. Bayley Silleck to Bill Edwards, October 17, 1968; Joanne Ney to Silleck (undated). EKA. In the end *Playboy* wasn't interested in either Pitt or Richard Burton. Canutt was another publicity target with *Time* and *Look* magazine reported as being interested though *Argosy* had turned down artwork as of inferior quality.
106. "Top Sellers," *Sunday Telegraph*, September 3, 1967. The book was a sensational seller. The paperback copy I read, printed in 1979, still with Richard Burton on the cover, was the 28th impression.
107. Photographs, March 9, 1969. EKA. These show various displays taking up entire bookstore windows for the Fontana movie tie-in paperback. Such displays were generally the responsibility of store staff rather than a standardized display created by a studio marketing department.
108. Letter, Kastner to Burton, July 3, 1967. EKA.
109. Letter, Lee Barker to Mark Levy, March 5, 1970. EKA.
110. Memo, Gershwin to Holt, September 23, 1969. EKA.
111. "MGM Producer/Participation Statement," February 13, 1971. EKA.
112. "Producer/Participant Statement," MGM, July 31, 1984. EKA.
113. Letter, Silverstein to Kastner, April 2, 1968. EKA. Silverstein, whose name was Maurice, always signed letters with his nickname "Red."
114. Letter, Silverstein to Kastner, April 2, 1968. EKA.
115. Press Release, "Clint Eastwood America's Toshiro Mifune Returns to Japanese Screens in MGM's *Where Eagles Dare*." In retrospect, Japan seems an odd choice for a world premiere for a British-made World War II picture. I'm assuming MGM couldn't find a London screen available, hence the arrangement with *Gone with the Wind* at the Empire. And I'm also assuming the U.S. release was held back to take advantage of publicity emanating from the British Royal Premiere. And I'm also assuming that *A Fistful of Dollars* (1964/1967)—a remake of Japanese classic *Yojimbo* (1961)—had been as big a hit in Japan as the western remake of *Seven Samurai* (1954) known as *The Magnificent Seven* (1960) which had gone down a storm,
116. "*GWTW* to Take Short Breather," *Kine Weekly*, November 2, 1968, 5.
117. By the time the movie was released, Eastwood had proved his marquee credentials through *Coogan's Bluff* (1968) and *Hang 'Em High* (1968).

Chapter Seven

1. Kastner to MacLean, July 5, 1968. EKA. William Goldman would top the Rose record with over $440,000 for *Butch Cassidy and the Sundance Kid* (1969) after it went to auction. MacLean's fees

covered *Deakin*, the pirate picture known as *Caribbean* at this point, and book rights and screenplay for *Fear Is the Key*. For *When Eight Bells Toll*, he was cut in on everything Kastner would receive, the producing fees and the profits, an unusual arrangement as, usually, as with *Where Eagles Dare*, his share only began once all principal investors had recouped their monies.

2. Kastner to the Aga Khan. EKA. According to records kept at the time *When Eight Bells Toll* cost $1.4 million, *A Severed Head* $1.6 million, *Tam Lin* $2.1 million and *The Walking Stick* $2.2 million. In his memoir Kastner put the cost of *When Eight Bells Toll* at $1.9 million.

3. Kastner to MacLean, July 5, 1968. EKA. There was some confusion over this as Kastner to Lee Steiner, May 15, 1970, suggests there would be three sequels rather than two to *When Eight Bells Toll*.

4. Jack Pitman, "Every Man a Picture Producer; Private Banking Spurs Indie Pix," *Variety*, September 1, 1971, 7.

5. "Winkast Stepping Up Prod Slate to Fill Anticipated Shortage," *Variety*, November 19, 1969, 27. The company had *The Walking Stick*, *A Severed Head* and *Tam Lin* also in production.

6. Unger vs. Winkast, U.S District Court Central District of California, 1976.

7. "Rich Man's Letters" (EKA) gave names and addresses for individuals with a tick against those who had replied.

8. Kastner to Howard Hughes, February 19, 1970. EKA.

9. Kastner to the Aga Khan (undated, assuming 1970). EKA.

10. A.J. Perenchio, to Kastner, July 1, 1970. EKA. He was responsible for kick-starting Elton John's U.S. career by booking him into the Troubadour.

11. Ivan Boesky to Kastner, October 12, 1970. EKA.

12. Jack Pitman, "Every Man."

13. Robert Pickett to Kastner, June 1971. EKA.

14. Elliott Kastner Memoir, 24. EKA. Riklis later married Pia Zadora and funded Kurt Unger's *Pope Joan* (1972)

15. Michael Feeney Callan, *Anthony Hopkins: In Darkness and Light* (Scribners,1994), 131.

16. A contract had been drawn up and signed by both parties for payment "for introducing" Winkast to Glen Alden Corporation and RKO-Stanley Warner which promised Unger five percent of "other territories net profit" (OTNP) for Britain and Italy plus five percent from U.K. distribution. The "aggregate" of payments was not to exceed $250,000. However, similar sums would be available should the initial film lead to sequels. EKA. It was hardly surprising that after receiving nothing at all for his endeavors Unger sought legal retribution. However, in Kastner's eyes, "profits" meant whatever was left once all costs and investors had been paid, while Unger interpreted this to mean a share of the entire revenues and in 1976 took Kastner and Gershwin to court (Unger vs. Winkast, U.S District Court Central District of California, 1976). The crux of the claim was that Unger sought a share of the revenues Kastner had received from the film's British and Italian distributors. Rank had paid Kastner as his share of the box office £154,795 and £6,690 had come from the Italian end. Unger sought the equivalent of $21,000 for his share even though Kastner explained that half of the Winkast profits went immediately to MacLean. Kastner stuck to the line that there had been "no profits." The actual Winkast company had been dissolved in 1973.

17. Unger vs Winkast, 1976. EKA.

18. *Ibid*.

19. R.M. Fletcher to Denis Holt, July 25, 1973. EKA.

20. Holt to Kastner, December 20, 1971. EKA. Holt was credited with £4,725 for 21 weeks work, Rosenberg £1,800 for 30 weeks and Jenni Lynton, whom Anthony Hopkins romanced, £630 for 21 weeks. Given the average U.K. salary at that time was £1,204, Holt earned about ten times that, Rosenberg about three times, while Lynton was marginally above average.

21. Unger vs. Winkast, 1976. EKA.

22. "Alden Gets Go-Ahead on Production of Film," *Box Office*, May 19, 1969, 5.

23. Callan, *Hopkins*, 129.

24. "London Report," *Box Office*, October 6, 1969, E5.

25. He was the male lead in *I Start Counting* (1970).

26. Both Robin Hawdon (male lead) and Drewe Henley (significant role) appeared in *When Dinosaurs Ruled the Earth* (1970).

27. "8 Bells Casting," undated. EKA.

28. Perier to Kastner, undated. EKA.

29. Marilyn Beck, "Whatever Will Be Will Be," *St Petersburg Times*, August 30, 1976, 5D. Hopkins met his next wife Jennifer Lynton on the picture. She was working as an assistant to the producer and had been sent to pick him up at the airport. They got off to a bad start but over eight weeks their attitudes softened.

30. Robert Sellers, *1971: 100 Films from Cinema's Greatest Year* (The History Press, 2023).

31. Marika Aba, "Hopkins Wants to Be Himself," *Los Angeles Times*, August 22, 1970, A8.

32. Press release, "On the Road at Six." EKA.

33. "Interview with Anthony Hopkins." EKA.

34. *Ibid*.

35. Press release, "Tony Hopkins and Philip Calvert." EKA.

36. Letter from Winkast clarifying Hopkins contract, September 1, 1969. EKA. Hopkins had made *The Looking Glass War* (1970) for Columbia, in which he was billed fifth. He was also on "The Roster of Promising British Actors," *Variety*, May 13, 1970, 30.

37. "Hollywood Report," *Box Office*, October 13, 1969, 12.

38. EKA Files. In today's equivalent Delon would be paid £276,000 with £5,100 in expenses—translating

Notes—Chapter Seven

into $662,000 plus $12,240. The equivalent for Hopkins in today's money would be just under £100,000 which equates to just under $250,000. So not a large amount of money in anybody's terms.

39. Ten weeks after the 1971 general release of *When Eight Bells Toll* in Britain, distributors Rank cashed in by putting it out on the Odeon chain (though anglicized to *The Samourai*) as support to *A Town Called Bastard*.

40. "Interview with Nathalie Delon." EKA. Where in similar interviews with director and star, the men were asked about upbringing and their careers, Delon was subject to just questions about her beauty regime and clothes.

41. Call Sheets, EKA. P.J Peacock to Rosenberg, December 18, 1969. EKA. The whole issue arose in the first place because it looks like she was asked to stay on for an extra couple of days at the end of the shoot and the producers planned to swap the days she hadn't worked for those ones.

42. Miriam Brickman to Kastner, undated. EKA.

43. "Artistes Budget and Cost as at Nov 24th, 1969." EKA.

44. "Interview with Etienne Perier." EKA. He had secured the services of Sophia Loren and Peter Ustinov. When it appeared in 1965, Loren was still the star, but Paul Newman had replaced Ustinov.

45. Press release, 1962. EKA.

46. Perier to Kastner, November 31 (*sic*), 1964. EKA.

47. "Interview with Etienne Perier." EKA.

48. Date shown on the screenplay. EKA.

49. "Interview with Etienne Perier." EKA.

50. Press release, "Midnight Madness." EKA.

51. Press release, "The Coolest Actor in the Business." EKA.

52. Donnelly, "New Hero?" EKA.

53. Denis Holt, "Production Cost Statement No 7." EKA.

54. Press release, "Just Another Job." EKA.

55. Lily Poyser to Leon Ross, October 31, 1969. EKA.

56. Jack Pitman, "Every Man."

57. "Jerry Gershwin Solo; Ex-Pards Carry On," *Variety*, December 2, 1970, 7.

58. "Winkast Welcome for Jay Kanter," *Box Office*, May 10, 1969, 30; "London Report," *Box Office*, May 19, 1969, 18. Winkast threw a party for him for 300 guests at Les Ambassadeurs restaurant in London.

59. "London Report," Box Office, March 31, 1969, E4. Three films were planned. Only one finally appeared—*Toys* later titled *Toys and Games* and finally *Tam Lin* (1970) starring Ava Gardner and directed by Roddy McDowell. The others were *Rose of Tibet* from the Lionel Davidson bestseller and *The Machine* to be directed by Louis Malle. "Winkast Purchase," *Kine Weekly*, May 10, 1969, 30, referred to *The Chill* by Ross Macdonald, a sequel to *The Moving Target/Harper* and coming complete with William Goldman screenplay. It was also never made presumably because Paul Newman rejected it though he did reprise the character in *The Drowning Pool* (1975).

60. Advert, Anglo-Amalgamated, *Box Office*, February 9, 1970, 3, listed as a forthcoming release *The Burden of Proof*, later retitled *Villain* (1971), "from the producers of *Where Eagles Dare*." This would appear under the Kastner-Ladd-Kanter aegis.

61. Lee Steiner to Kastner, May 19, 1970. EKA.

62. Kastner to Lee Steiner, May 15, 1970. EKA.

63. *Ibid*.

64. Lee Steiner to Kastner, May 19, 1970. EKA.

65. MacLean to Kastner, August 18, 1970. EKA.

66. Joseph Sugar of Cinerama to Gershwin, November 15, 1973. EKA. Cinerama held the rights until 1990.

67. Margaret Gardner (of PR firm Rogers Cowan & Brenner) to Delon, April 10, 1970. EKA.

68. Margaret Gardner to Leon Roth, March 12, 1970. EKA. Gardner had received a terse reply from Delon's manager George Baume.

69. "*When Eight Bells Toll* TV Film," July 3, 1969; Kastner to John Shirley, November 4, 1969. EKA. It would cost £7,250 for a four-week schedule that would purport to show the author returning to his childhood locales as well as include sequences from the film such as Calvert in both wet suit and Naval uniform, the fight in the cemetery, underwater footage, the love scene and helicopter scenery.

70. Maurice Silversteain to Kastner, November 19, 1969. EKA. He had touted the film to distributors in Tokyo, Hong Kong, Manila and Bangkok.

71. Press release, April 10, 1970. EKA.

72. Rosenberg to MacLean, May 18, 1971. EKA.

73. Memo, R.M. Fletcher, undated. EKA.

74. "Rapid-American vs. Winkast Ltd., Supreme Court of the State of New York County of New York," January 4, 1988. Rapid-American and Winkast jointly owned the movie. Kastner had been critical of the Cinerama deal of November 24, 1970 (Letter, Marc Toboroff to James Pollak of Rapid-American, undated) calling it "ill-advised and disadvantageous" and complaining further that Cinerama had made a "weak distribution" deal with Orion. EKA.

75. Holt to Kastner, November 1976. EKA.

76. "Receipt from Alistair MacLean," October 24, 1977. EKA.

77. Kastner to Carolyn Kean of Simon Olswang & Co., November 1, 1994. EKA.

78. Elwood A. Rickless to Kastner, June 7, 1995. EKA. There were two separate letters sent this day.

79. "License Agreement Between Roadshow Productions and Atlantic Films of Stockholm," March 28, 2001. EKA. Atlantic paid $6,000 to license the film for television and VHS in Sweden, Norway, Denmark and Finland. But that was a minimum guarantee against 12.5 percent of gross sales and rental revenue. Daniel Unger informed me he had been working on behalf of the investors.

80. Sharon Powell of Rochamn Landau to Andrew Sparrow of Lecote, June 15, 2009. EKA.

81. Bishop to Kastner, October 10, 1989. EKA.

"Any claims against you will be dropped," Bishop assured Kastner. Kastner owed the MacLean estate £11,547 and was due £8,630 in return (Bishop to Kastner, November 8, 1988; Bishop to Kastner, February 1, 1989, EKA) so Bishop wiped out the difference.
  82. Kastner to Bishop, November 19, 1988. EKA.
  83. Stott was one of the first transgender women, undergoing gender reassignment in 1972 and changing her name to Angela Morley.

Chapter Eight

  1. An error on IMDb is responsible for the pervasive belief that this film was released before *When Eight Bells Toll*. IMDb gives the same release date for both 1970 and 1971, whereas it's the latter that's correct.
  2. "Film Production Slump No Problem for Alistair MacLean," *Variety*, December 10, 1969, 35.
  3. *Ibid*.
  4. Ian Johnston, "Author Says He's Businessman," *Los Angeles Times*, December 24, 1972.
  5. "Film Production Slump."
  6. "MGM-Filmways Acquire *Golden Rendezvous*," *Box Office*, May 6, 1968, 3.
  7. "Film Production Slump."
  8. *Ibid*.
  9. Since advertising at this point scarcely qualified as filmmaking at all, the number of directors who made the jump from making commercials (itself in its infancy) to making movies was virtually nil. This was long before the Scott Brothers, Ridley (*Blade Runner*, 1982) and Tony (*Top Gun*, 1986), and Adrian Lyne (*Fatal Attraction*, 1987) established commercials as a feeder route for Hollywood,
  10. Webster, *Alistair MacLean*, 141–143.
  11. Webster, *Alistair MacLean*, 143–145. While living in Switzerland MacLean had placed his copyrights in a company called Gilach. But when he moved to Britain they—and rights to future books—were transferred to the Crewe Organization which ran a tax scheme under which artists handed over their earnings in exchange for an annual salary. For its fee, the organization took one-third of income. MacLean's annual pay was set at £10,000 at a time when he was bringing in £300,000 a year and if he wanted more he had to make application to Crewe. David Bishop was charged with extricating MacLean from the scheme which cost £100,000, raised from a bank loan and selling cheaply the rights to two books.
  12. Webster, *Alistair MacLean*,143.
  13. Webster, *Alistair MacLean*,152.
  14. Thomas Lask, "End Papers," *New York Times*, November 4, 1969, 43.
  15. Letter, Sam Arkoff to Kastner, June 23, 1969. EKA.
  16. By this point, ABPC had sold off the rights to *H.M.S. Ulysses* which, with the British movie industry also in a parlous state, it couldn't hope to fund.
  17. Webster, *Alistair MacLean*, 153, 154.
  18. *Ibid.*, 154
  19. "Indoctrination Kurt Unger for his London Chores," *Variety*, March 5, 1958, 26; "Under Exiting Britain, UA," *Variety*, September 5, 1958, 5; "Vidpix Chatter," *Variety*, April 1, 1959, 44. Unger had come into production via distribution and sales. After working for United Artists as head of distribution in Italy, he was promoted to head of European production in 1958. But he lasted only a few months. He then worked as sales chief of the European operation of National Telefilm Associates and then as an independent distributor in Israel before persuading Paramount to part with $3 million for *Judith*.
  20. Author interview with Daniel Unger, who later produced *Return from the River Kwai* (1989) with his father.
  21. *Ibid*.
  22. *Ibid*.
  23. Webster, *Alistair MacLean*, 154.
  24. "Set *Puppet on String* [sic] to Roll in Amsterdam," *Variety*, December 10, 1969, 34; "British Films Shooting," *Variety*, May 6, 1970, 27.
  25. Webster, *Alistair MacLean*, 155.
  26. Author interview with Daniel Unger.
  27. Webster, *Alistair MacLean*, 154–155.
  28. Webster, *Alistair MacLean*, 155.
  29. Eddy Darvas and Eddie Lawson, *Don Sharp*, The London History Project, November 1993.
  30. *Ibid*.
  31. *Ibid*.
  32. Author interview with Tom Reeve.
  33. Tom Reeve, correspondence with the author.
  34. Letter, Colin Leighton to Kastner, August 14, 1971. EKA.
  35. "Additional Sequences," July 1970. Margaret Herrick Library, Alexander Knox Collection, ID 71441222.
  36. Darvas and Lawson, *Don Sharp*.
  37. Author interview with Daniel Unger.
  38. The dance troupe from BBC's *Top of the Pops* music show.

Chapter Nine

  1. MacLean to Kastner, August 18, 1970. EKA.
  2. Derek Todd, "The Emperor of Elstree's First 300 Days," *Kine Weekly*, March 7, 1970, 6–8, 19.
  3. Advert, *Variety*, January 21, 1970, 12–13; "MGM-EMI in Joint Deal on British Filmmaking," *Box Office*, April 27, 1970, 7; "MGM Setting EMI CoProds," *Variety*, June 10, 1970, 3; "MGM-EMI To Produce 12 films Annually," *Box Office*, July 6, 1970, 6.
  4. "EMI Prepares 18 Films to Be Released in U.S. Theaters," *Box Office*, June 20, 1972, 1. Other films included *Dulcima*, *Henry VIII and His Six Wives*, *Lady Caroline Lamb*, *Baxter*, *Our Miss Fred* and *On the Buses*. Apart from Paramount, Cohen

had lined up a series of less prestigious distributors including Cinema V, Cinevision, Gold Key Entertainments and Group W, which might, with possibly fewer films to sell, give these movies a bigger push. *Fear Is the Key* featured in a Paramount advertisement ("Promises Made, Promises Kept," Paramount, September 27, 1972, 13).

5. Kastner to Nat Cohen, October 25, 1974. EKA. Working with EMI on *Villain* had proved a disappointment. Kastner wrote: "Our worst fears about film distribution proved to be true... results poorer than anyone could have expected... it is our belief that you have recouped your negative costs." The implication being that the expected share of box office had not been passed on to the producers. Kastner threatened to conduct an audit. "Then we're going to start in on *Fear Is the Key*, you've been giving our lawyers the runaround for months." In truth, *Villain* suffered because Richard Burton had squandered a great deal of his marquee value after *Where Eagles Dare*. *Staircase* (1970) had been a monumental flop, he had been fired from *Laughter in the Dark* and although Oscar-nominated for *Anne of the Thousand Days* (1969) that movie had not been a rollicking hit. His career remained in the doldrums until revived by Kastner with *Equus* (1977).

6. "MacLean Again," *Kine Weekly*, June 12, 1971, 11.

7. Alan Ladd, Jr., to Paul Newman, August 26, 1971. EKA. At that time, the producers had allocated just one week for the chase, and in Florida, with nine weeks in England.

8. As shown in Kastner's files he routinely sent Newman scripts for projects, none of which took the actor's fancy. EKA.

9. Robert H. Solo to Nat Cohen, October 13, 1971. EKA.

10. David Brown to Kastner, October 14, 1968. EKA. Having received a copy of the novel, Brown declared it was "something we would have to see packaged before we could even consider it, although it has a great action sequence." It was perhaps this initial admission of the book's qualities that sent the producers chasing Paul Newman, aware that *Butch Cassidy and the Sundance Kid* had been made by that studio,

11. Gordon Stulberg to Kastner, November 5, 1971. EKA.

12. "Belgravia Productions Agreement with Atlantic United Productions" (Winkast and Anglo-EMI). EKA.

13. Sylvaine Fretet, Canal +, to Sir Jay Kanter, May 19, 2010. EKA.

14. "Car Chase Outline—Louisiana Version," March 6, 1972. EKA.

15. Phil Gersh, to Kastner, November 18, 1971. EKA. While Fleischer's interest was clearly genuine, Gersh, in typical agent fashion, took the opportunity to promote other clients, namely Ken Annakin (*Battle of the Bulge*, 1965), Guy Green (*The Magus*, 1968)—especially if "you required a (British) director for quota purposes"—and American David Miller (*Hammerhead*, 1968) should Fleischer not be deemed suitable.

16. Rolf Kruger to Nat Cohen, September 24, 1971. EKA.

17. Paul Stader to Alan Ladd, Jr., January 19, 1972. EKA.

18. Ed Palmer to Kastner, May 23, 1972. EKA.

19. Philip Collins to Robert Carrington, September 10, 1971. EKA.

20. "Notes for Nat Cohen," Winkast, January 1, 1972. EKA.

21. He oversaw *Little Big Man* (1970) and *Le Mans* (1970) but ultimately the venture was not a success.

22. Nat Cohen to Lee N. Stiner of Hess Segall et al., January 1972. EKA. "I really took umbrage at their attitude," wrote Cohen.

23. Lee N. Steiner to Nat Cohen, December 27, 1971. EKA. EMI would be left with just the UK, Australia and New Zealand. In the U.S. and Canada and countries such as France, Italy, Germany, etc., where dubbing was required, the fee rose to 30 percent.

24. Elliott Kastner to Nat Cohen, October 25, 1974. EKA.

25. Agreement, Anglo EMI and Paramount, July 11, 1972. EKA. "Paramount Gets Release of *Fear*," *Box Office*, July 31, 1972, 11.

26. Advertisement, United Artists, *Box Office*, November 13, 1972, 20–21.

27. Jay Kanter was another agent-turned producer. His clients had included Marilyn Monroe, Marlon Brando and Grace Kelly. Alan Ladd, Jr., son of actor Alan Ladd, Kastner's other partner, had also been an agent. Later president of Twentieth Century–Fox, under Gordon Stulberg, he greenlit *Star Wars* (1977) and *Alien* (1979). His The Ladd Company produced *Blade Runner* (1982), and he won an Oscar for *Braveheart* (1995).

28. "Agreement, Winkast," October 20, 1970. EKA. "Agreement," December 15, 1972. EKA. Initially, when Kanter joined the team in 1970 shares were allocated thus: Gershwin had 46.75 percent, Kastner 38.75 percent and Kanter 15 percent. It was agreed that Gershwin could use any of the accumulated properties except for *Sometime Champs*. Two years later, when Gershwin was moving out of the company, the agreement between Gershwin and K&K allowed that between them they had 49 properties including *Force 10 from Navarone*.

29. With fees deferred, *The Nightcomers* (1971), was made for just $500,000 and then sold to mini-major Avco Embassy for $1 million. EKA. Other movies on the slate included *Night Watch*, *The Big Sleep*, and the unmade *Cherry* ("Scripter Wraps *Cherry*," *Variety*, May 24, 1971, 15) from German Hans Konigsberger.

30. "KLK Co Pick Up Pix Prod Pace VIA Outside Financing," *Variety*, September 6, 1971, 6. The company still maintained, "it can afford to move ahead with more important fall and winter projects without waiting for preproduction distrib deals to be firmed."

31. "Ladd-Kastner in Louisiana Locationing," *Variety*, May 24, 1972, 28.
32. "Wrap Key in London," *Variety*, July 19, 1972, 20.
33. Fred Wright, "Chitwoods Smash into Film," *Evening Independent*, June 28, 1973.
34. Paul Reynolds, "An Interview with Barry Newman," *Money into Light* blog, 2019.
35. "All Keyed Up in Berkshire," *Film Review*, September 1972.
36. Denis Holt to Alan Ladd, Jr., August 10, 1971. EKA.
37. Ann McMorrow to Gavrik Losey, March 21, 1972. EKA.
38. Agreement, Anglo EMI and Paramount, July 11, 1972. EKA.
39. Ladd to Judy Scott Fox of Wm Morris, October 24, 1972. EKA.
40. Agreement, KLK and Ian La Fresnais, 1972. EKA. He was provided with first-class travel to the United States.
41. "Second Draft Revisions to Be Made," June 28, 1971. EKA.
42. Agreement, Anthony A. Williams of the Wm Morris Agency to Alan Ladd, Jr., January 25, 1975. EKA.
43. Williams to Ladd, January 28, 1972. EKA.
44. Alan Ladd, Jr., to Douglas Rae of CMA, January 4, 1972. EKA. Tuchner's travel allowance was restricted to outside a 30-mile radius of Charing Cross in central London, and for that he would be supplied with car and driver.
45. In order to meet Clause 6 of the Alien Order, the producers had specified: "No British actor in the opinion of the producers and financiers can adequately meet the national and accent of the role particularly within the limited price range available for this particular role. The producers have done their best without success to cast the part from foreigners long resident here."
46. Mary Selway to Mr. Newman, April 28, 1971. EKA.
47. "Casting Advice Note," April 24, 1972. EKA.
48. Ladd to Tuchner, January 25, 1972. EKA
49. Ann McMorrow, Anglo EMI UK to Gary Dartnell, Anglo EMI U.S., February 15, 1972. EKA. The issue was resolved within the day.
50. Gavrik Losey to Philip Collins, March 1, 1972. EKA.
51. Ladd to Losey, February 1, 1972. EKA.
52. Losey to Collins.
53. Ann McMorrow to G.C. McLean of Pathé Equipment, March 2, 1972. EKA. Gavrik Losey to Keith Ward of Motion Picture Hire Facilities, March 21, 1972. EKA. You tend to get the impression when the budgets for movies are thrown around that money is no object. But, in fact, the opposite was true. Penny-pinching was the order of the day. Losey proposed paying Pathé £20pw for three rooms for 4–5 weeks, but he was told he would have to pay £250 for a month. Instead he went to Bayswater for four offices at £45pw from March 6 "until further notice." All incidental costs had to be accounted—including £55.45 for photocopying, £36.54 for fares and £27.95 for cables, telex and long-distance phone calls (R.M. Fletcher to Jay Kanter, April 18, 1972. EKA).
54. "Re *Fear Is the Key* Source Music," undated. EKA.
55. Philip Collins to Kanter, January 26, 1973. EKA.
56. "Re *Fear Is the Key* Source Music," undated. EKA.
57. Kanter to Fishman, February 5, 1973. EKA. To date there have been seven recordings of the OST. Pye released an album and an 8-track cartridge in the UK while Astor had the rights in Australia. In 1999 Cinephile issued a remastered CD and album and in 2010 Silva Screen brought out a CD and an LP.
58. Ladd to Farlan I. Myers, J. Walter Thompson, October 4, 1972. EKA. The movie had gone "considerably over budget" filming the chase and bought two additional Gran Torinos at cost, which were also "totalled."

Chapter Ten

1. Tom Reeve, author interview. He added, "My father regularly stayed in touch with Alistair, stayed by Alistair's side through all of it. Contrary to public perception, Alistair was very generous, and would be touched by people in trouble, wanting to help. In fact, the best thing my dad did was to stop him giving it all away."
2. "A Lantern Amidst London's Trade Gloom Held Aloft by Colombia Pics," *Variety*, October 29, 1969, 6.
3. "London Report," *Box Office*, November 3, 1969, 4; "London Report," *Box Office*, November 10, 1969, 15.
4. Webster, *Alistair MacLean*, 141.
5. Kastner to MacLean. EKA. Reeve would have to earn the credit. He was down to work for 40 weeks on each picture. Still, it was a very good deal for, at that time, an inexperienced wannabe.
6. Tom Reeve, author interview.
7. Morris-Adams ran a highly successful merchandizing business called CPM.
8. Author interview with Richard Morris-Adams.
9. Webb had been heavily involved in building the M1 motorway in Britian. He died tragically when the helicopter he was piloting out of Le Touquet plunged into the sea on May 30, 1978.
10. "U.K. Hybrids with France," *Variety*, November 23, 1983, 5. There were only five British-French co-production deals that year. This was a big improvement in previous years when the lack of trade agreements made this virtually impossible.
11. Author interview with Richard Morris-Adams.
12. Up to this point, he had one writing credit, for documentary short *Telegram for America* (1956).
13. Wheeler was credited in the movie for the screenplay and Wheeler for adapting the novel.

14. Oddly enough, Rampling had a small part in *Vanishing Point*, but it was cut. In his interview with me Tom Reeve recalls bumping into Rampling at the White Elephant Club in London in the company of Maude Spector who became the casting director for the film.
15. Author interview with Richard Morris-Adams.
16. "U.K. Hybrids"; "Perainos U.K. Pickup of *Vaccarès*," *Variety*, June 18, 1975, 22.
17. "U.K. Hybrids."
18. Author interview with Tom Reeve. He recalled this figure after discussions with his father. It's entirely feasible the confusion arose from Transatlantic miscommunication. The figure of $750,000 could have been mistaken for £750,000 in which case that would have translated into the larger sum.
19. "*Caravan* Rolls," *Variety*, October 10, 1973, 17; "*Vaccarès* Lensing Done," *Box Office*, January 7, 1974, E7.
20. "Film Sales in Foreign Markets Whole New Game: Ian Jessel," *Variety*, October 16, 1974, 31. Worldwide distribution had undergone a further change with "local product much stronger than imports."
21. *Ibid.*
22. Not to be confused with the British outfit that had made *Saturday Night and Sunday Morning*, 1960.
23. "Form Bryanston to Produce, Direct," *Box Office*, November 6, 1972, 9; "Bryanston to Distribute *Caravan to Vaccarès*," *Box Office*, July 7, 1975, C1; Advert, *Variety*, April 17, 1976, 15–17. The Bryanston slate for 1976 included *Teenage Graffiti* and horror films *Symptoms* and *The Bride*. Unfortunately, company president Louis Peraino was in 1976 indicted for distributing pornography ("Bryanston Regrouping After Court Ruling," *Box Office*, June 16, 1976, 11) which had a knock-on effect on all that year's releases, of which *Caravan to Vaccarès* was one.

Chapter Eleven

1. "Alistair MacLean." EKA.
2. Bishop to Kastner, January 25, 1968. EKA. Kastner to MacLean, August 24, 1970. EKA.
3. Westerns remained a booming industry for the publishing industry, but most were short and written quickly by journeymen authors who turned out three or four a year to make a living. Louis L'Amour, for example, wrote 105 books; J.T. Edson, 180. Occasionally, a literary critic would give them the nod and it might enter the lower reaches of the bestselling charts for a week or so; *True Grit* was one such example. None featured in the annual Top Ten of bestsellers any year during the 1960s.
4. "13 Film Book Tie-Ins Set By UA," *Box Office*, August 11, 1975, 13. Another Bronson western *From Noon 'Til Three* received the novelization treatment and around 1.8 million copies of source novels for *Dog Soldiers*, *One Flew over the Cuckoo's Nest*, *The Wilby Conspiracy* and *Semi Tough* helped market the movies through bookstalls.
5. Margaret Herrick Library. ID720176011 and ID720616670.
6. Margaret Herrick Library. ID71361865 and ID71330346.
7. Wisconsin, United Artists Internal Memo, Bill Bernstein to Arthur Krim et al; "Elliott Kastner Two-Picture Deal," October 29, 1971; Bill Bernstein to Files; "11 Harrowhouse," June 7, 1973; Bill Bernstein to Elliott Kastner, "*Rancho Deluxe*," February 25, 1974. All EKA. Before the deal for the first two was finalized Kastner had already paid out of his own pocket just over $45,000 on options and screenplays. Author Donald Westlake was due $80,000 plus a percentage for *Cops and Robbers* and the Raymond Chandler estate $75,000 with screenwriter Leigh Brackett earning $20,000. The deal for *11 Harrowhouse* was contingent on securing Walter Matthau and when that proved impossible the project shifted to Twentieth Century Fox. *Rancho Deluxe* was budgeted at $1.6 million and *Cops and Robbers*, $1.62 million. *Cops and Robbers* ("Results of Distribution of Released Pictures, UA, Wisconsin, Box 1, Folder 8") turned in an ultimate profit of $1.14 million and *Rancho Deluxe*, $1.44 million.
8. "Jerry Gershwin Back with Elliott Kastner in 2 Film Projects," *Variety*, December 17, 1975, 5. Although they were setting up *Fast Lane and Equus*, the former never appeared and when the latter was filmed it had only the Kastner imprimatur.
9. United Artists Archive, University of Wisconsin, Box 1, Folder 8. Audience appreciation of Bronson can be seen from figures notched up in Sweden. ("Hard Krona of Sweden Spells Impressive Totals," *Variety*, May 12, 1976, 342.) Swedish grosses included $2.4 million for *Death Wish* (1974), $1.45 million for *The Stone Killer*, $1.5 million for *The Streetfighter*, $1.77 million for *Breakout* and $1.33 million for *Mr. Majestyk*. These figures were gross not rentals—the rental figure would be about half the gross.
10. Brian Hannan, *In Theaters Everywhere: A History of the Hollywood Wide Release, 1913–2017* (Jefferson, NC: McFarland, 2019), 189.
11. Kastner Memoir.
12. "Breakheart Pass," *Time*, May 5, 1975.
13. UA Internal Memo, Bill Bernstein to Robert Geary, October 15, 1974.
14. *Breakheart Pass* script, 109 pages, Margaret Herrick Library. ID72061671.
15. "Revised screenplay by Alistair MacLean and Lorenzo Semple Jr.," February 4, 1975, with changes through March 10, 1975, 119 pages. Margaret Herrick Library. ID71361865.
16. UA Internal Memo, Lee Katz to William Bernstein, March 13, 1975.
17. "Indians Demand Equal Pay to Fight Cowboys," *Box Office*, March 10, 1975, W5. Production chief Don Guest denied there was inequality, saying all extras were paid the same and the Nez

Perce did not suffer a $20 shortfall. In fact, he said the extras were paid more than usual because they were filming in snow.

18. United Artists Archive, University of Wisconsin, Box 1, Folder 8.

19. Gershwin to Rosenberg, August 28, 1975. EKA.

20. Robert J. Landry, "Elliott Kastner: 34 Pics in Nine Yrs," *Variety*, June 25, 1975, 5.

21. "Productions Rediscover Trains," *Variety*, May 15, 1976, 28.

22. "*Breakheart* Tops Million Mark in First 2 Weeks," *Box Office*, May 15, 1976, 37.

23. "Boxcar Dinner Is Part of *Breakheart* Bally," *Box Office*, May 17, 1976, A32; "Train Set Giveaway Revs *Breakheart*," *Box Office*, May 31, 1976, 17

24. There are exceptions, of course. *The Sons of Katie Elder* (1965) spent quite a time wondering what's going on and another Hathaway piece, *Five Card Stud* (1968), was a detective story.

Chapter Twelve

1. Published by Doubleday in hardback in the U.S.

2. "Laurence Harvey Announces Four Major Film Projects," *Box Office*, May 23, 1966, 12.

3. "Harvey Huddles with Maugham on *Bondage*," *Variety*, May 15, 1963, 25.

4. "Laurence Harvey Announces," *Box Office*. The others were: *The Reason Why* from the Cecil Woodham-Smith book about The Charge of the Light Brigade originally published in 1953 and sci fi *The Long Loud Silence*. *The Reason Why* nearly brought him to his knees. He initiated a lawsuit against Woodfall Films, the makers of *The Charge of the Light Brigade* (1968). He didn't manage to prevent their version being made and as part of the settlement was given the role of a Russian prince, a part which was edited out of the completed version. He had directed his second picture by default when Anthony Mann died during the making of *A Dandy in Aspic* (1967) and he completed the shooting. He only directed one more film, *Welcome to Arrow Beach* (1973).

5. "MGM-Filmways Acquire *Golden Rendezvous*," *Box Office*, May 6, 1968, 3.

6. James Chapman, "Film Finances and *Golden Rendezvous* (1977): Financial Mismanagement, Personal Tensions and Political Scandal," *Historical Journal of Film, Radio and Television*, 42:4 (2022), 707–727, DOI: 10.1080/01439685.2021.2013019.

7. James Chapman, "Film Finances."

8. "Yank Films Weather O'Seas," *Variety*, May 23, 1973, 5.

9. James Chapman, "Film Finances."

10. Crossover from records into music was not unusual. Fantasy Films which produced *One Flew Over the Cuckoo's Nest* (1975) was an offshoot of Fantasy Records whose biggest act was Creedence Clearwater Revival and Robert Stigwood, producer of *Saturday Night Fever* (1977), started out in the recording industry.

11. Chapman put the budget at the lower figure, reports in the trade papers opting for the higher one: "MacLean *Rendezvous* $4.5-Mil Actioner Gets Rolling in Indian Ocean," *Variety*, March 2, 1977, 40; "*Rendezvous* Rolls on So Africa Site," *Variety*, March 16, 1977, 36.

12. "Pieterse Seeking *Rendezvous* with Distributors," *Hollywood Reporter*, February 2, 1978, 12.

13. James Chapman, "Film Finances"; "UA Ready for '78 with 29 Pix costing $100-Mil," *Variety*, November 23, 1977. *Golden Rendezvous* was promoted as a forthcoming release.

14. James Chapman, "Film Finances"; "Rank Leisure Reactivates Feature Film Financing," *Variety*, January 4, 1978, 7.

15. James Chapman, "Film Finances."

16. "Pieterse Seeking *Rendezvous*."

17. "MacLean *Rendezvous*."

18. "Pieterse Seeking *Rendezvous*."

19. James Chapman, "Film Finances."

20. James Chapman, "Film Finances."

21. "MacLean *Rendezvous*."

22. James Chapman, "Film Finances." Harris later settled for $20,000 for expenses but believes he was unfairly penalized on future films when part of his salary was put in escrow.

23. "Wayne Files Suit Over Film Score," *Variety*, June 13, 1979, 76.

24. James Chapman, "Film Finances."

25. "New-Look *Golden Rendezvous*," *Screen International*, February 4, 1978, 20.

26. James Chapman, "Film Finances."

27. Hemdale was founded in 1967 by British actor David Hemmings (*Blow-Up*, 1966) and insurance agent John Daly. Eventually, the business expanded into real estate, public relations, talent agency and restaurants but its core remained movie making. It either made in its entirety or part-funded films like *Melody* (1971), *The Triple Echo* (1972), *Tommy* (1975), *The Terminator* (1984) and *Platoon* (1986).

28. James Chapman, "Film Finances."

29. Review, *Variety*, December 14, 1977, 13,

30. James Chapman, "Film Finances."

31. "Wayne Files Suit."

32. "14th Sitges Horror Festival Entries," *Variety*, September 2, 1981, 6.

33. "Theatrical Movie Rankings 1981–82," *Variety*, September 29, 1982, 44. The period covered was from September 1, 1981, to August 31, 1982. It ranked ahead of Charles Bronson-starrer *Love and Bullets* (1979), Rock Hudson-Mia Farrow disaster picture *Avalanche* (1978) and drama *Comes a Horseman* (1977) with Jane Fonda and James Caan, all of which small-screen showings had been preceded by cinema release.

Chapter Thirteen

1. It was renamed *The Moving Target* in the U.K.

2. "*After Navarone*," *Kine Weekly*, April 15, 1967, 3.

3. "Carl Foreman *Navarone* Project," *Variety*, June 8, 1977, 6.

4. "Premise for Sequel to *The Guns of Navarone*, Devised by Carl Foreman and Supplied to Alistair MacLean," July 21, 1966. EKA.

5. *Ibid.* "Mallory and Miller are no longer active commandos in the field…and this should come as no surprise because…. [they] were considerably beyond the age of active commandos during the period." Their retiral is somewhat ingenuous given their age didn't enter the equation for their original adventure. Mallory heads up the commando school rather than, as in the film, in charge of catering while Miller is an explosives and sabotage instructor. Foreman wanted to see James Robertson Justice return as their boss. Andrea for some reason has been "virtually kidnapped" (shown in brief flashback). EKA.

6. *Ibid.*

7. *Ibid.*

8. "Six Films Re-Titled," *Box Office*, May 22, 1967, 11.

9. Advert, *Kine Weekly*, September 14, 1968, 12; "Hollywood Report," *Box Office*, September 16, 1968, 16.

10. "*Force 10* Project Goes Full Circle as Col Shifts It Back to Foreman," *Variety*, September 2, 1970, 43.

11. "*After Navarone*," *Variety*, April 19, 1967, 4.

12. "Carl Foreman Projects," *Variety*, September 11, 1968, 26.

13. "*Force 10* Project."

14. Carl Foreman to Kastner, January 15, 1966. EKA. Solely in his capacity as a writer, Foreman had taken up Kastner's invitation to take a shot at turning William Goldman bestseller *Boys and Girls Together* into a screenplay. In the end, Foreman did not proceed with the Goldman project, surmising that, thanks to the novel's permissiveness, "there was no way to get it on film at least in any way that would enable the film to remotely resemble the book."

15. "Carl Foreman Adaptation." Margaret Herrick Library. File 853, *Force 10 from Navarone*, ID7140346.

16. *Ibid.*

17. "Memorandum of a Meeting held on 27th May at 2.30pm at Columbia Pictures Corporation Limited, attended by Kenneth L. Maidment of Columbia, Alan Ladd Jr and R.M. Fletcher." The year was included in the covering letter, dated June 2, 1969, sent by Fletcher to Maidment. Maidment represented Columbia, Ladd was there on behalf of Winkast and Fletcher was the lawyer.

18. *Ibid.* The rights were sold by "a MacLean company, J.M.R. Productions."

19. *Ibid.* This would kick in once net profits exceeded $600,000. The studio had three years to recruit a director and star before the rights reverted back to the author.

20. *Ibid.*

21. *Ibid.* For a fee of $5,000.

22. *Ibid.*

23. *Ibid.*

24. *Ibid.* This broke down into $200,000 (with $50,000 deferred) for producer's fees, $25,000 in legal fees, $15,000 for publicity and $50,000 for overhead

25. Cinema Center was an offshoot of CBS which presented a challenge for existing legislation since not only did the Paramount Decree of 1948 prevent studios owning cinemas and vice-versa, but an earlier statute stopped studios owning television stations. The product shortage triggered a legal rethink and CBS followed fellow network ABC and cinema chain National General into the movie business.

26. Jerry Gershwin to Jay Kanter, May 14, 1970. This letter was written on Cinema Center letterhead. Gershwin and Kastner had gone their separate ways. Kastner had formed a new company with Kanter and Alan Ladd, Jr. EKA.

27. This is my assumption. In his correspondence (Gershwin to Kanter, "Comments on *Force 10* First Draft," May 14, 1970) Gershwin states, "John T agrees his people are lacking…" John T. Kelley's name came second in a list of screenwriters suggested. Ben Maddow was top of a list that included Walter Newman, Robert Towne, Stirling Silliphant and James Lee Barrett. EKA.

28. *Ibid.* Gershwin to Kanter, "Comments." Gershwin was calling for a rewrite and offering strong opinions as to how the characters should be developed and their interplay. "As the situation portion of the story unfolds utilizing surprise and suspense, we will also unfold the individual characters that make up the teams." EKA.

29. *Ibid.* Based on a true story, apparently.

30. *Ibid.*

31. *Ibid.*

32. "*Force 10* Project."

33. "Despite Industry Slide, Foreman Has More Projects Than Can Handle," *Variety*, January 27, 1971, 23.

34. Iain Johnstone, "War Is Hell but It Pays Off for MacLean," *Los Angeles Times*, December 17, 1972.

35. Carl Foreman to Gregory Peck, July 2, 1970. Margaret Herrick Library, File 853, *Force 10 from Navarone*, ID7140346.

36. "Col Releases in Next 10 Months," *Variety*, May 30, 1973, 4; "Columbia to Release 23 Features, Start Roll 26 in Six Months," *Variety*, June 4, 1973, 6.

37. "Foreman Goes Woolf; As to Col, Apart Not Divorce," *Variety*, February 12, 1975, 3; "Foreman to Script $12 Mil *Tai Pan* for Shaw Bros," *Hollywood Reporter*, April 30, 1975, 3; "Carl Foreman Muses on Mankind's Obsession with Terror Threats," *Variety*, January 16, 1976, 22 (this became *When Time Ran Out*, 1980). Foreman signed a three-year exclusive deal with Universal in February 1977.

38. "Foreman to Script."

39. "Carl Foreman Muses."

40. "Foreman Goes Woolf." Foreman planned to make *The Year of the Golden Ape* for Woolf.

41. "Unger, Foreman in Deal with Mondo for *Navarone* Pic," *Variety*, September 15, 1976, 4; "Hollywood Report," *Box Office*, October 11, 1976, 48.
42. "*Navarone* Coin Came Easy; Stars Maybe Not," *Variety*, September 29, 1976, 5.
43. "Unger Plans to Roll 2 Big Pix in Greece," *Variety*, August 18, 1976, 40.
44. "*Navarone* Coin Came Easy."
45. Colin Vaines, "Minus a Stiff Upper Lip," *Screen International*, January 21, 1978, 13.
46. "Unger, Foreman in Deal."
47. "Columbia to Distribute *Navarone* Abroad," *Hollywood Reporter*, June 2, 1977, 1. A three-year deal was signed on February 17, 1977. The first picture, *Kramer's War*, was never made.
48. "Geoff Reeve Line Producer," *Screen International*, December 4, 1976, 15; "International Soundtrack," *Variety*, December 8, 1976, 38. Reeve had now been working on this project off and on since it was first announced.
49. "*Navarone* Coin Came Easy."
50. Ibid.
51. "*Force 10 from Navarone* to Be Released by AIP," *Box Office*, October 3, 1977, W4.
52. "Columbia to Distribute *Navarone* Abroad," *Hollywood Reporter*, June 2, 1977, 1.
53. Ibid.
54. "Film Production," *Variety*, December 28, 1977, 24.
55. William J. Law and Helen M. Law, Petitioners, vs Commissioner of Internal Revenue, Respondent, Docket Nos 17315–82, 10054–83, United States Tax Court, 22 May 1986.
56. "*Force 10 from Navarone*."
57. Sam Arkoff to Kastner, June 23, 1969. EKA. This was when Kastner had briefly been involved in trying to find financing.
58. "*Way to Dusty Death* to Be AIP Production," *Box Office*, January 23, 1975, 7.
59. "HBO Sues Over *Force 10*," *Variety*, March 12, 1980, 66; "Theatrical Movie Rankings, 1979–1980," *Variety*, September 17, 1980, 52. HBO showed it on March 13, ABC on March 16.
60. "*Navarone* Coin Came Easy"; Rena Velisarriou, "Lotsa Inducements Lure O'Seas Filmmakers to Lense in Greece," *Variety*, January 19, 1977, 51.
61. "Hollywood Battles," *Sunday Times*, May 12, 2002, 18.
62. "Col Sets New O'Seas Sales Record," *Variety*, January 4, 1980, 3. It earned $31 million in domestic and $20 million abroad.
63. "Robert Shaw on Folly of an Actor Cutting Price," *Variety*, June 22, 1977, 34. He was also being sought for *Under the Volcano* and an Antonioni film.
64. Tom Buckey, "Robert Shaw Goes from War-Yarn Pillar to Spy-Thriller Post," *New York Times*, March 24, 1978.
65. Michael Blowen, "Harrison Ford Shuns *Star Wars*," *Boston Globe*, July 8, 1982, 1.
66. "*Navarone* Coin Came Easy"; "Foreman May Roll Force in Pakistan," *Variety*, 1977, 45; "Pakistan Buys Film Gear for Location Use," *Variety*, March 23, 1977, 42. The region had been used for *Bhowani Junction* (1956).
67. He was in charge of developing projects which had been on the Foreman slate for over a decade—*Insurrection* and *Holiday* and a new movie called *Arctic Submarine*. None were ever made.
68. "*Force 10*."
69. "*Force 10* to England, Malta Next," *Box Office*, December 19, 1977, 3.
70. "International Soundtrack," *Variety*, August 31, 1977, 38; "Film Production," *Variety*, December 28, 1977, 24.
71. "German Bank Group (Unnamed) Reported Backing Oliver Unger," *Variety*, December 21, 1977, 5.
72. Lee Grant, "Memories of Robert Shaw, A Gallant Man," *Los Angeles Times*, September 2, 1978, B5. It's unclear if Shaw was just speaking in general because he was seriously thinking of packing in the business and returning to his real love, writing.
73. Alan McKenzie, *The Harrison Ford Story* (Westminster, MD: Arbor House, 1984), 31.
74. Charles Champlin, "The Force Is with Him," *Los Angeles Times*, January 5, 1971, F1
75. "*Force 10* Begins Publicity Push," *Box Office*, August 21, 1978, 15.
76. "First Family Views AIP's *Force 10* at Camp David," *Box Office*, December 4, 1978, 7.
77. "Nearly 100 Feature Films Scheduled for Release During Next Few Months," *Box Office*, October 16, 1978, 12.
78. "AIP-Filmways Merger to Be Dropped," *Box Office*, December 18, 1978, 3.
79. "Robert Shaw Dead at 51," *Box Office*, September 4, 1978, 12. This wasn't his last film. That honor went to *Avalanche Express* (1979), in which he was second-billed to Lee Marvin.
80. "N.Y. Christmas Tree Again Overloaded," *Variety*, December 27, 1978. The 19 new movies had to compete against holdovers from November and perennial Yuletide faves.

Chapter Fourteen

1. Marion Rosenberg (Kastner's secretary) to Ian Chapman (of Collins) undated. EKA. Reply, Chapman to Rosenberg, January 21, 1976. EKA. Bishop to Holt, December 21, 1977. EKA.
2. Ibid.
3. *Don't Look Now* starring Donald Sutherland and Julie Christie was a critical and box office hit. *The Wicker Man* starring Christopher Lee was savaged by the critics and a financial flop and only entered cult territory decades later.
4. "International Sound Track," *Variety*, April 12, 1972, 26.
5. "Bear Island Script," Margaret Herrick Library. File 32, ID71430399.
6. Bishop to Holt, December 21, 1977. It looks like Bishop had hopes of Kastner, after the success of *Breakheart Pass*, coming back into the MacLean fold.
7. Sid Adilman, "*Bear Island*: Anglo-Canadian

Co-Prod Rolls in Alaska on Soviet Ship; Avoids Upfront Distrib Deals," *Variety*, February 14, 1979, 36.
   8. Sid Adilman, *"Bear Island."*
   9. "Snell Teaming with MacLean Maps Series Adventure Pix," *Variety*, April 4, 1979, 32.
   10. "Snell Teaming with MacLean."
   11. "UA Founding Father Max Youngstein Forms Prod'n Unit," *Hollywood Reporter*, October 5, 1977, 3.
   12. Colin Vaines, "Sharp Steers Course to Proven Success," *Screen International*, March 10, 1979, 40.
   13. *Ibid.*
   14. *Ibid.*
   15. Sid Adilman, *"Bear Island."*
   16. *Ibid.*
   17. *Ibid.*; *"Bear Island* Rolls in Canada," *Hollywood Reporter*, December 5, 1978, 17; "Snell MacLean Link Up on Multi Picture Prod Pact," *Variety*, November 21, 1979, 6.
   18. "Acquisitions," *Box Office*, October 15, 1979, 7.
   19. Sie Adilman, *"Bear Island."*
   20. Redgrave's career had been strewn with as many misses as hits—*Isadora* (1968) and *The Charge of the Light Brigade* (1968) chief among them. She had courted controversy in *The Devils* (1971) and the arthouse fraternity with *A Quiet Place in the Country* (1968) and *The Trojan Woman* (1971), none of which would endear her to mainstream Hollywood. Her political activities, also, at the time counted against her in certain quarters.
   21. Colin Vaines, "Sharp Steers Course."
   22. *Ibid.*
   23. Sid Adilman, *"Bear Island."*
   24. *Ibid.*
   25. "Hollywood Report," *Box Office*, August 25, 1980, 30.
   26. "Hollywood Report," *Box Office*, May 26, 1980, 9. I say unusual because United Artists had by far the greater experience as a distributor in the United States. But it's most likely that they could not match the Taft offer. As noted, independent distributors wishing to break into the big time often did so by taking a greater financial risk and offering more for distribution rights than a more established operator.
   27. "British Columbia Is Playing Big Part in U.S. Film Production," *Box office*, January 22, 1979.
   28. Sid Adilman, *"Bear Island."*
   29. *Ibid.*
   30. Colin Vaines, "Sharp Steers Course."
   31. Sid Adilman, *"Bear Island."*
   32. "Sudden Glacier Storm Traps Pic; Bad White-Out," *Variety*, November 22, 1978, 3.
   33. Christopher Lee, *Tall, Dark and Gruesome* (Boston: Vista, 1998), 368. He was filming *1941* at the same time and commuted between the two films.
   34. Sid Adilman, *"Bear Island."*
   35. Colin Vaines, "Sharp Steers Course."
   36. Robert Osborne, "On Location," *Hollywood Reporter*, September 7, 1979, 25.
   37. "Cinema Score Card," *Box Office*, September 1, 1980, 40. The movie itself didn't come off well. The survey of 224 adults, 57 percent male and 59 percent aged over 25, gave the movie an overall rating of C.
   38. "Snell MacLean Link Up."
   39. Colin Vaines, "Sharp Steers Course."

Chapter Fifteen

   1. Webster, *Alistair MacLean*, 217–218.
   2. Anne Head, "Tour de Force," *Screen International*, December 22, 1979, 9.
   3. Webster, *Alistair MacLean*, 223.
   4. "CBS Spends $80m on TV Movies for the Autumn Season," *Screen International*, September 15, 1979, 6.
   5. Webster, *Alistair MacLean*, 217–225. MacLean decided not to flesh out the outlines into novels but allowed his publisher Collins to hire another writer to novelize the material. John Denis did with *The Hostage Tower*. Alistair MacNeill undertook six and later Simon Galdolfini would complete other books based on original MacLean screenplays. The books were published with Alistair MacLean's name at the top and the other writer at the bottom. "Little Led Original to *Hostage Tower*," *Variety*, October 3, 1979, 77—*Variety* reported the budget as $6 million.
   6. "Bourne Purchases *Hostage Tower*," *Hollywood Reporter*, September 25, 1979, 1. She was lined up to play, presumably, the part essayed Celia Johnson.
   7. "U.S. Briefing," *Screen International*, October 13, 1979, 6.
   8. "Broadway Ballyhoo," *Hollywood Reporter*, November 5, 1979, 8. She would have played the president's wife, the role ultimately taken by Celia Johnson.
   9. Hank Grant, "Rambling Reporter," *Hollywood Reporter*, October 10, 1979, 2. She was to play a terrorist.
   10. She had a role in Peter Fonda crime caper *Killer Force* (1976).
   11. *Wicker Man* (1973), which is something of a cult these days, was a flop on original release.
   12. "Feature Casting," *Hollywood Reporter*, November 30, 1979, 17.
   13. "Julienne Stunting," *Hollywood Reporter*, December 18, 1979, 16.
   14. "Foreign Film Production," *Hollywood Reporter*, November 20, 1979, 16.
   15. Anne Head, "Tour de Force."
   16. "Jean Max Brand: *Hostage Tower* a Lift from His," *Variety*, December 12, 1979, 9.
   17. Anne Head, "Tour de Force."
   18. "Bourne Purchases." Syncom had the Norwegian rights.
   19. "Regina Films," *Screen International*, November 3, 1979, 14.
   20. Advert, *Hollywood Reporter*, May 13, 1980, C34.

21. "Bourne Purchases."
22. "*Hostage Tower* Slated for CBS," *Hollywood Reporter*, February 15, 1980, 14.
23. "*Hostage Tower* Slated"; Advert, *Hollywood Reporter*, May 13, 1980, C25. Neither Guzmán nor Lance were involved by the time *Air Force One Is Down* appeared in 2013.
24. "Tower Set for Foreign Release," *Hollywood Reporter*, July 8, 1980, 6.
25. *Ibid.*
26. "Less Activity at MIFED," *Hollywood Reporter*, November 4, 1980, 1.
27. "MIFED," *Screen International*, November 3, 1979, 15. Robert Little reported "heavy sales."
28. Anne Head, "Tour de Force."
29. "MIFED," *Screen International*.
30. Maud Adams graduated to female lead in Bond picture *Octopussy* (1983).
31. Blattner to Peck, November 20, 1973; Peck to Blattner, January 11, 1974; Peck to Blattner, January 29, 1974. Margaret Herrick Library. Gregory Peck Files. ID 71494438.
32. "Snell, MacLean Link Up on Multi-Film Prod. Pact," *Variety*, November 21, 1979, 6.
33. "Re *El Dorado* by MacLean," *Variety*, December 12, 1979, 28.
34. Advert, *Variety*, October 16, 1985, 70.
35. "Cannon's Showing at Cannes," *Variety*, May 7, 1986, 505.
36. "Hollywood Soundtrack," *Variety*, May 14, 1986, 30.
37. "Film Costs vs Domestic Rentals," *Variety*, February 21, 1990.
38. "Back Upriver, Interview with Steve Carver," *River of Death* Bonus Feature, MGM/UA DVD.
39. Roel Haanen, "Steve Carver Interview," *The Flashback Files*, 2020.
40. "New Film Starts," *Variety*, October 26, 1988, 6.
41. Haanen, "Carver Interview."
42. *Back Upriver*.
43. Harry Alan Towers, *Mr. Towers of London, A Life in Show Business* (Albany, GA: BearManor, 2013), 103. This was the nickname given to Towers by Hank Werba, Rome correspondent of *Variety*.
44. *Ibid.*
45. *Back Upriver*.

Chapter Sixteen

1. For later DVD release, the movie was retitled *Detonator: Death Train* to try and tie in with the second in the series featuring the same team which was renamed *Detonator II: Night Watch*.
2. *Ibid.*
3. Cable was booming—57.2 million subscribers compared to 16 million in 1980.
4. "USA Made-Fors Just Got Bigger," *Variety*, April 5, 1993, 40.
5. "USA Network Sets Up Film Unit," *Hollywood Reporter*, April 1, 1993, 1.
6. A subsidiary of the British-based Yorkshire Television.
7. This was a particularly lean year for the perennially employable Christopher Lee. *Death Train* was his only screen appearance in 1993 compared with five roles in 1990, three apiece in 1991 and 1992 and four in 1994.
8. Alistair MacNeill went on to write another half-dozen of the books in the UNACO series—*Night Watch*, *Time of the Assassins*, *Dead Halt*, *Code Breaker*, *Red Alert* and *Rendezvous*. Whereas John "Denis was working fairly heavily from the screenplays which had been written for the first two books"—*The Hostage Tower* and *Air Force One is Down*—for *Death Train* "MacNeill had a much more limited story line from which to develop the subsequent books" (Webster, *Alistair MacLean*, 227).
9. Susan King, "The New Adventures of Pierce Brosnan," *Los Angeles Times*, April 11, 1993.
10. York Membery, *Pierce Brosnan: The Biography* (London: Virgin Books, 1997), 141–142.
11. Susan King, "The New Adventures."
12. The dead child is now a five-year-old not unborn.
13. Webster, *Alistair MacLean*, 110.
14. Advert, *Variety*, May 7, 1975, 46
15. "*Way To Dusty Death* to Be AIP Prod," *Box Office*, June 23, 1975, 7. The start date was switched to September 1975.
16. "Hollywood Happenings," *Box Office*, April 5, 1976, W2; "Coming Releases," *Box Office*, November 1, 1976, A6; "Coming Releases," *Box Office*, August 1, 1977, A6.
17. "Peter Fonda, William Hayward Plan to Produce 12 films in 2 Years," *Box Office*, March 8, 1976, 5.
18. Darvas and Lawson, "Don Sharp Interview."
19. Bishop to Holt, December 21, 1977.
20. Bishop to Holt, July 13, 1981. He touted three titles that were "available if Winkast is interested."
21. Bishop to Holt, July 13, 1981; Holt to Bishop, July 14, 1981.
22. "Co-Prod'n Push Seen on Comglom Horizon," *Variety*, October 24, 1994, 54. The shorter movie version, which I saw, was made in order to qualify for tax credits in the U.K.
23. Author interview with Tom Reeve.
24. Although later Tom Reeve and Linda Hamilton became good friends, accounting for her presence in *Air Force One Is Down*, here Linda Hamilton was a straightforward piece of casting from ICM which had represented Sigourney Weaver when she starred in Geoff Reeve's *Half Moon Street* (1986).
25. Geoff Reeve produced a further two pictures starring Caine—*Shadow Run* (1998) and *Shiner* (2000) and was executive producer of the star's *Quicksand* (2013.)
26. Tom Reeve has since produced over 40 movies, his latest being *Midas Run* (2024), including *Dog Soldiers* (2002), *Blind Revenge* (2009) with Darryl Hannah and Tom Conti and *13 Hrs/Night Wolf* (2010). He directed *Diggity's Treasure* (2001) with Andrew McCarthy, *George and the Dragon*

(2009) starring James Purefoy, Patrick Swayze and Piper Perabo and *Holy Water/Hard Times* (2009) as well as the TV movie *The Laura Marlin Mysteries: Dead Man's Cove* (2024).
27. Tom Reeve had worked for NBC in the U.S. as executive producer reporting to Charlie Goldstein who shepherded home such productions as *Princess Daisy* (1982) with Lindsay Wagner and *Rage of Angels* (1982) starring Jaclyn Smith. This was an era when a miniseries like *Fatal Vision* (1984) starring Karl Malden and Eva Marie Saint could set a network back $16 million.
28. Author interview with Tom Reeve.
29. *Ibid.*
30. *Ibid.*
31. Author interview with Tom Reeve. MacCorkindale ended up with six producer credits including *Stolen Heaven* (1988) directed by Clive Donner, *That Summer of White Roses* (1989) starring Tom Conti opposite MacCorkindale's wife Susan George, and was co-executive producer of three television series including *Queen of Swords* (1999–20020 starring Tia Carrere.
32. Author interview with Tom Reeve.
33. *Ibid.*
34. Tony Scott, Review of *Night Watch*, October 2, 1995.
35. Not to be confused with *Air Force One Down* (2024).
36. Darvas and Lawson, "Don Sharp Interview."
37. Renamed Sonar Entertainment and now known as Halcyon Entertainment.
38. Author interview with Tom Reeve.
39. *Ibid.*
40. *Ibid.*
41. *Ibid.*

Chapter Seventeen

1. "G-K Productions; 5 to WB; 9 More Pend," *Variety*, November 30, 1966, 3.
2. It's worth pointing out how adventurous MacLean had become. He was diversifying in several directions at once. As part of the move towards becoming a screenwriter, not only had MacLean embarked on *Where Eagles Dare*, but it was almost as if he intended to blow apart publisher expectation by forays into the pirate and western genres, both screenplays intended to end up as novels. Having won a certain amount of creative independence after his self-imposed exile it's worth considering what route his career would have taken if he had immediately followed the publication of *Where Eagles Dare* with both *Breakheart Pass* and *Caribbean*.
3. Kastner to MacLean, July 5, 1968. EKA. Geoff Reeve would have to commit to 40 weeks' work.
4. "Alistair." EKA.
5. The standard measurement is that one page equates to one minute of screen time. In that state it would run for over three hours.
6. Denis Holt to MacLean, March 3, 1969. EKA.
7. Holt to MacLean, March 4, 1969. EKA.
8. Date on screenplay. EKA. Still at two-and-half-hours too long.
9. "Caribbean-MGM." Undated. EKA. This tallied "receipts" at $500,000 with "costs" (what Kastner had shelled out for the screenplay) at $150,000 producing "net profits" of $350,000. Kastner expected a payment of $335,000 on signing an agreement with the studio plus another $15,000 for a second draft of the screenplay. The remainder of the money would be paid in three equal instalments—at the beginning of filming, once the shoot was complete, and when Kastner delivered an answer print. Unfortunately, MGM did not bite.
10. "Status of Projects as at October 14, 1968." EKA. In a letter to Kastner dated June 8 (presumably 1968) Burton had "voiced interest" in the "pirate project." EKA.
11. Kastner to Louis F. Polk Jr., of MGM, June 5, 1969. EKA. Kastner noted there had been a "total turn-down" on *Swashbuckler*.
12. Rosenberg to Holt, October 14, 1969. EKA.
13. Kastner to the Aga Khan (undated, assuming 1970). EKA.
14. Kastner to Howard Hughes, February 19, 1970. EKA.
15. "List of Scripts Elliott Has Left with George Daris," October 4, 1968. EKA. The word "No" was scribbled next to *Caribbean*. Daris had also rejected *Tam Lin* and *Deakin* but there was a "maybe" against *Sandra Rifkin's Jewels* which was either never made or was an alternative title for another film. It's not clear whose handwriting this is.
16. Kastner to MacLean, August 24, 1970. EKA.
17. Holt to Kastner, June 10, 1971. EKA.
18. Bishop to Kastner, September 25, 1995. EKA. Bishop had written to offer to sell rights to the screenplay, obviously not realizing that Kastner had been involved in the Jennings Lang production. He pointed out, "your option to the screenplay expired something like 26 years ago" which would place it at 1969.
19. Ludlum published *The Scarlatti Inheritance* in 1971 and *The Osterman Weekend* in 1972. From 1977 onwards seven Ludlum novels were turned into movies and four into television mini-series or movies. But six of these were based on Jason Bourne, achieving the brand consistency that eluded Alistair MacLean.
20. Wheeler was later also credited for *Caravan to Vaccarès*.
21. Kastner to Ludlum, August 30, 1972. EKA. The tone of the letter suggests that Ludlum has sent the first section of the screenplay, at 63-pages that would be roughly half a finished work and was seeking some feedback while the producer wanted him to get on with it and not be discouraged by too detailed a critique.
22. Letter, Rosenberg to Dick Clayton IFA, undated.
23. Agreement between Winkast and Expert Promotions Ltd, November 21, 1973; Wheeler to Winkast, December 1973. Wheeler was paid $1,500

for the first draft, with the remainder only payable if the movie went ahead, a typical deal of the time.

24. Letter, Holt to Kastner, August 7, 1975. Wheeler had been sent a copy of the Ludlum effort in August 1973 (Rosenberg to Wheeler, August 21, 1973.

25. Kastner to Wheeler, December 17, 1973. EKA.

26. Holt to Kastner, March 25, 1974. EKA.

27. Holt to Kastner, August 9, 1975. EKA. "Final script has nothing to with Ludlum."

28. Bantam published a paperback original movie-tie in written by D.R. Benson in 1976. With Robert Shaw's picture on the cover and running 167 pages it was "based on the screenplay by Jeffrey Bloom and the story by Paul Wheeler." As noted, earlier, there would have been financial implications for excluding Ludlum from this particular slice of the pie. Even if an author didn't write the novelization, they were entitled to a percentage of the receipts.

29. Holt to Kastner, August 7, 1975. EKA.

30. Dean Rissner of UA to Kastner, December 18, 1973. EKA. Bizarrely, Rissner touted the notion of casting Italian duo Bud Spencer and Terence Hill and reworking the script to "fit into the comedic milieu."

31. Letter, Barry Spikings to Kastner, April 2, 1974.

32. Letter, M. Serafian to Frank Wells, March 31, 1974.

33. Kastner to Jack Nicholson, May 6, 1974. EKA. According to an undated ICM Memo from the Kastner archive Nicholson was also in the frame for the later *Pirates* (1986) which eventually starred Walter Matthau and was directed by Roman Polanski.

34. Kastner to Frank Yablans, June 24, 1974. EKA. Yablans was head of Paramount and had overseen production of *The Godfather* (1972) and *Chinatown*.

35. Kastner to Frank Yablans, Paramount.

36. Rosenberg to Bryan Forbes, September 11, 1974. EKA. Rosenberg wrote, "Elliott is in New York closing a deal for Raquel Welch to play Jane. Albert Finney is reading the script, but should he decide against it there will be no problem casting a suitable strong leading man."

37. Memo, "Constructive Thoughts Department," Holt to Kastner, March 21, 1974. EKA. At this point the movie was still known as *The Buccaneers*.

38. Telegram, Bryan Forbes to Kastner.

39. "*Satan's Ribbon* Casting Suggestions," February 27, 1973.

40. Telex, Henry Morrison to Kastner, undated.

41. Kastner to Jennings Lang, December 16, 1974. Jewison opted for *Rollerball* (1975) instead.

42. Telex, Henry Morrison to Kastner, undated.

43. Letter, Kastner to Norman Jewison, January 4, 1974.

44. "Casting Suggestions," July 8, 1975.

45. "Casting," August 23, 1974.

46. "Casting," January 15, 1975.

47. Letter, Kastner to Fernando Ghia, January 30, 1974; Kastner to Ghia, February 7, 1974; Ghia to Kastner, February 9, 1974. This was no mere fanciful notion, Spencer having read the script in February with the result that the actors were deemed the same month "agreeable" to the project.

48. Jeffrey Bloom to Joe Di Muro, MCA, Febraury 4, 1975; Mike Ludner to Joe Di Muro, MCA, February 12, 1975. Bloom was paid $18,000 for his first draft, $10,000 for two sets of revisions, plus $2,500 if he received sole or joint screenplay credit, and 2.5 percent of the profits.

49. Kastner to Lang, May 18, 1971. EKA. Kastner had asked Jennings Lang in 1971 to look after MacLean's son Lachlan on a Hollywood trip. Kastner said he would "greatly appreciate any courtesy you can extend to him."

50. Kastner to Jennings Lang, December 16, 1975. EKA. Location would be Spain or the Caribbean with Pinewood still essential to pick up Eady cash—*Where Eagles Dare*, Kastner reminded Lang, had picked up $700,000 from the Eady fund. He also asked if Lang "could arrange a meeting with Valerie Perrine," though whether that was in conjunction with this picture is unclear.

51. "Undated Memo." EKA. This compared expected income from *Rancho Deluxe*, *Breakheart Pass* and *Swashbuckler*. Even though *Rancho Deluxe* was the cheapest to make at $1.6 million, Kastner's fee was $215,000 plus 40 percent of the profits.

52. "Loanout Agreement," January 9, 1975. EKA. The deal was between the EK Corporation and Universal Pictures. For tax purposes, this was not done using Winkast, which was incorporated in Britain. Kastner was to be paid $25,000 on signing the legal documentation, $25,000 on delivery of the Paul Wheeler screenplay, $25,000 at the start of shooting, and $25,000 on completion of principal photography. The contract specified that the screenplay was written by Wheeler but revised by Jeffrey Bloom, who was entitled to one percent of the net profits out of Kastner's share.

53. Kastner to Lang, August 6, 1975. EKA.

54. Leo Steiner to George Chasin, September 9, 1975. EKA.

55. Undated scripts from the Kastner archive. EKA.

56. Memo, Winkast Programming, undated (assuming mid 1970s). EKA. Kastner was enamored enough of Bloom to commission other screenplays, *Cairo Christmas* and *A Man for Deajum's Wife*, which at various points featured on the Winkast slate in the mid-1970s though neither was made.

57. Anthony Jones of A.D. Peters (Wheeler's agent) to Rosenberg, undated. EKA. Wheeler had discovered his name was not even on the script being used to attract talent.

58. Paul Wheeler to Gloria Brinkman, October 22, 1975. EKA.

59. "Final Revised Set The Golden Hinde," September 17, 1975. EKA.
60. *Swashbuckler* screenplay. EKA.

Chapter Eighteen

1. "Acquisitions," *Box Office*, October 15, 1979, 20.
2. Bishop to Holt, July 13, 1981. EKA. He touted three titles that were "available if Winkast is interested."
3. "Letter, Bishop to Holt, July 13, 1981; Holt to Bishop, July 14, 1981.
4. "Article," *Box Office*, November 24, 1975, MC2.
5. *Ibid*.
6. "Offshore Oil Pic," *Variety*, November 12, 1975, 4.
7. "New York Sound Track," *Variety*, December 10, 1975, 32.
8. Bishop to Holt, July 13, 1981. EKA.
9. Hank Grant, "Rambling Reporter," *Hollywood Reporter*, December 21, 1973, 2; Hank Grant, "Rambling Reporter," *Hollywood Reporter*, September 12, 1974, 2.
10. "Fox Out-Races Hounds of TV," *Variety*, September 19, 1973, 5.
11. "Allen, Feld in $6-Mil Deal for 3D *Circus* Pic," *Variety*, October 10, 1973, 3.
12. *Ice Station Zebra* globally and *Where Eagles Dare* outside the U.S. had been presented as roadshows.
13. "Acquisitions," *Box Office*, October 15, 1979, 20.
14. Webster, *Alistair MacLean*, 117.
15. Interview with the author.
16. Screenplay. EKA.
17. Ali Jafaar, "Cassian Elwes, Andrew Gaines to Remake Classic Thriller *Fear Is the Key* Following Rights Deal with StudioCanal—Cannes," *Deadline*, May 14, 2016.
18. Author interview.
19. "Snell Teaming."
20. Webster, *Alistair MacLean*, 110.
21. "New Major AFD," *Hollywood Reporter*, October 27, 1978, 1.
22. "Sir Lew Grade Discloses ATV-ITC $97m Production Slate," *Box Office*, October 24, 1977, 10
23. "New Major AFD," *Hollywood Reporter*, October 27, 1978, 1.
24. "Associated Clarifies Itself," *Variety*, March 7, 1979, 6. Other movies on the slate included *Saturn 3*, *The Lone Ranger*, *Firepower* and *The Jazz Singer*, all of which were made, though most were flops.
25. "Rosemont," *Hollywood Reporter*, March 7, 1979, 17. Others planned included *The Scarlatti Inheritance* from the Robert Ludlum thriller and a remake of *All Quiet on the Western Front*, neither of which were made.
26. Advert, *Variety*, April 4, 1979, 48.
27. Advert, *Variety*, May 9, 1979, 440.

28. Hank Grant, "Rambling Reporter," *Hollywood Reporter*, February 21, 1978, 3.
29. Hank Grant, "Rambling Reporter," *Hollywood Reporter*, March 3, 1978, 3.
30. "Snell, MacLean Link Up."
31. "Acquisitions," *Box Office*, October 15, 1979, 20
32. "Pinewood-based U.S. Producer's Next Film at $12-Mil," *Hollywood Reporter*, February 12, 1980, 17.
33. "Sharp to Direct," *Hollywood Reporter*, October 15, 1979, 5.
34. Bishop to Holt, July 13, 1981. EKA.
35. "Letter, Bishop to Holt, July 13, 1981; Holt to Bishop, July 14, 1981.
36. Bishop to Kastner, January 25, 1968.
37. "Alistair MacLean Mulls *Guns of Suez*," *Variety*, March 4, 1970, 2.
38. Photo, *Daily Film Renter*, October 4, 1955, 6.
39. Webster, *Alistair MacLean*, 110.
40. "Film Production Slump No Problem for Alistair MacLean," *Variety*, December 10, 1969, 35.
41. "Venice Festival Founder's Son Gears into Film Biz with a Sports Car Pic," *Variety*, May 5, 1971, 25.
42. Advert, *Variety*, May 12, 1981, 60; Advert, *Variety*, May 3, 1972, 64. The biopic was to star Scott Holden (son of William Holden) and model Laura Bernard. Volpi owned two properties, this and *The Peking to Paris Race*. A feature film proved a step too far and what eventually appeared was the documentary *Drive to Win*, 1981 (Advert, Variety, October 17, 1978, 18.)
43. "George Brown to Roll *Assault* in June, Preps *Army* and *H.M.S. Ulysses*," *Variety*, April 29, 1970, 174. *Assault* starring Suzy Kendall was made, *Popski's Army* was not. Brown was father to magazine editor Tina Brown and the first husband of Maureen O'Hara.
44. Quentin Falk and Colin Vaines, "$160m Tempts in Top Teams." *Screen International*, May 17, 1980, 1. This was part of an announcement at Cannes, the amount mentioned being the combined investment from EMI and Rank.
45. "Klingers Sign," *Hollywood Reporter*, April 1, 1980, 26.
46. "Puttnam Package," *Screen International*, March 29, 1980, 13. Puttnam had assembled quite a slate. Apart from *Chariots of Fire*, which started shooting on April 14, 1980, he was prepping *October Circle*, *Last Chance* for Goldcrest based on a play by Rose Shaet and Anne Powell, *Axis* by Colin Welland from the Clifford Irving novel, and, for International Film Investors, "a very major piece," *The Life and Death of Dith Prang* which would appear four years later as *The Killing Fields*.
47. "Rank Eyes $36-Mil Outlay for 10 Pix," *Variety*, May 21, 1980, 5.
48. Email from Puttnam to the author, April 29, 2024.
49. Zoom interview with the author, April 26, 2024.
50. "Disappointing Market Place," *Screen International*, June 7, 1980, 12.

51. Zoom interview with the author, April 26, 2024.
52. Quentin Falk, "How It All Turned Sour," *Screen International*, June 20, 1980, 10.
53. "Chatter," *Variety*, July 7, 1982, 77. Brown's last film as producer was *Penny Gold* (1973) and he executive produced *Open Season* (1974), both of which had screenwriting input from David Osborn.
54. Robert Boris to Elliott Kastner, November 9, 1998. EKA.
55. Tampico Productions, Press Release, November 18, 1999. EKA.
56. "*H.M.S. Ulysses*, A Story Outline by Robert Boris, Producer, Elliott Kastner, November 8, 1998." EKA.
57. Borys Kit, *Hollywood Reporter*, May 6, 2013.
58. HarperCollins Archive.
59. "Snell Teaming with MacLean Maps Series Adventure Pix," *Variety*, April 4, 1979, 32.
60. "Review," *Variety*, May 25, 1960, 34. The serialisation ran for over two weeks in a late-night slot (starting at 11:10 p.m.) with actor John Slater reading.
61. "Pre-Finance the Key to Holding Off on O'Seas Deals," *Variety*, May 19, 1971, 27.
62. Author interview with Daniel Unger.
63. "J&M Scores Duigan Double," *Screen International*, May 12, 1995, 8; Advert, *Hollywood Reporter*, October 31, 1995, 7. Alexandra Paul and William Devane headlined, with no mention of Brosnan.
64. Nancy Tartaglione, *Deadline*, October 13, 2018.
65. "Snell Teaming."
66. Peter Noble, "On the Floor," *Daily Film Renter*, May 30, 1957, 4.
67. "London," *Hollywood Reporter*, February 20, 1958, 3.
68. "Angel Here to Cast 20th's British *Java*," *Hollywood Reporter*, January 15, 1959, 1.
69. Advert, *Variety*, January 8, 1986, 133. Also on the slate were *Lady Jane* (1986) and *A Prayer for the Dying* (1987). In terms of active agents, UNACO divided its field agents into groups of three, each named Strike Force, of which the Graham/Carver/Whitlock team was designated Strike Force Three.
70. "*Cabo Blanco*," *Hollywood Reporter*, October 20, 1978, 33.
71. Kastner to MacLean, July 5, 1968.
72. Pieterse ot Kastner, Mrch 7 1973.
73. Norman M. Tyre (MGM's attorney) to R.M Fletcher, August 3, 1973.
74. Fletcher to Holt, August 10, 1973.

Appendix

1. And in Sweden, in particular, Alistair MacLean pictures regularly beat those of Eastwood and Bronson at the box office.
2. That's a conservative estimate.
3. HarperCollins Archive.
4. In the U.S. in the 1960s and 1970s television sales were based on box office, although many movies were sold as part of a package. However, movies were only leased to television for a specific number of showings over a specific number of years, for example two screenings in three years, although for big blockbusters, to increase ad revenue, the networks would break movies into two parts shown on successive nights.
5. VHS and DVD, especially, released movies in the same way as studios had in the past released pictures, on a staggered price basis. On initial release, though wholesalers, the market would comprise rental companies who bought copies of movies at $60 apiece knowing they could rent them out for $2-$3 at a time until they wore out. Sometimes, rental companies sold off these as ex-rental copies, not paying any more to the distributor for doing so. But soon, studios realized that, as the sales of video machines boomed, if they dropped prices to, say, $40, they could make considerable inroads in direct-to-public sales through general retailers. Occasionally, some titles went out on first release with the price dropped to $29.99 or $24.99 as a means of expanding the market. Distributors soon realized they could lower the price step-by-step down to "bargain bin" releases at $4.99 several years after initial release and continue to attract steady custom. The life of a movie was greatly enhanced long after initial release, hence the "long tail." With each new phase of technology or market diversification, the same films were sold again and again. At its peak, Blockbuster had over 9,000 stores and each outlet might order 10–20 copies of new videos or DVDs.
6. "Warner Brothers Statement," September 30, 2014. EKA.
7. "Foreign Report to January 3, 1970." EKA. British rentals hit $1.29 million (plus an Eady contribution of $504,000) and Italy next with $1.13 million, then came Japan at $736 million, South Africa at $406,000, France at $331,000 and Sweden with $328,000.
8. Bill Atria, "Box-Office Business," *Kine Weekly*, 1969, February 1-March 8. The weekly figures were: £11,011, £11,966, £10, 969, £11,140, £10,389 and £10,078. In general release, it placed third for 1970 ("Box Office Winners of 1970," *Kine Weekly*, December 19, 1970, 6).
9. "MGM Producer/Participation Statement," April 20, 1969. EKA. "Half of Gina's share of net profits (20%) is subject to cross-collateralization with *The Walking Stick*."
10. Norman R. Tyre to R.M. Fletcher, June 8, 1971. EKA.
11. Bishop to Fletcher, June 4, 1971. EKA. "Do not see why MacLean should suffer," he wrote, "in result of cross-collateralization of *The Walking Stick* resulting in Gina receiving no profits and therefore being unable to pay the $100,000" which MacLean had originally deferred.
12. Bishop to Holt, October 1, 1973. EKA.

13. "TV Income Through Period Ending Aug 2, 1980." EKA. Revenue from the U.S. was $1.77 million compared to $272,000 from the UK, $91,000 from Japan and $50,000 from Australia, those countries being the leading earners.

14. Norman R. Tyre to Gershwin, August 31, 1981. EKA. *Breakheart Pass* brought in more from television, possibly because it had attracted a smaller cinema audience.

15. Bishop to Kastner, February 15, 1982. EKA.

16. Gary Conaff, Mitchell Silverberg and Knupp to Kastner, February 19, 1992; Albert Gaerish, Turner, to Kastner, February 1, 1996; Michael G. Edwards, WB, to Kastner, January 25, 2001. EKA.

17. Aaron R. Frosch to MGM, February 25, 1970. EKA; "Atlantic Programmes Ltd Examination of MGM *Where Eagles Dare* to February 12, 1970." EKA. Burton's company Atlantic Programmes had, at a cost of $25,000, audited MGM's books. Burton's initial million-dollar fee was seen as an advance against 10 percent of the profits. Once rentals reached $10 million, he was entitled to reap the rewards of his percentage. As a result of the audit, Burton was entitled to an extra $290,000. The audit specified that in the United States up to February 1970, there were 5,274 bookings totaling $6.189 million in rentals (an average of $1,173 per booking). It proved most popular in New York ($608,000 from 273 bookings), Los Angeles ($553,000 from 324 bookings), Chicago ($462,000/162), Dallas ($373,000/443), San Francisco ($338,000/204), Philadelphia (£329,000/242), Atlanta ($310,000/370), Boston ($256,000/200), Detroit ($211,000/164) and Minneapolis ($129,000/258).

18. "Turner Entertainment Producer/Participant Statement," July 31, 1987. EKA. Including $5 million from television, the total earnings were $32.5 million. Foreign rentals of $20.2 million far exceeded the domestic total of $7.3 million. By this point Atlantic Programming had earned $2.68 million, Mary Ure $56,000, and Eastwood had received his deferred $150,000. Gershwin-Kastner had received $1.4 million of which half went to MacLean. Of the remaining amount, Gershwin (55 percent) earned more than Kastner (45 percent).

19. "Warner Brothers Statement," September 30, 2014. EKA.

20. *Ibid.*

21. "*Force 10* Project Goes Full Circle as Col Shifts It Back to Foreman," *Variety*, September 2, 1970, 43. Overall, rentals will have shown an increase post–1970 judging not just by the results of various reissues but ongoing sales from television and home entertainment.

22. "*Guns* New Yardstick on British Hits," *Variety*, December 6, 1961, 13. It grossed $495,000 from the London West End alone comprising $195,000 in ten weeks at the Odeon Leicester Square followed by 23 weeks at the Columbia.

23. Advert, *Variety*, July 23, 1961, 23. Between the Criterion and Murray Hill, it set a new record of $108,000 in the first week, which it promptly broke by $2,000 in the second week. Studios took out these kinds of adverts to make exhibitors further down the line salivate at the prospect.

24. *Ibid.* Records were set at the State Lake in Chicago, Stanley Warner in San Francisco and in Detroit

25. "*Guns* New Yardstick." Records were set at 33 out of the first 58 cinemas in Britain where it played. From just 143 houses it had already earned $1.4 million and was just $300,000 shy of the all-time record held by *Bridge on the River Kwai* and had not yet entered general release.

26. "Hat Trick of Records," *Kine Weekly*, August 10, 1961, 24; "*Navarone* Held Over in Holland," *Kine Weekly*, December 7, 1961, 14. In first run in Amsterdam, Rotterdam and The Hague, the movie was held over for six weeks, the first time that had occurred since *Gone with the Wind* 15 years before.

27. Advert, "Paris 1st Week 1st Run," *Variety*, October 13, 1971, 13. *The Guns of Navarone* was incidental to this ad for *Red Sun* and was included since it highlighted the best opening weeks every year of the 1960s—it hit $171,000 from three—in order to include the figures from *Red Sun* ($170,000 from 10) in this elite group.

28. "French Market B.O. Champs '56-'79," *Variety*, October 15, 1980, 278.

29. "Movie Rankings for Previous Season," *Variety*, September 16, 1970, 60; "ABC TV Panic Cues Oldies Pix," *Variety*, October 9, 1974, 45. It had screened on September 1969—in two parts—November 1970 and October 1974. It remained sellable for television and the next year Columbia led with it as the main title (Advert, *Variety*, August. 1975, 40) out of a package of 27 being sold for syndication.

30. "London Box Office," *Variety*, 1974, April 17, April 24, May 1, May 8, May 15. Overall gross was $52,000.

31. "*Exorcist* in Thailand," December 4, 1974, 30.

32. "Hard Krona of Sweden Spells Impressive Totals," *Variety*, May 12, 1976, 342. These figures were gross not rentals—the rental figure would be about half the gross.

33. "*Geste* Strong 12G Port," *Variety*, July 27, 1977, 12.

34. "RCA/Col Sign Videodisk Pact," *Variety*, September 30, 1981, 70.

35. "Around the Home Video Track," *Variety*, December 16, 1981, 26.

36. "*Breakheart Pass* Producer/Participant Statement," April 8, 1996. EKA. Profits were put at $6.1 million.

37. "Box Office with David Thomas," *Screen International*, 1976, January 31–February 14. The opener of £15,300 dipped to £10,300 and a final week of £7,700.

38. Television audiences were, of course, much bigger nearly half a century ago. In the U.K. movies could not be screened on TV until five years after release. In January 1981, *Breakheart Pass* attracted an audience of 15.6 million on the BBC ("TV News," *Screen International*, January 24,

1981, 12) and another 9.45 million when repeated the following year ("National TV Ratings," *Screen International*, November 6, 1982, 16). It was the 10th most popular program for the week on its first week, and eighth in its second.

39. "*Breakheart Pass* Producer/Participant Statement," April 8, 1996. EKA.

40. United Artists, "Producer/Participant Statement," December 31, 1995. EKA. "New York Showcases," *Variety*, 1976, May 12-May 19. It hit $155,000 from 51 with, surprisingly, a second week increase to $154,000 from 50. "International," *Variety*, 1946, February 4-March 8. It ran for five weeks at the Odeon Leicester Square with figures of $30,000; $20,700; $15,300; $13,800 and $13,400. It was less impressive in Sweden ("Sweden B.O. Champs," *Variety*, May 11, 1977, 360), placing 43rd over the period July 1974–December 1976, below other Bronson-starrers *Death Wish*, *Breakout*, *The Streetfighter*, as well as *Caravan to Vaccarès*.

41. "N.Y. Christmas Tree Again Overloaded," *Variety*, December 27, 1978. The 19 new movies had to compete against holdovers from November and perennial Yuletide faves.

42. "Big Rental Films of 1979," *Variety*, January 9, 1980, 21.

43. "Col O'Seas Boom Paced *by Close Encounters*," *Variety*, August 1, 1979, 7.

44. "International," *Variety*, December 20, 1978, 44. The opening of $53,200 from the pair was deemed "none too fancy."

45. "British Pics at Home 1978-1979," *Variety*, January 9, 1980, 101; "*Grease* Paced Top Grossing Films in Sweden for '78-'79," *Variety*. February 20, 1980, 45.

46. "Theatrical Movie Rankings 1979–1980," *Variety*, September 17, 1980, 52. It ranked 50th for the year, proportionately better than it done at the box office.

47. "Gold in 'Abandoned' Films," *Variety*, July 9, 1969, 3; Advert, *Variety*, July 9, 1969, 21. It grossed just over $1.5 million in New York, Los Angeles and Miami in two weeks, the best showing for a general release in New York for MGM since *The Dirty Dozen* two years previously. Heightened box office expectation was blamed on the industry taking "a passing phenomenon for a permanent trend" after actioners like *The Dirty Dozen*, *Bullitt* and *Planet of the Apes* hit unprecedented box office for that genre.

48. This meant the biggest film of the year went out on initial release in cinemas not aligned to Rank. In Glasgow, for example, it played an unprecedented six months at the La Scala in the city centre.

49. Bill Atria, "Box-Office Business," *Kine Weekly*, from March 20, 1971, onwards. It broke Saturday night records and was moved over to the Odeon Kensington. In the suburbs "it lived up to expectations."

50. "Money Films Sweden 1971-1973," *Variety*, May 8, 1974, 215.

51. Eyles, *Odeon 2*, 216.

52. "London," *Screen International*, March 3, 1976, 43. It played the Astoria, heading up a revival double bill with comedy *Please Sir* (1971).

53. Advertisement, *New York Times*, May 28, 1971.

54. "Picture Grosses," *Variety*, June 1971. Canada counted as part of the U.S. box office. Sometimes movies opened there first to kick-start interest in a picture in the U.S., which was why this opened first in Toronto. Other figures were: "mild" $4,000 in Pittsburgh; "soft" $55,000 from 10 theaters in Detroit including $5,200 in a first run; and "fair" $10,500 in Cleveland. The problem with the *Variety* mode of reporting was it concentrated on the biggest cities and had little coverage of the south, Dallas box office, for example, never reported. And it primarily reported on first run or those cities that had established "showcase" release strands. If a movie played a chunk of dates in drive-ins in a less populated area of the country, its figures didn't come to light. For example, a simultaneous release in 100 cinemas in New England did not merit mention in *Variety* but was picked up by its rival *Box Office* ("When Eight Bells Toll at 100-Plus NE Theaters," *Box Office*, May 31, 1971, NE4).

55. "From $10-mil and Up Rentals," *Variety*, November 29, 1972, 5.

56. Joseph Sugar of Cinerama to Gershwin, November 15, 1973. Cinerama held the rights until 1990. EKA.

57. Walter Manley of Manley Productions to Steven Monas of Vestron, April 30, 1986. EKA.

58. "Contract Between Orion and Leonard Lane of Rapid-American." EKA. This was unsigned so I'm not sure if it went through or not. Either way, with the boom in demand for movies in the expanding markets of cable, video, videodisc and later DVD, this could be a lucrative deal. No company would agree to pay so much upfront if it didn't expect to recoup the money fairly quickly.

59. Dan Shimvra of Zazie Films to Kastner, October 7, 1994; Alex Massie of Angliak Films International to Kastner, March 27, 1995; Alex Massie to Kastner, October 30, 1995. EKA.

60. Holt to Kastner, January 27, 1982. EKA. Rank had taken up a 14-year license form 1971. It licensed the television rights to Granada for seven years from March 1976 and although no limit was placed on the number of television showings in fact it had only been seen once on network television (in March 1978) and one other network plus six regional screenings.

61. George J. Helyer of Rank to R.A. Shaw of Winkast Programming (the successor to Winkast). EKA.

62. Kastner to E.P. Turner of Rank, October 11, 1989. EKA.

63. E.P. Turner of Rank to Kastner, December 18, 1989; G.J. Belyer to R.A. Shaw, January 5, 1990. EKA. Rank receiving the rights (TV, video and cable) "in perpetuity."

64. Author correspondence with Daniel Unger.

65. "London West End Sees Puppet Smash $19,800," *Variety*, August 18, 1971, 25.
66. "International," *Variety*, August 18-September 29, 1971. The weekly figures at the Pavilion were: $19,800; $16,100; $14,100; $14,700; $12,500; $15,100 and $12,200. The increases in week four and week six were considered "remarkable."
67. "International," *Variety*, October 20, 1971, 28. The gross was $15, 878 from three cinemas.
68. "International," *Variety*, 1971, October 20-December 28. The Cinecenta only had 150 seats. The first week was $4,908, and even by the seventh week was still pulling in $3,300.
69. "Picture Grosses," *Variety*. April 19, 1972, 8. It took $30,000.
70. "New York Showcases," *Variety*, May 10, 1972, 8.
71. "Picture Grosses," *Variety*, 1972, April 26-May 24. Grosses were: $20,000 from three in Cleveland, $18,000 from six in Kansas City, $10,500 in Boston, $13,200 from three in Cleveland and $11,200 from three in Detroit.
72. "International," *Variety*, December 20, 1972-January 31, 1973. It played the ABC2 and scored as follows: $12,500; $11,200; $8,100; $10,900; $9,700; $6,000 and $4,700.
73. "New York Showcases," *Variety*, March 21, 1973, 8. It returned to the showcase a couple of months later as support to *Save the Tiger*, which knocked up $275,000 from 75 ("New York Showcases," *Variety*, May 30, 1973, 8).
74. "Picture Grosses," *Variety*, March 14-May 30, 1973.
75. "Money Films Sweden 1971-1973."
76. "Universal Patterns Two for Detroit Suburbs," *Variety*, April 26, 1961, 15. This was the beginning of an experiment to challenge the existing release structure which kept exhibitors in the nabes waiting until a movie had completed first- and second-run engagements in the big cities.
77. "Picture Grosses," *Variety*, 1961, April 19, May 3, May 10, May 24, May 31, June 7, June 14. The *Variety* comments put into perspective the various results; what appears a good figure might be well less of an achievement once you take into account the size of the cinema. The movie scored an "okay" $19,000 at the Palace on Broadway in New York running concurrently with the Translux on 85th St arthouse where it earned $6,500. The $11,000 in Cleveland was "only good"; $12,000 in St Louis "okay"; $6,000 in Louisville "good"; $4,000 in Omaha "modest"; $5,000 in Buffalo "dullish"; $5,000 in Providence "fair"; $12,000 from three houses in Los Angeles "modest"; and $10,000 in St Louis "fair." In Boston it played support to *Tammy Tell Me True*. Bear in mind these are all grosses not the rentals referred to elsewhere. Exhibitors closely monitored grosses to get an idea of how a movie might perform at their own operation. They might, therefore, be prepared for the worst or deny the picture a booking at all.
78. Josh Billings, "Your Films," *Kine Weekly*, June 15, 1961, 11. Agatha Christie attended the premiere. *Variety* tabbed the opening of $7,500 as "fair" rather than "promising" ("London," *Variety*, June 21, 1961, 10).
79. Advert, *Kine Weekly*, June 8, 1961, 12.
80. Allen Eyles, *Odeon Cinemas 2* (London: CTA, 2005), 208.
81. "Long Short," *Kine Weekly*, June 8, 1961, 5.
82. While it was taking $7,500 in its London opener, *The Guns of Navarone* captured $21,000 in its seventh week.
83. "Picture Grosses," *Variety*, April 14-June 2, 1961. "Sad" was for $8,000 in Philadelphia, "slow" was the $11,000 in Chicago, "okay" was $6,000 in Boston. Washington was "big" with $10,000 but Los Angeles brought in only $9,000 from two and Kansas City $15,000 from five. There was a second showcase week in New York of $114,000 from 23, which marked a relatively slow drop. But the problem with going wide was that momentum was stifled, the screens already book for another picture, whereas first run for the main part allowed a movie to sit there long enough to prove demand.
84. Bill Atria, "Box-Office Business," *Kine Weekly*, May 13, 1965, 7. That translated into just under $9,000, not much for one of the city's top venues.
85. Bill Atria, "Box-Office Business," *Kine Weekly*, May 27, 1965, 7.
86. Bill Atria, "Box-Office Business," *Kine Weekly*, June 17, 1965, 16.
87. Allen Eyles, *Odeon Cinemas 2* (London: CTA, 2005), 211.
88. United Artists Archive, University of Wisconsin.
89. "International," *Variety*, August 21-September 11, 1974. Grosses were: $27,800; $23,900; $20,000, and $19,700. *Variety's* verdict reflected the holding power—"showed solidly." It moved over to the Victoria. By comparison this low-budget picture opened in the same week as *Chinatown*, already a huge hit in the U.S., which took home $55.000
90. "Motion Pictures Rated by the Code and Rating Administration," *Variety*, September 15, 1976, 24.
91. "Picture Grosses," *Variety*, March 10, 1976, 18. That was a poor $3,461 in Toronto. I couldn't find any box office reports for the U.S. in *Variety*. However, Bryanston was the type of company whose movies often flew below the radar. I did find reports of bookings in Canada from *Box Office* magazine, but it didn't report actual tallies, rather just commented on performance. But screenings in Calgary, Winnipeg and Edmonton were all tagged "poor" (*Box Office*, 1976, March 1, April 12, June 14).
92. "Hard Krona of Sweden Spells Impressive Totals," *Variety*, May 12, 1976, 342. These figures were gross not rentals—the rental figure would be about half the gross.
93. "Swedish B.O. Champs," *Variety*, May 11, 1977, 360. *Caravan to Vaccarès* pulled in approximately £588,000.
94. "*Rendezvous* OK 24G in London," *Variety*, December 14, 1977, 35; "Pre-Yule Gloom Hits

London," *Variety*, December 21, 1977, 38. The opening salvo was adjudged to be "not bad for this time of year." The second week had a surprisingly low fall-off, down just $3,100 to $20,800—just over 10 percent—and the third week hit a "fair" $15,000 (a 25 percent tumble which would also be considered very low by modern standards).

95. "*Spy* Again," *Variety*, February 15, 1978, 37; "*Spy* Big $184,680 Leads Tokyo," *Variety*, March 1, 1978, 32; "*Spy*, $167,770 11th Paces Tokyo B.O." *Variety*, March 8, 1978, 52. The opening week managed $133,000 from three cinemas, the second $90,000, the third $82,000 and the fourth $78,000. Again, by modern standards, these were small declines. By comparison *The Spy Who Loved Me* scored $184,000 from six in its 10th week.

96. "Mutual Gets Distribution of *Golden Rendezvous*," *Box Office*, September 5, 1977, K1.

97. "*Cop* $242,412 3rd Leads Paris B.O.," *Variety*, February 22, 1978, 38. It took $77,000 from 15 cinemas.

98. "1977–1978 B.O. for Sweden," *Variety*, May 9, 1978, 44. Rentals came to approx. $653,000.

99. "National TV Ratings," *Screen International*, September 18, 1982, 32. It beat *Airport '75* and *The Driver*, screened the same week.

100. "Picture Grosses," *Variety*, September 10, 1980, 5.

101. "Picture Grosses," *Variety*, September 23, 1980, 17.

102. "Picture Grosses," *Variety*, September 23, 1980, 24; "Picture Grosses," *Variety*, November 26, 1980, 12; "Picture Grosses," *Variety*, January 21, 1981. $34,000 from nine in Cleveland; $45,000 in Detroit, $75,000 in Philadelphia and $3,500 in Washington.

103. "London," *Variety*, January 16, 1980, 42.

104. "British Top-Grossing Films on the U.K. Market," *Variety*, January 14, 1981, 142.

105. "Tokyo," *Variety*, February 20–March 6, 1980.

106. "Further Totals in Spain," *Variety*, February 25, 1981, 41.

107. "50 Top-Grossing Pix in Sweden," *Variety*, May 13, 1981, 306.

108. "New York Showcases," *Variety*, December 27, 1989, 17.

109. "Box Office," *Variety*, October 11, 1989, 41.

110. "*Hostage Tower* Slated for CBS," *Hollywood Reporter*, February 15, 1980, 14.

111. "Made for TV Rankings for 1979–1980," *Variety*, September 17, 1980, 60.

112. "New Films," *Screen International*, September 6, 1980, 13.

113. "*Gigolo*, *Being There* and *Shining* Big in Finland," *Hollywood Reporter*, November 4, 1980.

114. "Video Top 20 (Wholesalers)," *Screen International*, January 26, 1985, 27; "Around the Home Video Track," *Variety*, March 28, 1984, 40. It had been released the year before in the U.S. via Embassy.

Bibliography

The best book about Alistair MacLean's personal life, written shortly after his death, is Jack Webster's biography *Alistair MacLean: A Life* (Chapmans, 1991). *Alistair MacLean's War: How the Royal Navy Shaped His Bestsellers* (Pen & Sword Marine, 2022) by Mark Simmons investigates his war experiences.

Dillon Kastner made available to me the Elliot Kastner Archives (EKA). Sources at the Margaret Herrick Library were also useful.

Trade Press

Box Office
Hollywood Reporter
Kine Weekly / Cinema Today
Motion Picture Exhibitor
Screen International
Variety

Movie Magazines

ABC Film Review / Film Review
Cinema
Cinema Retro
Films and Filming
Films Illustrated
Movie
Photoplay
Sight & Sound

Books, Articles and Broadcasts

After the Battle, "The Guns of Navarone," Issue No 177, 2017, 46–54.
Alistair MacLean, BBC Alba, December 28, 2021.
Alistair MacLean, BBC1, July 7, 1972.
The Alistair MacLean Story, ITV, April 20, 1973.
Balio, Tino, ed. *The American Film Industry*, 2nd revised edition. Madison: University of Wisconsin Press, 1985.
Balio, Tino. *Grand Design: Hollywood as a Modern Business Enterprise, 1930–1939*. New York: Charles Scribner's Sons, 1993.
Balio, Tino. *United Artists: The Company Built by the Stars*. Madison: University of Wisconsin Press, 1976.
Balio, Tino. *United Artists: The Company That Changed the Film Industry*. Madison: University of Wisconsin Press, 1987.
Bergen, Ronald. *The United Artists Story*. London: Octopus, 1986.
Bernstein, Andrew. "The Exalted Heroism of Alistair MacLean's Novels." *The Objective Standard*, Spring 2008.
Binns, Daniel. *Hollywood War Films: Critical Observations from World War One to Iraq*. Chicago: University of Chicago Press, 2017.
Biskind, Peter. *Easy Riders, Raging Bulls*. New York: Simon & Schuster, 1998.
Blumberg, Joel, and Sandra Grabman. *Lloyd Nolan: An Actor's Life with Meaning*. Orlando: BearManor Media, 2010.
Book Programme, BBC2, May 4, 1976.
Booth, Rupert. *Not a Number—Patrick McGoohan, A Life*. London: Aurora Metro, 2011.
Borgnine, Ernest. *I Don't Want to Set the World on Fire, I Just Want to Keep My Nuts Warm: My Autobiography*. London: JR Books, 2009.
Bragg, Melvyn. *Rich: The Life of Richard Burton*. London: Hodder & Stoughton, 1989.
Bret, David. *Rock Hudson*. London: Pavilion Books, 2004.
Brierley, Dean. "The Espionage Films of Alistair MacLean." *Cinema Retro*, Issue 13, 2009.
Brierley, Dean. "The Espionage Films of Alistair MacLean Part 2," *Cinema Retro*, Issue 14, 2009.
Britton, Wesley. *Beyond Bond: Spies in Fiction and Film*. Santa Barbara: ABC-Clio, 2004.
Britton, Wesley. *Onscreen and Undercover: The Ultimate Book of Movie Espionage*. Santa Barbara: ABC-Clio, 2006.
Brown, Gene. *Movie Time: A Chronology of Hollywood and the Movie Industry from Its Beginnings to the Present*. New York: Macmillan, 1995.
Buscombe, Edward. *The BFI Companion to the Western*. New York: Athenaeum, 1988.
Calder, Jenni. *There Must Be a Lone Ranger*. London: Hamish Hamilton, 1974.
Callan, Michael Feeney. *Richard Harris: Sex, Death & the Movies*. London: Robson Books, 2004.
Cameron, Ian, and Douglas Pye, eds. *The Movie Book of the Western*. London: Studio Vista, 1996.
Cashin, Fergus. *Richard Burton*. London: Hodder and Stoughton, 1974.

Caspar, Drew. *Post-War Hollywood 1946–1962*. Hoboken: Wiley-Blackwell, 2007.

Cawelti, John G. *The Six-Gun Mystique*. Bowling Green, OH: Popular Press, 1971.

Chapman, James. "Film Finances and *The Golden Rendezvous*: Financial Mismanagement, Personal Tensions and Political Scandal." *Historical Journal of Film, Radio and Television*, Volume 42, Issue 4, October 2022.

Chibnall, Steve. *J. Lee Thompson*. (British Film Makers Series.) Manchester: Manchester University Press, 2001.

Child, Lee. "Foreword to *Alistair MacLean's War*" by Mark Simmons, see below.

Chudacoff, Helga. "Out of the Pages." *People*, September 12, 1977.

Cinema Retro Special Edition: *Where Eagles Dare*. Dorset: Solo Publishing, 2009.

Clapham, Walter. *Western Movies: The Story of the West on Screen*. London: Octopus, 1974.

"Conversation with Derren Nesbitt." Pictureville, Bradford, March 20, 2009. https://www.youtube.com/watch?v=P0P0HUgC_1M

"Conversation with *Where Eagles Dare* Film-Makers." 50th Anniversary Screening at the British Film Institute. https://www.youtube.com/watch?v=_KAWFJfpC3g&t=982s

Corkin, Stanley. *Cowboys as Cold Warriors—The Western and U.S. History*. Philadelphia: Temple University Press, 2004.

Dangaard, Colin. "The Art of Navarone." *Washington Post*, September 3, 1978.

Darvas, Eddy, and Eddie Lawson. *Don Sharp*. The London History Project, November 1993.

Davenport, Robert. *The Encyclopaedia of War Films*. New York: Checkmark Books, 2003.

Davies, Richard Rhys. *The International Spy Film Guide, 1945–1989*. Picture and Sound, 2016.

De Vries, Fred. alistairmacleanblog.com

Dick, Bernard F. *Engulfed: The Death of Paramount and the Birth of Corporate Hollywood*. Lexington: The University Press of Kentucky, 2001.

Downing, David. *Charles Bronson*. London: Virgin Books, 1982.

Dyer, Geoff. *"Broadsword Calling Danny Boy": On Where Eagles Dare*. London: Penguin, 2018.

Everson, William K. *The Hollywood Western*. New York: Citadel Press, 1992.

Exshaw, John. "Don Sharp, Director: An Appreciation." *Cinema Retro*, Issue 20.

Eyles, Allen. *The Western: An Illustrated Guide*. London: A. Zwemmer, 1967.

Falk, Quentin. *Anthony Hopkins: The Authorized Biography*. London: Ebury Publishing, 2004.

Falk, Quentin. *Too Good to Waste: Anthony Hopkins, A Biography*. London: Columbus Books, 1989.

Fishgall, Gary. *Gregory Peck: A Biography*. New York: Simon & Schuster, 2002.

Fonda, Peter. *Don't Tell Dad: A Memoir*. London: Pocket Books, 1999.

Foreman, Carl. "Dialogue on Film." *American Cinematographer*, April 1979.

Foreman, Carl. "The Road to *The Victors*." *Films & Filming*, 1964.

Frazier, Paul. *The Cold War on Film*. Santa Barbara: ABC-Clio, 2021.

Freedland, Michael. *Gregory Peck: A Biography*. New York: Wm Morrow, 1980.

Freeman, Mike. *Jim Brown: The Fierce Life of an American Hero*. New York: HarperCollins, 2006.

French, Philip. *Westerns: Aspects of a Genre*. Revised edition. Manchester: Carcanet, 2001.

Garfield, Brian. *Western Films: A Complete Guide*. New York: Da Capo Press, 1982.

Gow, Gordon. "Interrogation: An Interview with Carl Foreman." *Films & Filming*, 1972.

Grant, Barry Keith, ed. *American Cinema of the 1960s: Themes and Variations*. New Brunswick: Rutger University Press, 2008.

Haney, Lynn. *Gregory Peck: A Charmed Life*. London: Robson Books, 2005.

Hannan, Brian. *Coming Back to a Theater Near You: A History of Hollywood Reissues 1914–2014*. Jefferson, NC: McFarland, 2016.

Hannan, Brian. *The Magnificent '60s: The 100 Most Popular Films of the Revolutionary Decade*. Jefferson, NC: McFarland, 2022.

Hannan, Brian. *The Making of* The Guns of Navarone. Glasgow: Baroliant Press, 2013 (Revised Edition 2019).

Hannan, Brian. *The Making of* The Magnificent Seven: *Behind the Scenes of the Pivotal Western*. Jefferson, NC: McFarland, 2015.

Hannan, Brian. *1960s Movies, Behind the Scenes*. Glasgow: Baroliant Press, 2022.

Hannan, Brian. *1960s Movies Redux, Volume One*. Glasgow: Baroliant Press, 2022.

Hannan, Brian. *1960s Movies Redux, Volume Two*. Glasgow: Baroliant Press, 2022.

Hawkins, Jack. *Anything for a Quiet Life: The Autobiography of Jack Hawkins*. London: Elm tree Books, 1973.

Heston, Charlton. *An Actor's Life: Journals 1956–1976*. Penguin: London, 1979.

Higgins, Jack. "Review of *River of Death*." *Sunday Standard*.

Hillier, Jim. *The New Hollywood*. London: Studio Vista, 1993.

Holston, Kim R. *Richard Widmark: A Bio-Bibliography*. Greenwood Press, 1990.

Hudson, Rock, and Sara Davidson. *Rock Hudson: His Story*. London: Weidenfeld & Nicolson, 1986.

Hughes, Howard. *Stagecoach to Tombstone: The Filmgoers Guide to Great Westerns*. London and New York: I.B. Tauris, 2008.

Hunt, Bill. "Bill Hunt Interviews Director J. Lee Thompson." *The Digital Bits*, June 6, 2020.

"*Ice Station Zebra*, Film in Focus." *Cinema Retro*, Volume 17, Issue 51.

Ireland, Jill. *Life Wish*. London: Cornerstone, 1990.

Izod, John. *Hollywood and the Box Office*. New York: Columbia University Press, 1992.

Jenkins, Garry. *Harrison Ford: Imperfect Hero*. London: Kensington Publishing, 1998.

Jensen, Richard D. *The Nicest Fella: The Life of Ben Johnson*. IUniverse, 2010.
Johnston, Iain. "Author Says He's Businessman." *Los Angeles Times*, December 24, 1972.
Kassabuam, Bartlett Lee. *Becoming Richard Widmark*. Createspace, 2017.
Kirtz, William. "Out to Beat Bond." *New York Times*, June 23, 1966, 109.
Langley, Roger. *Patrick McGoohan: Danger Man or Prisoner?* Revised edition. Gwynned: Six of One, 2017.
Lardner, Ring, Jr. *I'd Hate Myself in the Morning: A Memoir*. New York: Thunder's Mouth Press, 2000.
Lee, Christopher. *Tall, Dark and Gruesome*. London: Vista, 1998.
Lee, Robert E. *Alistair MacLean: The Key Is Fear*. San Bernardino: Borgo Press, 1976.
Lloyd, Ann, ed. *Movies of the Sixties*. London: Orbis, 1983.
Lord, Graham. "Alistair MacLean Interview." *Sunday Express*, 1972.
Lovell, Glenn. *Escape Artist: The Life and Times of John Sturges*. Wisconsin: University of Wisconsin Press, 2008.
Loy, R. Philip. *Westerns in a Changing America, 1955–2000*. Jefferson, NC: McFarland, 2004.
Lucas, George, Alex Ben Block and Lucy Autry Wilson, eds. *Blockbusting*. New York: IT Books, 2010.
MacLean, Alistair. *Alistair MacLean Introduces Scotland*. London: Andre Deutsch, 1972.
MacLean, Alistair. "Introduction to *The Guns of Navarone*." London: Companion Book Club, 1958.
MacLean, Alistair. "The Rewards and Responsibilities of Success." *Glasgow Herald*, June 19, 1982.
Madsen, Axel. *The New Hollywood*. New York: Crowell, 1975.
McDonald, Archie P. *Shooting Stars: Heroes and Heroines of Western Film*. Bloomington: Indiana University Press, 1987.
McGilligan, Patrick. *Clint: The Life and Legend of Clint Eastwood*. New York: HarperCollins, 1999.
Membery, York. *Pierce Brosnan: The Biography*. London: Virgin Books, 2002.
Mirisch, Walter. *I Thought We Were Making Movies, Not History*. Madison: University of Wisconsin Press, 2008.
Monaco, James. *American Film Now: The People, the Power, the Money, the Movies*. New York: Oxford University Press, 1979.
Monaco, Paul. *The Sixties: 1960–1969*. New York: Scribner's, 2001.
Morden, Ethan. *Medium Cool: The Movies of the 1960s*. New York: Knopf, 1990.
Morley, Sheridan. *Robert, My Father*. London: Orion, 1993.
Muller, Jurgen. *Best Movies of the 1970s*. Cologne: Taschen, 2006.
Muller, Jurgen. *Movies of the 1960s*. Cologne: Taschen, 2004.
Munn, Michael. *David Niven: The Man Behind the Balloon*. London: JR Books, 2009.
Munn, Michael. *Richard Burton: Prince of Players*. Skyhorse Publishing, 2015.
Niven, David, *The Moon's a Balloon*. London: Penguin, 1994.
Norman, Barry. "The Best-Selling Sceptic." *The Observer*, September 5, 1971.
Pitt, Ingrid. *Life's a Scream: The Autobiography of Ingrid Pitt*. London: Cornerstone, 1999.
Quayle, Anthony. *Time to Speak*. London: Vintage, 1990.
Quinn, Anthony. *One Man Tango*. London: Headline Publishing, 1995.
Quinn, Anthony. *The Original Sin: A Self-Portrait*. London: W.H. Allen, 1974.
Richardson, Michael. *Guns, Girls and Gadgets: Sixties Spy Films Uncovered*. Powys: Quoit Media, 2021.
Rubin, Robert M. *Vanishing Point Forever*. Ride with Bob, 2024.
Sackett, Susan. *The Hollywood Reporter Book of Box Office Hits*. New York: Billboard Books, 1990.
Sarris, Andrew. *American Cinema—Directors and Directions 1929–1968*. New York: E.P. Dutton, 1968.
Schickel, Richard. *Clint Eastwood: A Biography*. London: Cornerstone, 1997.
Scougal, Murray. "The Adventures of Alistair MacLean—The Scots Author Who Invented the Thriller." *Sunday Post*, December 27, 2021.
Simmons, Mark. *Alistair MacLean's War*. London: Pen & Sword Maritime, 2022.
Slater, Jay. *Under Fire: A Century of War Movies*. Wythenshawe: Crecy Publishing, 2009.
Stanley, Allessandra. "In Praise of Alistair MacLean and the Male Romance." *New York Times*, February 13, 2018.
Steinberg, Cobbett. *Reel Facts*. New York: Vintage Books, 1968.
Towers, Harry Alan. *Mr. Towers of London: A Life in Show Business*. Albany, GA: BearManor Media, 2013.
Vermilye, Jerry. *The Films of Charles Bronson*. London: Kensington Publishing, 1980.
Webster, Jack. *Alistair MacLean*. London: Chapman Publishing, 1991.
Widmark, Richard. "Creating Without Compromise." *Films & Filming*, October 1961, 7–8.
Williams, Chris, ed. *The Richard Burton Diaries*. New Haven: Yale University Press, 2012.
Wojcik, Pamela Robertson, ed. *New Constellations: Movie Stars of the 1960s*. New Brunswick: Rutgers University Press, 2012.
Zinman, David. *Fifty Grand Movies of the 1960s and 1970s*. New York: Random House, 1988.

Index

ABC TV 69, 74, 113, 120, 177
Acropolis 24
Actors Strike 22, 23
Adams, Maud 139, 140
Aegean 5
Aga Khan 67, 160
The Agony and the Ecstasy 9
Aimée, Anouk 50
Air Force One 155, 159
Air Force One Is Down 138, 140, 155–159, 173, 182
Airport 47
Airport '75 163, 169
Airport '77 132
Alaska 7, 131, 133
Alien 177, 181
Alistair MacLean's Strike Force 172
All About Lawrence 39
All the President's Men 6
Allen, Irwin 131, 167
Allen, Patrick 83, 88
Amazon Jungle 7, 144, 145
Ambler, Eric 3, 15, 23, 82
American International Pictures 82, 120, 151
Amsterdam 5, 7, 82, 83, 87, 128, 134, 136, 169
Anderson, Michael 15, 23, 53
Andrews, Dana 37
Andrews, Harry 52
Andrews, Julie 40
Angel, Daniel 15, 111, 128, 172
Angelique 98
Anglo Amalgamated 74, 91
Anglo EMI 93
The Angry Hills 22
Anhalt, Edward 35, 38
Ann-Margret 49
Annakin, Ken 53
Apocalypse Now 146, 147
Arabesque 103, 112
Arctic 43, 136
Argentina 169
Arkoff, Samuel Z 82, 120
Arness, James 50
Around the World in 80 Days (1956) 15
Arrochar 43

Asimov, Isaac 13
Asner, Edward 36, 37
Assault on a Queen 11
Associated British 15, 16, 91, 169
Athabasca 131, 167
Australia 34, 112, 140
Austria 17, 20, 55, 56
The Avengers TV series 84

Bach, Barbara 122
Badel, Alan 122
Bahamas 11, 162
Balin, Ina 22
Ball, Vincent 52
Ballantine Books 11
Bancroft, Anne 50
Bandolero! 12
Bangkok 177
Bank of Montreal 131
Bantam Books 11, 12
Barkworth, Peter 59
Barrett, James Lee 13
Basehart, Richard 36, 37
Battle of Britain 121
Battle of the Bulge 53
Bear Island 4, 6, 7, 128–137, 148, 149, 151, 155, 159, 173, 181
Beatty, Robert 58
Beatty, Warren 49
Beau Geste (1966) 41
Becket 35, 49
The Bedford Incident 18
Belgium 156
Belle de Jour 12
Ben-Hur (1959) 55
Bergen 162
Berger, Senta 17–21
Bernstein, Elmer 93
Big Iron 167
Bill, Tony 44
Birney, David 4, 100, 103, 167, 173
Bishop, David 75, 81, 83, 104, 152, 161, 167, 169
Bitter Harvest 69
Black Sunday 38
Blattner, Gerry 142
Bloch, Robert 12
Bloom, Jeffrey 163

Blow-Up 132
The Bobo 49, 50, 67, 69
Bodle, Justin 156
Boesky, Ivan 67
Bolt, Robert 120
Bond, James 1, 3, 20, 37, 38, 44, 60, 66, 71, 76, 86, 94, 128, 131, 141, 149
Boone, Richard 50
Das Boot 46
Borehamwood Studios 55
Borgnine, Ernest 42, 43, 44, 46
Bosnia and Herzegovina 122
Boyle, Peter 143, 166
The Boys from Brazil 134
Bozzuffi, Marcel 100, 101
Brando, Marlon 50, 71, 129
Brands Hatch 152
Brass Target 134
Brazil 143, 144, 155
Breakheart Pass 2, 7, 74, 80, 91, 98, 100, 104–110, 128, 136, 167, 168, 173, 177, 180
Breakout 105, 169, 180
The Brides of Fu Manchu 144
Bridge on the River Kwai 22, 58
A Bridge Too Far 6, 122
Bridges, Lloyd 132, 134
The Bridges at Toko-Ri 15
Britain 22, 39, 74, 82, 83, 94, 100, 112, 143, 164, 176, 177, 178, 179, 181, 182
British Lion 129, 149, 154, 162, 172
British Touring Car Championship 152
Broccoli, Cubby 85, 128
Bronson, Charles 46, 52, 104–110, 138, 143, 146, 162, 168, 173, 175, 176, 177, 180
Brosnan, Pierce 149, 154, 155, 173
Brown, George H. 170
Brown, Jim 42, 44, 46
Brunston, Dave 152
Bryanston 100, 180
Bryant, Chris 112, 169
Budapest 17, 19
Budd, Roy 95

215

Index

budget 15, 17, 22, 26, 36, 41, 43, 49, 53, 55, 57, 72, 74, 82, 93, 100, 105, 106, 107, 111, 112, 119, 120, 131, 133, 138, 144, 148, 152, 156, 160, 163, 169
Bujold, Geneviève 166
Bullitt 86, 91, 94, 133
bullring 101
Burlinson, Tom 153
Burnett, W.R. 41
Burton, Richard 40, 49–67, 82, 92, 107, 160, 173, 176
Butler, David 129, 131, 136
The Buttercup Chain 83
Butterfield 8 111

Caan, James 120
cable car 55, 177, 182
Callas, Maria 22
The Camargue 98
Camelot 132
Canada 94, 95, 128, 132, 140, 181
Canadian Film Development Corp 131
Cannes Film Festival 170
Canutt, Yakima 53, 55, 108
Caravan to Vaccarès 5, 6, 80, 91, 98–103, 120, 128, 152, 167, 168, 173, 180
Caravans 132
Cardinale, Claudia 50
Caribbean 7, 80, 91, 96, 160–166
Caron, Leslie 52
Carradine, John 112, 114, 115
Carrington, Robert 93, 94, 97, 138, 142, 168
Carver, Steve 144
Casdagli, Penny 83, 87, 88
The Cassandra Crossing 38, 111
Cassavettes, John 54
Cast a Giant Shadow 18
Castle, John 69
Castle Keep 44
Cat Ballou 53
CBS 93, 138, 140, 182
The Ceremony 111
Chamberlain, Richard 162
Chandler, Raymond 115
Chapman, Ian 120
Chapman, Robin 120
Charade 41, 103
Chariots of Fire 170
Chato's Land 105, 107
Chayefsky, Paddy 40, 46
Child, Lee 33
Children of Sanchez 49
China 102
Chitwood, Tim and Joie 94
Christie, Agatha 4, 136, 137
Christie, Julie 33, 46, 58
The Cincinnati Kid 11, 40
Cinema Center 74, 93
Cinema Seven 167

Cinerama 1, 23, 35, 41, 43, 46, 74, 177, 179
Circus 131, 167
Clancy, Tom 47
Clark, Robert 15, 82, 168
Clarke, Arthur C. 13
Clavell, James 35, 38
Cleverings, Piet 83
CLT 151
Coburn, James 50, 83
Cohen, Larry 71
Cohen, Nat 91, 162
Cold Sweat 104
The Collector 11
Collins, Patricia 132
Collins, Wm 33, 34, 39
Columbia 5, 9, 11, 15, 16, 22, 24, 25, 27, 49, 69, 80, 82, 93, 98, 111, 117, 118, 119, 120, 131, 133, 167, 171
The Comedians 49
Commonwealth United 74, 119, 120
Connery, Sean 72, 83, 99, 120, 162
Cornwall 39
Corvette 93
Count Volpi 80, 128, 169
Creasey, John 33
Crenna, Richard 105, 107
Croatia 149, 154
The Cruel Sea 7, 71
Cummings, Constance 139
Custer of the West 61, 121
Cyprus 23

The Dam Busters 15, 23, 169
The Damned (1969) 99
Dancing Ledge Productions 171
Danger Man/Secret Agent TV Series 42
The Dark Crusader/The Black Shrike 34, 35, 128, 131, 156, 172
Darren, James 22–32
Dassin, Jules 53, 162
The Day of the Jackal (1973) 99, 122, 178
Days of Wine and Roses 13
Deadfall 162
Deadlier than the Male 61
Death Train 148–151, 154, 155, 158, 173, 183
Death Wish 105
Death Wish II 143
The Deep 121
The Deer Hunter 122, 177
Delacorte-Dell 13
Delfont, Lord Bernard 91
Deliverance 178
Dell Books 11
Delon, Nathalie 69, 70, 72, 74, 76
Delux 151

Denis, John 142, 143, 158
Denmark 140
Denver, John 111
de Ravin, Emilie 156, 157, 158
De Sica, Vittorio 49
Detroit 179, 180
Devane, William 154, 171
The Devil Rides Out 83
Dickens, Charles 115
Die Hard 115, 141
Diffring, Anton 52, 58
The Dirty Dozen 7, 42, 43, 57, 58, 60, 104, 132, 161
Dirty Harry 76, 162
distribution 43, 67, 74, 75, 92, 93, 100, 107, 111, 112, 119, 122, 133, 140, 178, 179
Doctor Faustus 49, 50, 52
Dr. No 53, 72, 82
Dr. Syn 42
Doctor Zhivago 11, 82, 120
Donen, Stanley 41
Don't Look Now 112, 129, 132
Doubleday 17
Douglas, Kirk 17, 50
Dudikoff, Michael 144, 145, 146
Duel 148
Duken, Ken 156, 157
Dullea, Keir 139, 140
Durning, Charles 105
Duvall, Robert 156

Earthquake 112, 163
Eastwood, Clint 48–65, 82, 104, 105, 107, 120, 162, 175, 176, 179, 180, 181
Easy Rider 139, 162
Eggar, Samantha 66
Eiffel Tower 138
Ekland, Britt 69, 139, 140
Elwes, Cary 167
Elwes, Cassian 168
EMI 91, 93, 95, 162
Empire, Leics Sq., London 57
The Empire Strikes Back 182
The Enforcer (1976) 181
Engel, William C. 11
Entertainment in Video 182
Escape from Alcatraz 181
Every Which Way But Loose 177, 181
The Exorcist (1973) 177

Faberge 67
Fail Safe 9, 41
Fairbanks, Douglas, Jr. 139, 140
Fantastic Voyage 13, 93
Fawcett Books 11
Fawcett-Majors, Farrah 169
Fear Is the Key 2, 3, 5, 7, 8, 19, 20, 33, 34, 66, 80, 89, 91–97, 101, 103, 197, 112, 115, 138, 141, 148, 167, 173, 179

Index

Ferrer, José 111
Film Finance 112
Film Fund Luxembourg 156
Film Trust Overseas 111
Filmways 39, 44, 111
Fingal's Cave 71
Finney, Albert 162
Fishman, Paul 95
A Fistful of Dollars 50
Fleischer, Richard 93
Fleming, Ian 46, 128
Flemyng, Robert 112
Floodgate 99, 168
Florida 7, 95
Fonda, Jane 49, 50, 162
Fonda, Peter 139, 140, 151
Forbes, Bryan 91, 162
Force 10 from Navarone 7, 66, 91, 98, 117–127, 132, 151, 173, 177, 181
Ford, Harrison 121, 122, 127, 156, 159, 173
Ford, John 18
Foreman, Carl 1, 5, 6, 16, 22–32, 41, 62, 81, 84, 117–127
Forest, Joseph 99, 168
Fox, Edward 121, 122, 152
France 52, 75, 98, 104, 128
Franciosa, Anthony 50
Francis, Anne 36, 37
Francis, Freddie 112
Frankenheimer, John 41, 143
Fraser, George MacDonald 121
Fraulein Doktor 94
The French Connection 86, 91, 100, 178
Friedland, Dennis 143
Friend, Ed 13
From the Terrace 22
Fuchs, Daniel 15, 172
Funeral in Berlin 11
Funny Girl 13
Furie, Sidney J. 53, 162
Futureworld 139

Gallipoli 170
Gardner, Ava 66
Gareloch, Scotland 43
Garner, James 50
Gay, John 36, 111, 151
Gellhorn, Martha 71
Geneva 74, 130
Germany 94, 119, 177, 181
Gershwin, Jerry 49, 53, 67, 74, 104, 106, 118, 176
Ghia, Fernando 163
Glasgow, Scotland 1, 5, 180
Glen Alden Corporation 67, 69, 72
Golan, Menahem 143
Gold Medal Books 12
Golden Gate 168
Golden Girl 169
Golden Rendezvous 7, 39, 80, 91,
111–116, 120, 132, 134, 136, 169, 173, 181
Goldfinger 38, 53
Goldman, William 6, 49
Goldsmith, Jerry 106
Golus, Yoram 143
Gone with the Wind 9, 57
Goodbye California 130, 131, 169
Goodbye, Mr. Chips (1969) 49, 50
Grade, Sir Lew 131, 168
Grafton Media 152
Grand Prix 43, 154
Grant, Cary 22
Graves, Rupert 156, 157, 158
The Great Escape 1, 7, 35, 41, 45, 91, 104, 144
The Great Race 13
Greece 23, 24, 25, 83, 119, 122, 160
Greene, Graham 3, 82
Greenland 15, 43
Greenwood, Bruce 132
Gries, Tom 105, 106
Griffiths, Leon 171
Gulf of Mexico 7
Guns for Butter 169
The Guns of Navarone 1, 3, 5, 6, 7, 15, 16, 22–32, 33, 39, 41, 46, 52, 59, 62, 77, 80, 81, 82, 101, 111, 117, 118, 122, 126, 132, 141, 142, 143, 144, 168, 169, 173, 176, 178, 180
Guzmán, Claudio 138, 140, 182

Hackett, Joan 36
Hailey, Arthur 47
The Hallelujah Trail 35, 36, 41, 46
Halmi, Robert 156
Hamilton, Guy 23, 53, 121, 122
Hamilton, Linda 152, 156, 157
Harper/The Moving Target 6, 49, 50, 67, 92, 117
Harris, Richard 6, 50, 111–116, 146
Harvey, Laurence 39, 42, 111
Haslemere, England 39
Hawden, Robin 69
Hawkins, Jack 69, 70, 76, 82
Hawn, Goldie 162
Hazlewood, Jean 17
Heath Productions 17
Hemdale 113
Hemmings, David 66, 82
Hennessey 120, 132
Hepburn, Audrey 50
Hepburn, Katharine 143
Heston, Charlton 35, 41, 120, 129
Heyes, Douglas 41, 117
High Noon 22, 41
Hill, Terence 163
Hillier, Erwin 142

Hitchcock, Alfred 12
Hohenwerfen 55
Holden, William 15, 22, 23
Holland 140
Holt, Denis 55, 69, 94, 160, 164
Hombre 50, 52
Home Box Office 113, 120
Homolka, Oscar 69
Hong Kong 140, 154, 155
Hopkins, Anthony 4, 66–79, 107, 162, 173
Hordern, Michael 52, 58
The Hostage Tower 138–142, 149, 150, 151, 155, 158, 182
Hour of the Gun 35, 41
House Un-American Activities Committee (HUAC) 22, 30
Houston, Donald 58
How the West Was Won 13
Huddleston, David 108
Hudson, Hugh 173
Hudson, Rock 39–47
Hughes, Howard 67, 160
Hungary 17, 20, 128
Hunt, Peter 129
Huston, John 53
Hutton, Brian G. 4, 48–65, 53, 55, 56, 61, 71, 163

Ice Cold in Alex 23
Ice Station Zebra 1, 4, 39–47, 48, 57, 62, 76, 81, 102, 111, 136, 170, 173, 177
Idaho 106
Ireland, Jill 106, 107
Isle of Mull 71
Israel 67, 171
Istanbul 67
The Italian Job (1969) 69
Italy 23, 67, 74, 75, 100, 105
ITC 171

Jackson, David S. 149, 154, 171
Jackson, Gordon 112
Jadran Films 149, 154
Jamaica Inn 39
Jameson, Jerry 169
Janssen, David 50, 112, 114, 115
Japan 57, 75, 177, 181, 182
Jaws 98, 121, 163
Jaws 3D 152
Jayston, Michael 69
The Jazz Singer (1980) 138
Jenkins, Geoffrey 33
Jenkins, Lewis 81
Jersey 122
Jewison, Norman 41, 53, 162
Johnson, Ben 105, 107
Johnson, Celia 139, 140
Johnson, Patricia 12
Joint, Alf 55, 93
Jones, L.Q. 146
Jourdan, Louis 22
Judith 82

Index

Juggernaut 111, 112
Julienne, Remy 139
Justice, James Robertson 28, 52

Kaleidoscope 49, 67
Kanter, Jay 69, 74, 93, 94, 95
Karlson, Phil 17, 35
Kastner, Dillon 167
Kastner, Elliott 2, 4, 6, 48, 49–67, 66–79, 80, 82, 91–97, 98, 100, 104, 107, 112, 117, 119, 120, 128, 129, 132, 151, 156, 160, 162, 163, 167, 169, 173, 176, 179
Kelley, John T. 118
Kelly, Grace 15
Kelly, Skeets 84
Kemeny, John 167
Kendall, Suzy 91–97
Kerr, Deborah 15
The Key 23
Khartoum 13, 53
King, Jamie Thomas 156, 157, 158
King, Stephen 4
King of Kings 13
King Paul of Greece 25
Kingsley, Ben 94, 96, 97
Kiss of Death (1947) 17
Klute 132, 179
Knox, Alexander 87, 88
Korean War 17, 38
Koscina, Sylva 69
Kruger, Hardy 52
Kubrick, Stanley 12

Ladd, Alan, Jr. 74
Lady L 71, 92
The Ladykillers (1955) 23
La Fresnais, Ian 94
L'Amour, Louis 13
Lancaster, Burt 17, 22, 23
Lanchester, Elsa 139
Lang, Jennings 163, 166
Lane, Leonard 67, 85, 86
Lardner, Ring, Jr. 40
Larson, Ania 83, 87, 88
Las Vegas 67
The Last Picture Show 105
Latin America 100
Lauter, Ed 105, 108
Lawrence of Arabia 53
Lawson, Leigh 112, 114
lawsuit 140
Lazarus, Ashley 112, 115
Lean, David 53, 82
Lee, Christopher 112, 132, 134, 149
Legrand, Michel 44
Leics Sq Theatre, London 180
Leider, Jerry 138
Leigh, Suzanna 83, 88
Lemon Popsicle 143
Leonard, Niall 156
Levine, Ted 149

Lewis, Simon 172
libraries 11, 12
Lieber, Perry 11
The Lion in Winter 69
Lisi, Virna 50
Little, Robert 140
Little Big Man 98, 107
Live and Let Die 86, 94, 178
Lloyd, Euan 18
location 23, 25, 35, 36, 37, 43, 55, 71, 84, 85, 94, 100, 106, 118, 122, 136, 140, 143, 144, 145, 154, 156, 161, 163
Loch Lomond, Scotland 43
Lollobrigida, Gina 138
Lom, Herbert 52, 144, 146
Lombino, Salvatore 33
London 28, 38, 49, 71, 74, 100, 176, 179, 180, 181, 182
London Pavilion Cinema 179
Lonesome Dove 156
The Long Goodbye 93, 104
Lonsdale, Michael 99, 100
Lord Jim 11
Loren, Sophia 23, 49, 82
Los Angeles 35, 36, 37, 43, 163, 179, 181
Losey, Gavrik 95
The Lost Continent 83
Louisiana 93, 96
Love Story 11, 162, 178
Lovell, Glenn 46
Lowe, Olga 52
Ludlum, Robert 161, 162
Lumet, Sidney 41
Luxembourg 152, 156
Lynx Productions 156

Maas, Hidde 153
MacCorkindale, Simon 152, 153
MacDonald, John D. 7
Macdonald, Ross 7, 49, 117, 128
Mackendrick, Sandy 23, 169
MacKenna's Gold 117
MacLean, Mary Marcelle 6, 129, 151, 169
MacNeill, Alistair 143, 149, 155
The Magnificent Seven (1960) 1, 28, 35, 45, 58, 93, 104, 144, 161
The Magnificent 60s 1
Maharis, George 4, 36, 50, 87, 173
Mainz 150
Major Dundee 18, 41
Malone, Dorothy 112, 114, 115
Malta 71, 122
A Man Called Horse 112
A Man for All Seasons 53
The Man with the Golden Gun 139
Mann, Abby 48
Mann, Michael 148
Mann, Stanley 144
Marathon Man 134

Marchant, Tony 171
marketing 10, 14, 28, 40, 57
Marooned 12
Marquand, Christian 100
Marshall, Bryan 69
Martin, Dean 22, 50
Marvin, Lee 50, 120, 132, 138
Mason, James 22, 52, 152
Mayerling 69
Mayne, Ferdy 71, 76
MCA 48, 71
McAnally, Ray 96
McBain, Ed 33
McCallum, David 54
McCarthy, Cormac 7
McGoohan, Patrick 42, 44, 46, 173
McGraw, Ali 162
McKinney, Bill 108
McPherron, Kent 55
McQuarrie, Christopher 170
McQueen, Steve 35, 40, 41, 42, 50, 174
McTiernan, John 115
McWhorter, Richard 52
The Mechanic (1972) 105, 107, 162
Medak, Peter 143
Mediterranean 5
Mediterranean Film Studios 122
merchandising 10
Meredith, Burgess 112, 114, 115, 116
Meteor 120
Mexico 163
Meyer, Nicholas 163
MGM 9, 11, 40, 43, 48–65, 71, 74, 82, 91, 92, 93, 111, 130, 160, 175, 176
Michener, James 3, 4
Miller, David 41
Mills, John 22
Minerva Films 169
Mirisch, Walter 35, 36, 41
Mr. Blandings Builds His Dream House 10
Mr. Majestyk 105
Mitchum, Robert 50, 143
Moore, Archie 106, 108
Moore, Roger 52, 132, 162
More, Kenneth 22, 52
Morley, Robert 69, 70, 76
Morris-Adams, Richard 98, 100
Mosquito Squadron 69
Motion Picture Association of America 53
movie tie-in 9, 11, 12, 14, 28, 57, 104
Murder on the Orient Express (1974) 107, 136, 137, 162
music 58, 76, 93, 95, 112
The Music Man 13
My Fair Lady 13

Index

Nassau 161, 168
National General 69
Native American 107, 108
NATO 12
Navarone Productions 120
NBC 74
Nero, Franco 122
Nesbitt, Derren 52, 58
Netherlands 152
New American Library 11
New York 28, 43, 53, 176, 178, 179, 180, 181
New York Times 43, 82
New York Times Review of Books 7
Newman, Barry 91–97
Newman, Paul 49, 50, 92, 117, 174
Nez Perce 107
Nicholson, Jack 162
Nicholson, James H. 120
The Night Porter 99
The Night Watch 154–155, 173, 182
Night Without End 15, 16, 39, 128, 130, 131, 136, 170
The Nightcomers 93
Niven, David 22–32, 41, 117, 121, 173
Nodella, Burt 128, 140
Nolan, Lloyd 44
Norman, Marc 169
North by Northwest 103
North Pole 43, 128
Norway 129, 140
Nova Scotia 7

Ochsenknecht, Uwe 152, 153
Odeon Leics Sq., London 177, 178, 180, 181
Odeon Marble Arch 177, 180
The Odessa File 134
Okun, Milton 111
On the Buses 91
100 Rifles 105, 162
Open Road Productions 120
Operation Crossbow 11, 13, 53
Orion 179
Osborn, David 170
Oscar 17, 22, 25, 28, 40, 41, 44, 53, 60, 112
Our Man in Havana 21
Our Man in Marrakesh / Bang! Bang! You're Dead 84
Outbreak 38
The Outlaw Josey Wales 181

The Pad 53
Page, Geneviève 69
Paint Your Wagon 13
Pakistan 122
Palance, Jack 22
Papas, Irene 22, 28
Paramount 11, 39, 49, 69, 120, 121, 128, 162

Paris 140, 176, 181
Paris Blues 11
Parkins, Barbara 83, 87, 88, 132, 134
Partisans 171
Patterson, James 4
Paul, Alexandra 149, 154, 171
Peck, Gregory 22–32, 41, 42, 107, 117, 119, 121, 126, 142, 173
Peckinpah, Sam 86
Penthouse Cinema, Broadway 178
Peppard, George 50
Perenchio, Jerry 67
Perier, Etienne 66–79
Perlberg, William 15, 170
Perrine, Valerie 162
Peters, Clarke 149
Philadelphia 180
Pieterse, André 111, 120, 132, 172
Pinewood 162, 169
The Pink Panther (1964) 13
Pitt, Ingrid 52, 57, 58
Pittsburgh 178
Planet of the Apes (1968) 12
Playboy 74
Playtex 67
Pleasence, Donald 144, 145, 146
Plymouth, England 122
Pocket Books 11
Point Blank 94
Ponti, Carlo 49
Popular Library 35
Port St. Johns, South Africa 144
The Poseidon Adventure (1972) 46, 93, 167, 179
Powell, Joe 55
Power TV 156
Price, Stanley 112
The Prize 9
The Proud and the Profane 15
Provence 7, 100
Psycho 11, 12
Publishers Weekly 9
Puppet on a Chain 3, 4, 5, 6, 7, 20, 67, 75, 80–90, 97, 98, 99, 120, 131, 132, 134, 136, 148, 152, 154, 156, 161, 171, 173, 178, 179
Puttnam, Sir David 170

Quayle, Anthony 22–32, 52
Queen Elizabeth II 28
The Quiller Memorandum 18, 41
Quinn, Anthony 22–32, 50, 117, 121, 126, 173

racism 122
RAF 126
Rampling, Charlotte 99, 100
Rank 22, 74, 111, 112, 170, 177, 178, 179, 180, 181

Ransohoff, Marty 39–47, 49, 80, 111
Rapid-American Corporation 67, 74, 75
RCA 177
Reach for the Sky 22
Red Alert 171
The Red Tent 163
Redgrave, Corin 69, 71, 75
Redgrave, Michael 52
Redgrave, Vanessa 132, 133, 134, 173
Reed, Carol 23, 58
Reeve, Darci 156
Reeve, Geoffrey 4, 6, 80–90, 98–103, 118, 119, 122, 151–154, 167, 168
Reeve, Tom 85, 99, 100, 151, 152, 155–159, 168, 173
reissue 177, 178, 180
Relyea, Robert 36
remake 167, 170
Remick, Lee 50, 66
rentals 105, 121, 176, 177, 180
Reynolds, Burt 161
Reynolds, Debbie 15
RHI 156
Rhodes 24, 25
"Rich Man's Letters" 67
Rider on the Rain 104
Rigg, Diana 50
Rilla, Wolf 19
Rio de Janeiro 155
Rio Lobo, 139
Risklis, Menushan 67, 75, 82, 85
Ritt, Martin 4
River of Death 120, 130, 181
RKO-Stanley Warner 67, 74
roadshow 4, 16, 35, 41, 57, 176, 178
Robards, Jason 41
Robbins, Harold 3
Roberts, Rachel 140
Rocky 112, 122
Rocky II 177, 181
Roeves, Maurice 71
Rome 49, 156
Rose, William 66
Rosemont 169
Rosenberg, Marion 69, 74
Roth, Philip 7
Rowling, J.K. 4, 33
Royal Navy 5
Run Run Shaw 119
Ryan's Daughter 82

St. Johns, Adela Rogers 13
salary 41, 49, 50, 52, 54, 55, 56, 66, 67, 70, 94, 95, 99, 104, 106, 107, 111, 119, 121, 138, 160, 161, 162, 163, 176, 177
Saltzman, Harry 85, 128
San Andreas 171

San Diego 43
San Francisco 7, 169
San Jose 181
Santorini 171
Sarandon, Susan 143
Sardinia 160
The Satan Bug 4, 5, 6, 7, 33–38, 41, 46, 87, 173, 180
Satan's Ribbon 161
Scala, Gia 22, 25, 28
Scandinavia 75, 179
Scene 2 cinema, London 181
Scheider, Roy 98, 99
Scholastic Publishing 11
Scotland 1, 7, 43, 44, 71, 72
Scott, Allan 112, 169
Scott, George C. 50
Scott-Thomas, Serena 153
Screen Actors Guild 24
screenplay/script 12, 30, 40, 41, 49, 54, 54, 62, 71, 85, 82, 94, 88, 93, 97, 98, 101, 104, 106, 111, 112, 118, 120, 129, 131, 138, 140, 143, 144, 156, 160, 163, 164, 167, 171
screenwriter 66, 71, 85, 82, 94, 88, 93, 97, 98, 101
Seaton, George 15, 171
Seawitch 131, 167, 171
The Secret Ways/The Last Frontier 4, 6, 7, 9, 15–21, 28, 87, 128, 132, 173, 179, 180
Segal, George 41, 50
Selkirk Communications 131
Sellers, Peter 91
Selway, Mary 95
Semple, Lorenzo, Jr. 104, 106
sequel 57, 74, 80, 117, 154, 158, 167, 171
Sergeants 3 11
Setton, Maxwell 80, 98
Seven Arts 11
Seven Days in May 9
70mm 1, 4, 35, 46, 57, 176, 177
Shalako 18
Sharp, Don 4, 84, 128–137, 131, 132, 134, 136, 151, 155, 169, 171, 173
Shaw, Robert 61, 118, 121, 122, 126, 163, 166, 173
Shepperton Studios 24, 25, 122
Sheybal, Vladek 83, 87
The Shooting Party 152
Shout at the Devil 132, 144
Shulman, Irving 13
Siberia 43
Sierra Nevada 7
Silver Streak 107
Silverstein, Maurice 53, 57, 74, 82
Simenon, Georges 33
Simmons, Bob 69, 72
Sink the Bismarck! 39
The Sisters 70

Sisto, Jeremy 156, 157
Sitges Festival 113
633 Squadron 58
Slovenia 149
Smith, Murray 136
Smith, Wilbur 143
S.N. Prodis 98–99
Snell, Peter 4, 6, 120, 128–137, 138, 149, 151, 154, 156, 167, 169, 171, 172, 173
Sol Madrid 54
Soldier Blue 197
Solo, Robert H. 92
Sommer, Elke 50, 52
The Sound of Music 1, 11
South Africa 111, 112, 140, 144
South by Java Head 15, 16, 33, 111, 128, 172
Spain 140, 161, 181
Spencer, Bud 163
Spillane, Mickey 3
The Spy Who Came In from the Cold 4, 49
The Spy Who Loved Me 122
Squire, William 59
Stader, Paul 71, 93
Staffa, Scotland 71
Star Wars 121
Steiger, Rod 50
Stephens, John M. 43, 44
Stewart, Jackie 151, 154
Stewart, Patrick 149
The Sting 121, 122, 163
Stott, Walter 76
Strasbourg 150
Stride, John 69
Strike Force 172
Stroyberg, Annette 22
Stuart, Ian 6, 33, 34, 35, 128
Studio Canal 168
Stulberg, Gordon 93
stunt 53, 55, 69, 93, 94, 106, 108, 139, 148, 152
Sturges, John 17, 35–38, 41–47, 163, 173
Summer of '42 139
Superman (1978) 177
Surrey, England 39
Sutherland, Donald 132, 134, 143, 162, 173
Swashbuckler 121, 160, 163, 166
Sweden 22, 82, 140, 169, 177, 178, 179, 180, 181
Sweet, Dolph 95, 96
Switzerland 39, 55, 56, 150

Taft Industries 133, 171
Tai Pan 119
Tam Lin 66, 119
Tammes, Fred 85
Tarnished Angels 112
Taube, Sven-Bertil 4, 80–90, 171, 173
Taylor, Elizabeth 40, 49, 50

Taylor, Rod 50
television 138, 148, 176, 177, 179, 181, 182
Templeton, William 17
The Terminator 152
Thompson, J. Lee 22–32, 35, 117, 143, 151, 163, 168, 169, 172
Thomson, Jim 13
Three Days of the Condor 104
Thunderball 72, 76
Time Limit 17
To the Devil a Daughter 132
Tobermory, Scotland 71
Tobruk 42
Tokyo 181
Topaz 12
Topkapi 53
Toronto 131, 178, 179
The Towering Inferno 112, 119
Towers, Harry Alan 84, 144
The Treasure of the Sierra Madre 143
Trio Productions 81, 82
True Grit (1969) 12
Tuchner, Michael 91–97
Turkel, Ann 112, 114
Turner, Fred 170
Turner Entertainment 176
Twentieth Century Fox 11, 12, 15, 92, 93, 119, 128, 160, 167, 172
Two Rode Together 18
2001: A Space Odyssey 13, 47, 57, 139

HMS Ulysses 5, 7, 15, 16, 33, 39, 80, 91, 128, 169
Unger, Danny 75, 82, 84, 87, 171, 179
Unger, Kurt 67, 74, 75, 80–90, 98, 119, 131, 171, 173
Unger, Oliver 119, 120, 122
United Artists 9, 11, 17, 35, 67, 74, 93, 104, 107, 111, 112, 120, 131, 162
Universal 17, 49, 74, 119, 121, 163
Up the Junction 94
Ure, Mary 52, 56, 58, 61
Uris, Leon 4
USA Pictures 149

Valentine, Anthony 153
Valley of the Dolls 9, 83, 132, 136
Vance, Leigh 140, 182
Vancouver 133
Vanishing Point 91, 93
Variety 80, 113, 175, 176, 178, 179, 180, 181
Vaughn, Robert 144, 145, 146
Venice Film Festival 169
Vernon, John 94, 95, 97, 112, 114
VHS 177, 179, 182
Vienna 17, 19, 29
Viertel, Peter 17

Villain 92, 93, 94
The Violent Land 54

Walken, Christopher 142, 144
The Walking Stick 66, 176
Ward, Sarah Maur 145
Ware, Cilla 156
Warner Bros 49, 74, 119, 120, 131, 142, 155, 162, 170, 175, 176
Warner West End Cinema, London 181
The Way to Dusty Death 85, 100, 120, 130, 131, 151–154, 156, 182
Wayne, Jeff 112
Weathers, Carl 122, 126, 127
Webb, James 13
Webb, Larry 98
Webber, Robert 41, 50
Webster, Jack 75
Welch, Raquel 162
Welles, Orson 69, 70
Wells, Frank 162
West Indies 164
West Side Story (1961)
Westheimer, David 13
Wheeler, Paul 98, 152, 161, 163
When Eight Bells Toll 2, 5, 7, 20, 49, 66–79, 80, 82, 92, 93, 99, 101, 103, 112, 120, 130, 141, 152, 161, 162, 163, 173, 178, 179
Where Eagles Dare 1, 3, 4, 6, 7, 8, 19, 48–65, 67, 76, 82, 87, 88, 92, 96, 101, 111, 115, 117, 120, 127, 132, 141, 142, 148, 161, 163, 172, 173, 175, 176, 178
Whitmore, Stanford 169
The Wicker Man (1973) 7, 129, 132
Widmark, Richard 7, 15–21, 39, 87, 111, 132, 134, 146, 173, 180
The Wild Bunch 44, 58, 107
The Wild Seed 53
Wm. Morris Agency 53
Williams, Billy Dee 139, 140, 182

Wilson, Richard 39
Wings Over Cairo 169
Winkast 49, 66, 74, 75, 80, 93, 117, 160
Winner, Michael 143, 162
Women in Love 12
Woolf, John 119
World War II 3, 7, 18, 49, 83, 129, 137
Writers Guild of America 12
Wymark, Patrick 52, 60

Yorkshire Television 149
Yugloslavia 7, 118, 122, 126
Yuricich, Matthew 43

Zagreb 154
Zandvoort 152
Zeta One 69
Ziemann, Sonia 17–19
Zinnemann, Fred 41, 53

www.ingramcontent.com/pod-product-compliance
Lightning Source LLC
Chambersburg PA
CBHW060342010526
44117CB00017B/2930